THE
COUPLE'S
GUIDE
TO
FERTILITY

Infertility Awareness Association of Canada
Suite 104, 1785 Alta Vista Drive
Ottawa, Ontario
K1G 3Y6

THE COUPLE'S GUIDE TO FERTILITY

*How new
medical advances
can help you
have a baby*

*Gary S. Berger, M.D.
Marc Goldstein, M.D.
and Mark Fuerst*

DOUBLEDAY

*New York Toronto London
Sydney Auckland*

acknowledgments

Many individuals—family, friends, patients, professional colleagues, and teachers—have contributed directly and indirectly to this book. It would be impossible to list them all by name. In particular, we would like to thank our wives and families for their support. Special recognition is due to Sandy Pratt, patient care coordinator, and Susan Tripp, medical transcriptionist, for their contributions and assistance through all phases of the book.

note on the collaboration

From information supplied by Dr. Berger and Dr. Goldstein, Mr. Fuerst prepared the basic manuscript, and then interviewed other experts and patients across the country to add to Dr. Berger's and Dr. Goldstein's medical insights. The third-person references to Dr. Berger and Dr. Goldstein are used to differentiate their opinions and experiences from those of other fertility specialists.

*We dedicate this book
to our wives and our parents, and to all
couples striving to
become parents.*

——

This book is not intended as a substitute
for professional medical advice on fertility,
infertility, or gynecological disorders.
The reader should regularly consult a physician
in matters relating to health and
particularly with respect to any symptoms that may
require diagnosis or medical attention.

——

Published by Doubleday, a division of
Bantam Doubleday Dell Publishing Group, Inc.,
666 Fifth Avenue, New York, New York 10103

Doubleday and the portrayal of an anchor
with a dolphin are trademarks of Doubleday,
a division of Bantam Doubleday Dell
Publishing Group, Inc.

Library of Congress Cataloging-in-Publication Data
Berger, Gary S.
The couple's guide to fertility: how new medical advances can
help you have a baby/Gary S. Berger, Marc Goldstein, Mark Fuerst.
—1st ed.
p.   cm.
Includes index.
1. Infertility, Human—Popular works.   I. Goldstein, Marc.
II. Fuerst, Mark.   III. Title.
RC889.B444   1989
616.6'92—dc20   89-7863
CIP

ISBN 0-385-24546-7.
ISBN 0-385-26390-2 (pbk.)

Printed in the United States of America
November 1989
First Edition
DC

CONTENTS

THE
COUPLE'S
GUIDE
TO
FERTILITY

PREFACE

To those of us who grew up in the 1960s and 1970s, it seemed a birthright to have two or three children by the time we reached our thirties. But for many among the baby boom generation, that's not the way it happened.

For various reasons, many of us put off even thinking about having kids until age thirty or beyond. Now, it seems that some couples may have waited too long. The orchestration of events necessary to make babies has some how fallen out of sync. A few discordant notes—a silent epidemic of sexually transmitted diseases, prolonged use of the Pill or IUD, sterilization operations, the stresses of making a living have hindered many people's ability to produce babies.

Over the past twenty years, as today's childbearing generation has come of age, there has been a tremendous increase in the number of couples seeking help for infertility. Today there are about 10 million infertile Americans, and this generation is the first in U.S. history that will not fully reproduce itself. The 73 million people born between 1946 and 1965—known collectively as baby boomers—now face some new facts of life.

Infertility in the 1980s carried the legacy of the "free sex" era of the 1960s and the career movement of the 1970s. It is clear that both periods have exacted a heavy price. The ravages wrought on our reproductive systems by sexually transmitted diseases like chlamydia, combined with contraceptives like the IUD and the Pill that provide no protection against infection, have caused part of the problem. And delaying pregnancy until late into their thirties has made conception appreciably more difficult for many of today's infertile couples.

The irony is that couples who have planned the past twenty years of their lives in order to "have it all" now face the fact that the baby they thought could be delayed may no longer be possible at all.

Infertility is pervasive. We all know someone or know of someone with a fertility problem. Even as new developments make the headlines and late-night news, infertility largely remains taboo. Most couples don't make cocktail conversation about their infertility. But let drop that you know of a fertility expert, and their ears perk up. Mention that you are writing a book about it, and they start to come out of the woodwork. Old college friends, next-door neighbors, and office colleagues all want to hear about anything you have to offer—a new procedure, an article to read.

Today's infertile couples have more treatments available than in the past. Just twenty years ago, there were no drugs to induce ovulation and no microsurgical techniques to unblock fallopian tubes, the vas deferens, or epididymis. In vitro fertilization was only a dream. There is now a growing array of infertility therapies and providers of such services.

And infertile couples, possibly more than any other health consumers, shop around. They are highly informed and carefully weigh their doctor's advice, along with tidbits garnered from the grapevine. If they have the opportunity, they talk with other infertile couples about the kinds of tests and treatments they have received and what combinations of drugs they have tried. They are determined to find a way to have their own babies.

And more men, who traditionally have found it difficult to express their feelings about infertility, are seeking help. Male feelings about producing an heir run deep, and the classic view of infertility as a woman's problem is on the way out. Infertility is a couple's problem, best treated with the full participation of the husband, who, like his partner, accounts for the fertility problem at least 30 percent of the time. The remaining 40 percent of cases are caused by a combination of male and female factors.

This is a book for couples. It examines how the *couple,* not just the husband or wife, can deal with the problems of infertility. It includes information from specialists in male and female fertility to show you how both husband and wife share the challenge of infertility. This way, you can understand what's happening to you as well as to your partner as you work through your fertility problems together.

We will lead you through a systematic, thorough evaluation and treatment of infertility. You'll find a detailed look at the step-by-step process by which infertility tests and treatments are conducted. You will see why certain tests should be performed at specific times so that you get the best use out of them and avoid visiting the doctor unnecessarily. You'll be taken on a day-by-day look at how your doctor determines where the baby-making problem lies and the treatments that will help produce healthy babies. Along the way, you'll learn about the multitude of new treatments and techniques now available to couples, including such novel approaches as in vitro fertilization "cousins," embryo freezing, and surrogate parenting. At the end of most chapters, you'll find a list of questions to think about and discuss with your doctor if you are considering whether to have a particular test or to go through a particular treatment.

In instances where we believe one test or treatment is superior to another, we tell you so. We try to make it clear that this is our opinion based on our own experiences. That opinion may not necessarily be shared by all fertility specialists.

While doing our research, we contacted more than fifty of the top medical experts in their fields for the latest developments in infertility diagnosis and treatment. But this book is more than a medical guide to fertility. We also consider social, psychological, religious, and legal perspectives on the latest fertility treatments, as well as recent statistics on treatment success rates.

We have focused on subfertile couples, who make up 95 percent of infertility patients. These people have a difficulty, rather than an inability, in making babies. Many of the newest treatments detailed in this book are designed specifically for these subfertile couples.

The Couple's Guide to Fertility seeks to show couples in our generation and generations to follow how they can restore the natural rhythms of life and fulfill their dreams of having a family. The book includes anecdotes from real people who describe, in their own words, what it's like to go through the sometimes trying times presented by infertility diagnosis and treatment.

We wrote this book to help all couples understand the newest infertility treatments and techniques. In order to do this, we have translated medical terminology into lay terms as often as possible. We also include a directory of fertility specialists throughout the United States and fertility clinics in Canada. Working with your family doctor, you can use the directory to help you determine which local specialist may be the best for your particular problem.

Note to the Reader

The anecdotes throughout the book derive from interviews with dozens of infertile couples from around the country. Everything contained in these anecdotes is genuine, except for the names and occupations, which have been changed to protect the couples' privacy.

Cindy's Story

"We had decided early in our marriage that we didn't necessarily have to have children," says Cindy, who owns a real estate agency with her husband. "I had been pregnant and had an abortion before I met Doug. When we decided not to have children, he had a vasectomy. After seventeen years together, we had settled into our marriage, done everything that we wanted. Then we changed our minds about children." Cindy, thirty-six, and Doug, thirty-seven, decided to try to have a baby through donor insemination of sperm instead of vasectomy reversal, and on their second attempt she became pregnant.

"It's important to be surrounded in the doctor's office with people who really care. Dr. Berger and his staff made me and Doug feel real comfortable about the procedure, even though both of us were embarrassed about it at first," Cindy says. When she was five months pregnant, she went back to visit Dr. Berger to tell him how well the pregnancy was going. "Everything had fallen into place for us," she says.

As Cindy left the doctor's office, a woman in the waiting area saw the spring in her step, as well as her obvious condition. "Did you get pregnant here?" she asked. Cindy beamed and nodded, and the woman smiled in response. "Then there's hope for me, too," she said.

Part One

WHAT'S GOING ON

1

THE ORCHESTRATION OF CONCEPTION

Like a good orchestra, reproduction requires an intricate combination of various parts synchronized to perform at just the right time. Reproductive organs produce the basic notes necessary for reproduction. Fertility hormones signal when and how long to play the notes that lead to fertilization.

The fertilization process begins with sperm entering through the vagina and swimming upstream through the cervix and uterus to the fallopian tubes. One sperm, one-thousandth of an inch long, swimming six inches to reach the egg, is analogous to a man swimming a hundred miles, or across the English Channel three times. No wonder, then, that among the millions that began the long journey, perhaps only a few hundred sperm will arrive at the egg. Only one will penetrate and enter it. As it is dividing, the fertilized egg must be transported into the uterus at just the right time to implant itself in a suitable spot for adequate nourishment, development, and growth over the months ahead.

Conception and Fertility

Before a couple can conceive naturally, several basic physiologic conditions must be met. The man must produce a sufficient number of normal, actively moving sperm. The woman must produce a healthy egg and must release the egg from one of her ovaries and have it picked up by the adjacent fallopian tube. The tube must be open so that the egg, after fertilization, can find its way into the uterus.

The man's sperm need open pathways so that they can pass from the testicles, where they are produced, out through the penis at the time of ejaculation. The man must be able to ejaculate and deposit the sperm into the vagina. The sperm have to travel up through fertile mucus produced by the cervix to reach the uterus and then through the fallopian tubes in order to reach the egg.

If the woman has ovulated and the egg has been released, the sperm must be able to penetrate and fertilize the egg. The woman's reproductive organs must be ready to receive the sperm and allow them to migrate from the vagina through the cervix and into a fallopian tube. Her tubes must be healthy and be able to help the sperm get to the egg. Then they will protect and nourish the fertilized egg to deliver it into the uterus, where it can develop fully.

The hormones that control production of sperm and eggs are called gonadotropins. These fertility hormones originate in the pituitary gland, a pea-sized extension of the brain located just behind the bridge of the nose. Men and women produce the same two pituitary gonadotropins, follicle stimulating hormone (FSH) and luteinizing hormone (LH). In men, these hormones stimulate production of sperm and testosterone in the testicles; in women, they stimulate production of eggs, estrogen, and progesterone by the ovaries.

FSH governs the first half of the menstrual cycle, stimulating the development of the egg and signaling the ovary to produce estrogen. On or about day fourteen of a normal twenty-eight-day cycle, the LH level suddenly rises to a sharp peak and then falls, stimulating release of the mature egg. Simultaneously, the egg-bearing sac or follicle begins producing progesterone. At this stage in the cycle, the follicle becomes known as the "corpus luteum."

Progesterone, along with estrogen, directs the lining of the uterus to produce a thick blanket of blood vessels and a lush endometrial lining to prepare for the arrival of the fertilized egg. Unless an embryo has implanted, about two weeks after the corpus luteum is formed it stops making progesterone, and the woman menstruates, shedding the uterine lining. The cycle starts over again the next month.

It is not surprising, with such complex signals and directions, that these finely tuned reproductive instruments fail to perform exactly right from time to time. There is a relatively short period in each cycle during which the egg may be fertilized—probably only about eight to twelve hours—so it's important that you and your mate have intercourse during the fertile time of the wife's cycle. You don't have to make love precisely on the day of ovulation (the day the egg is released from the follicle) since healthy sperm may survive for days inside a woman's reproductive tract. The most fertile time in a typical twenty-eight-day cycle is most likely between days twelve and fifteen.

Man and Woman: How They Are Similar

Most people assume that a man and a woman have two distinct, separate reproductive physiologies, but they actually are quite similar (see diagram). A man's sperm (the male gamete) develops inside his testicles (1) and then enters the epididymis (2). Similarly, a woman's egg (the fe-

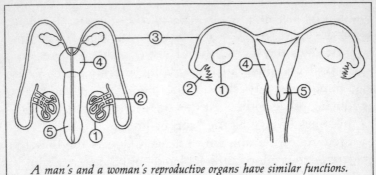

A man's and a woman's reproductive organs have similar functions. The testicles and ovaries (1) produce the gametes (sperm in man, egg in woman) that the epididymis and fimbria (2) pick up. The sperm or egg then travels either through the vas deferens or the fallopian tube (3). Both the man's prostate and the woman's uterus (4) produce substances that nourish the sperm or egg. Just as the sperm exit from the penis in a man, they enter into the vagina and cervix of a woman (5), the sites of exit and entry into the reproductive tract.

male gamete) first forms in the ovaries (1) and is picked up by the fringed ends, or fimbria (2), of the fallopian tube. As the sperm travels through the vas deferens (3) and the egg is transported through the fallopian tube (3), they both develop and grow during their time within these thin tubes. The man's prostate (4) and the woman's uterus (4), both about the same size and in the same approximate location within the body, produce nourishing substances for either the sperm or the egg. And just as the sperm exit from the penis (5), they enter the vagina and cervix (5)—the sites of exit or entry into the man's and woman's reproductive tract.

How the Man Contributes to Fertility

Although a man may not always be as verbal and forthcoming about infertility as a woman, today's husbands contribute just as much to the causes of infertility as do their wives. It can't be assumed, if a wife doesn't get pregnant, that it's her problem, or that her husband's reproductive system is normal. The male side of the fertility issue must also be examined, from the beginning of sperm production through the release of sperm into the ejaculate.

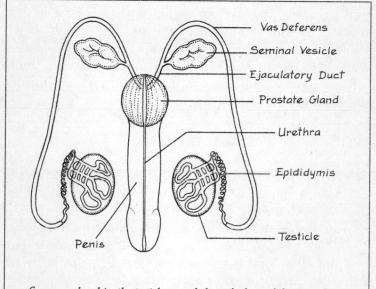

Sperm produced in the testicles travel through the epididymis and vas deferens. The seminal vesicles and prostate add their fluids to the sperm to create semen, which is ejaculated through the urethra and out the tip of the penis.

The glands, organs, and tubes that comprise the male reproductive system are located in three parts of the body —the scrotum, abdomen, and penis. The scrotum is the sac that holds a man's testicles. Sperm leave the testicles bathed in testicular fluid, enter a cluster of microscopic tubules at the top of each testicle, and then move into a tightly coiled, fifteen-foot-long tube called the epididymis.

From the epididymis, sperm enter the vas deferens, a fifteen-inch-long tube about as thick as a venetian blind cord, that rises into the abdomen. From the vas, sperm and testicular fluid enter the ejaculatory duct, formed by the end of the vas and the exit duct of the seminal vesicle, a gland that produces approximately 65 percent of the semen. The ejaculatory duct empties into the bulb of the urethra. Here, sperm from each testicle combine with a mixture of fluid produced in the prostate gland, which empties into the bulb of the urethra through a separate duct. Muscles surrounding the urethra contract rhythmically to cause ejaculation, the sudden spurt of semen from the penis.

Male Hormones

The male reproductive system takes its cues from male sex hormones (androgens). At puberty, these hormones trigger a man's pubic hair to grow, his beard to sprout, his voice to change, his muscles to bulk up, and his sex drive to escalate. Once he has matured, a continuous flow of testosterone and other androgens from his testicles helps maintain these secondary sexual characteristics.

Sperm Production in the Testicles

The main instruments of the male reproductive system are the testicles, which manufacture sperm, the tailed microscopic cells that carry a man's genetic potential to a woman's unfertilized egg. The testicles typically produce 50,000 new sperm every minute of every day until a man is well into his seventies.

Mature sperm take seventy-four days to evolve from primitive sperm cells. These early sperm forms divide several times while in the seminiferous tubules (the tiny tubes inside the testicles where sperm are produced) before they are fully mature. A mature sperm cell has one-half the chromosome content of all other body cells. About 50 percent of the sperm contain the genetic coding for maleness, the Y chromosome, and the other 50 percent contain the X chromosome, which specifies femaleness when paired with another X chromosome from the egg. A man has both an X and a Y chromosome, and a woman two X chromosomes.

When the fully mature sperm leave the testicles, they aren't yet able to swim on their own and aren't capable of fertilizing a woman's eggs. They acquire these abilities during their journey through the epididymis.

Epididymis

The epididymis is a tightly coiled, ultra-thin tube that fits into a two-inch space behind the testicle. The epididymis is like a swimming school for sperm. The sperm must spend some time in the epididymis to learn how to swim well and attain their full fertilizing potential. As they take their two-to twelve-day journey through the epididymis, the special environment within the epididymis accelerates their ability to swim and fertilize eggs.

Vas Deferens

The now-mature sperm enter the vas deferens in preparation for ejaculation. A vas deferens (the tube cut and tied off in a vasectomy) runs from the end of each epididymis upwards into the abdomen. Each vas is part of a sheath of veins, arteries, nerves, and connective tissues known as the spermatic cord.

Through its inner channel as thin as a hair on your

head, the muscular vas carries sperm from the testicle to the ejaculatory duct. The vas, along with the epididymis, stores an estimated 700 million sperm at a time. During ejaculation, the two tubes contract to propel the sperm and testicular fluid into the ejaculatory duct. There, the sperm join with the fluids, enzymes, and nutrients in the secretions of the seminal vesicles and prostate gland to form semen.

Seminal Vesicles and Prostate Gland

Each seminal vesicle secretes a fructose-rich substance that nourishes the sperm and forms the major portion of the ejaculate. The prostate, a gland that surrounds the bladder and produces additional seminal fluid, has its own exit ducts leading to the urethra. In preparing for an orgasm, the seminal vesicles and prostate pass most of their fluid into the urethra. That's why it takes a little while for most men to have a second ejaculation: the seminal vesicles and prostate need time to manufacture and emit more seminal fluid.

Ejaculation

Pleasurable sensations stimulate the penis to contract the muscles surrounding the base of the urethra and convey semen out of the penis. The urethra also conveys urine from the bladder, but urine can destroy sperm, so semen and urine never mix in a healthy male. The sphincter muscle contracts during sexual stimulation, closing down the exit from the bladder to the urethra, which is why it's difficult for a man to urinate when he has an erection.

Sperm Penetration and Fertilization

Only a small proportion of rapidly moving sperm may complete the journey to the egg; once sperm get to the egg, they also have to be able to penetrate it. Some men have normal sperm counts and motility (movement of the sperm or their ability to swim), yet their apparently normal wives don't become pregnant. The normal appearance of the sperm provides no clues to the man's ability to penetrate his wife's eggs. The fertilizing potential of even the fastest swimming sperm varies from one man to another and, just as sperm counts do, from one ejaculate to the next from the same man.

Sperm need energy for their long journey to the egg. They pick up a boost of energy as they pass through the epididymis. The energized sperm can now swim up to and burrow itself into the egg. But just getting to the egg isn't enough; the sperm needs another burst of energy in order to penetrate the egg. The sperm sustains this high energy state for a few milliseconds, less than a blink of the eye, to attach to the outer layer of the egg and burrow its way inside.

When sperm leave the testicles, they don't yet have the ability to fertilize an egg. In the 1950s, reproductive scientists began studying the interaction of sperm and egg in the laboratory, and soon found that sperm have to spend time within the woman's reproductive tract to become fully capable of fertilization.

Developing the capacity to penetrate an egg is called capacitation. Only capacitized sperm that have gone through this final stage of maturing can penetrate the membrane that surrounds the egg. This final stage is called the acrosome reaction, during which the "stocking cap" on the sperm head, called the acrosome, is removed, releasing enzymes that create a hole in the egg's cell wall so that the sperm can penetrate through the thick outer coat of the egg, known as the zona pellucida.

Once a sperm attaches to the zona pellucida, its tail begins to beat in a furious, whip-like motion, a sign of capacitation. Now the sperm can start penetrating the egg as it dissolves a tiny hole in the egg's outer membrane.

The egg doesn't just sit back passively. Once a single sperm has fused with the egg surface, the egg "grabs" the one sperm and helps bring it inside. At a certain point, the sperm's whip-like motion is no longer needed. Meanwhile, the egg immediately transforms its outer wall into an impenetrable barrier for all other sperm. Inside the egg, the chromosomes from the sole successful sperm fuse with those of the egg. The fertilized egg now has the genetic material needed to produce an entirely new person.

What the Woman Brings to Fertility

The design of the woman's reproductive system complements the man's, but keeps time to a different schedule. Under the supervision of gonadotropin hormones FSH and LH, one of the two ovaries normally produces a mature egg each month. Once released from the ovary, the egg must be gathered into the fallopian tube for its journey through the tube to reach the uterus. If the egg meets viable sperm on its way, it may become fertilized. If the fertilized egg then implants in the uterus, pregnancy has begun.

The functions of the various parts of the female anatomy must harmonize with the male's for a couple to achieve a pregnancy.

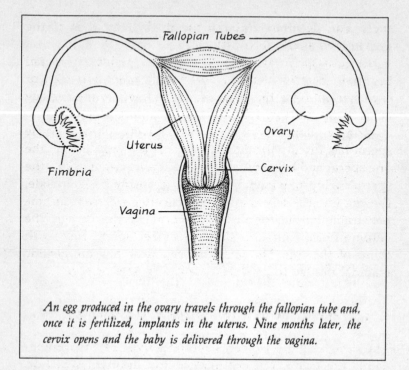

An egg produced in the ovary travels through the fallopian tube and, once it is fertilized, implants in the uterus. Nine months later, the cervix opens and the baby is delivered through the vagina.

Vagina

The vagina is a muscular, four-inch-long canal that provides an exit for menstrual blood and an entrance for semen. Normally flat, like a collapsed balloon, the vagina can stretch to accommodate a tampon, a penis, or a baby's head.

Cervix

The one-inch-long cervix lies at the top of the vagina and serves as the entrance to the uterus. In fact, it's more properly called the "uterine cervix." A mixture of powerful muscle and tough connective tissue, the cervix must remain closed throughout the pregnancy, but then has to expand to allow the baby's head to pass through during labor.

Most of the time, the cervix produces a barrier of mucus that prevents the invasion of bacteria and other organisms from the vagina to the uterus. Just before ovulation, however, sperm must be able to pass through the cervix. Only for a few days each month does the cervix become hospitable to sperm, allowing them to swim freely through to the uterus and enter the fallopian tubes.

Fallopian Tubes

The macaroni-sized fallopian tubes stretch about four to six inches from the uterus to the ovaries, where they feather out into ends called fimbria (which is Latin for "fringes"). Lining the fimbria and tubes are millions of tiny hairs, or cilia, that beat rhythmically thousands of times a minute to catch the egg at ovulation and move it through the tube to the uterus. Cells in the tube's lining produce mucus and fluid to help lubricate the egg's path and nourish it during its stay inside the fallopian tube. Once inside the tube, the egg meets sperm. If an egg doesn't become fertilized within eight to twelve hours after ovulation, the egg deteriorates and is absorbed and removed like any other dead cell in the body.

Not just a passive pipe or a conduit, the fallopian tube is an active organ with its separate locations performing separate functions. A muscular ligament, the fimbria ovarica, joins the end of the tube and the ovary; its contraction during ovulation pulls the fimbria immediately adjacent to the ovary. The fimbria then captures the egg and draws it into the tube. The middle section of the tube moves the egg and sperm toward each other by muscular contractions and the action of the beating cilia. The uterine end acts like a sphincter and prevents the egg from being released into the uterus until just the right time for implantation, which is about five to seven days after ovulation.

The Ovaries

The two almond-sized ovaries are perched just within the fallopian tubes' grasp. They are stocked with a lifetime of eggs at birth. Each month prior to ovulation, the brain triggers the release of follicle-stimulating hormone, which causes egg-bearing follicles to grow near the surface of each ovary.

Just as sperm struggle to survive the conception obstacle course, only one of the many eggs stimulated each month matures fully. The dominant follicle contains this egg and releases suppressor hormones to destroy all the other eggs that may be starting to mature each cycle. The egg in the dominant follicle matures fully; the rest shrivel and die.

The pinpoint-sized egg grows slowly its first week, then rapidly accelerates to about the size of a pencil point at the end of the second week as the cells around it begin releasing estrogen. Subsequently, LH released from the brain stimulates the one dominant egg to burst forth from the grape-size follicle and be scooped up by one of the fallopian tubes. Most women ovulate within twenty-four to thirty-six hours after the surge of luteinizing hormone. (Home test kits can measure hormone levels in the urine this way.)

The finger-like projections at the end of the fallopian tubes look a little like a catcher's mitt, but they don't always gather in an egg as easily as a catcher receives a pitched ball. Sometimes the egg isn't released near the ends of the tube, but may gently drop from the surface of the ovary and float in a puddle of fluid in the bottom of the pelvic cavity (the cul-de-sac). The egg can float for several hours in this area and still be picked up by the tube and be fertilized, since the cul-de-sac has a smooth surface that allows easy movement of the egg and the fimbrial ends of the tubes also float in the fluid in the cul-de-sac.

The release of eggs from follicles month after month leaves the ovaries' surfaces wrinkled and full of pits. At ovulation, a hole appears in the surface of the ovary. Following ovulation, the corpus luteum forms and produces progesterone during the second half of the cycle to prepare the uterus for a pregnancy. The corpus luteum ("yellow body" in Latin) leaves a yellow stain on the ovary. Normally, the ovaries have lots of scars and yellow stains from previous ovulations.

Uterus

The uterus, the shape and size of a pear, sits in the center of the reproductive tract. It consists of a narrow inner mucus-membrane lining surrounded by a thick wall of muscle. Usually the cavity holds less than a quarter of a teaspoon of liquid, yet it can expand up to the size of a watermelon during pregnancy.

The lining of the uterus first proliferates or thickens under the influence of estrogen early in the menstrual cycle. Later, under the influence of progesterone, the lining secretes nourishing substances to support a fertilized egg that's ready to implant and develop into a fetus.

For Some, Things Have Gotten Out of Tune

Because of the intricate sequence of events required for conception, it's not surprising that many couples' ability to reproduce has somehow gotten out of tune. Most likely, you have tried to have a baby with no luck, maybe even for years, and you probably know other couples who have experienced similar difficulties. You have read about infertility in newspapers and magazines, or heard couples discussing their infertility on radio or TV talk shows. Infertility has even become a popular subject for TV dramas and sitcoms.

If you are just beginning to investigate your fertility problem, you may feel frustrated, depressed, or hopeless and may also be somewhat afraid of the workup necessary to diagnose your problem. If you have already begun fertility treatments, you know how depressing they can be at times, with the lack of privacy at the doctor's office, the grind of sex on schedule, and the time lost from work for tests and treatments. The people who love you, your family and friends, may make insensitive remarks about making babies that hurt because you haven't told them about your infertility. Once you have told them, they may come to pity you or make light of something you must face every day. The worst part is that empty feeling when you've done all that you can, but you don't succeed, and the menstrual period starts again. Then you have to go through the whole process for another month.

National Fertility Surveys

Although most couples coping with infertility feel isolated, there are in fact millions of others struggling with the same problem. Near the end of the baby boom in 1955, university researchers conducted the first national surveys to collect information on fertility, family planning, and maternal and child health. The surveys proved so useful that the federal government began funding similar studies, seven in all, through 1982.

The 1982 survey, which included interviews with nearly 8,000 women, was the first to cover unmarried as well as married women. Applying national estimates, the survey represents the fertility status of 54 million women aged fifteen to forty-four.

The survey concluded that 2.4 million women were infertile, that is, unable to conceive after one year or more of intercourse without contraception. One million of these women were childless (what doctors refer to as primary infertility), and 1.4 million had one or more children before they subsequently became infertile (secondary infertility). Adding formerly married couples and never-married women of childbearing age, the number of infertile women rose to 4.5 million—including 1.9 million who were childless and 2.6 million who had one or more children but were unable to get pregnant again.

Our generation's predilection for delaying pregnancy until later in life has led to higher infertility rates. The 1982 survey showed that about one in seven American couples was infertile, and the risk for women aged forty to forty-four is one in four, about twice that of thirty- to thirty-four-year-olds. Now most experts consider the overall infertility rate to be higher than in 1982, with one in six American couples believed infertile.

After a preliminary look at the eighth national fertility survey, conducted in 1986 (with full results expected by 1990), the survey's director, Dr. William Pratt, anticipates that infertility will increasingly be a problem for couples in the 1990s.

2

THE
MEDICAL
FACTS

*What Stands in
Our Way of Making
a Family*

O ver the past few decades, we have witnessed an explosion in medical knowledge, including many exciting new ways to combat diseases and to control fertility through medications and operations. Unfortunately, not all of these advancements turn out to be as beneficial as originally intended.

Two Steps Forward, One Step Back

As the Pill came into widespread use in the 1960s, it became apparent that early versions had some serious side effects, including increasing a woman's risk of stroke and heart attack and, possibly, cervical cancer. So women in the 1970s began switching to intrauterine devices—until the reproductive damages of certain IUDs became well known and most of the devices were taken off the market.

Another birth control method, sterilization, was legalized in the early 1960s and became so popular that it is now the contraceptive method of choice among today's couples. As these operations grew more common, surgeons had to develop their microsurgical skills to reverse the operation if the individual had a later change of mind. Even so, only a little more than half of the more than 20 million people who have had sterilization operations can have them successfully reversed if they want to be able to have children again.

In the late 1960s, nearly every American city had an epidemic of gonorrhea that was at that time able to be treated effectively by penicillin. But now, cases of penicillin-resistant gonorrhea have become a new public health problem. Throughout this period, men and women infected with a still-obscure bacteria called chlamydia appeared at venereal disease clinics. Not until the early 1980s did infectious disease experts realize the full extent of the insidious fertility problems caused by chlamydia.

Although gonorrhea and chlamydia led the VD epidemic, a variety of other organisms also contributed to more pelvic infections. These infections eventually led to scarring of fallopian tubes, which in turn led to a dramatic rise in tubal pregnancies as well as miscarriages. The lifestyle that often exposed people to sexually transmitted diseases may also have primed their bodies' immune systems to attack and kill sperm.

The advent of new, more powerful medications dominated the pharmaceutical scene of the 1960s and 1970s. Several of these drugs, including two of the top sellers—one for ulcers, the other for heart disease—have side effects that reduce a man's fertility. The introduction of specific cancer treatments has contributed to a high cure rate for certain cancers, such as cancer of the testicles. But, again, serious fertility-reducing side effects make most cancer treatments a problem for couples who want to have babies.

To keep tabs on all these new drugs, the federal government in the mid-1960s began requiring drug companies to provide medical evidence to support all new drug claims. But this was already too late for the sons and daughters whose mothers had taken the drug diethylstilbestrol (DES) in the 1950s to prevent miscarriages. The link between DES exposure and deformities of both daughters' and sons' reproductive organs came to light during the 1970s. Many DES daughters were unable to conceive or couldn't carry to term.

The VD Epidemic

One of the primary causes of today's rising infertility rates, particularly among young men and women, is venereal infection due to a wide variety of sexually transmitted diseases (STDs). If left untreated, STDs that infect a woman's upper reproductive tract can cause scar tissue and can damage or destroy the delicate membranes lining the uterus, fallopian tubes, and ovaries. In the man such infection can damage the delicate ducts of the epididymis.

Even a single venereal infection can permanently damage the lining of the fallopian tubes or epididymis and partially or totally block them. With each episode of STD, the chances of blocked tubes in both men and women increase. A woman who has been infected is more likely to have chronic pelvic pain than other women, and she is more susceptible to repeated infections and an ectopic (tubal) pregnancy if she does get pregnant.

The sheer number of these sexually transmitted infections is astounding. In the United States each year there are more than 4 million cases of chlamydia infection, 1 million cases of gonorrhea infection, and millions of viral infections. STDs from common bacteria, such as streptococcus, and other organisms—mycoplasma, ureaplasma, trichomonas—and viruses such as cytomegalovirus can all lead to infertility.

These STDs may affect the fertility of both women and

men by scarring either the fallopian tubes or the sperm-carrying tubes. In women, the uterus and fallopian tubes usually become infected by organisms traveling up from the vagina and cervix. The body's response to the infections may cause scars (adhesions) to form in and around the tubes. These scars may prevent sperm from meeting the egg inside the tube or prevent the tube from transporting the fertilized egg to the uterus, which can lead to a tubal pregnancy. For men, the scar formation may close off the epididymis, the sperm-carrying tube on top of each of the testicles.

Pelvic inflammatory disease (PID), inflammation of the uterus, fallopian tubes, or ovaries, seems to hit the upper reproductive tract with a one-two punch of infections. First, gonorrhea or chlamydia bacteria infect the tubes, followed closely by infections with other bacteria from the vagina or cervix. Bacteria from the vagina and cervix may also ascend to the uterus during menstruation. Just as an open cut on your finger can become infected, the open blood vessels of the uterus are more susceptible to an attack by bacteria once the uterine lining has been sloughed off. A viral infection, such as cytomegalovirus, may also tax a woman's immune defenses, allowing a bacterial infection to establish itself more easily and do damage.

When a sexually active woman complains of lower abdominal pain or shows signs of pelvic tenderness, the diagnosis of pelvic inflammatory disease is often suspected. Acute pelvic infections usually begin with pain in the lower abdomen that becomes increasingly worse over two or three days. The pain may become so severe that a woman has trouble walking and urinating. If not treated properly, an abscess may form, and if the abscess ruptures, the infection may spread throughout the woman's abdominal cavity, requiring emergency surgery. The male equivalent of PID is epididymitis, which can also lead to chronic pain and permanently scarred and blocked ducts.

How Many Become Infertile from STDs

Infectious disease experts estimate that after one episode of PID, 35 percent of women become infertile. After two episodes, the infertility rate is 50 to 60 percent, and after three episodes, more than 75 percent.

Nearly 8 million American women have had PID during their lives. Experts estimate that chlamydia infections cause at least 300,000 new cases of PID among women and 250,000 cases of epididymitis (infection of the epididymis) among men each year.

These statistics become even more staggering when we realize that they represent only symptomatic cases. No one knows how many additional millions of cases go undetected or unreported. Probably at least as many women have had asymptomatic pelvic infections and didn't know it until they tried, unsuccessfully, to get pregnant.

One of the most authoritative estimates for STD-related infertility comes from the federal government's Centers for Disease Control (CDC) in Atlanta. The CDC's Dr. Willard Cates, Jr., estimates that 125,000 women become infertile each year due to STDs and that about 2 million American women have had their tubes blocked by PID.

Dr. Cates's figures don't include men who become infertile from STDs, but it is likely that there are an equal number of men whose fertility has been compromised by STD-related epididymitis.

An Unrecognized, Pervasive Problem

One reason chlamydia has become the fastest-growing sexually transmitted infection is that its pervasiveness wasn't recognized until the mid-1980s. In the 1970s and early 1980s, the CDC was recommending that a woman with an inflamed cervix (cervicitis) who had a proven gonorrhea infection first receive treatment with penicillin antibiotics rather than with tetracycline-type antibiotics that would also eradicate chlamydia. Even the country's most authoritative epidemiologists and STD specialists didn't recognize how widespread the growing chlamydia problem was. A large percentage of doctors still prescribe outdated, ineffective antibiotics that don't properly attack chlamydia infections.

Prior to the 1980s, chlamydia infections were known to cause conjunctivitis (an inflammation of the eyes) among newborns, which was transmitted from the mother's genital tract during birth. But chlamydia wasn't thought of as a common STD. We now know that, besides causing cervicitis, the bacteria can lead to an inflammation of the lining of the uterus (endometritis), the fallopian tubes (salpingitis), and of the ovaries that can lead to scarring of these reproductive organs.

"Silent" Symptoms

Because its symptoms are often "silent," chlamydia can cause more severe damage than other infections. Although men may notice a burning sensation during urination and a pus-like discharge from the penis within a week of infection, most women don't feel any symptoms and consequently don't seek treatment. About 70 percent of women infected with chlamydia show *no* symptoms; the rest may notice only a yellowish cervical discharge. About half of the men with so-called non-gonococcal urethritis (inflammation of the urethra *not* due to gonorrhea) and nearly half of those with acute epididymitis are infected with chlamydia.

In addition, both men and women can carry PID-causing organisms without showing symptoms. These carriers may unwittingly pass the organisms on to their sex partners, who may carry the bacteria for weeks, months, or years. About half of the women with closed fallopian tubes report no history of PID, which either means that they never had severe enough complaints to make them visit a doctor or that the doctor failed to make the diagnosis.

Epidemiologists now recognize that a chlamydia infection often accompanies a gonorrhea infection. About half of the women who have an acute inflammation of the fallopian tubes harbor both chlamydia and gonorrhea infections, and 15 to 30 percent of heterosexual men infected with gonorrhea who have an inflamed urethra have a simultaneous infection with chlamydia. That is why, during an initial workup, some fertility specialists routinely order screening tests to detect the presence of both chlamydia and gonorrhea, as well as other harmful, disease-causing bacteria.

Other Organisms

In women, gonorrhea and chlamydia infections cause about 85 percent of all cases of PID. The rest come from a variety of other bacteria in the vagina and cervix, frequently carried "piggyback" by sperm into the uterus. Insertion of an intrauterine device (IUD), a dilatation and curettage (D&C) operation, and other procedures that involve passing an instrument through the cervix into the uterus may also carry bacteria into the upper reproductive tract.

Infections with mycoplasma and a related organism, ureaplasma, may be associated with ectopic pregnancies, spontaneous abortions, and premature births. In males, mycoplasma or ureaplasma infections can cause urethritis and also impair sperm production and motility.

Sex and PID

In the 1960s and 1970s, more people started having sex at an earlier age than in prior decades. They were also more likely to have had more sexual partners, which exposed them to more STDs. Since infertility often goes unrecognized until five to ten years after tubes have been infected, much of today's increase in infertility can be related to the increase in sexually transmitted infections acquired over the past two decades.

The sobering news for the victims of PID is that once an infection has damaged the tubes, medications can't repair the damage. (Surgery may be successful, depending on the extent of the problem.) So new antibiotics, even those active against chlamydia, cannot control the infertility epidemic. To have a sizable impact on STD-related tubal infertility, infections have to be stopped before they reach the fallopian tubes. One way to accomplish this is to prevent the spread of infection from one partner to another by screening for "silent" infections of the lower reproductive tract before they can cause damage higher up.

Regular use of condoms also reduces the risk of sexually transmitted infections. Latex (rubber) condoms have proven effective in preventing not only bacterial infections, such as chlamydia and gonorrhea, but also viruses, including the herpes virus, human papilloma virus, cytomegalovirus, hepatitis B, and the AIDS virus.

Water molecules are much smaller than viruses, so if

water can't get through a condom, then a virus can't either. The AIDS virus is small at 120 nanometers (billionths of a meter) in diameter compared with the much larger gonorrhea bacteria at 1,000 nanometers. Sperm, in comparison, are huge at 3,000 nanometers in diameter. The failure of condoms to protect against STDs is more often due to not using the condom than to a defect in the condom itself.

Despite the rising concern about AIDS and other, less deadly, STDs, condom use remains low among our sexually active population. The partners of only 16 percent of sexually active unmarried women and 15 percent of married women actually use condoms, according to a 1987 survey of 10,000 reproductive-age American women conducted by the Alan Guttmacher Institute, a New York family planning institute. And a greater percentage of never-married women are having sex than before—76 percent in the 1987 survey, up from 68 percent in a similar Guttmacher survey conducted in 1982. Since there has been little significant change in condom use to prevent STDs, the same infectious climate that led to today's high tubal infertility rates persists.

The Risks of a Tubal Pregnancy

As the number of STDs has risen dramatically in the 1980s, so has the incidence of ectopic pregnancies, or pregnancies outside of the uterus, usually in the fallopian tubes. The primary reason for the increased incidence of tubal pregnancies is the large number of women with pelvic inflammatory disease. Because of damage to the delicate lining of the fallopian tube, which helps transport the egg to the uterus, PID can cause fertilized eggs to implant in the tubes before they reach the uterus. Women with a history of pelvic infection have four times the risk of ectopic pregnancy than women without a history of infection, and there is a tenfold increased risk of ectopic pregnancy among women with tubal damage. About half of the women who have ectopic pregnancies become infertile.

The rate of ectopic pregnancies has more than tripled since 1970, according to the Centers for Disease Control, when fewer than five out of every 1,000 births were ectopic compared to more than fifteen per 1,000 births in 1985 (the latest government figures available).

The most common cause of ectopic pregnancy is previous salpingitis, with about half of all ectopic pregnancies due to PID. But any condition that prevents the fertilized egg from reaching the uterus predisposes a woman to an ectopic pregnancy. Problems may arise from IUD use, fallopian tube surgery (such as plastic surgery to repair damaged tubes), surgery to remove all or part of a tube (salpingectomy), or tubal sterilization and previous tubal pregnancy. Other factors associated with a higher risk of tubal pregnancy include: abdominal or pelvic surgery, acute appendicitis, induced abortion, endometriosis, and exposure to DES in utero. Women who douche during the week after they ovulate, and cigarette smokers, too, may also have a higher risk of ectopic pregnancy.

During the 1970s, over 10 million women had legal abortions, and some used abortion as their only means of birth control. Many of these women who had abortions now have obstructed fallopian tubes and pelvic scarring due to often "silent" infections following the abortions. This fact wasn't fully appreciated at a time when the emphasis fell more on making abortions legal and safe. While deaths due to poorly supervised, illegal abortions were virtually wiped out, the more subtle problem of tubal infertility from asymptomatic infections was not.

The rising incidence of ectopic pregnancies can partly be attributed to better recognition. In the past, many early ectopic pregnancies weren't diagnosed before the fallopian tube ruptured and caused internal bleeding. Only those cases that progressed to a painful, serious, or life-threatening stage were diagnosed. Today early pregnancy testing (including highly sensitive, specific assays of the pregnancy hormone human chorionic gonadotropin or hCG and high-resolution ultrasound scans) and diagnostic laparoscopy have led to diagnosis of ectopic pregnancy within a week or two after a woman misses her period.

Prolonged Use of IUDs and the Pill

New contraceptives introduced in the 1960s and 1970s added to fertility woes in the 1980s. While today's couples enjoy new sexual freedom with highly effective contraceptives, they contract more STDs by exposing themselves to more sex partners, and by not using condoms, which can help prevent infection. The widespread use of intrauterine devices (IUDs) has been associated with an increase in pelvic inflammatory disease and infertility due to scarred fallopian tubes. And some women who stayed on the Pill for years and then went off once they planned to have a family have found that they are not ovulating and require fertility drugs to stimulate ovulation.

IUDs became the most popular form of birth control in the late 1960s and early 1970s when the safety of the Pill came into question. The high-dose oral contraceptives then available carried risks of increasing the chance of heart attack, stroke, and possibly cervical cancer. The switch to IUDs in the 1970s, along with a decrease in the use of condoms and diaphragms, contributed to the rise in infertility.

An IUD works by causing an inflammatory reaction inside the uterine cavity, which prevents the embryo from implanting in the uterus.

Only after millions of American women were already using IUDs in the 1970s was the association between IUD use and an increased risk of PID fully appreciated. Thousands of women are believed to have suffered pelvic and uterine infections, ectopic pregnancies, and infertility while using the Dalkon Shield, which was removed from the market in 1974. Because of the legal problems encountered by the Dalkon Shield's manufacturer, most other IUD manufacturers withdrew their devices from the market. Now, there are only two IUDs remaining, one copper IUD and one medicated, hormone-carrying IUD.

Many studies have linked IUD use to tubal infertility. Two recent American studies report that childless women with tubal infertility were two to three times more likely to have used IUDs than women who have one child. IUD wearers with more than one sexual partner had a three to four times higher risk of tubal infertility, while IUD users with only one partner had no increased risk.

Inserting an IUD may increase a woman's risk of developing PID by giving bacteria and other organisms from the vagina and cervix access to the upper reproductive tract. The bacteria may "wick" their way up on the tail of the IUD through the cervix and into the uterus, then move on into the fallopian tubes. The longer menstrual bleeding time associated with IUDs may also allow bacteria to enter upper reproductive tract organs.

In the rare instance when an IUD user becomes pregnant with an IUD in place, the pregnancy is likely to be ectopic. The device is highly effective in preventing pregnancies within the uterus, but not those outside the uterus. IUD users have three to four times the rate of ectopic pregnancies, compared to women who don't use IUDs. (When several IUDs were available, women who used the steroid-containing Progestasert IUD appeared to have more tubal pregnancies than those who wore other IUDs.)

In contrast to the IUD, the Pill may protect women from developing PID to a certain extent. The hormones in oral contraceptives tend to reduce menstrual flow and produce a sticky cervical mucus that provides a barrier to infectious organisms, reducing their upward spread into the uterus.

On the other hand, long-term Pill users may not menstruate or ovulate after they stop using the Pill. This condition, known as "hypothalamic amenorrhea," occurs because the Pill disrupts the natural rhythmic flow of hormones from the hypothalamus to the pituitary to the ovaries. This may pose a special problem for older women who have been on the Pill for many years because their ovaries may have become resistant to resuming ovulation.

Furthermore, the oral contraceptive "minipill," containing only the hormone progestin, has been associated with an elevated risk of tubal pregnancy.

Sterilization Operations

Millions of people had sterilization operations over the past quarter-century, some to gain more sexual freedom, others to curb the population explosion. Still others recognized the dangerous side effects of the high-dose Pill then in use and chose a more permanent form of birth control.

Many environmentally conscious young people of the Woodstock Generation who thought sterilization would aid zero population growth now regret having been sterilized, and they want their fertility back. Others have found out that sterilization did not solve their emotional, sexual, or marital problems.

Fortunately, with the advent of microsurgery, which

uses high-powered microscopes and surgical thread thinner than a hair, doctors can now sew back together previously cut or tied-off fallopian tubes in women and sperm-carrying vas deferens in men, with up to 50–60 percent success rates in the best of hands.

Each year since around 1970, about one million people have opted for sterilization operations, the nation's most popular form of birth control. By the end of 1989, more than 22 million Americans will have chosen sterilization as their means of contraception. Yet, as many as 10 percent each year not only regret having had these sterilizations but would like to have them reversed, according to family-planning expert Richard Lincoln, formerly senior vice president of the Alan Guttmacher Institute in New York. Most do nothing about it mainly because they don't know that these "permanent" procedures often can be reversed.

The pace of sterilizations—731,000 female sterilizations and 419,000 vasectomies in 1984—remains about the same. That means that couples are still choosing sterilization, and will continue to do so until a better, safer contraceptive is developed. And, concurrently, we can expect that the number of attempted sterilization reversals will continue unabated.

More Chances for More Miscarriages

The idea behind contraceptives is to prevent the sperm and egg from meeting, or to prevent the fertilized egg from implanting in the uterus. Even without contraceptives most fertilized eggs never develop into a live baby. About one-third of all pregnancies end in miscarriages, two-thirds of these within two weeks after conception—*before* a woman or her doctor becomes aware of the pregnancy.

Miscarriage has become an increasing problem for

today's infertile couples. More women have postponed having children, and since the risk of miscarriage rises with the mother's age, miscarriages have become more common.

Traditionally, a woman had to have at least three miscarriages before a doctor would attempt to find the cause of "habitual spontaneous abortion." The rationale was that most women who have one or two miscarriages will eventually bear healthy babies without any need for treatment. However, for couples who delay having a baby until their thirties, many fertility specialists now investigate the problem of recurrent miscarriages sooner and won't arbitrarily wait until the wife has lost three pregnancies.

If a childless woman keeps miscarrying, this may suggest that she, her husband, or both of them, are passing along a genetic defect. A chromosome analysis, called a karyotype, of each partner's blood can confirm a genetic problem. However, chromosome analysis is costly—as much as $1,000 for the couple—and provides an explanation for less than 5 percent of recurrent miscarriages. (About half of all miscarriages are due to abnormal chromosomes, infections, hormone irregularities, immune system, or anatomic problems, while the other half go unexplained.)

Combining sperm and egg to form a fetus is one of nature's most intricate processes, and can go awry in many ways beyond incompatible chromosomes between husband and wife. An otherwise healthy woman can have a deficiency of the hormones she needs to sustain a growing fetus. A woman with an abnormally shaped uterus, or a woman with a septum in her uterus, may lose her pregnancy. Fibroids, or hard nodules, in the uterus can also lead to miscarriage by preventing the embryo from implanting. Even if the embryo somehow becomes implanted, it probably won't receive an adequate supply of blood to survive. Also, wearing an IUD or having an elective abortion or a

D&C procedure can scar the uterus, making it difficult for a fetus to implant or grow.

Genital tract infections are also associated with miscarriage. Bacteria "piggybacked" on sperm can infect the lining of the uterus and sabotage the growing fetus. Viruses and bacteria from anywhere in a pregnant woman's body may also travel through the bloodstream and infect the fetus, or produce enzymes that trigger the release of prostaglandins, chemicals that can cause her uterus to contract and send her into early labor.

A woman's immune system can also malfunction, rejecting the embryo as a foreign body, since one-half of the fetus's genes come from the father. Normally, a pregnant woman's immune system must produce blocking factors to shield the fetus from her usual immune defenses. If a woman has repeated spontaneous abortions, her immune system may not recognize that she is pregnant and may not turn on its blocking response. She will reject the pregnancy, usually within a few weeks.

Sperm Busters

The immune system is like a night watchman prowling the spacious warehouse of our bodies from head to toe, checking out substances to see if they are friend or foe. Normally, friends are left alone, while foes get attacked by watchdog-like antibodies (blood proteins made by the immune system's white blood cells, to protect the body against invaders). Once the body has identified an invader, the immune system produces a specific antibody against it to fight it off.

A man's body sometimes sees his own sperm as invaders and produces antibodies against them. These antisperm antibodies can attach to the sperm's surface and alter the sperm's ability to fertilize eggs. Women may also produce antibodies against sperm, interfering with sperm function and fertilization.

Antisperm antibodies don't necessarily kill sperm, but more likely stop the sperm in their tracks or cause them to clump together. The antibodies can also interfere with fertilization by preventing sperm from penetrating through cervical mucus or by interfering with the sperm-egg interaction in the fallopian tubes, barring sperm from attaching to the egg or penetrating it.

Depending on where they attach themselves on the sperm, antibodies can interfere either with sperm movement or fertilization. When antibodies attach to the sperm tail, the sperm can't swim as well. When antibodies attach to the sperm head, they are more likely to interfere with the sperm's ability to fertilize an egg.

No one knows why some women produce antisperm antibodies while others don't. Some women may be born with a genetic susceptibility that makes them react more to sperm, while others may turn on production of antisperm antibodies later in life.

A sexually active woman may be exposed to more than a trillion sperm in her lifetime. When too many sperm die within the reproductive tract or reach the abdominal cavity, the body acts to dispose of them by sending white blood cells to gobble them up. Once the immune system is turned on, it can produce antibodies against the sperm.

A woman who has had many sex partners is more likely to contract STDs. Her immune system reacts to these genital infections by producing antibodies against them. When the microorganisms attach to sperm, antibodies may form against both the bacteria and the sperm. In fact, some sperm antibody diagnostic tests give mixed results because they can't distinguish between antibodies against bacteria and antibodies against sperm with bacteria attached.

Animal studies suggest that anal intercourse may lead to antisperm antibody production whereas exposure to a healthy vagina or oral sex usually does not. When sperm come into contact with blood vessels in the rectum, the immune system may have a greater opportunity to "see" the sperm. Once discovered, the "invading" sperm may then have antibodies produced against them.

Antibodies might play a role in miscarriages. Women who have recurrent miscarriages tend to have high levels of antisperm antibodies. Some doctors suspect that the antisperm antibodies interfere with implantation and embryo development. On the other hand, women who develop antibodies against sperm may also develop other antibodies, and perhaps these other antibodies are directly involved in causing miscarriages.

Men produce antibodies against sperm only when their sperm come in contact with their own blood. When men are born, they have no sperm, and so their immune systems don't recognize sperm as "self" when they are produced later in life. Sperm develop within the testicles and are normally kept from exposure to the man's own blood (where antibodies could be produced against them) by a physical separation called the "blood-testis barrier." So, as far as the immune system is concerned, sperm develop "outside" the body.

When sperm get into body tissues—for example, after a vasectomy or trauma to the testicles, epididymis, or vas deferens—the body recognizes them as "foreign" and develops antibodies against them. These antibodies don't always impair a man's fertility, since men who have had vasectomies and then had them reversed have gotten their wives pregnant, but most men who have had vasectomies do develop sperm antibodies.

As in women, a genital infection can bring white blood

cells into a man's genital tract and activate antibody production to fight off the infection. If the infection damages his genital tract, allowing sperm to come into contact with the blood, then antibodies may be produced against his sperm as well.

Two other conditions may also lead to antisperm antibody production in men. Cystic fibrosis, an inherited disease, may block normal sperm passageways; and a twisting of the testicles, called torsion, can damage them. As with a vasectomy, these two problems may lead to antibody production by allowing sperm to escape into the bloodstream and be recognized by the immune system.

The location and number of antisperm antibodies also determines how damaging they may be. Antibodies attached to sperm cause more male fertility problems than antisperm antibodies circulating in the blood. And if less than 50 percent of the sperm have antibodies bound to them, the chances of a conception remain good if the sperm are otherwise normal.

New Medications, New Treatments

Many commonly used prescription drugs have been associated with infertility, mostly among men. Two popular drugs, the ulcer drug cimetidine (Tagamet) and the heart drug digitalis (Crystodigin), reduce a man's level of sex hormones and depress normal sperm formation. A medication used to treat ulcerative colitis, sulfasalazine, causes low sperm counts, decreases sperm motility, and increases the number of abnormally shaped sperm. Nitrofurantoins (Furadantin), antibiotics used to treat urinary tract infections, inhibit sperm formation. The anti-gout drug colchicine may lead to azoospermia (a zero sperm count). And the diuretic spironolactone (Aldactone) interferes with the synthesis of male hormones. (Every gray cloud has a silver lining: this action of spironolactone makes it a useful treatment for some infertile women who produce increased amounts of male hormones.)

Not as many medications lower a woman's fertility, but the use of decongestants may affect a woman's ability to conceive. One woman who was in the habit of taking oral decongestants for her sinus troubles reduced the flow of her cervical, as well as nasal, mucus. The lack of fertile cervical mucus over two years prevented her husband's sperm from reaching her eggs. Once she stopped taking the decongestants, she became pregnant.

More likely, a woman may have had a surgical treatment that interferes with her fertility. Freezing or burning the cervix to treat some cervical abnormalities detected by an abnormal Pap smear can damage the mucus-producing glands and limit a woman's ability to reproduce.

Cancer Therapies

When David began having constant back pains, he went to his doctor, who found a small mass on his back that turned out to be cancerous. A further investigation revealed that David had testicular cancer that had spread into his back. For the next year, he went through a series of chemotherapy and surgical treatments to cleanse his body of the cancer. Because of the treatment, David's sperm count was low, but gradually rose to nearly normal about two years after treatment. In that time, the single salesman met his future wife Judy, aged thirty. "Now that I have been disease-free for three years, we are thinking about starting a family," says David, who adds that Judy plans to visit her gynecologist for a basic fertility workup.

Cancer treatments frequently cause infertility. Radiation and chemotherapy treatments can save the lives of 90 percent of men with testicular cancer. But the treatments that cure the cancer often cause the men to become permanently sterile. Even with careful shielding during radiation of a man's lymph nodes, his testicles often receive a dose of radiation that irreversibly damages his sperm-producing cells. Chemotherapy, designed to kill rapidly multiplying or dividing cancer cells, also damages the cells that produce the hundreds of millions of new sperm every day. Some men regain their fertility several years later if some of the sperm-producing cells survive the therapy.

Treatment for other cancers can also make a man sterile, at least temporarily. Some men treated for leukemias, lymphomas, and solid tumors who became sterile have shown renewed sperm production, some as early as seven months after their treatment stopped. The more drugs used in chemotherapy and the longer the treatment lasts, the greater the odds against the man becoming fertile again.

About half of all women who receive radiation and chemotherapy for Hodgkin's disease suffer from premature ovarian failure (menopause) because of damage to their eggs and egg-bearing follicles. Some women have only a temporary disruption in their menstrual cycles lasting from a few months to a few years. Those women treated with a combination of radiation and chemotherapy seem to have more damage than those exposed to either therapy alone.

The Damage Done by DES

Soon after Tina got pregnant the first time, she noticed she was spotting. She miscarried a few weeks later. Within five months, the thirty-two-year-old book agent was pregnant again and miscarried again. Her third pregnancy that year also ended in miscarriage. "I knew I had been exposed to DES. When I was fifteen, my mother told me she had taken the drug throughout her pregnancy with me because she had miscarried twice before," Tina says. "Since there was nothing I could do about it, and I was still young, it wasn't an immediate worry." Then she and her husband, Tom, a thirty-eight-year-old engineer, decided to make an appointment with a doctor who handles high-risk pregnancies.

She had an X-ray examination, which showed that Tina had a T-shaped uterus, probably caused by the DES exposure. The doctor told her to keep trying to get pregnant, and eventually an embryo would find a place to implant itself in her malformed uterus. "He told me he could put a stitch in my cervix to help prevent a miscarriage, and that I would have to stay in bed for the first six months of pregnancy," she says. "I told him, 'No way, I'd go crazy.'" Instead, Tina and Tom went through an adoption agency and now have a six-month-old son.

When women in the early 1950s took a new fertility drug, diethylstilbestrol (DES) to prevent miscarriages, they never dreamed the drug could kink up their daughters' fallopian tubes, cause vaginal cancer and a malformed cervix and uterus, and cause their sons to have abnormal testicles. Prescribed for more than thirty years to women with high-risk pregnancies, DES, a synthetic hormone, was touted as a wonder drug. More than 8 million American daughters and sons were exposed to the drug in utero (during their development as a fetus inside their mother's uterus).

Most people know of the limb deformities caused by the drug thalidomide since the deformities are all on the outside of the body. With DES exposure, the deformities are on the inside, where they aren't so obvious. Some studies estimate that the reproductive organs of 40 percent of DES daughters are malformed, including deformities of the vagina or cervix, an abnormal, T-shaped uterus, and abnormal fallopian tubes. Some DES daughters have ovulation problems; others have an increased risk of ectopic pregnancy, repeated miscarriages, and premature delivery. A small number have also developed a rare form of cancer of the vagina, called adenocarcinoma. DES sons also have fertility problems, including low sperm counts, decreased sperm motility and abnormal sperm forms. Some have small penises or undescended testicles (a risk factor for testicular cancer).

In response to the drug's far-reaching effects, DES mothers, sons, and daughters founded a national consumer group called DES Action USA. With headquarters in New York and San Francisco and affiliates in twenty-two states, DES Action USA provides educational information and support to those exposed to DES as fetuses.

More than five hundred lawsuits have been filed on behalf of DES daughters and sons, covering the myriad problems caused by DES exposure, according to Aaron Levine, a Washington, D.C., lawyer who heads the DES Litigation Group. Hundreds of lawsuits from daughters who are cancer victims or are unable to bear children have been settled out of court. In 1985 Eli Lilly and other drug manufacturers settled 240 cases at once in Detroit for an undisclosed amount.

As DES daughters have moved into their childbearing years, additional suits have been filed on behalf of the children of DES-affected people who were able to conceive. Most of these third-generation suits involve the children of DES daughters and sons born prematurely.

A DES daughter who becomes pregnant is usually considered to have a high-risk pregnancy. Since DES daughters are at increased risk of an ectopic pregnancy, they need to confirm the location of the pregnancy as soon as possible to prevent the serious problem of a ruptured tube, which leads to internal bleeding. They also have an increased risk of miscarriage, signaled by bleeding or spotting, cramping, and loss of breast tenderness while pregnant.

As you can see, a variety of medical problems may lead

to a couple's inability to conceive or bear a child. In addition, social factors play at least as important a role. These various medical problems can be best understood within their social context, which we discuss in the next chapter.

3

THE
SOCIAL
FACTS

*Why Is This Generation
Different from All
Other Generations?*

With the first public sale of birth control pills in 1960, the sexual revolution was off and running, followed closely by the free-spirited drug culture and the rock 'n' roll music era. Those days of free love and hedonism may have taught us to live life to the fullest. But many former swinging singles now want a family and have learned—too late —that sexual freedom may have lowered their fertility.

The 1960s was also an era of environmental consciousness. Rachel Carson's *Silent Spring* caused an uproar over pesticides, but the publicity did little to protect the fertility of pesticide workers and others exposed to harmful chemicals at the worksite.

Further problems arose, including reports of genetic damage to people who "dropped acid" (LSD) repeatedly. And although the Surgeon General warned us about the health hazards of cigarettes, he failed to mention that smoking can reduce fertility.

Social trends of the 1970s added a further variable to the fertility equation. Former activists began building careers. An increasing number of women delayed childbearing to become lawyers and doctors, and the equal rights movement encouraged women to take greater control of their own lives. The single, working woman became the image to be emulated.

The "Me decade" also brought an increased emphasis on exercise and healthy eating habits. But some women who worked too hard at working out stopped menstruating, while others found that strict diets and health foods were detrimental to their reproductive systems.

And in the 1980s, so-called yuppies, striving to one-minute manage their lives, found that a lack of control over their reproductive systems can be frustrating. The factors that can affect fertility have finally caught up with many of us. Now that some are ready to reproduce, they find out that they can't. The first step is to cease potentially harmful behavior immediately. Then you may have to seek the help of a fertility specialist.

Pregnancy in Their Thirties, Not Their Twenties

One of the basic reasons why today's couples have trouble making babies is that they have waited until their thirties before trying. As the body ages, conception becomes more of a gamble. Just how much of a gamble depends on your lifestyle, general health, and personal history. And just as most of us can run faster, stay up later, and eat more without gaining weight when we're younger, a woman's body is more apt to cooperate in conceiving a baby at age twenty than at thirty or forty.

Since the mid-1960s, the proportion of married women under thirty who have never had a baby has more than doubled, from 12 percent to 25 percent. The primary reason is that couples are marrying later and delaying childbearing. More than half of women aged twenty to twenty-four and one-quarter of those twenty-five to thirty had never married in 1985, more than twice the percentages of never-marrieds among those age groups in 1960, according to the Office of Population Research at Princeton University.

Postponement of pregnancy represents a significant change by our generation. Women have their first child, on average, three years later than women did twenty years ago. In other words, when today's women try to conceive, they are already three years older than their counterparts of past generations.

In addition to the natural decline in fecundability (the ability to become pregnant) with increasing age, the longer a woman puts off becoming pregnant, the more she risks having her fertility threatened for various other reasons—including sexually transmitted diseases and complications due to conditions like endometriosis. Since a woman carries all her eggs from birth, her eggs also have to survive all the drugs, chemicals, and X-rays that she has been exposed to during her life. The extra years of exposure to different agents play a role in the increase in abnormal cell division seen in a woman's eggs as she ages. Older women, particularly those over age thirty-five, have a greater chance of bearing a child with birth defects, even though mother nature has a way of screening out most of these defective embryos in older women: she rejects them through miscarriages.

Despite the body's changes, women in their thirties now account for an increasing percentage of births. Mothers older than thirty had one out of four U.S. births in 1985, nearly twice as many as teenage mothers. And between 1980 and 1990, population experts anticipate a 46 percent rise in the number of births to women over thirty-five.

Some of these older women are self-supporting singles who want a child before their biological clocks run down.

The birth rates of unmarried women in their thirties and forties has increased steadily over the past twenty years, which may be a function of the increased number of unmarried women in their thirties today. In 1974, about one in seven women age thirty to thirty-four was unmarried; in 1984, the figure had risen to one in four.

Cohabitation without marriage has become an acceptable way for young couples to live. But the earlier days of free sex and swinging singles parties may have caused unwitting damage to a significant number of never-marrieds. Reluctant to settle for less than their ideal mates, many searched and searched, playing the field. Some women used repeated abortions as a means of birth control, which in some cases led to infection and scarring of the uterus and fallopian tubes. And after years of exposure to sperm, some women have produced antisperm antibodies—one more obstacle to fertility.

A man's fertility may also decline with age. A promiscuous twenties can lead to a sterile thirties, due to the ravages of venereal diseases affecting the epididymis. Alcohol and marijuana are proven gonadotoxins (toxic to the testicles), and long-term substance abuse can reduce fertility. Also, men with varicocele, a collection of abnormally enlarged veins draining the testicles, may be fertile when they are younger, but because a varicocele slowly damages the testicle's ability to make healthy sperm, they become infertile later in life.

Economics

"Whatever I do, I feel I have to do well," says Ginger, a forty-two-year-old sales representative. "Everything I work hard at, I achieve. I worked at having a baby, but didn't achieve it. That's been hard to take." Ginger has wanted to have a baby with her second husband, Steve, since they were married two and a half years ago. After two

miscarriages, she was referred to Dr. Berger, who diagnosed a hormonal problem.

"I have read every book on fertility, and had a thorough history and practically every test conceivable," says Ginger, who has made notes about all of her fertility tests, treatments, and their outcomes "to see if I can shed some light. I feel that I have done all that I could, that I have left no stone unturned."

After three consecutive cycles of hormone stimulation with Pergonal without a pregnancy, Ginger has decided to take a break from treatment for a few months. "I will probably try to get pregnant until I'm fifty. I'm not going to give up until I'm sure we have exhausted all of our resources. I see it as a crapshoot—sometimes you win, sometimes you lose. Eventually, your number is going to come up. I'm going to rest up, and then go for it again."

Changes in the work world have given women more economic independence, which in turn has led more couples to postpone marriage and childbirth. Many couples have waited until both the husband and wife have established careers and they can afford to start a family. But the stress and anxiety of making a living in a competitive economic climate, even with two incomes, have taken their toll on men's sperm counts and altered the delicate balance of women's reproductive hormones.

Many infertile couples want to control their reproductive lives just as they do their business lives. With two incomes, these couples usually have the money and motivation to seek the top fertility experts. Women executives are more likely than other women to plan their pregnancies carefully. More than one in four women executives use home pregnancy and ovulation test kits, according to a survey by Warner-Lambert's Early Pregnancy Information Center.

For these high achievers and technology believers, it is especially frustrating when a pregnancy doesn't happen on schedule. Those who thought they could overcome any obstacle in life keenly feel the disappointment of infertility.

An acronym that has been used to describe the millions of baby boom couples who work for wages and, so far, don't have children is DINKs—Double Income, No Kids. Executives studying demographic changes for marketing opportunities have now identified a large segment of the baby boom generation as worthwhile targets. An extreme example is "Video Baby," a videotape of a newborn, which is being pitched to couples who don't have a child of their own.

Several factors have fed the DINKS trend. First, there is the surging presence of women in the workforce. From 1965 to 1985, the number of women with jobs almost doubled. Among married couples aged twenty-five to thirty-four, two-thirds of wives work, compared with fewer than half ten years ago. And about half of all women are working before their child's first birthday.

Back in the 1940s, 1950s, and even the 1960s, newlyweds normally took a brief year to start a family. It was unusual for the wife to work. Today, it's not unusual for wives to earn more than their husbands, or for couples to wait ten years before having a child. By postponing a family and having two incomes, these DINKS have found that they can achieve their high material aspirations.

Today's middle-class wife is used to having control over her life. So if something goes wrong and she can't have a child, she faces a profound sense of guilt and failure. But most biological problems that cause infertility are not within her control. And the treatment of infertility adds stresses of its own.

Stress and Its Effects

"I tried all my life to prevent pregnancies, starting on the Pill when I was a teenager," says Jan, aged twenty-eight. "I was in college a long time, then worked hard to save some money. I thought everything was in place. I had a good job as a nurse, a house, a good husband. After so many years of marriage, we were going to have a baby. It was all calculated."

What Jan and her husband Larry, aged thirty, hadn't counted on was a combination of fertility problems. Her obstetrician-gynecologist ordered tests and found that her mucus was "hostile" to Larry's sperm, which had a high percentage of abnormal forms. An artificial insemination attempt was unsuccessful, and so they went to see Dr. Berger. An endometrial biopsy and hormone studies revealed that Jan had a luteal phase defect. After hormone treatments, another artificial insemination failed. Jan decided to stop fertility treatments, and she and Larry have applied to an adoption agency.

"I had to stop. It was getting too stressful," says Jan. "I quit my job, even though I loved it, because I found myself slipping away from work, not giving 100 percent, thinking about having a baby. I'm trying to slow down, not put any pressure on myself. I've always been a go-getter. But when I got to the point of feeling like I was losing control, it scared me."

The infertile couple grapples with a problem that is stressful for them physically, emotionally, and financially. Both husband and wife are distressed by a loss of choice and control over the direction of their lives, feelings of being damaged or defective, and over their personal and sexual identities.

Some sociologists attribute the high amount of emotional turmoil experienced by the current generation of prospective parents to their large numbers. Because of supply and demand, a large age group—baby boomers, who total nearly one third of all Americans—faces lower wages, higher unemployment, and less upward job mobility than smaller-sized age groups. Most of today's young couples have high material expectations because they grew up in prosperous times. To achieve their expectations in a highly competitive job market, many have stayed single, or formed families with working spouses and few, if any, children.

Our generation may feel more stressed and clinically depressed earlier in life than previous generations. Female baby boomers have a 65 percent greater chance than earlier generations of being clinically depressed at some time in their lives. The suicide rate among women aged fifteen to twenty-four in 1980 was nearly three times that of a comparable age group in 1950. Depression has changed from a disease of people in their forties, fifties, and older to one of people in their twenties and thirties.

Chronic stress can have detrimental effects on the reproductive system, just as it can on any other organ system. It has been associated with lowering a man's sperm count, motility (how well sperm swim) and morphology (the percentage of normally shaped sperm). Depressed testosterone levels have been linked not only with the stress of combat or combat training but also with the stressful business climate today's men face everyday.

Stress has been known to lower semen volume and raise the percentage of abnormal sperm forms. The additional stress of an infertility evaluation and treatment particularly for an in vitro fertilization (IVF) program, can further lower a man's semen quality.

Stress also affects a woman's reproductive function and her ability to become pregnant. Chronic stress can reduce the output of gonadotropin releasing hormone (GnRH) from the hypothalamus, which in turn causes the pituitary to reduce its output of the gonadotropins (FSH, LH). Because of the reduced signals to the ovaries from the pituitary gland, ovulation may not occur.

Women under stress may suddenly stop having their periods. For example, when a woman moves to a new city to change jobs or go to school, it's relatively common for her next period to be delayed.

Even extremely healthy people are susceptible to the reproductive ravages of stress. Both male and female athletes who put themselves through intense, ofttimes stressful training periods may have disrupted reproduction.

Health Kicks

The national obsession with fitness and health has had its reproductive repercussions. The search for the "runner's high" has led some female athletes to become prone to scanty or missed periods, and some male athletes to have lowered testosterone levels and impaired sperm production. Women who diet to become fashionably slim may run a risk of compromising their reproductive function since too little body fat can impair a woman's ability to ovulate.

Strict vegetarian diets may also have hurt today's fertility rates. Low protein diets, particularly those lacking in meat, may affect a woman's fertility. Seemingly healthful vegetarian diets often lack essential nutritional requirements, such as zinc, which a man needs in sufficient amounts to produce sperm.

Once prevalent mainly among ballet dancers who felt the pressure to be thin, amenorrhea (no menstruation) has been spread by the exercise boom to runners, swimmers, and gymnasts. A decade of research has shown how exercise can disrupt a woman's hormonal balance and her menstrual cycle, particularly among competitive athletes: Regular exercise can delay a girl's first period, cause her to have irregular periods (oligomenorrhea) or no periods at all (amenorrhea). Older women athletes who become excessively thin can also experience menstrual irregularities or have no periods at all. Many women who began running in their mid-teens and have run long distances through their twenties have found that they are having trouble getting pregnant in their thirties.

Lack of body fat is one of the causes of this type of infertility. The body's fat tissues store and convert hormones, including reproductive hormones. To allow the natural rise and fall of hormones during the menstrual cycle, a woman must maintain a body fat content of about 22 percent. Too much exercise, along with an excessively rigorous diet, may reduce a woman's body fat and cause her to have ovulation problems. Runners with a body fat content of 17 percent or less don't menstruate.

Aside from body weight or fat content, exercise itself can disrupt the pattern of hormone pulses that initiate the menstrual cycle. Normally, the "master" regulatory gland in the brain, the hypothalamus, emits pulses of gonadotropin releasing hormone (GnRH) every 90 to 120 minutes in women as a message to the pituitary to release luteinizing hormone (LH) and follicle stimulating hormone (FSH). But during strenuous exercise, the brain signals to the hypothalamus are altered, so the pulse pattern of GnRH becomes irregular. As a result, the pituitary puts out less than normal amounts of FSH and, in turn, the ovaries produce less estrogen (required for endometrial proliferation and for good cervical mucus production) and less progesterone (needed to make the uterine lining receptive for implantation). Also, a woman may not have a surge of LH during the middle of her menstrual cycle. Without these hormonal fluctuations, a woman may not ovulate or menstruate.

Another change in hormones found among competitive women athletes is an increased output of the stress-related adrenal hormone cortisol. The emotional stress of a strenu-

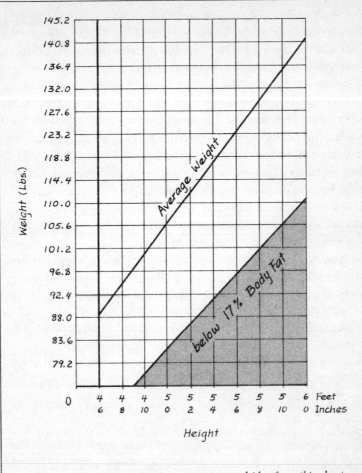

If you are not menstruating, you can get a good idea from this chart whether your body fat content is too low, based upon your height and weight. Women need more than 17 percent body fat (above the shaded area) to menstruate regularly.

ous training lifestyle, along with boosts in cortisol production, has led some women athletes to lose weight and stop having their periods.

The normal production of gonadotropins may also be hindered by increased production of endorphins in the brain. The release of these natural painkillers is thought to cause the so-called "runner's high."

Most of these athletes can reverse their infertility by simply gaining some weight. In fact, some women athletes who monitor their weight carefully know that if they gain some weight, their periods will return. The accompanying height and weight chart, devised by Harvard's Dr. Rose Frisch, shows you how much women of different heights need to weigh to maintain menstruation.

For example, if you are 5'8" tall and weigh ninety-eight pounds, your body fat level is less than 17 percent. Looking at the chart, you can see that you fall beneath the 17 percent body fat cutoff line. Lack of body fat may be the reason why you aren't menstruating. But if you gained ten pounds and weighed 108 pounds, you would be above the 17 percent body fat line. You would have the body fat necessary to store hormones and begin menstruating again.

Men, Exercise and Fertility

Strenuous exercise can cause a man's testosterone levels and sperm production to drop, also by interfering with the brain's signals that control hormones. It takes greater alterations in hormone levels to affect a man's fertility, however, and it usually takes a man longer than a woman to notice the symptoms of hormonal changes. If a man's testosterone level falls far enough over a long period, he will eventually lose his libido, and his sperm count will drop drastically.

Regular long-distance running may produce changes similar to those experienced by women long-distance runners. Prolonged periods of intense exercise can interfere

with a man's rhythmic release of GnRH from the hypothalamus and, subsequently, the release of pituitary hormones LH and FSH, just as in women. For a man, the result
can be reduced testosterone levels and a lower sperm
count.

This may explain why men who run 200 or more miles
each week often complain of a low sex drive. (They also
may be tired from running nearly thirty miles a day!) New
research shows that men who run twenty-five to thirty-
five miles a week have a 20 to 30 percent drop in testosterone levels and a slightly impaired sperm count.

A study of competitive wrestlers shows that their testosterone levels were higher after the season, when they
gained weight, than during the season, when they were
fighting to make their weight class. This correlation between change in body fat combined with intense, stressful
competition and falling hormone levels parallels that of
women athletes striving to stay slim.

Food and Fertility

Coupling exercise with a severely restricted diet can add to
a man's or woman's chance of reduced fertility. Anorexia, a
nervous disorder in which a person loses his or her appetite
and eats very little food, is rarely a problem for men. But a
man may go on a low-calorie diet as he starts a strenuous
exercise program in order to reduce his weight, which may
reduce his testosterone level.

More often, it's fashion-conscious women pursuing to-
the-bone thinness who compromise their fertility through
dieting. Some of these extremely thin young women with
unexplained infertility or menstrual problems have sex
hormone levels that match those of anorexic women.

A woman's weight normally increases with age.

Healthy women in their twenties and thirties who emulate teenage fashion models are trying to achieve an image that's not normal for their stage of life. As a result they are often underweight and may not ovulate or menstruate.

Young women in their twenties starving down to high-fashion figures may even hormonally repeat the experience of puberty. Researchers have found a general tendency for the LH level in the blood and the ratio of LH to FSH to increase as these underweight women begin to approach their ideal body weight. Just before a pubescent girl starts menstruating, the LH jumps way up and is maintained at this elevated level for several months, then drops down into the normal adult range. Women below their ideal body weight may become suspended in a hormonal state similar to puberty. Once they gain a few pounds, however, their pituitary gland function generally returns to normal.

Another factor may be what's in the diet. Nonmenstruating women athletes tend to consume less protein and take in fewer calories each day than menstruating women athletes. A Tufts University study shows nonmenstruating athletes consume an average of thirteen grams less protein per day than menstruating women athletes of the same height and weight. (One turkey sandwich and an eight-ounce glass of skim milk usually provide an adequate daily protein intake for an adult, say the Tufts nutritionists.)

A lack of meat in the diet can also affect ovulation. A German study of nine healthy young women on a balanced, meat-filled diet and nine women on a vegetarian diet found that seven of the vegetarian dieters stopped ovulating during a six-week weight loss program compared to only two of the meat-eating weight watchers. In addition, the menstrual cycles of all the vegetarians became significantly shorter than those of the nonvegetarians. The researchers at the Max Planck Institute in Munich suggest that inadequate amounts of protein in the vegetarian diet may have contributed to the athletes' hormone problems.

A strict vegetarian diet has also been linked to male infertility due to a zinc deficiency. In fact, a low sperm count may be a tip-off to a mild zinc deficiency. Some men with low sperm counts have been successfully treated with high doses of zinc.

Men who are strict vegetarians and who want to father children may need zinc supplements to give their fertility some zest. Although certain foods included in a typical vegetarian diet, such as whole grains, nuts, and legumes, contain zinc, animal protein is considered the best source of this element. The widespread use of bran in non-meat diets may counterbalance zinc intake: Bran attaches itself to zinc in the intestine and stops it from being absorbed.

Substance Abuse

Drug abuse has so permeated our society that the use of marijuana, alcohol, cocaine, and other mood-altering substances has become commonplace among young adults. An estimated 5 to 10 percent of women of childbearing age use illicit drugs on a regular basis, and another 5 percent have more than two drinks a day.

Drugs that affect the central nervous system (see accompanying list) will affect the control of gonadotropin secretion. Because of their actions on the central nervous system, these drugs can modify the brain's output of hormones that control the production of reproductive hormones. Changes in concentrations of the pituitary hormones LH, FSH, and prolactin can result in reduced libido, sexual dysfunction, and infertility.

Marijuana's effects on reproduction have been well established. Studies show that women who smoke marijuana

---

Drugs That Affect the Central Nervous System

Stimulants	Depressants
Amphetamines	Alcohol
Caffeine	Anesthetics
Cocaine	Barbiturates
Nicotine	Benzodiazepine Tranquilizers
Phencyclidine ("Angel Dust")	Heroin
	Marijuana

---

have shorter menstrual cycles and shorter luteal phases, particularly when they smoke during the late phase of the cycle. Men who are long-term marijuana smokers produce less sperm, and tend to have lower testosterone levels, lower sperm motility, and more abnormally shaped sperm than nonsmokers. Chronic marijuana smokers may also have chromosome damage, which may lead to problems in conception or to birth defects.

Likewise, chronic use of cocaine inhibits gonadotropin production, and elevates prolactin concentrations, resulting in impairment of a man's fertility by suppressing testosterone and sperm production, as well as his libido.

Alcohol, another commonly abused substance, may also adversely affect the reproductive system. As with other chemicals, alcohol's effects on fertility depend on the amount consumed. Chronic alcohol abuse in men can lead to reduced secretion of testosterone. In addition, chronic drinkers who have liver damage commonly have small sex organs, enlarged breasts, and irreversible impotence.

Both short- and long-term drinking can lead to abnormal sperm production. A man's sperm may have heads with deformities, curled tails, and swollen midpieces after a binge. Sperm from chronic alcoholics show high numbers of abnormal shapes.

Women alcoholics also may suffer from infertility and menstrual disorders. And sexologists at Rutgers University have found that the intensity and frequency of orgasms among women drop rapidly as their alcohol level rises.

Other drugs that affect the central nervous system— such as barbiturates and phencyclidine (PCP or "angel dust")—also show signs of impairing fertility. Barbiturates inhibit both LH and FSH production, and therefore depress reproductive hormone secretion.

"Angel dust" affects many areas of the brain. PCP has been shown to depress both testosterone and LH levels in the blood of animals. Although there aren't any studies of PCP's effects on reproductive function in humans, its effects are probably comparable.

Smoking

Smoking tobacco can also affect the physiologic functions necessary for reproduction.

Smoking alters a woman's estrogen metabolism and depletes her egg production. It can lead to cervical problems since cervical mucus production depends on estrogen production. What's more, high levels of nicotine, found in female smokers' cervical mucus, can be toxic to sperm.

Inhaling tobacco smoke may also impair the ability of the lining of the fallopian tubes to fight off infections. Nicotine and other components in cigarette smoke affect the cilia lining the tubes, and may alter the way the tubes' lining responds to inflammation. This may allow more infections of the tubes and pelvic inflammatory disease, which can lead to tubal damage and ectopic pregnancy.

Women who start smoking before age sixteen and smoke an average of more than half a pack a day show an increased risk of tubal infertility. If these women have used IUDs or had more than five lifetime sex partners, their infertility risk rises significantly. Women smokers have twice the risk of tubal pregnancy compared to women who have never smoked. They also have more frequent miscarriages and premature deliveries than nonsmokers.

Men who smoke are not immune to the harmful effects of tobacco on reproduction. They have significantly lower sperm counts and sperm motility and a significantly greater percentage of abnormally shaped sperm than nonsmokers.

Environmental and Workplace Hazards

Some of the industrial chemicals introduced in the 1960s have been implicated in fertility problems, especially in lowering a man's sperm count. In some instances, doctors and hospital personnel in contact with radioactive materials, radiation, and anesthetic gas have also suffered low fertility rates.

The testicles are the most sensitive organs in a man's body when it comes to exposure to environmental agents. Radiation, pesticides, and industrial solvents may all harm his sperm production. Many of these agents interfere with male hormone production and sperm formation, causing a loss of libido and impotency, or infertility.

Many toxic substances, including radiation and cancer drugs, have their greatest effect on cells with the highest metabolic rates, that is, cells in the process of growing and dividing. That's why the testicles, which make new sperm every day, are so prone to damage.

Of the 60,000 chemicals in widespread commercial use today, only three are regulated based on their documented effects on human reproduction: metallic lead, the pesticide dibromochloropropane (DBCP), and the pharmaceutical solvent ethylene oxide. Most of the remaining 59,997 chemicals haven't been as thoroughly studied, so no one knows what their effects on sperm production might be.

Infertility due to occupational hazards has been less well studied among women, although women who work in the manufacture of oral contraceptives may have altered menstrual function. And pesticides may produce ovarian problems, possibly leading to early menopause.

If a woman becomes pregnant, exposure to various chemicals may damage her developing embryo. Substances having the potential to cause early miscarriage include: ethylene oxide, used in the chemical sterilization of surgical instruments; vinyl chloride, used in the plastics industry; chemical solvents used in manufacturing industries; nitrous oxide exposure among anesthetists, operating room nurses, veterinarians, dentists, and dental assistants; and metallic compounds of manganese, arsenic, and nickel.

What's more, the sex partners of men chronically exposed to lead, DBCP, vinyl chloride, and anesthetic gases, particularly nitrous oxide, may be at increased risk of a miscarriage. Several insecticides, including DDT, chlordecone, and methoxychlor, and metals, including organic lead, copper, cadmium, and zinc, can prevent implantation of the fertilized egg.

Pregnant women who work with video display terminals (VDTs) may also have an increased risk of miscarriage. About a dozen unexplained "clusters" of miscarriages among VDT users have been reported since 1980, but so far the cause of the miscarriages hasn't been authoritatively linked to VDTs. One study by researchers at the Kaiser-Permanente Medical Care Program in Oakland,

California, reported that clerical workers who used VDTs for more than twenty hours a week had almost twice as many miscarriages as women who did other kinds of office work. However, women executives who spent as much time in front of VDTs as the clerical workers didn't have an increased miscarriage rate. So it's not clear yet whether exposure to VDTs is truly associated with more miscarriages.

Heat and Infertility

Intense exposure to heat in the workplace may cause significant fertility loss among men. Workers at risk of heat-provoked infertility include men involved in the smelting of metals and the manufacture of glass, those laboring in the engine rooms of ships, and possibly bakers, farm laborers, and long-distance truck drivers exposed to engine heat.

Normally, the temperature of the testicles is between 93 and 95 degrees Fahrenheit, or 34 and 35 degrees Centigrade. Temperatures above normal body temperature (98.6 degrees F or 37 degrees C) can impair a man's sperm count and motility and cause him to produce abnormal sperm forms. Although the impact on sperm production is generally reversible, a worker exposed on a daily basis, year after year, could experience long-term or even permanent impairment, according to Dr. Richard J. Levine, chief of epidemiology at the Chemical Industry Institute of Toxicology in Research Triangle Park, North Carolina.

A man's testicular temperature tends to be higher when he is sitting than when he is standing. The poor semen quality of paraplegics has been attributed, in part, to elevated testicular temperatures because they are forced to sit in a wheelchair, Dr. Levine notes. Others who sit for long periods, such as long-distance bus drivers and workaholic executives, may also be at increased risk of infertility.

The connection between exposure to heat and male infertility has also been noted outside the workplace. A high fever has long been associated with impaired sperm production. In tropical and subtropical climates, fewer women tend to become pregnant during the hot seasons, and men seem to have higher sperm counts during the winter.

How to Prevent Further Damage

Although you or your mate might fit into one of the above categories, that doesn't mean that you won't ever have a baby. Even if your lifestyle or habits have led to damage, you may still be able to prevent further damage to your fertility.

Obstetrics textbooks specify that a thirty-five-year-old woman who gets pregnant for the first time is considered to be an "elderly primigravida," which reflects the medical profession's concern with the medical and obstetric complications accompanying delayed childbearing. The ideal time, from a physical standpoint, for a woman to become pregnant is in her early or mid-twenties when her body is physically mature, her reproductive system is most responsive, and her chances of producing a genetically abnormal child are minimal.

From a socioeconomic view, however, delayed childbearing may be more advantageous. Studies supported by the National Institute of Child Health and Human Development have found that older mothers tend to have more education, higher status jobs, and better incomes than do mothers five or ten years younger. They also are likely to have higher aspirations for their children and more money to provide material goods and a quality education.

There have been many babies born to women in their late thirties and early forties, both naturally and through advanced reproductive technologies such as IVF. Perhaps the most unusual example is Pat Anthony, a forty-eight-year-old woman who gave birth to her own grandchildren —triplets conceived in vitro by her daughter and son-in-law—which she carried for them, proving the reproductive power of at least one over-forty woman to do what her daughter, who had had a hysterectomy, couldn't do.

When it comes to stress, a woman whose job or life circumstance places her under excessive pressure would be wise to delay pregnancy until she can reduce that stress, if at all possible.

The degree to which stress and exercise affect a man's testosterone level or sperm count depends on the individual man. Usually, hormonal changes in men who exercise regularly aren't severe enough to cause a loss in libido. For a man who exercises strenuously, is having difficulty fathering a child, and has a low sperm count, cutting back on exercise may help. Male athletes, particularly those involved in ever-popular "ultrasports," such as triathlons, may need to moderate their activity levels. Keeping body weight within normal limits, including a body fat content above 5 percent, will likely maintain a man's fertility.

People with an already damaged reproductive system will compound their fertility problems if they use illicit drugs. The type and amount of drug taken, how often it's taken, and the amount of active ingredient (which varies widely in street drugs), all affect the degree of reproductive, as well as general health, risks. Other factors include the user's age and the duration of use.

Fortunately, most drugs have a temporary effect on the central nervous system pathways necessary for normal production of gonadotropins. So when you stop using drugs, the harmful effects on your reproductive function are likely to be reversed.

Infertile couples who smoke cigarettes should quit if they want to improve their fertility potential, not to mention their general health and the health of their baby.

The problems of workplace reproductive hazards underscore the need to know the occupational history of each partner as part of the fertility workup. The history may also help in planning treatment. For example, it may take several months for a man to recover sperm production after an environmental insult, so periodic semen analyses are often useful in monitoring his response.

Assessing the significance of workplace exposures is often difficult. Occupational exposures are usually not isolated to one chemical, and the dosage may vary according to the particular job, tasks on the job, and accidents and spills. Exposure to potentially harmful agents is not routinely monitored in most workplaces.

One potential problem—excessive heat—can usually be overcome. If a man has sperm problems, he should minimize his exposure to heat.

The possible association of video display terminal use and miscarriage is potentially serious, since about half of the estimated 10 million people who use VDTs on the job are women of childbearing age. These women can use protective screens over their VDTs to absorb radiation. Pregnant women who work with computers for more than half the working day should take frequent breaks from the machine, interspersing non-VDT work with VDT work. Some pregnant women who operate VDTs have arranged with their employers to let them do other kinds of work or to cut down their hours at the computer during their term of pregnancy.

When to Seek Help from a Specialist

You and your spouse may have been trying to have a baby for a few months and are wondering, "Do we have a fertility problem?" There are simple tests that your family doctor, ob-gyn, or urologist can perform to give you a clue about your fertility before going through a full workup by a fertility specialist. With the ovulation predictor kits now available in drugstores, you can determine when you are ovulating, and can have sex around this most fertile time. Keeping a basal body temperature (BBT) chart may also help identify your normal ovulation days and hormonal cycles.

Remember that the odds of a woman getting pregnant are only about one in four each month, even under optimal conditions. That's why most couples should wait at least six months before seeking medical help.

The American Fertility Society recommends waiting two years for women under thirty and one year for women over thirty before seeking a specialist. But the view shared by many doctors is that a full year's wait isn't justified for couples in their thirties since fertility naturally declines with age. Because women in their thirties may be fighting their biological clocks, a wait of one year may waste precious time. Most fertility specialists recommend an evaluation if the wife is over thirty and the couple hasn't conceived after six months of frequent intercourse without birth control. Couples under thirty should seek medical counseling if they haven't conceived after one year of unprotected intercourse.

When the woman is over thirty, or if either partner has reason to believe there is a risk factor in their background —a history of genital infections, a DES mother, irregular periods, unusual sexual development—this certainly justifies an early evaluation. Women who have a history of two or more miscarriages and no live births may want to seek out a fertility specialist.

If you are over thirty or have clues from the past that you might have a fertility problem, and you still don't get pregnant after optimizing your chances by timing sex around ovulation, then you need not wait as long as six months before seeking medical help.

Part Two

WHAT
YOU CAN
DO

4

GETTING STARTED WITH A FERTILITY SPECIALIST

Sandy, a thirty-five-year-old musician, was referred to a gynecologist who had recently helped her friend through a miscarriage. He found that Sandy had a hormone deficiency. Her writer-husband, Jeff, aged thirty-six, had a normal sperm count. But after six months, Sandy and Jeff went looking for a fertility specialist. "My ob-gyn didn't treat me badly," says Sandy. "He picked up the ball, but he couldn't run with it. He wasn't able to do the more sophisticated tests we needed. His office was set up to provide care for pregnant women rather than deal with infertile couples."

Another friend recommended that Sandy see a doctor at a medical center, who suggested she and her husband try artificial insemination. "I asked him, 'What are the odds that this will work?' He said, 'I can't tell you that. Every patient is different.' So I went to the medical library. I found no evidence that artificial insemination made any sense in our situation. We could have done things nature's way without the stress of artificial insemination. Without a more thorough evaluation, artificial insemination was as sensible as having us do it standing on our heads."

Sandy and Jeff put their names on a waiting list at a big university hospital. Meanwhile, Jeff interviewed a doctor for a story. "I liked the sound of him. I knew he was running an in vitro fertilization (IVF) clinic, and was pretty sure he was a bona fide fertility specialist," Jeff says. "He was at a teaching hospital and was involved with federally funded research. By the way he spoke, I could tell he knew about Sandy's condition and that he could help us.''

Finding the right fertility specialist can be a frustrating and confusing process. The American Fertility Society (AFS), a medical society open to all doctors who have an interest in fertility, has more than ten thousand members. But not all of these doctors specialize in treating infertility. With the information in this chapter, however, and the directory of fertility specialists in the back of this book, you should be able to find a doctor in your geographic area who will be likely to meet your infertility needs.

How to Find the Right Doctor

A couple should expect to see their fertility specialist frequently during a period of intensive testing and treatment, maybe even as often as they see their friends. If you don't feel comfortable with your doctor, you probably will not get the most out of your treatment. You should be able to ask questions and get answers that you can understand and that make sense to you. If not, you will probably not have a successful interaction with that doctor.

Some couples find it hard to leave their primary care doctor to look for a fertility specialist. They may feel disloyal about asking for a second opinion or transferring their care to another doctor. But it's your body and your future. Your relationship with your doctor is a professional, not a personal, one. Just because your previous doctor's treatments have not succeeded doesn't mean he is a bad doctor.

The first doctor you may talk with about wanting to get pregnant is your family doctor. *Family practitioners* (FPs) and *general practitioners* (GPs) are trained as generalists. They deal with a wide variety of diseases as well as health maintenance. Part of their training is to identify and treat a wide range of conditions and, if need be, make referrals to specialists. FPs and GPs may have you start a basal body temperature (BBT) chart or suggest a semen analysis.

Your primary physician may be an *internist,* who has had additional residency training in diagnosing and treating medical disorders. There are many subspecialties within internal medicine—cardiology to treat the heart, gastroenterology for intestinal organs, oncology for cancer treatments—but none specifically for fertility. The closest subspecialty is medical endocrinology, which requires an internist to take additional training in diseases that affect the endocrine system. If a *medical endocrinologist* sees a patient with excess hair growth (hirsutism), this may indicate a coexisting fertility problem. Some thyroid diseases can also affect fertility. But most medical endocrinologists, like general internists, FPs, and GPs, are neither specially trained nor often willing to provide in-depth care for infertile couples.

Women who are having trouble getting pregnant usually go to their *obstetrician-gynecologist* (ob-gyn) for basic fertility studies. The ob-gyn is a specialist in the evaluation and treatment of diseases of women and in providing care for pregnant women, and has three or more years of residency training in these areas. If your ob-gyn has passed the required written and oral examinations and been in clinical practice for the additional years required by the American Board of Obstetrics and Gynecology, he or she will usually display a certificate or show on the practice's stationery that he or she is a certified specialist or diplomate of the American College of Obstetrics and Gynecology. Sometimes, after a board-certified doctor's name, you will see the letters "FACOG," which stands for Fellow of the American College of Obstetricians and Gynecologists.

The basic tests performed by most ob-gyns include a pelvic exam, a check of basal body temperature (BBT) charts, and the monitoring of some baseline hormone levels, such as prolactin and progesterone levels during the luteal phase. In addition, most ob-gyns will perform a postcoital test (PCT), endometrial biopsy, or diagnostic laparoscopy.

The *urologist* is the male's counterpart to the gynecologist. The urologist has completed a residency training of at least three years in the evaluation and treatment of disorders of the kidneys, urinary tract, bladder, and male reproductive organs, in addition to having at least two years of general surgical training. To become certified by the American Board of Urology, a urologist must also have practiced urology for eighteen months, including twelve months of urologic surgery. Board-certified urologists may become Fellows of the American College of Surgeons and use the initials "FACS" after their names.

For fertility patients, urologists will perform semen analyses, look for varicoceles (varicose veins in the scrotum), check hormone levels, and order lab tests to check sperm quality. Often, however, they only see the husband and have little idea about his wife's fertility problems, just as the gynecologist may see only the wife and have little knowledge of the husband's problems—which may interfere with coordinating the couple's workup and treatment.

Some ob-gyns take additional subspecialty training and become certified as *reproductive endocrinologists.* The American Board of Obstetrics and Gynecology certifies reproductive endocrinologists who have completed two additional years of training beyond their ob-gyn residency, passed oral and written exams, shown they are competent in managing reproductive endocrinology problems in their practice, and published a report in a peer-reviewed medical journal. Most certified reproductive endocrinologists are also members of the AFS's subspecialty group, the Society of Reproductive Endocrinologists. To join, a doctor must be an active member of the AFS and be certified as a reproductive endocrinologist.

Reproductive endocrinologists primarily are subspecialists in the treatment of hormonal diseases of women, including disorders involving the pituitary, thyroid, and adrenal glands, as well as the ovaries. A reproductive endocrinologist is likely to use the full range of hormonal treatments available, including Pergonal, Metrodin and gonadotropin releasing hormone (GnRH). In addition, a reproductive endocrinologist also conducts in-depth workups for further evaluation of ovulation problems, such as polycystic ovarian disease (PCOD). He or she usually has received some training in reproductive surgery.

A second group of subspecialists who deal with fertility problems are *reproductive surgeons.* A reproductive surgeon is specially trained and qualified to treat anatomical problems such as tubal obstruction, endometriosis, uterine abnormalities, and any other reproductive organ disorder requiring surgery. A reproductive surgeon can be either a gynecologist or a urologist, but in either case must be familiar with the principles of microsurgical reconstructive surgery, applying these principles to the reproductive organs.

More often ob gyns than urologists, reproductive surgeons look to conserve and restore reproductive potential. They are the most well-trained and experienced doctors to perform complicated reconstructive operations to restore fertility when it has been impaired by tubal blockage (including tubal ligation), scarring from pelvic inflammatory disease (PID), endometriosis, or blocked ducts in men.

Reproductive surgeons can also become members of an AFS subspeciality group, the Society of Reproductive Surgeons. As of 1989, doctors must complete a fellowship either in reproductive endocrinology or reproductive surgery and be in practice for at least three years in order to become eligible to join the Society of Reproductive Surgeons. A minimum of half of their case load must be reproductive surgery for infertility, and they must have been sponsored by two members of the society who have scrubbed and performed surgery with them. Physicians who became members of the Society of Reproductive Surgeons prior to 1989 were admitted based on their training and demonstrated experience in reproductive surgery before formal fellowship training was established.

Another type of specialist dealing with male fertility is the *andrologist*. The andrologist may be either a clinical or basic scientist who studies various aspects of male reproductive function, such as the semen or hormones. Andrologists often are laboratory specialists rather than medical doctors (MDs), and may have earned a Ph.D. (Doctorate of Philosophy) degree in biochemistry, endocrinology, or physiology. They often direct the laboratory procedures for testing sperm.

Andrologists are analogous to reproductive endocrinologists in the sense that these doctors focus on physiologic, hormonal conditions. Urologists are more like reproductive surgeons, since both deal mostly with anatomic problems. Some urologists are also andrologists.

Membership in the American Society of Andrology is open to any professionally qualified physician or scientist who makes a contribution to the field of andrology. Currently, andrologists are discussing how better to define their specialty and debating whether andrology should become a subspecialty of either the urology or fertility society. They would like to set up criteria similar to other specialty groups, with both written and oral exams and clinical fellowships as a prerequisite for certification.

Once the sperm gets together with the egg, it has entered the bailiwick of the *embryologist.* Embryologists watch over the fertilization process through early embryo development. They collaborate with andrologists to work with sperm up to the point of fertilization. They are usually not medical doctors, but may have advanced degrees such as a Ph.D. and tend to work more in the laboratory than directly with patients. An embryologist is trained to handle eggs, monitor development of fertilized eggs in the lab until they are transferred back into the body, and study the development of the embryo.

There is a pyramid of access to the above fertility specialists. As you go from generalists to specialists there are fewer to choose from. Of the more than 460,000 physicians in the country, about 147,000 are generalists, including FPs, GPs, and internists; about 30,000 are ob-gyns; and about 5,000 are urologists. The numbers drop off drastically when we get to the fertility subspecialists. In the United States there are currently about 300 reproductive endocrinologists, 250 reproductive surgeons, 800 andrologists (300 MDs) and less than 100 embryologists. There are, however, many other capable physicians who treat infertility problems and who are not members of one of these professional groups.

Getting to a Fertility Specialist

When Polly called the state medical society asking about a fertility specialist to treat her endometriosis, she was told there were none in her home town of Raleigh, N.C. Then she saw the name of an Oregon specialist in a woman's magazine and called the Endometriosis Society to check him out. They said he was a reputable doctor, and Polly went to Oregon for treatment. He performed laparoscopic surgery to remove adhesions and some areas of endometriosis, and sent her home. Not wanting to travel back West for follow-up, Polly looked for a doctor in the Yellow Pages directories of nearby cities, and found a nearby fertility specialist.

Sometimes a couple's primary care physician may not refer them to a fertility specialist, even after prolonged, unsuccessful treatment. In that case, the doctor is not acting in the couple's best interest. Sometimes couples want to stay with their primary care doctors even when they may be better off going to a specialist. That's all right as long as they are aware of available alternatives.

Your doctor may be an excellent physician and you may have a good relationship with him, yet he may not know how best to evaluate and treat your infertility, or may have ideas that don't fit with how you and your spouse envision your treatment. That's why you need to learn as much as you can about your condition. Listen carefully to what the doctor says and make sure his answers make sense to you.

If your doctor says, "Come in on day thirteen for a postcoital test—except if it's the weekend," then you are probably going to the wrong doctor for fertility treatment. A fertility specialist has to provide medical care at the right time of the cycle, *especially* when you are ovulating, which includes weekends, in order to check the cervical mucus, test hormone levels, and provide appropriate treatment when you are ovulating, not just when it's convenient. If your doctor is unavailable at the time these tests or procedures need to be done, find another doctor who takes these issues seriously enough to deal with them every day of the week, including weekends and holidays.

Your doctor should talk to you in a logical, unhurried fashion so that you can understand what he is thinking and develop confidence in him. You should also pay attention to your gut feelings. If you don't get "good vibes" when you see him, you may have a harder time with treatment.

You should recognize what's important to you in your relationship with your doctor. For example, do you want your doctor, who knows you and your history, to be on call (available to you) the majority of the time, or is a "covering" doctor or an associate acceptable? What do your friends, neighbors, colleagues, or any fertility patients you know like about their doctor? What don't they like about the doctor?

You may want to make initial appointments with more than one doctor to get a sense of what they are like, to learn about their staff and to get a feeling for what it will probably be like to deal with them. Try to get a sense of how comfortable you will feel with the doctor. Listen carefully to the answers to your questions—not just the words, but also the feelings and messages behind the words.

It's best to arrange your first visit as a couple. If the doctor doesn't want you to do this, that's usually not a good sign. When you come for your initial visit, talk with other couples in the waiting room, if possible. Ask how long they typically have to wait before being seen. Is the doctor available by phone? Does the doctor answer questions willingly? How much time does the doctor spend with each patient? Are there other physicians in the practice? If so, what are his associates like? Knowing what they now know, ask whether they would choose this doctor again if they were to start over with their fertility treatment.

Talk to the nurses since they will probably interact with you the most. For example, in a private office setting, they draw the blood, perform various tests, and call you with test results and instructions.

If you feel your doctor is not listening to you, don't hesitate to make your concerns known. Ask the questions that are on your mind. According to Dr. Mack Lipkin, Jr., director of the National Task Force on Medical Interviews, studies have shown that patients who ask forthright questions receive better medical care than passive patients.

Here are some of the ways you can actually go about locating a fertility specialist:

- Get a recommendation from your primary care family doctor, obstetrician/gynecologist or urologist.

- Check with the local medical society for names of specialists in your area.

- Contact the directors of private fertility clinics as well as those at nearby medical schools or hospitals.

- Ask a friend for a recommendation, and then check out the doctor yourself.

- Look in the phone book for doctors who limit their practice to fertility services.

- Consult the directory in the back of this book.

- Contact the American Fertility Society or, in Canada, the Canadian Fertility and Andrology Society.

As you embark upon your search for a specialist, keep in mind that fertility treatment is an ever-changing field. Your condition may now be treatable even though you were once told you had no chance. New treatment options continue to become available through private practices specializing in the treatment of infertility, as well as through university medical centers. Become familiar with doctors in your community whom you see, hear, or read about. They may have new techniques appropriate for treating your situation.

Insurance Issues

Betty and Bill had gone through a basic fertility workup, and after two artificial inseminations failed they were advised to try in vitro fertilization. Their first IVF attempt was unsuccessful. The second one worked and Betty, aged thirty-two, became pregnant. Their joy was tempered somewhat when their insurance company failed to cover their second IVF procedure. "They told us we could bill for a total of three inseminations, whether they were artificial or in vitro," says Bill. He and Betty ended up paying out of pocket nearly the full amount for the last procedure.

Besides questioning the doctor, you should ask your insurance carrier what types of fertility treatments, if any, it excludes from your coverage. Insurance companies resist covering new treatments, but several states have now passed laws mandating coverage of infertility and its often innovative procedures. It is up to you to know what your company does and does not cover.

With appropriate testing, most fertility specialists will establish specific diagnoses underlying your infertility. Some health insurance companies may not reimburse a couple for infertility, but will cover the costs of diagnosis and treatment of a specific condition, such as endometriosis, polycystic ovarian disease, or varicocele.

Usually, the infertility diagnosis comes only after tests of your reproductive physiology and anatomy. A woman with tubal infertility may have had salpingitis and developed tubal obstruction and/or pelvic adhesions due to a sexually transmitted infection, such as chlamydia. The farther back in the chain of events the doctor goes in establishing the diagnosis, and the more specific the diagnoses he can make, the better chance he has of suggesting the best fertility treatment and the more likely your insurance company may be in providing coverage for your tests and treatments.

Most insurance companies will reimburse you only if your doctor uses the standard diagnostic terms and number codes specified in the *International Classification of Diseases,* published by the National Center for Health Statistics. Similarly, for tests or treatments there is a standard book called *Current Procedural Terminology* published by the AMA. The classifications change every year, so your doctor has to keep up with the codes.

If you are denied insurance coverage for an infertility treatment, ask your doctor to write a letter to your insurance carrier to help you receive the reimbursement you believe is due you. Insurance companies sometimes make mistakes and may deny a payment that you are entitled to. It's well worth your time to read your health insurance contract carefully and to stand up for your rights. You or your employer have paid the premiums for the insurance and you are legally entitled to the coverage specified in the contract. In most states, unless your contract specifically excludes coverage for a particular problem, you should be reimbursed for treatment of that condition.

What to Expect

When Leslie and her husband, Lou, both aged forty, decided to have a baby, they tried for six months, then went to their family doctor. He suggested they keep trying for a year on their own. Worried that she was running out of reproductive years, Leslie found a fertility specialist, who immediately put them both through a fertility workup.

The fertility specialist told Leslie she had endometriosis, and that she would have to undergo a diagnostic laparoscopy under general anesthesia. Leslie read all she could about endometriosis, including that the diagnostic surgery could be done under local anesthesia. She asked her doctor if he would perform the surgery under a local, and he told her, *"Absolutely not."* *That's when Leslie went looking for another doctor who was comfortable with performing diagnostic laparoscopy using local, instead of general, anesthesia.*

She found two other infertility specialists in the phone book, and called each one. Both said they could do her diagnostic surgery under local anesthesia, but one doctor offered to let her watch via video, which appealed to her. "He listened to all my questions, telling me my options, explaining how he made his choices," she says. She felt even more confident when she met the doctor and his staff. "I liked the way they treated me. He made an effort to be personable, and was responsive to details. He didn't seem too busy to talk."

It's important for you to understand as much as you can about your condition and the possibilities for treatment. If you know about your body and how it works, you can interact with, not just react to, your doctor. Well-informed, educated couples can discuss their situation more specifically with the doctor and his staff, which helps facilitate making the best choices in diagnostic tests and treatments.

A fertility workup does not have to be a long, drawn-out process. Within one or two months, a fertility specialist should be able to give you a diagnosis of what's wrong, tell you what can be done about the problem, and give you an idea of your chances of pregnancy.

For every diagnostic procedure the doctor suggests, you ought to know what to expect from the procedure and what alternatives are available. In the case of treatments, you ought to know the doctor's success with it and, if it doesn't work, what the next step may be.

An infertility practice isn't like a family practice or general ob-gyn or urology practice. A fertility specialist can't see thirty or forty patients a day, spending only five to ten minutes with each patient. Even if your doctor is busy and can't always be available to review your situation with you at each visit, this doesn't mean that your treatment should suffer. These doctors have to build up a staff around them to collect and disseminate information, answer questions, and perform certain procedures. But the doctor should always be available in the event that problems arise that only he can respond to appropriately. The clinic staff may screen the doctor's calls and provide routine information over the phone. You should be able to get in touch with a nurse or a counselor easily and, if need be, see or talk to the doctor.

Most fertility specialists do the least invasive, simplest procedures first, then go on to more complicated procedures. Yet, some people want the most aggressive treatment right away. Your individual circumstances and needs help you and the doctor make the right choice.

Sometimes couples ask their doctor, "What would you do if you were in this situation?" Considering the medical facts, he may say, "I would do this." But he is not you. Besides intellectual concerns, emotional and social issues have to be considered. You and your spouse should be able to come to your own decisions about what seems best for you, given your particular circumstances. The doctor can help you make a decision, but if you ask him to make it for you, when you look back on your treatment later on you may wish you had actively participated in the decision-making process.

It's unrealistic for you to expect your doctor to take full control of your care. You have to take some responsibility for yourself. The first thing you can do is to learn about the diagnosis of your infertility and the available treatments so that you can discuss things intelligently with your doctor.

Trust is an important element in your care. You shouldn't blindly trust your doctor. But if you don't have enough confidence or trust in your doctor you probably will not be able to undergo the complex tests and treatments that may be necessary to help you have a baby.

Use your intellect and know as much as you can about your treatment, and don't lose sight of your goals. If you listen, think, and communicate well with your doctor, you will be able to decide when it's appropriate to question a doctor's decision or to call his office.

If the communication between you and your doctor is not going well, if you feel uncomfortable, or if you aren't getting what you want from the doctor or his staff, be explicit and say what's bothering you. If you still don't feel right, consider finding another doctor.

What Is a Good Fertility Center?

"When I visited my fertility doctor's office, I felt like I was in a living room, not a doctor's office," says Sandy. "I got a warm, cozy feeling, which helped me feel comfortable about being there."

A good fertility center will have an on-site fertility laboratory equipped with the latest medical technology. Some also offer on-site surgery. Typically, there will be several examination rooms, one of which may be reserved exclusively for ultrasound examinations. Another may be exclusively for artificial inseminations, keeping it "clean" from other patients who may have infections. There should also be a "masturbatorium," a private room stocked with appropriate erotic materials for the collection of semen specimens. It should be quiet, where the man won't be disturbed, and be roomy enough for both the husband and wife if she wants to assist in obtaining the semen sample.

The clinic's professional staff, including the lab and operating room personnel, must be available *seven days a week*. This is critical, since certain tests and treatments have to be administered at precisely the right time of the woman's cycle. Such tests and treatments include hormone assays, ultrasound exams, cervical mucus exams, and sperm washing preceding artificial insemination. The doctor should also be able to perform a semen analysis and immunologic and microbiologic studies whenever he desires.

When a new couple comes into a fertility center, the doctor will perform certain basic studies in order to determine what treatments can help them have a baby. Ideally, both the man and woman should undergo prenatal screening for infectious diseases, including blood tests for the AIDS virus, hepatitis B virus, and documentation of immunity to rubella (German measles). If a woman lacks immunity to rubella, she should be given a vaccination and then avoid becoming pregnant for three months until she has developed immunity. This simple procedure will eliminate the risk of her contracting rubella during pregnancy, which could result in the birth of a malformed baby.

Some basic equipment necessary for the appropriate laboratory procedures includes culture media, an incubator, a dissecting microscope, and a fluorescent microscope. Sperm banking should be offered, with frozen donor sperm stored in a liquid nitrogen tank. In some places, fresh samples are made available from local semen donors, although this raises specific risks that will be discussed later.

If the clinic offers IVF or other assisted reproductive technologies, it needs a highly specialized laboratory for handling human eggs outside of the body. This laboratory should be set up in or near the operating room where the egg retrievals take place. To become a member of the Society of Assisted Reproductive Technology of the American Fertility Society, an IVF clinic must have on staff a reproductive endocrinologist, a reproductive surgeon, and an embryologist familiar with human cell culture techniques. The clinic must have performed at least forty procedures and had at least three live births. An IVF laboratory must be more meticulous about every detail in performing procedures than a standard clinical laboratory.

A proper office waiting room will be designed for comfort and privacy, with several couches and easy chairs, some plants and paintings, maybe even colorful wallpaper. At Chapel Hill Fertility Center, the waiting room also serves as a patient education area containing books and pamphlets on fertility, as well as a variety of popular magazines.

Most fertility specialists schedule thirty to ninety minutes for new couples in order to become acquainted with their histories and determine the course of their initial evaluation. Couples returning for, say, an ultrasound exam or a blood test require less scheduled time and may only need to see a trained nurse or technician. But if you need to discuss something with your doctor, make sure you ask for sufficient time on the appointment schedule for that day.

Besides the physician(s), the staff often includes nurses, lab technicians, a counselor or patient care coordinator, and various clerical personnel. If there is no reproductive urologist on staff, then the clinic should offer a referral to a urologist who treats male infertility.

The First Consultation

Before your first consultation, get all your medical records together, or have them sent ahead to your new doctor. The doctor should review with you the past records of tests and treatments at the initial interview. He may start by asking, "What brings you here?" You can give specifics—"I have blocked fallopian tubes and my internist recommended seeing a fertility specialist." You should convey to your doctor whatever you feel are the most important issues or concerns on your mind.

Some standard questions the woman may be asked are: What cycle day is this for you? Have you kept a basal body temperature chart? Have you noticed any symptoms of ovulation? Do you develop premenstrual symptoms, such as fluid retention, tender breasts, or headaches, and how far in advance of your period?

Some standard questions for the man may include: Have you ever fathered a child before? When you ejaculate, how much fluid comes out? Do you feel any pain in your testicles when lifting heavy objects? How many hours a week do you work (an indication of stress or possible on-the-job exposure to toxins that may impair fertility)?

For both partners, questions may include: How long have you been trying to have a baby? Are you taking any medications? Are you under treatment for any kind of medical problem? Do you feel any pain during intercourse? What kind of pain, and where is it located? Have you ever had any sexually transmitted diseases? How often do you have sexual intercourse?

After the initial interview, Dr. Berger introduces the couple to his patient care coordinator, Sandy Pratt, a trained counselor who listens to him summarize and discuss the couple's history, explain what tests he thinks need to be done, and how to treat the problems already identified. Then she discusses what the tests and treatments mean in practical terms. If they want to proceed, the couple can start the diagnostic workup that day. They may choose to make another appointment, allowing them some time to discuss how they feel about their initial visit before taking any action.

You should never feel you are being pressured by your doctor into any particular treatment. The doctor's and his staff's role is to evaluate your situation, discuss it with you, and offer suggestions and recommendations. Dr. Berger often writes letters to summarize test results so that couples have a record of important test results and recommendations, which they can refer to later in case they don't remember certain points discussed during their visits.

After the initial visit, Dr. Berger often schedules the couple's next appointment at the fertile time of the wife's cycle, determined by having her run a simple home test that detects a surge in luteinizing hormone (LH). He likes to see couples on the day of the wife's LH surge since this is the optimal time to check the cervical mucus, perform a postcoital test, perform an ultrasound exam to document the presence of follicles, and draw blood to measure levels of LH, prolactin, and estradiol. In this single visit, he can diagnose many different conditions that cause infertility and begin to establish a treatment plan with the couple.

Taking Your Medical History

The medical evaluation starts by focusing on the most common causes of infertility. Both partners need to have a complete history and physical taken. The history and physical are important because general health problems involving weight, nutrition, and health habits can lead to infertility. Also, both work and play habits such as stress, excessive alcohol drinking, or cigarette smoking can contribute to infertility, as mentioned earlier.

The man's medical history begins with questions about childhood illnesses, current medical problems and their treatments, previous injuries or surgeries (including vasectomy), and the size of the man's immediate family. Infections along the reproductive tract can contribute to a male fertility problem, as well as common infections that cause fevers, such as a flu or dental abscess. The doctor will also ask about the man's general health, whether he is under stress, has been exposed to toxic chemicals, uses any drugs, drinks alcohol, or takes any long-term medications. A sexual history includes questions about the frequency, timing, and technique of sexual intercourse.

The woman's medical history will include questions about abdominal and pelvic surgery as well as any pregnancies. A menstrual history will include questions about when she began menstruating, what her cycles are like, when her last period started, and if she experiences any physical or psychological changes at ovulation or before or during menstruation. A sexual history will include questions about the frequency and timing of sex, if she feels any discomfort during sex, and what type of birth control she has used in the past. Pain during intercourse, or dyspareunia, is a symptom that should always be taken seriously; it might be due to a pelvic infection or endometriosis. A careful history should elicit details about the pain and determine if it's related to a particular time of the menstrual cycle.

Endometriosis may cause pain with intercourse, as well as pain immediately before and during menstruation and sometimes at ovulation. With endometriosis, the lining of the uterus (the endometrium) grows outside the uterus on or in other pelvic organs, and often leads to scar formation. During menstruation, the areas of endometriosis become engorged with blood. The more filled with blood and the closer the areas of endometriosis are to nerve endings in the reproductive tract, the more likely a woman is to feel pain.

Pain at ovulation may have to do with changes in the size of the ovary during ovulation. The microscopic follicle expands to about an inch in diameter during the week before ovulation as it fills with fluid. If scar tissue encloses the ovary, as the follicle expands it may push against the restricting scar tissue and cause pain.

Unfortunately, in many cases the diagnosis of endometriosis comes after the disease has been present for years and has advanced beyond its earliest stages. Frequently, the only symptom of endometriosis is infertility, and therefore this condition should always be considered during a fertility evaluation.

The Physical Exams

During the physical exams, general body appearance, fat and hair distribution, and breast development may reveal hormonal imbalances. For the man, the consistency of the testicles and prostate gland may indicate a hormone imbalance or infection. The physical may reveal a varicocele or an undescended testicle. For the woman, a pelvic exam may reveal infections of the vagina or cervix, or previous pelvic inflammatory disease, or suggest abnormalities of the uterus, fallopian tubes, or ovaries.

The Man's Physical

A complete physical and detailed examination of the testicles can give a fertility specialist a good clue to a man's reproductive function. Hormonal deficiencies are often reflected by an abnormal or "feminized" body shape, poorly developed pubic hair, or enlarged breasts. Sperm production is often reflected in the size and consistency of the testicles. Small, soft testicles generally denote a man has poor sperm production, while large, firm testicles usually mean he has good sperm production.

If a man has testicles of normal size and consistency, yet no sperm in his semen, this suggests that he is making sperm but they can't get out. On the other hand, a man with small, soft testicles who has a low sperm count or produces no sperm at all suggests a sperm production problem, which could be hereditary or due to a varicocele.

Just as cardiologists have their stethoscopes to listen to the heart and neurologists their rubber hammers to check the reflexes, male infertility specialists use orchidometers to measure the testicles. Like measuring spoons on a string, the orchidometer has various sized plastic orbs tied together. Your doctor simply matches each testicle to the appropriate-sized orb hanging from the orchidometer. A normal testicle is about the size and shape of a small hen's egg.

If your doctor finds you have testicles of normal size and consistency, he will feel for the ducts that run behind them—the epididymis and vas deferens—to make sure they are present. About one in a thousand men is born without any vas deferens. This condition cannot be surgically corrected, but a new experimental procedure gives these men a small chance at fertility. A few men have had sperm surgically extracted from the epididymis and then used in an IVF or Gamete Intra Fallopian Transfer (GIFT) procedure to make their wives pregnant.

VARICOSE VEINS IN THE SCROTUM • Once your doctor has determined that a man's testicles and ducts are normal, he will examine the scrotum for a varicocele. A varicocele is an enlarged or dilated vein in the spermatic cord within the scrotum, like a varicose vein in the leg. The enlarged vein causes pooling of blood and a rise in temperature in the testicles. This temperature rise is thought to inhibit sperm production, and may affect fertility.

A varicocele is probably the most common, identifiable cause of male infertility. Between 30 and 40 percent of infertile men have a varicocele, usually on the left side, since the vein on that side is longer and has a higher inner pressure than the vein on the right side. A varicocele in both testicles is relatively rare, and is even rarer on the right side alone. About 15 percent of all men, fertile or infertile, have a varicocele, so just having one doesn't mean that your sperm production will necessarily be impaired.

No one knows why certain men with varicoceles are infertile, but recent research suggests that the pool of stagnant blood heats up inside the testicle's vein. In an animal model, varicoceles have been associated with increased testicular temperature and increased blood flow within the testicle. The high temperature impairs normal sperm production and motility, leading to infertility.

Dr. Goldstein has proven that in humans varicoceles do indeed raise testicular temperature. This had been suggested by temperature studies of the surface of the scrotum, but Dr. Goldstein has recently measured the temperature inside the testicle. His studies show that a varicocele in one testicle raises the temperature within both testicles. What's more, his data also document that repairing these varicoceles causes a drop in testicular temperature, confirming animal studies of varicocele repair.

The basic exam for a varicocele is similar to the simple "turn-your-head-and-cough" testicle check. The doctor has the man stand upright in a warm room (the warmth relaxes the scrotum) and cough to make the veins in the scrotum stand out. (By the way, the doctor has him turn his head only so he doesn't cough right on the doctor.) This will allow an experienced doctor to detect a large varicocele. Then he has the man do what's called Valsalva's maneuver, in which he strains as if he were having a bowel movement. The squeezing makes the veins bulge out even more so that the doctor can detect smaller varicoceles.

A rectal exam completes the man's evaluation, allowing the doctor to detect abnormalities of the prostate and seminal vesicles which contribute most of the fluid to a man's ejaculate.

The Woman's Physical

The woman's physical exam starts with a check for vaginal infections. Examining the discharge from the vagina may help identify the presence of bacteria and other microorganisms that can contribute to infertility.

The exam begins with the doctor removing a sample of vaginal secretion to check on the vagina's pH (acidity level). A look through a microscope at the sample may reveal a high white blood cell count, which indicates that the woman has an inflamed vagina. The doctor can also perform a simple test, dissolving cells from the vaginal fluid in a salt solution of potassium hydroxide, to identify yeast organisms, and also perform a "wet prep," covering a slide with salt water solution to identify the rapidly moving organism called trichomonas.

It's essential for you and your mate to know the specific causes of a vaginal infection. Some bacteria can damage the upper genital tract (the uterus, fallopian tubes, and ovaries); yeasts are more benign, although the symptoms of vaginitis from a yeast infection are just as irritating as from a bacterial infection. When pathogenic or potentially harmful bacteria may infect the lower genital tract (the vagina and cervix), a woman may notice a creamy gray or yellow discharge and an unpleasant odor. But more often, these lower tract infections produce no symptoms at all.

In Dr. Berger's opinion, it's important to make sure that you have no active infection of the lower genital tract before performing any invasive tests in the fertility workup. These tests include injecting dye into the uterus to take an X-ray (hysterosalpingogram), pushing a solution through the fallopian tubes (hydrotubation), taking a fragment of the uterine lining (endometrial biopsy) or looking into the uterine cavity through a tiny telescope (hysteroscopy). These tests, often necessary to evaluate the extent of pelvic problems, can spread a lower tract infection farther up the woman's reproductive tract where it may cause damage to the uterus, tubes, and ovaries.

Viruses that cause vaginitis can be difficult to diagnose, except for the herpes virus, which typically causes blisters that become ulcers on the vulva. (Parasitic organisms, such as trichomonas, are usually more easy to diagnose than viral infections.) Another common viral infection of the vagina, with human papilloma virus (HPV), causes genital warts, or condyloma. While genital warts can become quite large on the vulva (the outer part of the vagina), these lesions are often too small to see in the vagina or on the cervix except through a colposcopic examination. This exam involves using a magnifying instrument to get an enlarged view of the vagina and cervix.

The papilloma virus itself is not thought to cause pelvic inflammatory disease, but often is accompanied by other bacterial organisms that do. Women with genital warts are more likely to have infections with chlamydia, ureaplasma, gonorrhea, and anaerobic bacteria that can inflame the fallopian tubes and lead to infertility. (If a woman has genital warts, her partner should also be examined and treated for penile warts.)

Vaginal adenosis, a disorder related to exposure to diethylstilbestrol (DES) in utero, has also been associated with fertility problems. Even if you have no known history of DES exposure, if your fertility specialist sees adenosis (folds of cervical mucus membrane in the vagina), you may have an anatomical defect higher up the reproductive tract, such as a hood covering the cervix, a ridge (septum) down the center of the cervix or uterus, an abnormally formed, T-shaped uterus, or cysts on your tubes.

CERVICAL EXAM • A cervical exam usually begins with the fertility specialist looking for anatomical abnormalities and seeing whether the cervix looks red or bleeds when touched with a sterile Q-tip, which suggests an inflammation called cervicitis.

One of the most important tests is the postcoital test to see whether you are producing "fertile" mucus that allows your mate's sperm to swim through it. Dr. Berger performs this test on the day of the LH surge, which can be determined using a simple at-home test kit.

Fertile mucus looks like the white of an uncooked egg: it's clear and transparent. It also is elastic and stretches about four inches, has a low viscosity (is not too gel-like) and a relatively high (alkaline) pH to allow sperm to survive in it. Nonfertile mucus is cloudy, sticky, not stretchy, has white blood cells in it, has a low (acidic) pH, and will prevent sperm from entering the upper reproductive tract. (See illustration of fertile mucus.)

A woman may have scanty or no mucus due to an infection of the cervix that involves the mucus glands or possibly due to a treatment required after a previous abnormal Pap smear or a hormonal problem. Either cryocautery (freezing the cervix to treat cervical dysplasia or warts) or a cervical conization (surgery to cut out a cone-shaped portion of the cervix) may damage the mucus glands, causing them not to function properly.

The cervix, as well as the vagina, can be affected by in utero exposure to DES, causing cervical adenosis. The mucus membrane lining the cervical canal or endocervix grows on the outer surface of the cervix or vagina, creating an abnormality at the junction between the two. The growth of this mucus membrane where there should be epithelium can continue out into the vagina, causing vaginal adenosis.

If the same kind of thing happened to the lining of your respiratory tract, the mucus membrane which lines the inside of the nose would grow onto the outside of the nose. In many ways, the mucus in the reproductive and respira-

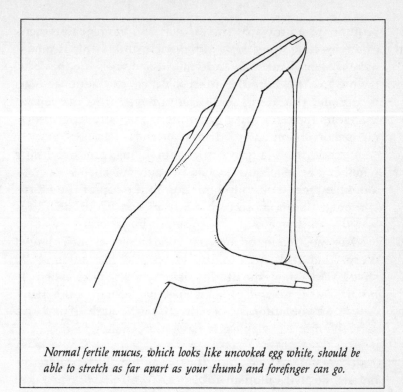

Normal fertile mucus, which looks like uncooked egg white, should be able to stretch as far apart as your thumb and forefinger can go.

tory tracts function similarly. Mucus in your nose protects the lungs by catching dust, smoke, bacteria, and viruses. In the cervix (which, incidentally, feels like and is about the size of the tip of the nose), mucus also traps microorganisms and foreign agents including sperm, except when the mucus changes consistency near ovulation to allow sperm to pass through it. Disorders such as infections, surgical trauma, hormonal deficiencies, or DES-related abnormalities can prevent the cervix from producing fertile mucus.

THE UTERUS • A physical examination of the uterus may show whether its position, shape, or size is abnormal. In most cases, the uterus is in a mid or anterior (forward) position, tilted towards the bladder. If a woman's uterus is in a retroverted position—tilted backwards—this is a suspicious sign of possible endometriosis or pelvic adhesions. If the area next to the uterus, called the adnexa, feels tender and the uterus isn't easily moved, this may mean that scars have formed on the uterus, usually from previous pelvic inflammatory disease or endometriosis.

Occasionally, a physical exam alone can determine whether a woman's uterus has an abnormal shape—such as a double uterus, or an indentation in the top of the uterus—though this is more commonly picked up on an ultrasound scan, hysterosalpingogram, or by laparoscopy.

The most common uterine abnormality is an enlarged uterus that feels firm to the touch and has an irregular shape. This suggests uterine leiomyomas, also called fibroids. But it may also mean that the woman is pregnant. Any time your uterus is enlarged, particularly if it's also soft, the first thing to do is have a pregnancy test!

FALLOPIAN TUBES • Unlike the other female reproductive organs, normal fallopian tubes can't be felt on a physical exam even if a woman is very thin. If the doctor can feel a tubular structure, or thinks he can, this commonly indicates that the woman has fluid in the tube. This condition, called hydrosalpinx ("hydro" for water, "salpinx" for tube) is easily detected on a vaginal ultrasound scan, a hysterosalpingogram, or diagnostic laparoscopy.

THE OVARIES • During a pelvic exam, your doctor feels for an enlargement on the ovaries, such as a cyst or firm nodules. If both ovaries are enlarged, you may have polycystic ovarian disease (PCOD), which is characterized by many enlarged, smooth ovarian cysts. This finding is easily diagnosed by an ultrasound scan and a check of hormone levels, which tend to show elevations of luteinizing hormone throughout the cycle as well as high amounts of androgens.

Once you have found a fertility specialist and had your initial history and physical, you and your doctor can sit down and discuss the tests and possible treatments to overcome your particular fertility problems.

Questions You May Have About Your Doctor

Is the doctor board-certified in obstetrics and gynecology, reproductive endocrinology, or urology?

Is he or she a member of the American Fertility Society? If so, then is the doctor a member of any AFS speciality societies, such as the Society of Reproductive Endocrinologists or Society of Reproductive Surgeons?

Does the doctor limit his or her practice to the treatment of infertility? If not, what percentage of his or her practice is related to the treatment of infertility?

How many infertile couples has he or she treated, and what is his or her overall success rate?

Questions You May Have About His or Her Practice

If I phone your office, will I speak with you or an assistant? When will I hear back from you?

Do you have special hours to answer phone questions? (Be prepared for a busy signal during these times.)

What are your office hours?

What are your fees?

What medicines and diagnostic tests do you often prescribe?

How do you handle medical insurance?

If the doctor is part of a large practice: How often will I see you and how often will I see associates?

What happens if I ovulate on a weekend or holiday?

Do you have a person on your staff to help couples deal with the stress and emotional impact of infertility?

Does your staff provide educational and written materials about tests and treatments?

Do you involve the infertile *couple* in the treatment?

Questions Your Doctor Is Looking to Answer in the Initial Workup

For the man

Is he producing enough sperm?

Are his sperm moving fast enough in a forward progressive fashion? Are they normally shaped?

Are his sperm passages clear and open?

Does he ejaculate high in the vagina near the woman's cervix?

Has he had or does he have any diseases, infections, or congenital problems that may affect his fertility?

Does he have a varicocele?

For the woman

Is she ovulating?

After ovulation, is the uterus properly prepared to receive the fertilized egg?

Are the fallopian tubes blocked, diseased, or bound up with adhesions?

Does the cervix produce an adequate amount of favorable mucus to receive the migrating sperm?

Has she had or does she have any diseases, infections (particularly pelvic or cervical), or congenital problems that may affect her fertility?

5

THE
FERTILITY
EVALUATION

The Basic Tests

Once you have found a fertility specialist and gone through a history and physical exam, the likelihood of your achieving a pregnancy depends largely on a full, coordinated evaluation involving both partners. In 40 percent of infertile couples, *both* the husband and the wife contribute to their infertility problem. So both partners need a complete, thorough fertility investigation, starting with a series of basic tests.

Before you start, let's recognize that there is no "perfect" score for these tests. The range of normal values for various diagnostic tests may vary widely from couple to couple. Frequently, a man and a woman each have "low normal" test results which, when put together, mean that they have been unable to have a baby. Improving, and hopefully optimizing, each partner's low or abnormal fertility test scores will maximize your chance of becoming parents.

The probability of a pregnancy is based on a number of independent variables multiplied together. Consider the common situation where the husband and wife each have conditions that impair their fertility. For example, the husband's fertility, based on a reduced sperm count due to a varicocele, is 50 percent of normal values. His wife's studies show that she ovulates only in 50 percent of cycles and that one of her fallopian tubes is blocked. With only three relative infertility factors, their probability of conception is: 0.5 (varicocele) × 0.5 (ovulation factor) × 0.5 (tubal factor) = 0.125 or 12.5 percent of normal.

Now, realize that even normal, fertile couples have only a 25 percent probability of conceiving in any one cycle if they don't use contraception and make love at the wife's most fertile time of the cycle. So this couple's chance of conceiving in any given month, *without treatment,* is only 0.25 × 0.125 = 0.03125, or 3 percent! Thus, independent variables multiplied together can magnify the odds against a couple achieving a pregnancy. *In order to maximize the chances of conception, each partner's contributing infertility factors must be corrected or improved as much as possible.*

In addition, most procedures, such as varicocele surgery or endometriosis treatments, create a "window" of optimal fertility. Therefore, both partners' treatment must be coordinated to ensure that their fertility problems have been evaluated and treated properly and, if possible, simultaneously.

It makes sense to evaluate one partner's fertility potential completely before the other undergoes major treatment, such as surgery, to improve fertility. For example, repairing a woman's blocked fallopian tubes surgically will do nothing to enhance a couple's fertility potential if her husband produces no sperm. If either partner is irreversibly sterile, the couple should know this in order to consider such alternatives as adoption, or artificial insemination.

Initial Lab Tests for Women

Most fertility specialists begin testing new couples with the most simple, least painful procedures to diagnose the most common and easily corrected problems, and then treat each problem as soon as it's recognized. If the woman doesn't get pregnant within a specified number of cycles, then the "workup" moves on to the more difficult problems or conditions that require more invasive tests and more aggressive treatments.

At Chapel Hill Fertility Center, the workup begins with a prenatal blood screening of both partners. This includes testing for infection with hepatitis virus and the AIDS virus, typing their blood, checking for rubella immunity, and a multichemistry panel to assess their general health. The screening checks heart, liver, and kidney function, cholesterol levels, blood sugar, and provides a complete blood count.

Cervical Cultures

At the time of her initial appointment with Dr. Berger, the first laboratory test for the woman is usually a variety of bacterial cultures of the cervix. Samples from the cervical canal are obtained with sterile swabs or brushes and examined to identify the various potentially harmful genital organisms, such as chlamydia, mycoplasma, neisseria (gonorrhea) and gardnerella, as well as various other aerobic and anaerobic bacteria.

Few clinics offer complete bacterial screening, although most now screen specifically for chlamydia. Many physicians perform limited cultures only when a symptom is present, but many genital tract infections have no symptoms. Until recently, the only method available to diagnose chlamydia used cell culture techniques, a time consuming, technically demanding, and expensive process. This type of testing was often available only in research laboratories.

Now, various rapid screening tests are available that don't require growing the chlamydia in tissue cultures. Using these tests, a doctor or lab technician can quickly identify the presence of chlamydia.

Because infectious conditions are easy to diagnose and treat, it's usually the best place to start an infertility evaluation. If the tests reveal potentially harmful bacteria, then both partners should be treated simultaneously with appropriate antibiotics. Treating infections is one of the easiest ways to eliminate a problem of "hostile" cervical mucus —when a woman's mucus kills off her husband's sperm due to inflammation of the cervix (cervicitis).

A wide variety of bacteria may be found in a healthy woman's genital tract, including anaerobic bacteria (which survive with little or no oxygen) and aerobic bacteria (which need higher concentrations of oxygen to survive). The primary anaerobic bacteria of the reproductive tract include bacteroides, peptococcus, peptostreptococcus and clostridia. If they find their way up to the uterus or fallopian tubes, they are especially dangerous since they may cause major pelvic infections. For that reason, Dr. Berger prefers to eradicate anaerobic bacteria in the lower genital tract before they gain access to the upper genital tract.

The harmful aerobic bacteria frequently found in the cervix include: group D streptococcus, or enterococcus, which may cause cervical bleeding and inflammation (a tip-off of infection) and may interfere with cervical mucus production; group B beta hemolytic streptococcus, which can infect, and even kill, a newborn baby if a mother carries the infection during the baby's birth; and staphylococcus aureus, which has been associated with toxic shock syndrome, a serious and potentially fatal form of blood infection first associated with the Rely superabsorbent tampon.

Dr. Berger also cultures the man's semen at the time of the first semen analysis. (There's more about testing the husband later in this chapter.) In most cases, the same organisms that appear in the wife's cervix also are found in the husband's semen. This shouldn't be surprising, since sexual partners expose each other to bacteria in each of their genital tracts. That is why, in order to clear an infection in either partner, it is *essential that both sex partners be treated together.* (This is one example of why the *couple* is the infertility specialist's "patient.")

Cervical Mucus Tests

Warren and Bernadette tried to have a baby for more than a year before they were referred to a fertility specialist in New York City. "The doctor had all the up-to-date equipment and, being a real go-getter, he suggested we try an intrauterine insemination (IUI) before performing any tests," recalls Warren, aged thirty-eight, a guidance counselor. Bernadette, a thirty-six-year-old teacher, did not get pregnant. After testing his sperm penetration in Bernadette's mucus, Warren says, "the doctor told us there was something in my sperm fluid that was preventing the sperm from being mobile, but he didn't know what it was." Two other IUI attempts failed.

Then the couple moved to North Carolina, and were referred to Dr. Berger. "He systematically and thoroughly checked everything out before continuing with treatment," says Bernadette. He diagnosed irregular ovulation for her and low sperm motility for Warren. But a postcoital test timed around Bernadette's ovulation showed that Warren's sperm were unable to penetrate her mucus. "We had never done a home ovulation test, and had only estimated when Bernadette was ovulating, which was difficult to do with her irregular cycles," Warren says. "Our first doctor had timed the IUIs two or three days too early. Dr. Berger knew the right time for insemination almost down to the hour." After only one IUI attempt at Chapel Hill Fertility Center, Bernadette became pregnant.

"I was surprised she got pregnant the first try," says Warren. "After the IUI, I didn't want to lift my hopes up again. Then we did the home pregnancy test, and it was positive, and Dr. Berger confirmed it." Bernadette, in her sixth month of pregnancy, says, "We're going to go for as many children as we can."

A cervical mucus examination should be performed when a woman is most likely to have fertile mucus, that is, on the day of the surge of luteinizing hormone (LH). (See diagram of hormones through a normal menstrual cycle.)

The simplest test samples the wife's cervical mucus several hours after intercourse to see whether the sperm are swimming freely. This basic test of sperm interaction is called the postcoital test (PCT). It indicates whether a man's sperm can penetrate and survive in his wife's mucus. It should be performed on the day before his wife ovulates, which she identifies by detecting her LH surge with a home urine test kit.

Your doctor should ask you when you last had intercourse before performing the test. This is essential to interpreting the results of the postcoital test. For example, if a couple made love thirty-six hours before coming in for their visit, and the doctor sees sperm moving in the cervical mucus, that's an excellent sign that the wife's mucus isn't "hostile" to her husband's sperm. But if only a few sperm are moving two hours after the couple had intercourse, then they have a sperm-mucus interaction problem.

Another mucus penetration test, called the Penetrak test, may be performed if the husband's sperm have trouble penetrating his wife's mucus. Sperm are allowed to migrate up thin tubes filled with bovine (cow's) cervical mucus to see how far they penetrate over a specific time, (ninety minutes). If this test reveals normal sperm penetra-

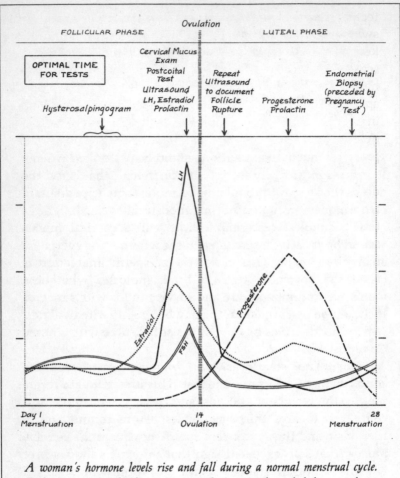

A woman's hormone levels rise and fall during a normal menstrual cycle. Performing various fertility tests at specific times in the cycle helps your doctor gain the most information from them.

tion but a properly timed postcoital test reveals only dead sperm, then the wife's cervical mucus is likely to be contributing to poor sperm survival or motility.

Yet another test places the husband's sperm and the wife's mucus side by side on a glass slide, and a laboratory technician checks whether the sperm can penetrate and swim freely in the mucus. The sperm-mucus mixture is kept at body temperature and looked at under the microscope periodically. A man with a good sperm count who hasn't been able to impregnate his wife might have good sperm survival for an hour, but then the sperm stop moving or die before they ever reach her eggs. A look at how quickly sperm die in this slide sperm-mucus interaction test may explain this couple's infertility.

If the postcoital and slide penetration tests reveal only dead sperm even though the wife's mucus appears to be fertile, and the Penetrak test reveals normal sperm penetration through the cow's mucus, this implies that there is something about the wife's mucus that's "hostile" to her husband's sperm. Infections and antibodies are frequently found to be the culprits. If sperm become immobilized both in the wife's mucus and cow's mucus, the husband's fertility needs more studying. Additional tests may use donor fertile mucus with the husband's sperm and donor sperm with the wife's mucus, placed together on a glass microscope slide, referred to as a "cross-match" test.

Since cervical mucus is receptive to sperm migration for a limited time during the menstrual cycle, these tests should all be performed when the mucus sample is most likely to reveal its actions upon the sperm, that is, on or around the day of the LH surge. Unfortunately, in many medical offices, *one of the most frequent causes for an abnormal PCT is that it was performed during the wrong time of the wife's cycle.* Remember that the mucus normally assumes its fertile quality and permits sperm survival only around the time of ovulation. Like any test, the PCT can provide extremely useful information, but only if it's performed at the proper time of the cycle.

Ultrasound Scans

The next step in the evaluation is an ultrasound (US) scan to look for pelvic abnormalities and monitor follicle development to assure that a woman is ovulating. In the past, an ultrasound scan involved applying a probe to the outside of the woman's abdomen over a full bladder in order to scan the ovaries and assess the size of her follicles. Now, with newer vaginal ultrasound scans, the tip of the probe is placed into the woman's vagina near her cervix so that it comes closer to the pelvic organs.

The high frequency sound waves, at this close distance, produce much clearer, sharper pictures, and can even enable imaging of the fallopian tubes if filled with fluid or blood. Although the images may look to you like a fuzzy weather map from a satellite scan, your doctor should be able to read them clearly.

For a vaginal scan, the US probe is covered with a clean condom and sterile lubricant. The woman's bladder should be empty (just the opposite of an abdominal scan, which requires a full bladder to enhance the ultrasound image), and the covered probe inserted by the woman into the vagina like a tampon.

The vaginal US exam can reveal fibroids practically down to the size of the letter "o" on this page. These small benign tumors embedded in the uterine lining have a characteristic appearance: they are well-encapsulated, firm nodules that can appear either in the uterine cavity (submucosal), in the muscle of the uterus (intramural), or on the uterus's outer surface (subserosal). A pea-sized or smaller fibroid may not be evident on a physical exam, but can be seen with a vaginal US scan.

A scan can determine how thick the uterine lining is, which is particularly useful on the day of the LH surge. A scan at that time can provide information about how well a woman's uterus is responding to hormone production. If the lining is thin, that indicates either that she is not producing adequate hormones or that her uterus is unable to respond to the amount of hormones she does produce.

Vaginal ultrasound is a safe, practical, noninvasive alternative to laparoscopy for diagnosing luteinized unruptured follicle (LUF) syndrome. From 5 to 30 percent of women with "unexplained" infertility have eggs that ripen but don't release from the follicle at ovulation. A vaginal ultrasound scan on the day of the LH surge enables a doctor to measure the size of the follicle, and a second scan two or three days later can confirm whether or not the follicle has ruptured.

In addition, this useful test can identify uterine abnormalities such as a double horned uterus or a uterine septum, and identify the presence of polyps in the uterine lining. These conditions should be confirmed either with an X-ray dye study of the uterus (hysterosalpingogram) or a direct look through a telescope-like device placed into the uterine cavity through the cervix (hysteroscopy).

A US examination of the ovaries also helps diagnose one of the most common ovarian abnormalities—endometriosis. The ultrasound scan can be used to measure the size of the ovaries and look at cysts or solid growths within the ovaries. US pictures of endometriomas, or blood-containing endometrial cysts in the ovaries, have a different appearance than the clear fluid-containing follicles. A test for antiendometrial antibodies in a woman's blood is also helpful in screening for endometriosis.

Endometriosis afflicts as many as 10 million American women. It develops when tissue from the inner lining of the uterus, the endometrium, grows outside its normal location. The cells form patches and scars throughout the pelvis and around the woman's ovaries and fallopian tubes. The disease can cause severe menstrual cramps, painful intercourse, and abnormal menstruation. But frequently endometriosis causes no symptoms at all beyond infertility.

The longer the disease persists without treatment, the slimmer are a woman's chances of conceiving when she wants to. Sometimes women and their doctors overlook the warning signs. Fortunately, endometriosis is a treatable cause of infertility, especially if it is diagnosed early.

No one knows why some women, but not others, develop endometriosis. Many women experience "retrograde menstruation," in which menstrual blood and tissue back up through the fallopian tubes and spill out into the pelvic cavity. The stray tissue from this retrograde menstruation may implant outside the uterus and continue to grow, reacting to each cycle of hormonal stimulation, just as the lining inside the uterus does. It isn't known why some women who experience retrograde menstruation have endometriosis while others don't.

Another way endometriosis can arise is from misplaced cells scattered about a woman's abdominal cavity during her fetal development. According to this theory, beginning at puberty some of the cells become stimulated by the release of estrogen in each ovulatory cycle, and the "ectopic" cells grow and implant in tissues outside the uterus.

Ovulation Monitoring

Because of her husband's male factor problems, Suzie, a forty-two-year-old caterer, went through five months of unsuccessful artificial insemination attempts by another doctor before going to see Dr. Berger. She had been testing her urine once a day with home kits, but was unable to detect whether she was having an LH surge. On Dr. Berger's suggestion she began running the test twice a day with an improved test kit.

The day before she had an artificial insemination, Suzie tested her urine in the morning (it was negative) and again that night. "I could tell from the weak color of the kit that I had not surged yet," she says.

*After an ultrasound exam confirmed that she had a preovulatory folli-
cle present, and a blood hormone test run that day in Dr. Berger's lab
indicated that the timing was right for ovulation, his nurse gave her an
injection of hCG to release her egg. Because she had fertile cervical
mucus, he inseminated some of her husband Bob's sperm into her
cervical canal later that day. The following day, another scan showed
that the egg had, indeed, been released by the follicle, and he inseminated some more of Bob's sperm into Suzie's uterine cavity and fallopian tubes. "I felt good knowing that some sperm had been put inside
before the egg was being released, and then some after," says Suzie,
who is awaiting the results of her pregnancy test.*

Most women have ovulation tests on the same day as
their mucus exams and ultrasound scans. During their initial visit to his office, couples learn from Dr. Berger's staff
how to use a simple, at-home ovulation testing kit. He
then asks them to schedule their second office visit on the
day of the wife's LH surge.

Another simple, widely used method to check on ovulation is the basal body temperature (BBT) chart. The basal
body temperature is one's temperature upon waking up.
First thing in the morning before getting up or doing anything else, the woman records her temperature on a daily
chart. A special BBT thermometer with an expanded, easy-
to-read scale, is available at most pharmacies or fertility
clinics. If you have been keeping a BBT chart at home, be
sure to bring it with you to the doctor's office on your
initial visit.

In a normal twenty-eight-day cycle, from day one of
the cycle (the first day of menstruation) through days
twelve to fourteen, a woman's BBT is usually between 97.2
and 97.6 degrees F (between 36.2 and 36.4 degrees C). From
just after ovulation, at mid-cycle, through to the onset of
the next period, the BBT rises as much as one degree.

This temperature change results from fluctuations in hormone levels. Estrogen, predominant before ovulation, tends to lower body temperature. Progesterone, produced after ovulation by the corpus luteum (the crater left after the follicle releases the egg) tends to raise body temperature. So the temperature early in the menstrual cycle will be low, and when the woman ovulates and progesterone is released, the temperature will rise. The BBT chart should reflect this rise in temperature: the curve on the chart normally is low in the early part of the cycle, rises at, or right after, ovulation, and remains high until the woman's next cycle.

The rise in temperature at ovulation can happen suddenly in one day, or slowly over several days. If a woman's temperature stays elevated for sixteen days or more, she probably is pregnant, since the corpus luteum usually stops producing progesterone after thirteen to fifteen days.

The BBT pattern is useful *in retrospect,* but not too helpful in telling whether a woman is about to ovulate. Unfortunately, the temperature changes are obvious only *after* ovulation, so it's like someone telling you, "Get off the bus the stop before me."

BBT charts aren't 100 percent accurate in confirming ovulation, but they can be useful in making educated guesses about ovarian hormone production. If the BBT chart shows no temperature rise, she may not have the typical hormone fluctuations through the cycle, and may not be ovulating. A BBT rise that lasts less than twelve days after the LH surge suggests luteal phase defect (LPD), in which the uterine lining fails to develop and be maintained properly after ovulation.

Your fertility specialist may order another ultrasound scan on your second visit to confirm ovulation. The advantage of US over the other methods used to detect ovulation —keeping a BBT chart or measuring the progesterone level in the blood—is that it can pinpoint the day of ovulation and document follicle rupture rather than simply reflect increased progesterone production (which can occur even without follicle rupture if a woman has luteinized unruptured follicle syndrome).

In addition, a series of US exams can provide valuable information about the progressive growth and development of the follicles. In a normal cycle, when the diameter of a woman's follicle reaches about 20 millimeters she is about to ovulate. Eggs released from small follicles may not be healthy, fertilizable eggs. Ultrasound monitoring of the follicles' growth can help time artificial insemination or stimulation of egg release using hormone injections.

Most fertility experts now use vaginal ultrasound not only to time ovulation but also to monitor early pregnancy and to spot a suspected ectopic (tubal) pregnancy. The vaginal scan is more sensitive than the abdominal exam, and can detect a pregnancy developing in the uterus within a week after a woman misses her period, thus ruling out the diagnosis of a tubal pregnancy.

Hormone Screening

On the day of the couple's first follow-up visit (the day of the wife's LH surge), Dr. Berger also tests the woman's blood for hormone levels, including LH, estradiol (the major biologically active estrogen), and the pituitary hormone prolactin, to check her ovulation response. He asks the wife to return again to check hormone levels *exactly seven days later* during the mid-luteal phase of the woman's cycle. This is the best time to measure progesterone, which should be at its peak, and prolactin as well.

Additional hormone studies depend on the woman's history and physical exam. For example, a baseline level of

LH and FSH early in the cycle helps identify women with polycystic ovarian disease (PCOD), who have a high LH to FSH ratio, as well as a high production of male hormones (androgens). To correct PCOD, which includes no or irregular ovulation, these women have to reduce their androgen production.

In the case of PCOD patients or other women with a suspected excess of androgens, the doctor will likely order an androgen panel to check the levels of free and total testosterone, dihydroepiandrosterone sulfate (DHEAS) and androstenedione. DHEAS is an androgen produced primarily by the adrenal gland, and a high DHEAS level suggests too much adrenal androgen output. High production of androstenedione and/or testosterone along with normal DHEAS levels indicates that the ovaries are the probable source of the excess androgens. Some PCOD patients produce excess androgens from the ovaries and the adrenals.

Almost all of a woman's hormone abnormalities can be picked up by doing the appropriate studies on these two specific days of the menstrual cycle—the day of the LH surge and seven days later in the mid-luteal phase. After two visits and two days of testing, Dr. Berger already has determined whether a woman has fertile cervical mucus, a normal preovulatory follicle, normal hormone levels accompanying ovulation, and a normal luteal phase of her cycle.

With these first two follow-up visits, he will not yet have evaluated all potential anatomic problems, but at this early point in the woman's workup he will have detected ovulation defects, hormone abnormalities, infectious problems and male factor infertility. As soon as Dr. Berger gets all of this information, he can institute appropriate therapies to correct any abnormalities and follow up with an evaluation in the next cycle to confirm that the abnormal conditions have, in fact, been corrected.

Female Hormones—Normal Values

Phase of Cycle

	Follicular	Day of LH Surge	Mid-luteal
Luteinizing Hormone (LH)	<7 mIU/ml	>15 mIU/ml	—
Follicle Stimulating Hormone (FSH)	<13 mIU/ml	>15 mIU/ml	—
Estradiol	—	>100 pg/ml	>60 pg/ml
Progesterone	—	<1.5 ng/ml	>15ng/ml

At any time

Prolactin	<25 ng/ml
Thyroid Stimulating Hormone (TSH)	0.4–3.8 uIU/ml
Free T_3	1.4–4.4 pg/ml
Free T_4	0.8–2.0 ng/dl
Total Testosterone	6.0–86 ng/dl
Free Testosterone	0.7–3.6 pg/ml
DHEAS	35–430 ug/dl
Androstenedione	0.7–3.1 ng/ml

< = less than
> = greater than
mIU = milli International Units
ml = milliliter
pg = picograms
ng = nanograms
uIU = micro International Units
dl = deciliter
ug = micrograms

Values from Chapel Hill Fertility Center laboratory. Normal values may vary in other laboratories.

These tests—cervical cultures, cervical mucus tests, ultrasound scans, ovulation monitoring, and hormone screening—are the standard opening gambit in diagnosing a woman's fertility problems. Further testing depends on the results of these initial tests. Depending on the couple's history, your fertility specialist can go in several different diagnostic directions. For example, if a man's sperm score well on the Penetrak test, but don't move easily through his wife's mucus, then the suspected diagnosis may be a cervical mucus abnormality, which could be due to an infection, a hormone deficiency or an immunological problem, each of which needs to be investigated further. If a man hasn't had a semen analysis Dr. Berger recommends that he have one on the day of the couple's first visit and that Dr. Stephen Shaban, a reproductive urologist at Chapel Hill Fertility Center, begin the husband's evaluation.

Initial Lab Tests for Men

Regardless of his wife's results, every husband should also be evaluated to assess his fertility status. Initial evaluation of the male is simpler than the female.

Certain male risk factors alert the physician to a potential problem in the man: a history of mumps, an undescended testicle, previous urologic surgery, previous genital infections, and exposure to environmental toxins. A semen analysis and a hormone profile should be obtained on the man's initial office visit to the fertility specialist, or soon after and, if warranted, his semen should be cultured as well. Additional testing of sperm penetrating power, antisperm antibody levels and a check of the testicles for sperm production may be reserved for specific situations. Usually, additional testing isn't required if the man has at least two normal semen analyses, negative cultures, and a good score on the postcoital test. A more intensive evaluation by a male fertility specialist is advisable for men if these tests prove abnormal.

Don't Count on "Sperm Count"

The first person to see live sperm was Dutch scientist Anton van Leeuwenhoek, the inventor of the microscope. One of the first things he looked at in 1677 was sperm, which he believed carried the progenitors of man inside them. More than three hundred years later, doctors still look at sperm through the microscope at the start of a fertility investigation to count the number of sperm in the ejaculate and to assess what the sperm look like and how well they move.

Analyzing the ejaculate to judge a man's fertility has changed little over the years. The volume of the semen, the sperm count (the amount of sperm in a certain volume of semen, properly known as the sperm concentration or sperm density), sperm motility (the percentage of actively moving sperm) and sperm size and shape (morphology) remain the foundations of semen analysis. Yet, these classic parameters are sometimes too crude to judge a man's fertility potential.

"Sperm count" has become a nebulous term that sometimes means the total number of sperm (the total sperm count), and other times the number of sperm per milliliter (the sperm concentration). One way to take into account various factors—including the total sperm count, percentage of sperm with normal forward motility and normal appearance (morphology)—is the "effective sperm count."

Although not too many doctors are accustomed to using it, at Chapel Hill Fertility Center the effective sperm

119

count is considered the man's "bottom line." It's the one number that can be used accurately to compare different semen samples and compare a man's sperm quality to that of other men. The effective sperm count is calculated by taking the number of sperm in the entire ejaculate (the total sperm count) and multiplying that by the percentage of motile sperm, by the percentage of forwardly progressive motile sperm, and by the percentage of normal sperm forms.

Let's take an example. Both Allen and Bob appeared at Chapel Hill Fertility Center with reports from their urologists that they had "normal" sperm counts. Each had a sperm concentration of 60 million (sperm per milliliter), well above the normal lower limit of 20 million per milliliter. Both had been told they were fertile, but on further analysis based on effective sperm count, Dr. Berger found that Allen was very fertile, while Bob was subfertile.

After getting a semen sample from each man, he calculated their effective sperm counts:

Allen

60 million sperm per milliliter
6 milliliters in the ejaculate
50% motility
90% forward motility
60% normal morphology

Bob

60 million sperm per milliliter
3 milliliters in the ejaculate
25% motility
45% forward motility
30% normal morphology

Allen: 60 million $\times$ 6 $\times$ .50 $\times$ .90 $\times$ .60 = 97.2 million effective sperm count

Bob: 60 million $\times$ 3 $\times$ .25 $\times$ .45 $\times$ .30 = 6 million effective sperm count

Allen's effective sperm count is more than fifteen times higher than Bob's. Bob's effective sperm count of 6 million means that he and his wife might need artificial insemination. This example shows how a man's sperm count can be, and often is, misinterpreted by couples, as well as by physicians who are not fertility specialists.

Sperm count alone can be a misleading indicator of fertility. In his experience treating infertile men with hormone replacements at the National Institutes of Health (NIH), Dr. Richard Sherins, former director of reproductive medicine, says that most have been able to father children, even though 75 percent had low sperm counts. Men with low sperm counts not only have too few sperm, but often have sperm that don't function properly, he says.

Although a man's fertility is related to the number of normal sperm in his ejaculate, researchers have found a surprisingly wide range of sperm counts among men with proven fertility. About 20 million healthy sperm per milliliter used to be considered the minimum concentration needed in the ejaculate to produce a baby, but it now appears that the necessary effective sperm count is even lower, between 5 million and 10 million normal sperm. And men with sperm counts as low as 1 million sperm per milliliter can father children with the help of new technologies such as intratubal insemination (ITI), IVF, and Gamete Intra Fallopian Transfer (GIFT).

Knowing, as we now do, that sperm quantity does not necessarily equal sperm quality, how do we determine what are normal sperm, that is, sperm capable of penetrating and fertilizing eggs? One of the first measures is sperm motility. The proportion of sperm with rapid, forward progressive motility is more important in determining a man's fertility than is the total number of sperm in his ejaculate. Under the best conditions only a limited number of sperm with good tail movement get through the female reproductive tract to reach the egg.

But motility alone doesn't determine a man's fertility

either. A high sperm count may compensate for a low motility. Like Allen and Bob, two men may produce the same concentration of sperm, but with a widely different volume of semen, sperm count, and motility.

New computer assisted sperm assessments may also help correlate motility with fertility. Looking at sperm by eye through the microscope, doctors get only crude estimates of good or bad sperm motility and whether sperm motion is forward. Using the computer to track sperm through the microscope, they can quantitatively assess sperm speed and how straight they swim.

Semen Analysis

In a normal ejaculation, the total volume of semen is between a half and a whole teaspoon. It typically contains between 40 million and 300 million sperm. A well-developed sperm can propel itself up a woman's reproductive tract at a rate of more than two inches an hour.

It takes about ten to twelve weeks from the initiation of new sperm formation for fully mature sperm to appear in the ejaculate. The urologist or fertility specialist must therefore consider any significant events in the man's history as far back as three months or more before the semen analysis.

The doctor may advise a man who is scheduled for a semen analysis to abstain from sex for three days beforehand. There is no hard-and-fast rule as to how long he should abstain, but urologists like to have a standard interval so that they can compare results. Three days is consistent with the average frequency of intercourse—about two or three times a week for most couples. Also, studies have shown that bacteria attached to sperm or in the semen are more accurately detected after at least three days of abstinence.

A man should have the results of the semen analysis back from the doctor the same or the next day. The first thing the doctor or laboratory technologist looks at is the appearance of the semen, the time it takes to liquify, and the volume in the ejaculate. A normal volume is about 2 to 6 milliliters (ml). A very low volume, under 1 ml, may mean that the semen doesn't contain all of the normal components. The seminal vesicles make about 60 to 65 percent of the ejaculate, including the proteins that cause the ejaculate to coagulate and come out looking like a clotted gel. About 30 percent of the seminal fluid is made by the prostate gland, which produces enzymes that cause the ejaculate to liquify.

If the semen doesn't come out as a clotted gel, this suggests that the man's seminal vesicles are malfunctioning or absent. If the semen doesn't liquify, this suggests a prostate disorder. Only 3 to 5 percent of the seminal fluid comes from testicular fluid and sperm. Because so little comes from the testicles, there is often nothing noticeably different in the ejaculate of a man with a zero or very low sperm count compared with a man with a normal count.

If a man has an extremely low semen volume, the seminal vesicles may not be making enough fluid, or these ducts may be blocked. When the seminal vesicles are blocked, it usually occurs where they enter into the ejaculatory ducts. This commonly happens to men born with no vas deferens, a rare condition called aplasia of the vas deferens. These men may also be missing a kidney since the vas derives from the kidney ducts. (Men without vas deferens should have an ultrasound scan or X-ray to check whether they have both kidneys.)

A low volume may also signify a low testosterone output, with not enough testosterone available to stimulate the seminal vesicles to produce fluid.

A high semen volume also can have its drawbacks. An abnormally high semen volume is frequently associated with an infection. For example, when the prostate gland is inflamed, seminal fluid increases. This extra fluid will dilute the sperm concentration in the semen. Even normal sperm don't function as well when their concentration has been diluted, or when the seminal plasma contains a high concentration of white blood cells and other inflammatory components. The concentration of round cells can be determined at the same time as the sperm concentration. There shouldn't be more than 1 million round cells in any one semen sample. Special stains must be performed to determine whether the high numbers of round cells represent white blood cells associated with infection and inflammation, or immature sperm.

A pH test to determine the acidity of a man's semen can help detect an infection. The normal pH range of semen is 7.5–8.1. If the sperm sample has a pH higher than 8.1, then an infection may be present. If the pH is less than 7.5, and a man has no sperm in the sample, then his vas deferens, seminal vesicles, or epididymis may have developed improperly.

As part of the semen analysis, the doctor—or, more commonly, a laboratory technician or andrologist—will determine the number of sperm present in the ejaculate. A normal sperm concentration falls between 20 million per ml and 200 million per ml. The lower normal limit of total sperm in the ejaculate should be at least 40 million. Between 20 million and 40 million sperm is considered a borderline low count, and under 20 million is definitely a low count. More than 1 billion total sperm, a rare condition, is considered an abnormally high concentration since the sperm can clump together, causing a motility problem.

The technician looks at how well the sperm are moving and will count the total percentage of motile sperm by figuring how many sperm per hundred are moving. At least 50 percent of any given sperm population should be moving. Then the sperm motion is qualified. The observer gives no movement a grade of 0. If the sperm stay in place and vibrate, that's considered Grade 1; if they are moving very slowly or meandering along, that's Grade 2. Sperm that are moving well in a straight line receive a Grade 3, and sperm that race across the microscopic field in a straight line are Grade 4. Normal, forwardly motile sperm are rated either Grade 3 or 4. More than half of all motile sperm should have forward, progressive motility of Grade 3 or 4.

Finally, the shape, or morphology, of the sperm will be determined. Sperm heads should be oval-shaped without irregularities. If the sperm are too narrow or thin, they are considered tapered. Men with an elevated testicular temperature, frequently due to a varicocele or exposure to excessive heat, often have tapered sperm. If the sperm have a large, round head, they may be missing the acrosome, the packet of enzymes at the tip of the sperm head that allow sperm to bore through the coating of the egg.

The midpiece, the part that connects the sperm head to the sperm tail, should also look normal. The tubular midpiece contains the mitochondria that provide the energy to make the tail move. The whip-like tail itself should be normal sized and have a wave-like motion.

Of all the parameters of semen analysis, shape is the most subjective. So assessment of morphology varies from one lab to the next. The same semen sample may be interpreted as normal in one lab, and abnormal in another. Motility assessment is also somewhat subjective. The sperm count is the easiest to quantitate objectively and accurately.

Even with computer assisted semen analysis, there is a

fair amount of error, particularly when a man's sperm count is low. The computer can rapidly assess the sperm count and sperm motility in men who have normal amounts of sperm to begin with. But computerized systems tend to overestimate the sperm count, sometimes by as much as 30 percent. So a computer may analyze a man's sperm count as "normal" when it actually is low. At this time, computerized systems don't assess sperm morphology accurately, but they do show promise for the future.

Most experts recommend that men undergoing fertility evaluation have three separate semen analyses performed, with at least two to four weeks in between analyses. If a man has the flu, a high fever, or is under excess stress, he may have a temporarily reduced sperm count. Even a normal, fertile man who has a semen analysis done every month for a year might have two or three analyses showing an abnormality in at least one of the three basic semen parameters—count, motility, morphology.

The only exception to the three analyses rule is a man with a zero sperm count. In this case, two semen analyses are enough. If a man has a zero count, his semen should be tested for the presence of the fruit sugar fructose, which is produced by the seminal vesicles. If fructose is absent from the semen, this suggests a blockage along the reproductive tract—preventing sperm from getting into the ejaculate. The semen of a man with apparently no sperm at all should be centrifuged and the pellet in the bottom of the test tube examined to see whether it contains any sperm. A careful look at the pellet may turn up an occasional sperm. It's important to distinguish a blocked duct, with an occasional sperm in the ejaculate, from an absolutely zero sperm count caused by other conditions, such as hormonal or testicular abnormality. Most andrology labs spin down the semen from a zero count, but general clinical labs often do

Comprehensive Semen Analysis Report

Patient: Spouse:

Date of Specimen: Time Specimen Produced:

Time Analysis Begun: Method of Collection:

Days Since Last Ejaculation: Any Portion of Specimen Lost?

Present Medications:

Parameter	Results	Normal Values
Color		Gray/Translucent
Coagulate?		Yes
Liquify?		Yes
If Yes, Time in Minutes		$\leqq 30$
Volume (ml)		2–6
Viscosity (1, 2, 3, 4)		1
pH		7.5–8.1
% Motility		$\geqq 50\%$
% of 3–4+ Forward Motile Sperm		$\geqq 50$
Sperm Concentration (× 1 Million per ml)		20–200
Total Sperm Count (× 1 Million per ml)		$\geqq 40$
Total Motile Sperm (× 1 Million per ml)		$\geqq 20$
White blood cells (× 1 Million per ml)		$\leqq 1$
Agglutination (0, 1, 2, 3) Clumping of sperm to sperm		0
Clumping of sperm to round cells		0
% Normal Morphology		$\geqq 50\%$
Penetrak Score (mm)		$\geqq 30$

ml = milliliter

mm = millimeter

$\leqq$ = Less Than or Equal to

$\geqq$ = More Than or Equal to

not. What may be reported as a zero sperm count in one lab, therefore, may not be so in another.

Sperm motility appears to be a more sensitive indicator of male fertility than sperm count. Time exposure photography through the microscope and, more recently, videotaping through the microscope are now available to assess motility. The camera's eye accurately catches swimming speed and direction in a totally objective measurement. A video allows for simultaneous measurement of length and width of sperm heads, and can be analyzed by a computer within one minute for a closer inspection of sperm.

The Hormone Profile

The next set of lab tests measures the hormones contained in a man's blood. Just as in women, the release of the key pituitary hormones—FSH and LH—is regulated by the release of pulses of gonadotropin releasing hormone from the hypothalamus. The bloodstream transports FSH and LH to the testicles where they stimulate the production of sperm and testosterone. The blood also is tested for testosterone itself. Testosterone is the male hormone that provides the sex drive, promotes hair growth and muscle development (the secondary sexual characteristics), stimulates the prostate and seminal vesicles to make their secretions, and provides the impetus for erections. Working in concert with FSH, testosterone helps produce sperm. So a man needs normal concentrations of both FSH and testosterone within his testicles to produce an adequate number of sperm.

Another pituitary hormone that an infertile man should have measured, as should his wife, is prolactin. High levels of prolactin (hyperprolactinemia) inhibit testosterone and, subsequently, sperm production. Microscopic-sized pituitary tumors, called prolactinomas, are often associated

---

Male Hormones—Normal Values

Testosterone	300–1,100 ng/dl
Prolactin	7–18 ng/ml
Luteinizing Hormone (LH)	2–18 mIU/ml
Follicle Stimulating	
Hormone (FSH)	2–19 mIU/ml
Estradiol	< 60 pg/ml

ng = nanograms
dl = deciliter
ml = milliliter
mIU = milli International Units
pg = picograms
< = less than

Values from the Endocrinology Laboratory at New York Hospital.
Normal values may vary in other laboratories.

---

with high prolactin levels. Hyperprolactinemia appears to be a less common disorder among men than women, but this may be due in part to the fact that tests looking for this disorder are obtained much more frequently among women than men.

The "female" hormone estradiol should be measured in men as well. All men produce this hormone, just as all women have some testosterone present in their blood. High levels of estradiol may lead to breast enlargement in men, which usually is associated with decreased sperm production. The estrogen feeds back to the brain and turns off production of LH and FSH, which in turn halts production of testosterone and sperm. High levels of estrogen often occur among men with testicle or adrenal gland tumors or those with liver diseases that prevent the normal metabolism of estrogen.

Because the hypothalamus sends pulses of GnRH to stimulate FSH and LH release frequently during the day, it may be necessary to sample a man's blood and measure his gonadotropin levels more than once to assess accurately the function of his hypothalamus or pituitary.

Semen Culture and Antisperm Antibodies

Depending on the results of these initial studies, the urologist or fertility specialist may recommend more sophisticated tests. If the man has sperm clumping (agglutination) or physical signs of a sexually transmitted disease, the doctor may want to culture his semen. It is crucial that semen cultures be obtained *before* any form of artificial insemination or assisted reproductive technology like IVF is performed with the husband's sperm.

The semen is placed in growth media and incubated at body temperature to check for growth of any disease-causing organisms, such as mycoplasma, ureaplasma, or gonorrhea, that may affect fertility. Other bacteria, such as those that cause staph infections or a strep throat, may also appear.

If the man's sperm agglutinate, and he has no signs of infection, then the doctor may recommend an antisperm antibody test. Until recently, tests to detect sperm antibodies relied on measuring sperm clumping or immobilization. New tests have been developed that can localize and quantify specific antibodies in the blood, semen, and on the sperm's surface. Greater availability and standardization of these highly specific tests should help clarify the role of antisperm antibodies in male infertility.

It is important to know where the antibodies attach to

the sperm, since antibodies stuck to the head of the sperm can prevent penetration of an egg; antibodies coating the sperm tail can prevent the sperm from moving properly to get to the egg. Antibody assays may also be performed in the blood and seminal fluid, as well as in the wife's blood and her cervical mucus.

Sperm antibody tests are also in order if a man has consistently poor sperm motility even if he shows no sperm agglutination, particularly if his doctor suspects a blockage along the reproductive tract ducts or if he has a varicocele. Some fertility specialists, like Dr. Goldstein, check for antibodies routinely. His Cornell group discovered that varicoceles are often associated with sperm antibodies by testing all infertile men who appeared at the clinic.

Questions to Ask Your Doctor About Basic Lab Tests for Women

Do my cervical cultures show any harmful organisms?

Does my cervical mucus appear to be fertile? (It should look like raw egg white.)

Is my cervical mucus receptive or "hostile" to my husband's sperm?

Did my ultrasound exam reveal any abnormalities (fibroids, ovarian cysts, fluid-filled fallopian tubes)?

Does my BBT chart show normal temperature fluctuations?

Does the ultrasound exam show I am ovulating normally and that I have normal size follicles?

Are the hormone levels in my blood within normal ranges?

Does my blood or cervical mucus show any evidence of antisperm antibodies?

Questions to Ask Your Doctor About Basic Lab Tests for Men

Is my sperm concentration within the normal range (20 million to 200 million sperm per milliliter)?

What is my total sperm count (normal = 40 million to 300 million sperm)?

Is the volume (amount) of my semen within the normal range (2 to 6 milliliters)?

Do I have a high white blood cell count in my semen (a sign of an inflammation)?

Was a special stain applied to tell the white blood cells apart from immature sperm cells?

What percentage of my sperm are actively moving (more then 50 percent is normal)?

Do my sperm look like they have normal shapes (more than 50 percent should have normal shapes)?

Are the hormone levels in my blood within normal ranges?

Does my semen culture show any harmful organisms?

Do I have any sperm antibodies in my blood, semen, or attached to my sperm?

6

THE
EVALUATION
CONTINUES

Advanced Tests

After you have gone through the basic fertility evaluation, your fertility specialist will have an idea of how best to proceed to complete your workup. Many of the initial tests and procedures are designed to evaluate a single physiological or anatomical aspect of either a woman's or a man's reproductive function. Some doctors, once they discover an abnormality, will put off further testing and begin treating that one particular problem. But this approach can be misleading since, in most cases, a couple has more than one factor contributing to their fertility problem.

Although the husband's fertility evaluation may be simpler than his wife's (because his reproductive organs and sperm are more accessible for examination than her reproductive organs and her eggs), this doesn't mean that there are more or better infertility treatments available for "male factor infertility." In fact, the reverse is true. Although semen analysis allows a simple evaluation of several aspects of a man's reproductive function, doctors still don't know much about how to predict whether a man's sperm will fertilize his wife's eggs. Even with all of the

---

sophisticated technology available today, no fertility test can positively predict a couple's ability to conceive or maintain a pregnancy. Actually having a baby is the only way of verifying your fertility as a couple.

Testing the Woman

Several simple tests using X-rays and tiny telescopes and examining a woman's endometrial development in the late luteal phase can give the doctor a better idea of exactly where a woman's fertility problem may lie.

The Dye Test (Hysterosalpingogram)

When a couple with a history of prolonged infertility has completed the basic, initial lab tests, the fertility evaluation usually proceeds with a dye study of the wife's upper reproductive tract. This study is called a hysterosalpingogram (HSG), an X-ray of the uterus (hystero) and tubes (salpinges). Basically, this involves flushing the cervical canal with a radiopaque dye, which appears white on an X-ray.

The hysterosalpingogram shows the shape of the internal cavity of the uterus and whether the fallopian tubes are patent (open). As the uterus fills and the dye moves out through the fallopian tubes, the X-ray can reveal different types of abnormalities, such as blocked areas due to adhesions (scar tissue) and growths, polyps, or tumors. In normal, healthy fallopian tubes, the dye fills the lengths of the tubes and quickly spills out through the far end. If a tube is blocked at its fimbrial end near the ovary, then the tube will enlarge as the dye is pushed into it, just as a balloon grows larger when it is blown up with air.

The dye test can be painful, particularly if there is a

blockage of the fallopian tubes. Dr. Berger recommends that a woman take 600 mg of ibuprofen (three Advil or Nuprin tablets) thirty to sixty minutes prior to the HSG to minimize her discomfort.

The major risk of an HSG—the possibility of spreading an unrecognized infection from the cervix to the upper reproductive tract—can be avoided by making sure that cervical cultures show no pathogenic bacteria before scheduling the HSG. If the woman has a cervical infection, then he postpones the exam, and she and her partner are put on appropriate antibiotic treatments. Only once the lower tract infection has cleared does he proceed to a hysterosalpingogram. In addition, for two days before the HSG and two days afterward, the woman routinely receives a broad spectrum prophylactic antibiotic, such as doxycycline. She also uses a betadine douche to cleanse her vagina immediately before going in for her X-ray, as an added precaution. (Betadine is a powerful antiseptic preparation used by most doctors to kill any bacteria on the skin prior to surgery.)

Hysteroscopy

If he suspects an abnormality of the uterus, Dr. Berger considers further evaluation with a hysteroscope, a thin, fiberoptically lighted telescope inserted through the cervical canal into the uterus. Through the hysteroscope's eyepiece, the doctor can see abnormalities inside the uterine cavity, such as fibroid tumors, adhesions, a septum, a double shaped uterus or the T-shaped uterine cavity associated with DES exposure while in utero. Pictures taken through the hysteroscope can document the condition of the uterine cavity, and are filed in the woman's permanent medical record.

Hysteroscopy is a simple procedure that can be performed using local anesthesia. The doctor places the hysteroscope through the woman's cervical canal, and then distends her uterus with either a gas such as carbon dioxide or a liquid medium to push the walls of the uterus apart and allow a panoramic view of the uterine cavity.

In many situations, Dr. Berger will combine hysteroscopy and laparoscopy to confirm the exact location and type of uterine abnormality, as well as to determine if the woman has any other abnormal conditions involving the uterus, fallopian tubes, and ovaries, such as pelvic adhesions or endometriosis.

The hysteroscopic examination is often performed early in a woman's menstrual cycle before her uterine lining (endometrium) has become fully developed. At that time, the doctor can get the clearest view of the uterine cavity, including the opening into each fallopian tube. (Later in the cycle, the exam may be more difficult to perform because the endometrium thickens and can obscure the view of the openings of the fallopian tubes.)

However, the decision when to perform hysteroscopy during the woman's cycle also depends on whether the doctor wants to obtain an endometrial biopsy to study the maturation of her uterine lining. In this case, the hysteroscopic examination is best performed late in the luteal phase of the cycle when an endometrial biopsy is most useful.

Before proceeding to diagnostic laparoscopy and endometrial biopsy, the woman should always have a pregnancy test to make sure that she isn't already pregnant. For fear of harming the early pregnancy, no couple or doctor would want to perform an invasive examination of the uterus for infertility only to find out that a fertilized egg had already implanted itself.

Laparoscopy

Several cycles after Wendy had a hysteroscopy and still wasn't pregnant, her doctor suggested that the thirty-year-old skin care specialist undergo a diagnostic laparoscopy as a further investigation. While she watched on a television monitor in the operating room, he inserted the laparoscope through a small puncture in her abdomen. "It was amazing. I could see streams of adhesions pulling the tube out of position," says Wendy, who had received a local anesthetic and intravenous sedation. "I couldn't feel the instruments inside me, but I saw him pick up my ovary and examine it. I never realized how small the ovaries really are."

The single procedure that provides the most information about a woman's reproductive anatomy is diagnostic laparoscopy. A diagnostic laparoscopy involves inserting a narrow fiber optic telescope into the woman's abdomen to get a direct view of her pelvic organs—the uterus, fallopian tubes, and ovaries—and to look for endometriosis or pelvic adhesions.

Dr. Berger usually schedules diagnostic laparoscopy in the late luteal phase, two or three days before the woman is expected to menstruate and late enough after ovulation (ten to twelve days later) to check her hormone levels in the blood to make sure she isn't already pregnant before proceeding with the examination.

A "second look" diagnostic laparoscopy is also sometimes performed to check the results of reconstructive surgery. In cases where extensive scarring has been corrected through microsurgery, the laparoscope may be used for a second look at the pelvic organs between three and six weeks after reconstructive surgery to assess the results and to remove any new adhesions that may have developed after the surgery.

The fiber optic laparoscope, introduced into the abdominal-pelvic cavity through a half-inch or smaller incision just below the navel, comes in different types and sizes. A thin 4 millimeter (mm) diameter laparoscope (about as thick as a darning needle) is adequate for most examinations, but an intermediate size laparoscope 6 to 8 mm in diameter (about as thick as a ballpoint pen) provides more light, which is required for video or photographic recording of findings. A larger 10 to 12 mm diameter operating laparoscope (about as thick as a fountain pen), which has a channel that can be used to introduce instruments into the abdominal cavity, is usually required to correct any abnormalities. With the larger scope, the doctor can cut away adhesions with scissors, or burn away endometriosis with an electric probe or a laser beam.

To enhance his view of the woman's reproductive organs, the doctor will place gas (carbon dioxide or nitrous oxide) into the abdominal cavity to lift up the anterior abdominal wall (the skin, muscles, and other soft tissues). Then the woman lies on the operating table so that her head is slightly lower than her pelvis, which helps the bowel fall away from the pelvic organs so that they can be examined more easily.

Frequently, the doctor needs to insert a second instrument through the abdomen to move various organs while he looks through the eyepiece of the laparoscope. Dr. Berger inserts a thin, blunt-tipped needle about two inches above the pubic bone. With this probe, he can move the fallopian tubes and ovaries to see all surfaces of those organs completely. Another probe placed inside the woman's uterine cavity through the cervical canal allows him to move the uterus for a thorough pelvic inspection.

Dr. Berger follows a routine during a laparoscopic exam, beginning with a look at the uterus, then moving along systematically to the fallopian tubes and ovaries. Using the laparoscope and needle as extensions of his fingers,

Dr. Berger traces along the right fallopian tube adjacent to the uterus. When he gets to the tube, he is looking for an enlargement, thickening, or obstruction in the segment of the tube adjacent to the uterus (the isthmic segment).

He then examines the rest of the tube, tracing it out to its fimbrial end near the ovary. This end, which has the bell-like shape of a trumpet and fringed ends, normally is open and its lining appears lush and healthy.

Sometimes the fimbrial end of the tube is partially closed. Think of the tube as an arm with the hand and fingers (fimbria) at the end. Pelvic inflammatory disease (PID) or salpingitis can cause the tube's fingers to close, preventing the spread of infection out into the abdominal cavity. If the fingers draw together completely like a shut fist, then dye can't pass through the end of the tube, and the tube becomes enlarged with the accumulation of the distending dye, giving it the shape of a "clubbed tube."

The laparoscopic examination also involves inspection of the ovaries. Ovulation requires the rupture of a follicle from the ovary's surface, which subsequently leaves a small pit or depression in the ovary. A small ovary with a very smooth surface suggests that a woman hasn't been ovulating regularly. When laparoscopy is performed in the post-ovulatory phase of the cycle, a yellow stain can be seen in the corpus luteum—the hole in the surface of the ovary where an egg has been released. Spotting this confirms ovulation. The ovary also is examined for endometriosis, adhesions, cysts, and other abnormalities.

After examining the right fallopian tube and ovary thoroughly, Dr. Berger points the instrument down behind the uterus in the cul-de-sac and along the broad ligaments on both sides of the uterus, looking for endometriosis. If the cul-de-sac contains fluid, he removes the fluid and continues the search for endometriosis. Then he moves along to the woman's left side and performs a similar evaluation on the left fallopian tube and ovary.

Hydrotubation

If there is any doubt about whether one or both tubes are open, Dr. Berger injects a sterile solution of indigo carmine dye and saline up through the cervical canal and uterus to check for the free spill of the dye from both tubes. This procedure is called hydrotubation.

The doctor places a cone-shaped instrument up against the woman's cervix to help prevent the flow of the dye solution back out through the cervical canal. When dye comes out of the fimbrial end of the fallopian tube, that proves that the entire length of the tube is open.

Tuboscopic Exam

An infection can destroy the cilia, or tiny hairs, lining the fallopian tube, transforming the tube's inner lining into a glassy, polished—and nonfunctioning—tube. Without the hair propellant, the egg may enter the tube and be stopped short, like a car stuck in a car wash with no power to the conveyor belt. If the egg is fertilized, it may not be transported into the uterus, resulting in a tubal pregnancy.

The problem of cilia damage is insidious because infections of the fallopian tubes frequently produce no symptoms. Many infertile women are found to have scarred fallopian tubes, but had no history to suggest when the infection happened. A high percentage of these women have antibodies to chlamydia, indicating that they have been infected with this organism in the past.

The longer and more severely the tube has been damaged, the less likely the cilia will return. The earlier the infection is diagnosed and treated with antibiotics, the less damage to the tube's lining and cilia.

A new diagnostic device, called a tuboscope, can help detect cilia damage once it's suspected. Through an ordinary laparoscope, one can only see part way into the fimbrial end of the fallopian tubes. But with the tiny telescopic tuboscope, designed to be threaded directly into the fallopian tubes through a small incision in the woman's abdomen, the entire inner lining of the fallopian tube can be examined. A hysterosalpingogram may show that the tubes are open, but a tuboscopic exam may reveal that the cilia in the tubal lining are missing. The tuboscope is a promising new tool but isn't yet commercially available to North American doctors.

Endometrial Biopsy

"Of all the things I had done to me, the endometrial biopsy procedure was the most uncomfortable," says Paula, a thirty-year-old illustrator. As part of her workup, she had undergone several hysterosalpingograms, hysteroscopies, and laparoscopies. The endometrial biopsy was performed in the doctor's office. "The same day I had the biopsy taken, I went on to work, and late in the afternoon I was bent over with cramps. I had to go into my office and shut the door until the pain went away," she recalls.

An endometrial biopsy involves scraping a small amount of tissue from the endometrium for examination by a pathologist. A woman can have the endometrial biopsy right in the doctor's office to monitor her endometrial development in the luteal phase and to determine the presence of a luteal phase defect (LPD). But because of the discomfort associated with the procedure, Dr. Berger prefers to perform an endometrial biopsy at the time of hysteroscopy or laparoscopy, when the woman already has received suitable anesthesia. Then the biopsy doesn't cause any discomfort.

An endometrial biopsy is most helpful in diagnosing luteal phase defect. The doctor suspects this condition when a woman's luteal phase of the cycle lasts for twelve days or less from the surge of luteinizing hormone, or her mid-luteal progesterone level is low. The pathologist studies the fragment of endometrium removed at biopsy to see how the tissue has developed. To insure proper interpretation, the biopsy material must be related to the date of the LH surge and to the time of the next period. It should be performed ten to thirteen days after the LH surge or one to four days before the next expected period, and only after a negative pregnancy test of hormone levels in the blood.

Testing the Man

Paralleling the woman's tests, the continuing analysis of a man's fertility also includes X-ray studies and examination of his sperm-producing tissues, as well as several tests of the health of his sperm.

Beyond Semen Analysis

Since semen analysis doesn't measure sperm function—only the quantity of sperm, what they look like and how they move—other tests of sperm function have been developed to aid the male fertility investigation. Some tests check for components of the seminal fluid that the sperm swim in; other tests measure the sperm's ability to survive in and move through cervical mucus. Still others determine whether a sperm can penetrate the coating around an egg and fertilize it.

THE SUGAR TEST • If a man has no sperm in his semen at all—that is, a zero sperm count—the doctor should perform a simple test for the presence of fructose (fruit sugar) in his semen. If he has no fructose in the semen, then his seminal vesicles are not functioning properly or, more likely, the ducts along the semen's path are blocked or absent, preventing the secretions from the seminal vesicles from mixing with his sperm.

To do the test, the seminal fluid is mixed with chemical reagents. If the mixture turns a pink-orange color (a positive test), then fructose is present and the secretions of the seminal vesicles are getting into the semen. If there is no color change (a negative test), then there is no sugar in the semen. Since the majority of the fluids in semen are made by the seminal vesicles, a negative test usually means that nothing is coming out of the seminal vesicles, or that ducts from the seminal vesicles are blocked or not working properly. A negative sugar test almost always parallels low semen volume of less than 1 ml. Further investigation of the man's reproductive tract ducts is necessary to try to locate blockages and determine whether they can be repaired.

THE ORANGE DYE TEST • Men who have normal numbers of sperm, but sperm that don't move well, may have denatured or inactivated deoxyribonucleic acid (DNA), which makes up the chromosomes. The orange dye test can distinguish between living, nonmotile sperm and genetically "dead" sperm.

The test involves mixing sperm with a dye called acridine orange. When viewed through a fluorescent microscope the dye glows green if bound to normal, double-stranded DNA and red if bound to denatured, single-stranded DNA. Normal sperm heads show a green tinge, while "dead" sperm heads appear red. A high percentage of green-tinged sperm indicates a high proportion of live sperm, while an abnormally high percentage of red sperm heads correlates with decreased fertility.

Mixing in various activating solutions may revive immotile sperm in the laboratory. Solutions of various albumins (proteins found throughout the body), such as the albumin found in human or cow blood, as well as the culture media used to grow cells, such as Ham's F10 or F12, have occasionally restored some men's motility. Other substances have been tried, including kinins (which make blood vessels open up) and even caffeine. These substances may make sperm move better in the test tube, but they don't necessarily improve the sperm's ability to penetrate an egg. So adding caffeine to an insemination cup or drinking lots of coffee before making love or producing a sperm sample for insemination won't make a man's sperm more effectual.

THE HAMSTER TEST

Lucy and Bill came to Chapel Hill Fertility Center after many years of trying, unsuccessfully, to have a baby. They already knew that Bill, a forty-three-year-old writer, had a low sperm count. Lucy, a psychotherapist, wanted to have his sperm penetration checked out right away. "We did not want to use donor sperm, and if Bill had no sperm penetration, I didn't want to continue treatment," says Lucy. Bill's hamster test showed good penetrating ability. "That renewed my interest in treatment. I couldn't go on not knowing," Lucy says.

The best test currently available to determine the fertilizing ability of a man's sperm is the sperm penetration assay, or hamster egg penetration test. It is like a trial run of in vitro fertilization, using a hamster's egg instead of the woman's eggs. This test determines one thing: whether human sperm placed immediately adjacent to hamster eggs can penetrate them. To penetrate an egg, sperm must have a healthy acrosome, the packet of enzymes at the head of the sperm. These enzymes dissolve the coating around the egg. The sperm head must also be free of antibodies and have an intact energy factory so that it has the power to move.

Instead of using human eggs, which are difficult to obtain, fertility researchers have turned to hamster eggs. Hamster egg penetration generally correlates with how well sperm can penetrate human eggs. Using enzymes, a lab technician removes the coating around the hamster egg (zona pellucida). This coating, also found on a human egg (ovum), prevents interspecies fertilization and must be removed before human sperm can penetrate the hamster egg. (That's also why you may hear the test called a hamster zona-free ovum or HZFO test.) Once the zona is removed, the sperm are mixed with hamster eggs; the technician then collects the eggs and checks to see how many have been penetrated by sperm and how many sperm penetrated each hamster egg. (Without the protective coating, more than one sperm can penetrate an egg.)

The hamster test is most valuable when the man has an apparently normal semen analysis and his wife has no defined fertility problem, yet they have failed to conceive. It also has use to check whether an artificial insemination attempt may be worthwhile for men with very low sperm counts. If his sperm can't penetrate an egg when they are placed immediately beside it, then intrauterine or intratubal insemination or assisted reproductive technologies like in vitro fertilization (IVF) will probably be of little value.

Like any test, the hamster test is not perfect. Although there is a good correlation between a sperm's ability to penetrate a hamster egg and its ability to penetrate human eggs, about 5 to 10 percent of men who have negative hamster tests still can get their wives pregnant with assisted reproductive technologies. So human eggs may be easier for human sperm to penetrate than hamster eggs.

On the other hand, some men who score well on the hamster test can't impregnate their wives, and show no evidence of fertilizing their wives' eggs during IVF treatment. Perhaps this is due to some abnormality in the wife's eggs. The hamster test provides a good, but not perfect, correlation with human fertility, and is of no value in diagnosing disorders involving poor transport of sperm to the egg or of post-fertilization abnormalities. Like any test, it can provide useful information, but it has its limitations.

Also, there are problems with the hamster test as most laboratories currently perform it. Egg penetration will vary depending on the culture medium used in the test. Performing the test with different types or concentrations of albumin to supplement the media will produce different penetration results from the same ejaculate. So it's often difficult to compare results from one lab to the next. Baylor University's Dr. Larry Lipshultz has developed a "cold-shock" version of the hamster test in which the sperm are subjected to a rapid temperature change. This test, called a sperm capacitation index, may provide a more accurate estimate of fertilizing success, and it may become the standard. Doctors also have to recognize that egg penetrations may vary from one ejaculate to the next from the same man. One hamster test, like a single semen analysis, may mislead a doctor to draw the wrong conclusion about a man's fertilizing potential.

THE ULTIMATE FERTILITY TEST • The ultimate fertilization question is, "Can a man's sperm fertilize his wife's egg?" Aside from a pregnancy, a couple can get an answer during treatment by in vitro fertilization. Since the couple's sperm and egg are placed together directly in a petri dish, this minimizes fertilization problems caused by mucus barriers, moderately low sperm counts, and low sperm motility (although some sperm with normal motility must be able to move to and attach to the egg within the dish).

Other sperm penetration tests, such as the hamster egg test, can provide good clues about a couple's fertilization potential, but IVF uses both of the couple's gametes (sperm and egg), not just the man's sperm and a hamster's egg. Also, IVF uses eggs with the zona pellucida intact, not removed, which better represents the true physiologic state of an unfertilized egg.

Therefore, IVF can be viewed as both a diagnostic and therapeutic procedure. As a diagnostic test, it determines whether the husband's sperm will penetrate his wife's egg. If the sperm penetrate and the egg divides, but the embryo doesn't implant, then it's worth trying another IVF procedure. If his sperm don't penetrate her eggs, there may be little point in the couple continuing with further IVF attempts, and donor insemination may be a better option.

If sperm fertilize the eggs in vitro (outside the body in a laboratory environment), that's good evidence that sperm *can* fertilize, that the eggs *are* fertilizable, and conception could happen naturally as well. In fact, IVF programs report a high spontaneous pregnancy rate. As many as 30 percent of women who become pregnant in IVF programs conceive during a non-IVF cycle! The success of IVF procedures relates to the care that's taken to regulate induction cycles, the maturation of more than one egg, optimal timing of insemination and support of the luteal phase with hormones, as well as fertilization outside of the body. If a woman ovulates and has functional tubes, she may be able to get pregnant without having to mix sperm and egg in a laboratory environment. As long as his sperm fertilizes her egg, the couple can be reassured that IVF or other treatments offer them the potential for conception.

As a diagnostic test, IVF holds most value for couples with unexplained infertility. If all other tests fail to explain why a couple is infertile, then an IVF attempt may provide the explanation. If eggs can be successfully retrieved from the woman, and her husband's sperm penetrate them, then they could have a child together, possibly through an IVF procedure or, for a woman with repeat miscarriages, through a surrogate to carry the baby to term for her. If his sperm don't penetrate her eggs, the couple's only options using the husband's sperm are experimental procedures, such as drilling through the zona to allow easier sperm penetration or microinjection of a single sperm (see Chapter 9).

In addition to the cervical mucus, other secretions from the female reproductive tract also play a role in how well sperm function. The fluids found in the uterus and follicles are potent inducers of the acrosome reaction, the biological change the sperm must go through to become "capacitated" and be able to penetrate eggs. The ability of sperm to undergo the acrosome reaction can be tested in the laboratory.

There is another new lab test of sperm fertilizing potential that holds promise as a predictor of a man's chances of fathering a child through IVF. Researchers at the Jones Institute for Reproductive Medicine in Norfolk, Virginia, have been able to identify couples with male fertility factors who would most likely succeed, or fail, in IVF treatment using what they call a hemizona assay.

Using eggs donated for research by women who had pelvic surgeries for various reasons, the Jones researchers have tested the binding of sperm to the zona pellucida. The eggs are split in two. One half is tested with the infertile man's sperm and the other half with sperm from a man with proven fertility. After the sperm are washed and allowed to "swim up" in a nutrient medium for one hour, they are recovered, and a drop of sperm is added to each half of an egg. After incubation for four hours, each egg half is rinsed to dislodge loose sperm, and the sperm still bound to the hemizona surfaces are counted.

In the experiments, the hemizona assay showed a high correlation between sperm binding to the zona pellucida and IVF fertilization rates. (Tight sperm binding to the zona pellucida is the first critical step in sperm-egg interaction.) After more experience with the test, Jones Institute researcher Dr. Gary Hodgen says that "we should be able to use it to distinguish subfertile from fertile sperm."

Testicular Biopsy

A man with a zero sperm count either isn't producing sperm or the sperm he produces can't get out into the ejaculate. If his testicles are small and soft, and his FSH level is high—more than twice normal—his doctor can presume he is not manufacturing sperm. If examination by an experienced male fertility specialist reveals that his vas deferens are absent from birth, he knows the sperm are being blocked. But if his physical exam is normal, then a testicular biopsy may be necessary to find out whether he is producing sperm.

If a man has no sperm in the ejaculate but has a normal semen volume along with normal FSH levels, a vas deferens on each side, and normal-sized testicles, then a testicular biopsy is definitely indicated. The doctor removes a small sample of tissue from each testicle and examines it under a microscope to see whether adequate numbers of sperm are being produced. If they are, but no sperm are present in the semen, then an obstruction exists somewhere along the tubes between the testicle and his penis.

Microscopic examination of the testicular sample allows the doctor to identify sperm in their various stages of development. This is a simple outpatient procedure. When Dr. Goldstein does a testicular biopsy, the cuts in the testicle are so small that no stitches are required. Most patients are back to work in one or two days. The biopsy results are usually ready in four to seven days.

If the biopsy shows that a man is making sperm, the next step is to find the blocked duct and open it surgically. But if the biopsy shows no signs of sperm production, then the man may have arrested sperm maturation or a condition called "Sertoli-Cell-Only" syndrome, which is characterized by slightly smaller than normal testicles and a zero sperm count. Presuming that his reproductive hormone levels are normal, no current treatment can stimulate his sperm production.

The doctor must make sure not to miss a hormonal cause of azoospermia, such as hypogonadotropic hypogonadism. Under this condition, a man's pituitary doesn't signal the testicles to produce sperm. This is analogous to a woman not ovulating because she lacks the proper hormonal signals from the brain to the ovaries. A man can be treated with the same drugs used to induce ovulation in women—Pergonal, human chorionic gonadotropin (hCG), or GnRH.

Karyotyping

Another test that is sometimes performed is a chromosome study (karyotyping). In men who have abnormally small testicles and a feminine body shape, a chromosome analysis may reveal a congenital, nontreatable condition, such as Klinefelter's syndrome, which halts sexual development.

Vasogram

A urologist or male fertility specialist should be able to diagnose a blockage with a testicular biopsy. If the biopsy shows a man has normal sperm production, but no sperm in the ejaculate, then it's obvious that the man has a blockage somewhere. The man's reproductive surgeon can explore the vas and epididymis under the microscope and, if necessary, perform a vasogram to find out exactly where the vas is blocked.

A vasogram involves making a small incision in the scrotum and exposing the vas deferens. Contrast dye is injected into the vas or the ejaculatory duct, and X-rays are taken from various angles. This is particularly useful in locating the exact spot of an obstruction since it gives an outline of the sperm transport system.

A vasogram isn't quite the same as an X-ray study of the fallopian tubes. The vas's tiny ducts are only one-third of a millimeter in diameter. Even the smallest needle placed in the vas to inject the X-ray dye can injure the pinpoint-sized duct. The needle itself can end up blocking the vas, and doing the vasogram before or at the time of a testicular biopsy can damage a man's vas ducts. Yet, some urologists routinely perform a biopsy and vasogram together. If your doctor suggests doing the vasogram along with a biopsy, obtain a second opinion from a male fertility specialist.

A vasogram should only be performed by a physician experienced in the technique, with an operating microscope available and only when the blocked ducts can be repaired immediately. That way, if the vas is damaged during the test, the reproductive surgeon can repair the damage right away by cutting out the segment of vas and sewing the two ends together.

In most cases, a vasogram is rarely indicated. To check for a blockage, the doctor can make a microscopic opening in the vas and take a sample of fluid to see if it contains sperm. If there are sperm in the fluid, then he knows there's a blockage. He can also inject saline into the vas. If it flows easily through the vas, then he knows the vas is open. When the saline doesn't flow easily, he can pass a thin catheter up into the vas. Where the catheter stops is where the vas is blocked. Only when these tests are inconclusive is an X-ray necessary to find the blocked spot.

Questions to Ask Your Doctor About Additional Fertility Tests for Women

Does my hysterosalpingogram show any abnormalities of my uterus or fallopian tubes (uterine adhesions, polyps, tumors, or blocked tubes)?

Does my hysteroscopic exam show any abnormalities (uterine adhesions, fibroids, a septum, or abnormally shaped uterus)?

What did my laparoscopic exam reveal about my uterus, fallopian tubes, and ovaries?

Do I have endometriosis or pelvic adhesions?

Did hydrotubation show my fallopian tubes are both open?

Did my endometrial biopsy show I have a luteal phase defect?

Questions to Ask Your Doctor About Additional Fertility Tests for Men

(In general)

How well did my sperm do on the hamster egg test?

Do my wife and I need to try in vitro fertilization to achieve a pregnancy and to learn whether my sperm can fertilize her eggs?

Does my chromosome analysis reveal any abnormalities?

(For men with low sperm motility)

Do my sperm appear to be sticking to each other?

Are my sperm coated with antibodies?

(For men with no sperm in the semen)

Does my sugar test show I have fructose in my semen?

If my FSH is normal, do I need a testicular biopsy to determine whether my ducts are blocked?

7

HORMONE
TREATMENTS

A s one important step during their fertility workups, both partners will have their hormone levels checked and, if need be, take fertility drugs designed to stimulate ovulation or sperm production. Hormones are chemical messengers produced in one organ, an endocrine gland, and released into the bloodstream, which carries them to another (target) organ, where they have their effect.

Hormones and Feedback

Hormone regulation is analogous to the way a thermostat and heater feed information back to each. As the temperature increases, the thermostat shuts off, signaling the heater to reduce its heat output. When the temperature falls below the thermostat's setting, the thermostat signals the heater to turn up the heat again.

A similar signaling relationship exists between the pituitary gland and the ovaries in women, and testicles in men. As the concentration of gonadotropin hormones in the blood rises, this signals the woman's ovaries or the man's testicles to increase hormone output. When the hormone

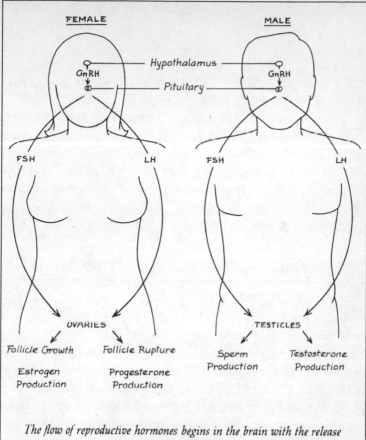

The flow of reproductive hormones begins in the brain with the release of gonadotropin releasing hormone (GnRH) from the hypothalamus, which stimulates the pituitary to release follicle stimulating hormone (FSH) and luteinizing hormone (LH) in both men and women. In a woman, FSH induces follicle development and estrogen production within the ovaries, while in a man FSH stimulates sperm production in the testicles. LH causes follicle rupture and progesterone development in women and testosterone production in men.

levels of estrogen (for women) or testosterone (for men) reach a certain point, the pituitary gland slows its production and release of gonadotropins.

Just as you work the gas and brake pedals on your car, the body steps up or holds back hormone production when appropriate. When the body's hormone production or regulation breaks down, or becomes sluggish, powerful fertility drugs can move it into action. Up to 75 percent of couples with fertility problems that are correctable by hormone treatments eventually achieve pregnancies.

Hormone Treatments for Women

When there is an imbalance in the interaction of hormones between the hypothalamus, pituitary, and ovary, a woman may ovulate irregularly or not at all. This is a frequent cause of infertility. Various hormone treatments for women can now correct the flow of hormones along the ovulation pathway. Other fertility drugs can help time exactly when to release the egg to become fertilized and, once the woman becomes pregnant, help maintain and support the pregnancy to prevent an early miscarriage.

A woman can also take medications that affect hormone production to alleviate such conditions as endometriosis, fibroids, and polycystic ovarian disease.

Clomiphene Citrate (Clomid, Serophene)

Some women can't get pregnant because they don't secrete enough LH and FSH at the right time during the cycle and, as a result, they don't ovulate. For these women, the first drug doctors often prescribe is clomiphene citrate (Clomid, Serophene). This synthetic drug stimulates the hypothalamus to release more GnRH, which then prompts the pituitary to release more LH and FSH, and thus increases stimulation of the ovary to begin ovulation.

Clomiphene is a good first choice drug when a woman's ovaries are capable of functioning normally and when her hypothalamus and pituitary are also capable of producing their hormones. In short, the woman's reproductive engine is in working order, but needs some revving up.

Structurally like estrogen, clomiphene binds to the sites in the brain where estrogen normally attaches, called estrogen receptors. Once these receptor sites are filled up with clomiphene, they can't bind with natural estrogen circulating in the blood and they are fooled into thinking that the amount of estrogen in the blood is too low. In response, the hypothalamus releases more GnRH, causing the pituitary to pump out more FSH, which then causes a follicle to grow to produce more estrogen and start maturing an egg to prepare for ovulation. Typically, a woman taking clomiphene produces double or triple the amount of estrogen in that cycle compared to pretreatment cycles.

If a woman is menstruating, even if irregularly, clomiphene is usually effective, particularly if she develops follicles that aren't reaching normal size. Usually, a mature follicle is about 20 millimeters in diameter, or about the size of a small grape, just before it ruptures and releases its egg. Clomiphene may help small, immature follicles grow to maturity.

A low estradiol level in a woman's blood correlates with an inadequately stimulated, small follicle. A woman having a spontaneous ovulation cycle (that is, ovulating without the aid of fertility drugs) generally has peak estradiol levels ranging from 100 to 300 picograms (one trillioneth of a gram)/ml. A woman may have enough hormones to produce an egg, but if her estradiol production by the follicles is low (less than 100 pg/ml), she may not adequately stimulate her cervix to produce fertile mucus or stimulate her endometrium to get ready to accept a fertilized egg for implantation. Clomiphene could boost her weak signals from the hypothalamus to the pituitary to the ovaries.

A woman who ovulates infrequently—say, at six-week intervals or less often—is also a good candidate for clomiphene therapy, since clomiphene will induce ovulation more frequently. The more a woman ovulates, the more opportunities her mature eggs have to be exposed to her husband's sperm and, therefore, the greater her chance to become pregnant.

Clomiphene is also often effective for a woman with luteal phase defect (LPD). A woman with LPD may begin the ovulation process properly, but her ovarian function becomes disrupted, resulting in low production of the hormone progesterone in the luteal phase of the menstrual cycle. Following ovulation, the ovary produces progesterone, the hormone needed to prepare the uterine lining for implantation of the fertilized egg, which has divided and entered the uterine cavity. A fall in progesterone levels in the blood during this critical time can interfere with early embryo implantation or, even if a fertilized egg has already implanted, cause a woman to menstruate too early and end a pregnancy within a few days after implantation.

Keeping a basal body temperature (BBT) chart is often helpful for a woman taking clomiphene. The chart will show her whether the luteal phase of her cycle is shorter than the normal fourteen days. The luteal phase of the cycle, the length of time from ovulation until she menstruates, has a normal range of thirteen to fifteen days. Clomiphene often can "tune up" the hypothalamus and pituitary so they keep producing the hormones the ovary needs to manufacture progesterone throughout the luteal phase.

Of women whose only fertility problem is irregular or no ovulation at all, about 80 percent will ovulate and about

50 percent will become pregnant within six months of clomiphene treatments. About 3 percent of women on clomiphene have a multiple pregnancy, usually twins, compared with about 1 percent in the general population.

If a woman responds to clomiphene and develops a mature follicle (determined by adequate estrogen production and ultrasound examination), but has no LH surge by cycle day fifteen, then injection of the hormone human chorionic gonadotropin (hCG), which acts like LH, can be given to stimulate final egg maturation and follicle rupture, releasing the egg. The woman tends to ovulate about thirty-six hours after the LH surge or hCG injection, which can be confirmed by further ultrasound scans.

Clomiphene is a relatively inexpensive drug, and is taken orally for only five days each month. The doctor attempts to initiate clomiphene therapy so that the woman ovulates on or around day fourteen of a regular twenty-eight-day cycle. The simplest, most widely used dose starts with one daily 50 mg tablet for five days starting on cycle day three or five. If a woman ovulates at this dose, there is no advantage to her increasing the dosage. In other words, more of the drug isn't necessarily better. In fact, more may be worse, producing multiple ovulation, causing side effects such as an ovarian cyst or hot flashes, and, most commonly, interfering with her fertile mucus production.

If a woman doesn't ovulate after taking one clomiphene tablet for five days, then her doctor will usually double the daily dose to two tablets (100 mg) in her next cycle, and if she still doesn't respond, then triple the daily dose to 150 mg, or add another fertility medication such as human menopausal gonadotropin (Pergonal) in the next cycle. Some doctors increase the dose up to 250 mg a day, but this is not recommended by either of the drug's two manufacturers. Women tend to have side effects much more frequently at higher doses.

If the dose of clomiphene is too high, the uterine lining may not respond completely to estrogen and progesterone stimulation, and may not develop properly. As a result, a woman's fertilized egg may not be able to implant in her uterus.

SIDE EFFECTS • Because clomiphene binds to estrogen receptors, including the estrogen receptors in the cervix, it can interfere with the ability of the cervical mucus glands to be stimulated by estrogen to produce fertile mucus. Only "hostile" or dry cervical mucus may develop in the days preceding ovulation. If this occurs, adding a small amount of estrogen beginning on cycle day ten and continuing until the LH surge may enhance cervical mucus production.

Some women taking clomiphene experience hot flashes and premenstrual-type symptoms, such as migraines and breast discomfort (particularly if they have fibrocystic disease of the breasts). Visual symptoms such as spots, flashes, or blurry vision are less common and indicate that treatment should stop.

The hot flashes are just like the hot flashes women experience at menopause when the level of estrogen circulating in the blood is low. The clomiphene fools the brain into thinking that blood estrogen levels are low.

Clomiphene is a very safe medication with relatively few contraindications. Preexisting liver disease is one contraindication since clomiphene is metabolized by the liver. Enlarged ovaries also are a contraindication since clomiphene may occasionally produce hyperstimulation of the ovaries.

CLOMIPHENE ABUSE • Too often, doctors give clomiphene to women with unexplained infertility before the couple has a fertility workup, or even after they have a workup, but there is no evidence of an ovulation disorder. This empiric therapy may create new problems, such as interfering with fertile mucus production, and often delays further evaluation that can lead to a specific diagnosis and proper treatment.

For a woman who has normal, spontaneous ovulation, driving the pituitary harder with clomiphene won't make ovulation any more normal. If a woman has taken clomiphene for several cycles without becoming pregnant, then she and her fertility specialist should investigate other conditions that may be preventing her pregnancy.

After noting a good postcoital test (PCT) during a fertility workup, some doctors fail to repeat the test after placing a woman on clomiphene. A PCT needs to be repeated to check the quality of the woman's cervical mucus while she is on clomiphene, since 25 percent or more of women who take the drug develop cervical mucus problems. It's important for a woman to monitor her cervical mucus production during every cycle while trying to become pregnant, including her cycles while taking clomiphene.

Human Menopausal Gonadotropin (Pergonal)

Women who fail to respond to clomiphene become candidates for treatment with human menopausal gonadotropin (hMG, trade name Pergonal). This fertility drug is made from equal amounts of purified FSH and LH. These natural gonadotropins are produced in very high amounts by women after menopause, and are extracted from the urine of women who have stopped menstruating. Unlike clomiphene, Pergonal induces ovulation by directly stimulating the ovaries, and can be used in women who don't have normal hypothalamic or pituitary function.

Pergonal therapy is effective for a woman who has ovaries that are capable of responding normally to FSH and LH, but who doesn't have a normal flow of hormones from the hypothalamus to the pituitary to the ovaries. The FSH provided through a Pergonal injection goes through her blood into the ovaries to stimulate follicle growth.

Pergonal offers the advantage over clomiphene of producing fertile cervical mucus (if the woman's mucus glands are normal) since it doesn't interfere with the body's estrogen receptors.

Two other less common indications for Pergonal include a woman with two ovaries but only one normal healthy fallopian tube, and the 5 to 10 percent of women with regular menstruation who have luteinized unruptured follicle (LUF) syndrome. For a woman with two ovaries and one healthy tube, Pergonal can enhance the probability that both of her ovaries ovulate simultaneously in the same cycle, which facilitates egg pickup by the normal tube. For LUF, in which an egg matures but the follicle doesn't rupture and release it, Pergonal, plus hCG to stimulate ovulation, seems to be more effective than either hCG alone or clomiphene plus hCG.

A woman with long-standing "unexplained" infertility may have abnormal FSH and LH levels despite normal estrogen and progesterone secretions. Pergonal may allow her to conceive by overriding these abnormal gonadotropin patterns.

Like clomiphene, Pergonal can also be taken along with hCG to induce ovulation to time artificial insemination. In addition, Pergonal is the primary fertility drug used for "superovulation": intentionally stimulating a woman's ovaries to produce multiple eggs during a cycle. Also called controlled ovarian hyperstimulation, this concept was originally developed for IVF. It has now been applied to other assisted reproductive technologies, most commonly combined with timed insemination techniques. The rationale is simple: Any time a woman produces more than one egg, she increases her chances of having a pregnancy, since more eggs are available to become fertilized.

For the proper candidates, about 90 percent will ovulate and about 50 percent will become pregnant through Pergonal therapy. The main drawback of Pergonal is the increased risk of multiple pregnancy. The multiple pregnancy rate is higher than with clomiphene-induced cycles because of the larger number of eggs produced by Pergonal stimulation. The risk of bearing three or more babies has been about 5 percent, but by careful monitoring of estrogen levels and using ultrasound scans, that risk can be reduced to 2 percent or less.

Gauging the amount of Pergonal that will properly stimulate ovulation without overstimulating the ovaries is an intricate process. The amount of hormone that must be given each day, and the number of days of treatment, varies greatly not only from one woman to the next, but may vary from one course of treatment to another for the same woman. Usually, however, once an adequate dose is established, a woman will generally respond to a similar dose in subsequent cycles.

HYPERSTIMULATION • Because of its potency, Pergonal stimulation must be carefully monitored during each cycle to avoid the risk of hyperstimulation syndrome, in which too many follicles are stimulated and the ovaries enlarge dangerously.

The majority of women only become mildly hyperstimulated, experiencing pelvic discomfort and ovaries enlarged to about the size of golf balls. Moderate hyperstimulation will enlarge the ovaries to baseball-size and cause a woman to gain weight and have a tender tummy.

A severe case may enlarge a woman's ovaries to grapefruit size or even larger, and may require that she spend time in the hospital to monitor her fluids and electrolytes. This is a rare but potentially serious complication. Just as the most potent heart drugs should be prescribed by cardiologists, Pergonal should be prescribed only by experienced fertility specialists.

Once a woman's ovaries begin responding to Pergonal, the fertility specialist will monitor her with frequent, often daily, estradiol blood tests, ultrasound scans, and cervical mucus examinations. Dr. Berger starts administering Pergonal on cycle day two or three after obtaining a baseline ultrasound scan to ensure that the woman has no ovarian cysts. By cycle day eight, he takes daily measurements of her estradiol, LH, and progesterone levels in the blood, monitors the number and size of her developing follicles, and examines her cervical mucus to determine whether she needs more Pergonal or if the conditions are right to induce ovulation with an hCG injection.

If the woman responds too much to Pergonal stimulation, he takes her off the drug and forestalls giving her hCG to prevent hyperstimulation. Her ovaries are allowed to rest until they completely return to normal size before she undertakes another attempt at ovulation induction.

The risk of hyperstimulation is related to the number of developing follicles and to the blood level of circulating estrogen produced by these follicles. Since each stimulated follicle puts out its own estrogen, blood levels of estradiol will be noticeably higher if there are an excess number of follicles.

Ultrasound examinations will tell a woman how many mature follicles she is developing. Dominant follicles during Pergonal treatment are generally 15 millimeters (mm), or the size of a plump raisin, in diameter, or larger. Follicles that reach 10 to 12 mm in diameter should be monitored daily, with the woman returning to the fertility specialist's office often to decide when to stop the Pergonal and give her the final injection of hCG.

The risk of multiple pregnancies is directly related to the number of dominant follicles. When two follicles exceed 16 mm in diameter, a woman has about a 2 to 4 percent chance of having twins. If she has three or four large follicles, the risk increases. The couple should understand the risks of multiple pregnancies before Pergonal treatment is administered. (Many couples go ahead with ovulation induction by Pergonal even though there may be an increased risk of twins or triplets because it's so effective in increasing the couple's chances of achieving a pregnancy.) By tightly monitoring Pergonal stimulation, Dr. Berger has yet to have a woman give birth to more than twins, but the risk of multiple pregnancies is always a possibility.

Examining the cervix also provides a method of rapidly monitoring the amount of circulating estrogen. Women often notice an abundance of cervical mucus while taking Pergonal because each follicle puts out estrogen, which in turn stimulates cervical mucus. As the blood level of estradiol increases, the cervix becomes soft, opens up, and produces copious amounts of watery, clear, fertile mucus. This indicates that the cervix has shifted into a fertile time of the woman's cycle, and is called the "clinical shift." Once a woman has undergone the clinical shift, she can usually expect to receive an hCG injection within one or two days to induce ovulation.

In addition to estradiol, Dr. Berger monitors a woman's LH and progesterone levels to check for "premature luteinization." Luteinization is the process by which an ovarian follicle transforms into the corpus luteum, which produces the progesterone needed to mature the endometrial lining for pregnancy. About 20 percent of women taking Pergonal luteinize their follicles before, and not after, an hCG injection, frequently due to a spontaneous surge in

LH production. If this happens, the woman's eggs may not fertilize, or if they do, her endometrium may not be receptive for implantation at the right time of the woman's cycle.

Dr. Berger also has a woman use a home urinary LH kit to learn when she is having a spontaneous LH surge, particularly if she has to time an artificial insemination attempt or an egg retrieval for Gamete Intra Fallopian Transfer (GIFT) or IVF. If a woman starts to develop an LH surge on her own while taking Pergonal, the doctor then instructs her to take an hCG injection, and then times the insemination or egg retrieval procedure from the onset of the LH surge.

THE COMMITMENT TO PERGONAL

Emma, a forty-year-old actress, went to a fertility specialist because she hadn't had her period in six months. After reviewing her history and physical examination, the doctor found she had low gonadotropin production, and put her on clomiphene. When clomiphene alone failed, she added Pergonal to her drug treatment. Once her follicles began to approach maturity, she began daily ultrasound exams.

"When you make a commitment to go on Pergonal, you have to plan your life around the treatment," says Emma. "My husband, Fred, wanted to make plans to go off together one weekend when I was taking Pergonal, and I told him I was sorry, we couldn't go because I had to go in for an ultrasound exam."

When monitored properly, Pergonal is a highly effective and safe drug. But without precise monitoring and controlled use, it can be dangerous. Pergonal stimulation requires much more time and commitment on a woman's, and her doctor's, part than ovulation induction with clomiphene. While she is being monitored, a woman can expect to make four or five office visits during a cycle to evaluate the drug's effects.

The couple should thoroughly discuss Pergonal treatments with their fertility specialist. To minimize the number of office visits, a nurse may train the husband to give his wife the injections. This ability to receive injections at home comes in handy, especially since the hCG injection is usually given late at night. For the couple to time an insemination procedure around midday, the wife has to receive the hCG injection after midnight the day before.

Pergonal treatment is expensive, with each vial costing $50 or more. The cost adds up quickly when a woman takes two or more vials a day for seven to ten days in each treatment cycle. Fortunately, most insurance companies cover treatment with Pergonal.

Pure FSH (Metrodin)

The success of Pergonal treatments to induce ovulation mostly results from the action of FSH. So its manufacturer, Serono Laboratories, has recently developed a purified form of FSH (Metrodin) free of the LH that is also present in Pergonal preparations.

Pure FSH helps induce ovulation in some infertile women who have too high an output of LH compared to the FSH they produce. It is specifically approved by the FDA for clomiphene-resistant women with polycystic ovarian disease (PCOD), who characteristically have an elevated LH to FSH ratio and are also prone to hyperstimulation. For these women, it can successfully initiate adequate follicle growth and reduce the risk of hyperstimulation associated with Pergonal.

A woman takes Metrodin the same way as Pergonal, by injection starting early in the cycle and continuing daily until her follicles start to respond, usually within six to ten days. She must be closely monitored during stimulation just as with Pergonal. And as with Pergonal, when pure FSH is used to stimulate ovulation, a woman usually won't have a spontaneous LH surge, and an hCG injection is usually given to cause her eggs to mature and her follicles to rupture.

Pure FSH is even more expensive than Pergonal, costing $60 or more per vial. If the price comes down, it could replace Pergonal as a more frequently used drug to stimulate ovulation.

The Egg Releaser—Human Chorionic Gonadotropin (hCG)

Once Pergonal or Metrodin have stimulated the growth and maturation of a woman's follicles, she then takes an injection of human chorionic gonadotropin (hCG) to stimulate release of the eggs from the follicles. Human chorionic gonadotropin is structurally similar to luteinizing hormone. Its primary function is to support the corpus luteum, which is what remains of a follicle after its egg has been released. The corpus luteum produces progesterone, which prepares the uterine lining for implantation of the fertilized egg and maintains the pregnancy. Once a woman is pregnant, she produces her own hCG, which stimulates the corpus luteum to produce progesterone to keep the pregnancy going and prevent her from menstruating.

Purified LH is not yet available for injection in large enough amounts to trigger ovulation. However, since hCG has a structure similar to LH, it can be given to women to stimulate the release of an egg from a mature follicle. In ovulation induced cycles, releasing the egg from the follicle usually requires an injection of hCG (5,000 to 10,000 units), most often given one or two days after the last dose of Pergonal. A woman ovulates, on average, about thirty-six hours after taking the hCG injection.

Some fertility specialists also provide repeated hCG injections to a woman with luteal phase defect as a means of stimulating her ovaries to keep producing progesterone late in the cycle so that menstrual bleeding doesn't occur prematurely, before the pregnancy can establish itself adequately in the uterus.

CONFUSED PREGNANCY TESTING • Since hCG is the same hormone detected by pregnancy tests, one problem with treating a luteal phase defect with hCG is that the injections can cause confusion. When a woman has a pregnancy test of the hormone levels in her blood, and hCG is identified, it's not known whether the hCG derives from the injections or pregnancy.

Not being able to differentiate the source of the hCG makes it more difficult to detect repeated, early miscarriages. When repeated hCG injections are given, it takes at least two blood tests—the second showing an increase in hCG over the earlier one—to establish that a woman is pregnant. If the initial test simply measures hCG left in the blood from a previous injection, then the second test will show a fall, not a rise, in the hCG level.

SIDE EFFECTS • If a woman has developed a large number of mature follicles, then an hCG injection may cause her to feel some tenderness in her lower abdomen due to enlarged ovaries. Occasionally, women complain of redness and tenderness at the site of injection or experience hot flashes.

Gonadotropin Releasing Hormone (GnRH)

When a woman's hypothalamus fails to produce pulsating bursts of gonadotropin releasing hormone (GnRH) to signal the pituitary to secrete LH and FSH, she will fail to ovulate. One solution is to provide supplementary GnRH, which mimics what happens naturally in the body. The drug can be administered through a vein or just under the skin in pulses (one every ninety minutes) delivered by a controlled-rate infusion pump, about the size of a cigarette pack, worn on a belt around the waist.

GnRH therapy is generally indicated for women who have failed to ovulate on clomiphene or Pergonal. The best response has been found among women with a weak signal within the hypothalamus–pituitary–ovary system. Less common indications include women who have underdeveloped ovaries due to lack of hormone stimulation (hypogonadotropic hypogonadism) and delayed puberty. GnRH can also stimulate ovulation in physically active women whose menstrual cycles have ceased due to excess exercise and occasionally in women whose reproductive years have been cut short by premature menopause.

Pulses of GnRH infused throughout the menstrual cycle can also be used to treat a luteal phase defect that is unresponsive to clomiphene and progesterone. This treatment has quite successfully corrected hormonal deficiencies both at the beginning and end of the cycle, promoting normal follicle development and normal luteal function after ovulation occurs.

An alternative to pulses of GnRH is to have the woman inject the drug into a muscle every other day, which seems to increase responsiveness to clomiphene. Some women who don't respond to clomiphene and take several GnRH injections may then respond to clomiphene and ovulate without the need for any more GnRH. This seems to be more effective for women who haven't menstruated for under one year than it is for women who are in a later stage of ovarian failure and have gone longer than one year without menstruating.

Among women who can tolerate a needle in their vein for a few weeks and are appropriate candidates for GnRH therapy, two out of three become pregnant within four months, assuming there are no other uncorrected fertility factors. GnRH administered subcutaneously carries about a 40 percent pregnancy rate. Most women find subcutaneous administration more acceptable and easier to manage. Intravenous infusion can be effective for some women who have failed to respond to subcutaneous GnRH.

Unlike Pergonal and Metrodin, which produce multiple follicles, GnRH-induced cycles usually result in the development of a single, dominant follicle accompanied by an LH surge. But these cycles need continual hormonal support through the luteal phase. The GnRH must be provided through the luteal phase or low doses of hCG must be injected after the pump is withdrawn. Or progesterone itself can be given. If the drug is discontinued, the corpus luteum will promptly wither, ending the pregnancy.

Therapy with GnRH is even more expensive than treatment with Pergonal. An infusion pump costs $2,000, but can usually be rented from the pump's manufacturer or from the physician providing treatment.

SIDE EFFECTS • GnRH therapy has few contraindications. As with any ovulation-inducing agent, it shouldn't be used if a woman is already pregnant. Meticulous monitoring of estradiol levels and ultrasound evaluations is less important than in Pergonal or hCG–induced ovulation, since ovarian hyperstimulation is not as much of a problem with GnRH treatment.

Side effects may include pain, swelling, drainage, and

infection at the injection site. Intravenous infusion carries a risk of phlebitis (inflammation of the vein) and requires careful inspection and frequent changes of the infusion site to prevent this potential problem.

GnRH Agonists

Scientists have developed synthetic versions of gonadotropin releasing hormone that are sixty times as potent as the natural hormone. These chemical copies of GnRH, called GnRH agonists, are similar in structure and action to the natural hormone. Initially, they cause greater release of LH and FSH from the pituitary gland. But with continued use, and due to their longer duration of action than the natural hormone, GnRH agonists quickly deplete the pituitary gland of LH and FSH. They therefore have an advantage over Pergonal in controlled ovarian hyperstimulation by preventing a spontaneous LH surge or premature luteinization that interferes with the proper timing of egg retrieval in an IVF or GIFT cycle.

The only GnRH agonist currently available in the United States is leuprolide acetate (Lupron). The woman takes Lupron as a once- or twice-daily injection just under the skin. Lupron is also available for injection in a depot form, which requires only one injection a month. Other versions of GnRH agonist can be given as a nasal spray taken several times a day, which has been used successfully in Europe, or as a thirty-day skin implant, which is currently under clinical investigation.

Currently, the main use of GnRH agonists for infertility is to suppress pituitary function. As an aid in ovulation induction, GnRH agonists can, in effect, wipe the hormone slate clean before a woman takes ovulation inducing drugs.

GnRH agonists also may assist ovulation induction for

women with polycystic ovaries. After GnRH agonist treatments shut down ovarian function, Pergonal stimulation allows a woman to produce more acceptable estrogen levels and develop follicles with less chance of hyperstimulation.

ENDOMETRIOSIS AND FIBROIDS • Some physicians are now using GnRH agonists to treat endometriosis and shrink uterine fibroids. The growth of endometriosis and fibroid tumors is stimulated by estrogen, and GnRH agonists stop estrogen production.

About 40 to 50 percent of women with endometriosis who give themselves injections of GnRH agonist for six months will become pregnant, about the same as those who take Danazol, the most common medical treatment for endometriosis. But GnRH agonists do not cause the masculinizing side effects of Danazol.

Some doctors biopsy endometriosis lesions to determine their drug binding capability. If the endometriosis lesions show no receptor binding with Danazol, a GnRH agonist may be a more useful treatment than Danazol.

GnRH agonists are also effective in reducing the size of uterine fibroid tumors. Some physicians advocate using Lupron to reduce the size of fibroid tumors before removing them surgically. Other doctors say that pretreatment with GnRH agonists makes it more difficult to remove the tumors because of fibrosis forming around them.

The side effects of GnRH agonists parallel those of menopause: calcium loss, hot flashes, decreased sex drive, and vaginal dryness. Some studies show that GnRH agonists also cause some loss of bone mass, although the loss appears to be reversible once a woman stops the drug.

Bromocriptine Mesylate (Parlodel)

Excess production of another pituitary hormone, prolactin, can interfere with normal production of LH and FSH, and disrupt a woman's menstruation and ovulation. Suppressing prolactin with the drug bromocriptine (Parlodel) allows the hypothalamic–pituitary–ovarian relationship to return to normal.

Elevated levels of prolactin in the blood (hyperprolactinemia) have been associated with a variety of fertility dysfunctions. A woman may not ovulate, or may ovulate infrequently, have a luteal deficiency, decreased production of estrogen by her ovaries, and irregular or no menstruation (oligomenorrhea/amenorrhea). As prolactin levels become more highly elevated, she may become stimulated to produce breast milk. Any woman who produces breast milk and isn't pregnant should be checked for hyperprolactinemia.

Bromocriptine, the same drug used to treat Parkinson's disease, is effective in suppressing prolactin secretion. The drug is useful for women who have elevated prolactin levels and don't menstruate or ovulate. From 60 to 80 percent of women with an ovulation problem caused by higher than normal prolactin levels become pregnant after bromocriptine treatments if they have no other fertility problems. Parlodel may also be used in conjunction with other fertility drugs, such as clomiphene, Pergonal, Metrodin, and hCG.

Some fertility specialists advocate using the drug to treat women who are ovulating spontaneously, but have only mild or intermittent elevations of the prolactin levels in their blood. If a doctor orders a prolactin level test randomly during a menstrual cycle, he may miss a transient prolactin elevation. These occur most frequently about the time of ovulation or in the mid-luteal phase. That's why

Dr. Berger routinely tests for prolactin levels on the day of the LH surge and seven days later. If he identifies an elevated prolactin level, he prescribes the smallest dose of bromocriptine that will correct the problem.

Blood tests for prolactin should be performed in the morning, when elevations are most likely to be detected. A woman's levels of prolactin in the blood fluctuate throughout the day. Some doctors consider a prolactin level of 15 to 20 ng/ml as borderline high. Yet, the stress of an office visit may be enough to elevate prolactin levels. Other things can stimulate prolactin elevations, such as breast stimulation. A woman shouldn't have blood drawn for a prolactin measurement following a breast examination by the doctor or herself.

A borderline high prolactin level can be easily corrected. Dr. Berger puts his patients on a small dose of bromocriptine, usually from 1.25 to 3.75 mg daily, which is half or less of the standard dose for women with high prolactin levels. As with most drug treatments for a hormone abnormality, rather than use a standard dose, he individualizes the amount of drug needed to achieve normal blood levels. A mild prolactin elevation may inhibit follicle maturation and is frequently seen among women with luteal phase defect, who usually have low estrogen and progesterone production. Side effects, frequent during the first few days after drug treatment has begun, include nausea, headache, dizziness, fatigue, and nasal congestion.

BROMOCRIPTINE VS. SCANNING • Many medical text books say that all women with elevated prolactin levels should have a brain scan, such as a computerized tomogram (CT scan) or magnetic resonance imaging (MRI) scan, to look for prolactin-secreting, benign pituitary tumors. This aggressive monitoring and heightened awareness of pituitary tumors is a function of our advanced medical technology.

Only within the past fifteen years have doctors been able to measure prolactin levels in the blood. And only within the past ten years have newer, more accurate brain scans been available to detect these tiny tumors. So doctors have "discovered" a condition that probably existed long before these diagnostic techniques were available.

Small pituitary tumors, less than 10 mm in diameter (microadenomas), are best treated with bromocriptine, and can be safely monitored with blood levels of prolactin. If the tumor is growing, the level of prolactin in the blood will increase. The doctor can follow these blood levels and treat the woman with bromocriptine without subjecting her to repeated X-ray examinations. If the levels rise substantially, imaging studies can then be performed to look for tumor growth. A sudden rise in prolactin may also indicate that the woman has been taking another medication—such as a phenothiazine for anxiety, or a high blood pressure medication—that shuts off the prolactin inhibiting factors in the brain.

A woman with high prolactin levels should also have her level of thyroid stimulating hormone (TSH) checked, since an underactive thyroid (hypothyroidism) can result in increased brain production of TSH, which leads to increased prolactin release. If the underlying problem is hypothyroidism, administering synthetic thyroid hormones is the correct treatment, and will bring a woman's prolactin levels down to normal.

Progesterone

Becoming and staying pregnant requires a delicate balance of hormones. A progesterone deficiency may explain why some women fail to become pregnant despite adequate egg development, or why they fail to maintain a pregnancy to term. Without the right levels of progesterone, a fertilized and dividing egg may be unable to implant itself successfully in the walls of the uterus. Or if it does implant, the uterine lining may be shed via menstruation, resulting in a pregnancy loss so early that the woman may not even know that she was pregnant.

A woman may safely take progesterone supplements (by injections, suppositories, or under-the-tongue tablets) to support an implanted fetus and maintain an early pregnancy. The supplements can also prevent a miscarriage due to inadequate corpus luteum function.

If a luteal phase defect is found after a woman with normal preovulatory hormones ovulates, then progesterone supplementation is in order following ovulation. Also, if a woman develops spotting or cramping during pregnancy and she has low progesterone levels, then progesterone administration plus other medications that stop uterine contractions may help prevent a threatened miscarriage.

Although the Food and Drug Administration hasn't approved progesterone supplementation during the first trimester of pregnancy, most fertility specialists prescribe the drug for women with inadequate luteal phase function to reduce their risks of miscarriage. The progesterone supplements may mask a missed abortion, but monitoring with hCG assays will detect a fetus that has stopped developing. If the fetus stops growing, the woman should stop taking progesterone supplements. She usually will begin to bleed from the uterus, aborting the pregnancy, or a D&C can remove the abnormal pregnancy from the uterus.

A hormone deficiency in the follicular (preovulatory) phase of a woman's cycle requires a different type of treatment, and here clomiphene or Pergonal with hCG are most helpful. Even with these drugs, a woman may still need additional progesterone in the luteal or post-ovulatory phase of the cycle to achieve and maintain a pregnancy.

Unfortunately, some women with problems beginning in the follicular phase are treated only with progesterone late in their cycles, which usually ends up being a wasted effort. If these women don't ovulate, then late progesterone supplementation is just that—too late to do any good. They need early hormonal therapy first to get them ovulating and to prepare the endometrial lining for progesterone's action later in the cycle.

Danocrine (Danazol)

Probably the most frequently prescribed drug to treat endometriosis is danocrine (Danazol). Danazol is a synthetic derivative of testosterone that counteracts the effects of estrogen and decreases its synthesis by interfering with the production of FSH and LH. By putting the body into a "pseudomenopausal" state, Danazol inhibits buildup of the endometrium, and thereby reduces the growth and spread of endometriosis.

A woman typically takes 200 mg of Danazol three or four times a day for six to nine months. The pregnancy rates quoted for Danazol treatments range from as high as 75 percent for mild endometriosis, to 50 percent for moderate endometriosis, to 25 percent for severe disease. These pregnancy rates may be optimistic for women with severe disease, who usually have such widespread endometriosis that they require surgery as well as medication. It's unclear whether treatment with Danazol is truly superior to treatment with a variety of other drugs, such as the synthetic progestins medroxyprogesterone acetate (Provera) or megestrol acetate (Megace), or to treatment by surgical methods alone. Another new treatment uses a once-a-month injection of Lupron depot, which reduces estrogen production.

SIDE EFFECTS • Although doctors consider Danazol an effective treatment for endometriosis, more than half of the women who take it develop side effects. A woman may grow facial hair, gain weight, develop acne, hear a deepening of her voice, show a decrease in breast size, experience muscle cramps and muscle enlargement, and raise her blood cholesterol level. Basically, Danazol produces masculinizing effects, since it is an anabolic steroid.

Androgens

Women and men both produce the steroid hormones called androgens in their adrenal glands, and in the ovaries for women and testicles for men. They are often thought of as "male" hormones because androgens are the primary hormones circulating in a man's blood, leading to masculine sexual characteristics, while estrogens are the primary circulating hormones in women.

In some women, the ovaries or adrenal glands produce more than normal amounts of androgens. In exceptional cases, androgens can reach such high levels that they may cause clinical masculinization of a woman—her voice deepens, her muscle mass increases, she grows hair on the face and chest, and she may even lose hair on her head in a male baldness pattern. In dramatic cases like this, it's important for the physician to perform appropriate tests to determine whether the woman has an androgen-producing tumor of either the adrenal glands or ovaries.

Much more frequently, androgen levels are only mildly elevated in women, but can still interfere with a woman's normal reproductive cycles. Since androgens tend to block the actions of estrogen, they can prevent normal follicle development, ovulation, and cervical mucus production.

Increased androgens are frequently seen in women with prolonged anovulation, such as in women with polycystic ovarian disease.

The most commonly measured androgens are testosterone, androstenedione, and dihydroepiandrosterone sulfate (DHEAS). If testosterone and androstenedione levels are elevated, but DHEAS levels are normal, this suggests that the ovaries are the source of the excess androgens. A high DHEAS level suggests that the adrenal glands are responsible.

When the adrenal glands are the source of high androgens, adrenal gland activity should be reduced by treatment with steroid medications such as prednisone or dexamethasone. These medications reduce the secretion of adrenocorticotropic hormone (ACTH) from the pituitary, which in turn reduces the adrenal production of hormones.

If the source of excess androgens is the ovaries, then medical treatment consists primarily of administering the drug spironolactone (Aldactone). This drug binds to the androgens, and therefore reduces the amount of androgens available to affect the ovaries, uterus, and cervix.

When ovaries and adrenal glands are both producing excess androgens, a combination of spironolactone and steroid treatment may be required. Medical management of high androgen production usually requires continued treatment, month after month, until a woman gets pregnant.

Hormone Treatments for Men

Although urologists have traditionally focused on the surgical management of male infertility, the majority of infertile men have disorders that don't lend themselves to surgery. Disorders interfering with hormone flow from the hypothalamus to the pituitary to the testicles are among the most treatable causes of male infertility.

Men and women produce the same sex hormones, but in different concentrations. Men make testosterone in the testicles and adrenal glands and women make it in their ovaries and adrenals. Men have about ten times as much testosterone as women, which is what gives them their secondary sexual characteristics. (It follows that testosterone is considered a "male" hormone.)

The same hormones that induce ovulation in women also occur naturally in men and play a role in male reproduction. LH and FSH stimulate the testicles to produce testosterone. Men with inadequate amounts of FSH and LH may produce insufficient testosterone, resulting in too few sperm or sperm of poor quality.

And just as men and women share reproductive hormones, the same hormonal therapies can be used to cure a man's infertility due to hormonal deficiencies—although the doses and lengths of treatment may differ.

Clomiphene

Clomiphene is one of the most commonly prescribed drugs for infertile men. The drug increases a man's levels of LH and FSH, which stimulate his testicles to produce testosterone and sperm. Men with low FSH or LH levels often show increased sperm counts after clomiphene treatments, but clomiphene alone hasn't been proven effective in increasing pregnancy rates.

The group of men who seem to benefit the most from clomiphene have low sperm counts and low or low-normal gonadotropin levels. They usually receive a dose of 25 mg per day for twenty-five days per month for three to six months. While taking clomiphene, a man should have a semen analysis and testosterone, LH, FSH, and estrogen levels checked every three months. If his estrogen level rises above normal, his sperm production may slow down. Too much estrogen in the blood signals the pituitary to stop gonadotropin secretion, which will worsen, rather than improve, the man's situation. In these cases, tamoxifen, a drug similar to clomiphene, may be effective.

HCG and Pergonal

If a man's hypothalamus or pituitary gland is malfunctioning, and he is secreting inadequate amounts of FSH and LH, the quality or quantity of his sperm may not be sufficient to fertilize his wife's egg. Treatment with hCG, followed by Pergonal, is the most direct way to correct the problem. HCG treatment stimulates the testicles to produce testosterone. Pergonal can be added to increase sperm production.

This combination therapy is most effective for men with hypogonadotropic hypogonadism. Men with this rare condition lack production of GnRH, and are diagnosed by finding low levels of LH, FSH, and testosterone in the blood, along with physical findings such as small testicles, breast enlargement, and often the lack of a sense of smell (Kallman's syndrome).

Initially, a man takes hCG injections three times each week for six months. If the size of his testicles increases and his testosterone levels reach normal, then he adds FSH, in the form of Pergonal, by mixing in two ampules with his hCG injections three times each week. If he doesn't respond after four months, then his doctor will double the Pergonal dosage. Once he has achieved adequate sperm output, he can stop taking Pergonal and will continue with hCG treatments alone. The Pergonal can be added again when the couple wants to maximize his sperm output to achieve a pregnancy.

Although inconvenient, there are few side effects with this combination therapy. Almost 50 percent of the treated men will impregnate their wives even though their sperm counts are rarely above 10 million per ml. The sperm produced, however, usually have good motility and normal morphology.

GnRH

Since men with hypogonadotropic hypogonadism lack GnRH, the ideal replacement is GnRH itself. GnRH can be effectively delivered subcutaneously or intravenously through a pump with pulses every 120 minutes (compared to every ninety minutes for women).

For men who can tolerate the portable infusion pump, the therapy is highly effective. About 75 percent who have had three to thirty months of therapy with natural GnRH show sperm in their ejaculates, and 50 to 60 percent of these men have impregnated their wives. Once the couple has achieved a pregnancy, the husband can return to hCG or testosterone therapy to maintain his secondary sexual characteristics. If the couple wants another child, he can use the GnRH pump again.

Bromocriptine

High prolactin levels can also affect a man's fertility. A high prolactin output inhibits LH and FSH secretion, probably because it inhibits secretion of GnRH. The lack of these reproductive hormones leads to impotence and a low sex drive, as well as a lowered sperm count and sperm production. In other words, elevated prolactin can adversely affect both sexual performance and fertility.

High prolactin levels among men can be due to a pituitary tumor, hypothalamus disorders, hypothyroidism, or drug treatments. In most cases, bromocriptine can reduce blood levels of prolactin to normal, restoring testosterone levels as well as a man's potency and fertility. Bromocriptine also shrinks pituitary tumors that secrete prolactin.

For men with high prolactin levels, bromocriptine often succeeds in restoring potency and fertility where testosterone therapy has failed. This is believed to be due to the increases in FSH levels after bromocriptine treatments. (Testosterone often doesn't increase FSH levels.)

Bromocriptine's side effects for men are the same as those for women. They include nausea, dizziness, headache, and fatigue, usually experienced only during the first few days of treatment.

Other Drugs

Hypothyroidism can be associated with low LH, FSH, and testosterone concentrations, in addition to a low sperm count and decreased sperm motility. A man with low thyroid levels should be treated with thyroid replacement, which may correct his infertility without any other treatment being required.

Testosterone has been prescribed for infertile men, but with little success. Too much testosterone can reduce sperm production. Testosterone is sometimes administered to impotent men, but rarely helps overcome the problem if the man already has normal gonadotropin and testosterone levels. Other, more successful, treatments include eliminating medications and recreational drugs that lower the libido and, as a last resort, penile implants. Tamoxifen, a drug similar to clomiphene, is an antiestrogen that increases sperm counts but has shown no clear improvement in pregnancy rates for the partners of infertile men.

Vitamins (such as vitamin C), minerals (zinc, in particular), and amino acids have been recommended for the treatment of unexplained male infertility. While these treatments have few risks, they probably have little value unless the man has a specific deficiency.

Future Drugs

Several new drugs, some still experimental, are on the horizon as infertility treatments for hormonal problems.

PURE LH • A pure version of luteinizing hormone has recently been produced through genetic engineering. The hormone is purer than hormones extracted from the pituitary gland or the urine of postmenopausal women.

Pure LH could have value for both women and men. Instead of receiving hCG on the day of the LH surge, a woman would receive pure LH to stimulate ovulation induction. It may also stimulate sperm production.

GnRH ANTAGONISTS • Another way to shut off pituitary gonadotropin output is with gonadotropin releasing hormone (GnRH) antagonists. These synthetic drugs, still experimental, cause a very rapid decrease in circulating gonadotropin levels, even faster than their chemical cousins, the GnRH agonists. While GnRH agonists lead to low GnRH by depleting the pituitary gland of the hormone, the antagonists block the effect of GnRH at the level of the pituitary gland and prevent further production of GnRH by the hypothalamus. Thus, the antagonists work more quickly (within a day) than the GnRH agonists (within a week) to lower gonadotropin levels. They may be used along with Pergonal to induce ovulation since they would probably be effective in preventing a woman's spontaneous LH surge or premature luteinization.

PROGESTERONE ANTAGONISTS • Progesterone antagonists, or antiprogestins, are a new class of steroids that compete with progesterone within the body. The most well-known is the controversial abortion pill RU486. Experts predict that within the next decade progesterone antagonists will be available to obstetrician-gynecologists to help control hormone-dependent tissue growth such as endometriosis.

ACTIVIN • Exciting possibilities have emerged with the recent discovery of a new hormone called activin. First, researchers looking into the action of FSH identified a hormone called inhibin in women's ovarian follicular fluid and in men's testicular fluid. This hormone inhibits FSH secretion. Then researchers found a potent activator of FSH secretion, which they termed activin.

Activin may have a role in increasing egg production. It has led to a doubling of the number of eggs produced in animal experiments. In addition, it may be useful in lowering the levels of androgens and the high LH to FSH ratio found among women with polycystic ovaries, which may then permit these women to have normal ovulation. Since activin also increases progesterone and hCG levels, it may also be useful in rescuing pregnancies in women with poor luteal function. For men, activin may be able to stimulate the body to produce more FSH, which in turn stimulates sperm production.

A limited supply of man-made activin produced in the lab is now available to a few researchers. Once we have a larger supply, it may take less than five years for it to become available to clinicians for infertility treatment.

RELAXIN • A newly identified component of semen is the hormone relaxin. This hormone enhances sperm motility. If and when more tests confirm its usefulness, relaxin may be a tool for the treatment of male infertility, especially for men with low sperm counts or poor motility.

Women also produce relaxin, which helps to reduce the strength of uterine contractions during pregnancy. Relaxin may also play a role in the relaxation or "softening" of the cervix in preparation for labor. Its potential for therapeutic uses, such as to stop premature labor, have not yet been determined.

Questions to Ask Your Doctor About Hormone Treatments

Both women and men may want to ask some basic questions about the hormones they are taking, including:

Why am I a good candidate for this hormone treatment?

How much of the hormone do I need to take each day, and for how many days?

What are the potential side effects of the hormone?

How much does the treatment cost?

In your experience, what are our chances of conceiving?

Specific Questions for Women
About Specific Hormones

Clomiphene

Do I have any contraindications that make clomiphene an inappropriate drug for me?

How will I know the drug is working, or not working?

Is the drug interfering with my cervical mucus production?

Pergonal

How will you monitor my drug taking to know how much I need to ovulate and to avoid hyperstimulation?

What are my risks of multiple pregnancy?

Do I have any contraindications that make Pergonal an inappropriate drug for me?

Human Chorionic Gonadotropin

How will I know the proper time for an hCG injection?

Will you teach me (or my husband) how to administer the injection?

Gonadotropin Releasing Hormone

Will I have the needle under my skin or in a vein?

How do I know whether I am developing a blood clot in the vein or an infection where the needle enters my body?

Where do I get an infusion pump?

Bromocriptine

Do I have an elevation in my prolactin levels, even mild or intermittent?

Do I need a brain scan to rule out a pituitary tumor?

Progesterone

Am I at risk of an early miscarriage?

Do I need progesterone supplements after I ovulate?

Danazol

Why do you recommend Danazol, and how does it compare with other treatments available for endometriosis?

Specific Questions for Men

How often will I need a semen analysis and blood tests while on hormone therapy?

Will the hormones I take affect my potency or sex drive?

8

OTHER MEDICAL
AND SURGICAL
TREATMENTS

After your situation has been adequately evaluated, your fertility specialist may recommend certain other medical and surgical treatments. Once you have a diagnosis of your fertility problem, you should sit down with your doctor and discuss how to try to resolve it. Consider your treatment options as carefully as you chose your doctor. Ask your doctor why he or she has decided this is the best treatment. Find out how to learn more about your diagnosed problem and the particular therapies available to you.

Antibiotics

If the early part of the infertility evaluation reveals that either partner has a genital tract infection, both partners should be treated with antibiotics, and then have follow-up cultures taken to be sure that the bacteria have been eradicated. Once the infection has been cleared from both the man's and woman's genital tracts, then it's safe to proceed with other treatments, including surgical or advanced laboratory methods.

The antibiotic treatment of choice for chlamydia is tetracycline for men and nonpregnant women. Erythromycin is the first choice for treating chlamydia infections in pregnant women, and offers the advantage of being effective against tetracycline-resistant mycoplasma organisms that may also be involved. Acute infection can be treated with a ten- to twelve-day course of antibiotics; chronic cases, however, may require longer treatment with more than one course of antibiotics.

According to the Centers for Disease Control, a combination of tetracycline and ampicillin may be more cost-effective than either antibiotic alone. These two antibiotics combined may also work against an incubating syphilis infection and are recommended for women with pelvic inflammatory disease (PID) who can be treated on an outpatient basis.

Mycoplasma and ureaplasma infections can be more difficult to eradicate with antibiotics than gonorrhea and chlamydia. Couples often receive an inadequate dosage or duration of treatment with tetracycline, or the organism may be resistant to the medication used. About 85 percent of mycoplasma organisms appear to be resistant to erythromycin. Don't assume that you are free of mycoplasma until you have negative cultures at least three months after your last antibiotic dose.

Aggressive antibiotic treatment can prevent the complications of PID, but only if therapy is begun very early, perhaps within days of an acute infection, or better, if the infection is discovered and treated before it causes symptoms. If treatment is delayed, the fallopian tubes may close partially or totally or scar tissue may form around the tubes and ovaries, impeding the egg's journey to the tubes and uterus. Antibiotics can eliminate bacteria, but they have no beneficial effect on already damaged tubes and ducts or on scar tissue.

Even today, many doctors don't recognize the importance of routine screening to diagnose and treat asymptomatic lower genital tract infections to prevent salpingitis and subsequent infertility. Most doctors tend to treat patients only *after* they have developed symptoms, and even then may treat for a presumed chlamydia infection without the benefit of appropriate, simple tests that tell them exactly what organisms may be causing the symptoms.

Treating the Woman

Treatments for fertility problems in women have grown by leaps and bounds lately. The advent of microsurgical techniques in the 1970s allowed reproductive surgeons to remove adhesions, including the scars formed by endometriosis, from a woman's upper reproductive tract. In addition, microsurgeons began performing delicate operations on the fallopian tubes, including reconnecting tubes "tied," burned, or cut during sterilization procedures. In the 1980s, the movement towards laparoscopes and surgery through hysteroscopes improved the correction of other anatomic abnormalities.

Microsurgery

Spectacular advances in microsurgery since the mid-1970s have helped restore many women's fertility. Just as the invention of the microscope opened up new horizons to scientists more than three hundred years ago, the development and application of special microscopes vastly expands the horizons of modern surgery. Microscopes were first used in human surgery in the 1920s. Although the magnification of the microscope gave doctors a better view of tiny structures, the lack of small needles and surgical thread held back further development of microsurgery.

By the 1960s, surgical manufacturers were producing needles as thin as a human hair and surgical thread virtually invisible to the naked eye. With the new technology came the need for new skills. Surgeons had to learn how to sew using a specially adapted jeweler's forceps or tweezers while looking through the eyepieces of a microscope. After practicing for hundreds of hours on animals, microsurgeons began performing previously impossible medical feats, such as repairing ultrathin nerves and blood vessels and removing tiny tumors from the brain.

Reproductive surgeons began adapting microsurgery to meet their patients' needs. For women, microsurgery can remove the scar tissue from the ovaries or other pelvic locations, destroy active areas of endometriosis, and repair damaged fallopian tubes.

TUBAL SURGERY • If a woman has an obstruction in the middle of the fallopian tube, most often due to a tubal ligation, she must have that portion of the tube removed. A skilled microsurgeon can remove the obstruction and stitch together the adjacent open ends of the tube in what's called an anastomosis.

The most common operation on the fallopian tube is a fimbrioplasty. The fimbria, the flared ends of the tubes near the ovaries, can become infected and scarred, and may need reconstruction. If the fimbria become tied up with adhesions, the adhesions must be removed or the tube cannot pick up eggs released from the ovary. If the fimbrial end of the tube is blocked and the fallopian tube is enlarged with fluid (a hydrosalpinx), then reconstructive surgery through an open incision (laparotomy) may be necessary.

The portion of the tube that begins to enter the uterus

is often a more difficult area to repair, and requires a different surgical approach than a blocked fimbria. If a woman has this portion of the tube damaged or diseased, she may need to have the portion removed and the remaining section of the normal tube placed in a newly created opening into the uterine cavity, a procedure called a tubouterine implantation. After the damaged part is removed, if the damage is in one small area the tube can be rejoined microsurgically.

A subtle condition called salpingitis isthmica nodosa causes an outpouching of bumps (diverticulae) at the junction of the tube with the uterus. This part of the tube controls when the fertilized egg is delivered into the uterine cavity. These inflamed nodules in the fallopian tube can prevent sperm from passing through the tube to meet the egg or, after the egg has been fertilized, can prevent the fertilized egg from traveling into the uterus for implantation. The affected portion of the tube has to be surgically removed to restore normal function.

Shortening an elongated ligament between the fallopian tube and the ovary back to its normal length using microsurgery may allow it to move the fimbrial end of the tube over the ovary, pick up an egg when released at ovulation and eventually, lead to a pregnancy.

STERILIZATION REVERSAL

The month after Jenny's divorce from her first husband was final, she married Peter, a thirty-seven-year-old engineer. "I thought we wouldn't want any more children," says Jenny, aged forty, who had been sterilized after she bore two sons. But a few years into their marriage, they decided they would like to have a baby. A surgeon at a fertility clinic told Jenny it may take several operations in the hospital to reverse her sterilization, and "I didn't want to go through that," she says.

Later that year, she read an article in Redbook *magazine about*

Dr. Berger's success with outpatient sterilization reversals. "He told me he could do the procedure, and I decided to go right ahead," Jenny says. "On the day of the surgery, I came into the outpatient center at ten o'clock, walked out to meet Peter in the car at noon, and was home before one." Their daughter Deborah is now three years old, and Jenny is pregnant again.

One of the most dramatic ways microsurgeons apply their skills is to reverse sterilization operations. As many as 10 percent of women who choose to be sterilized have second thoughts about it later on and want a reversal to make them fertile again. Most sterilized women don't know how simple, and effective, sterilization reversal surgery can be.

The women most likely to want a sterilization reversal and have a child are in the twenty-five to thirty-four-year-old age bracket. In general, women who were sterilized in their twenties want a reversal more often than those who were thirty or older when they were sterilized. Also, women who had a tubal ligation within the past five years are significantly more likely to say they want a reversal than those who had the surgery more than five years ago.

Women whose lives have changed due to separation, divorce, or death of a husband, and who are considering remarrying also want reversals much more often than women who have remained married to the same spouse. And when sterilized partners divorce and remarry, they, too, are highly motivated to seek reversals. More than 90 percent of the couples who ask Dr. Berger to reverse a sterilization have remarried and want to start a second family.

In addition to using microsurgical techniques, Dr. Berger has adapted the concepts of out-of-hospital surgery to sterilization reversals. Instead of the usual four- to seven-day hospital stay and four- to six-week recovery period,

Dr. Berger's patients recuperate at home a few hours after surgery and are back at work within two weeks.

So far, of the more than fifty women Dr. Berger has operated on in this manner and followed for one year or more after the procedure, 90 percent have clear and open tubes and more than 75 percent have become pregnant.

Outpatient Surgery

Besides reversing sterilizations, outpatient surgery can now be used to treat many anatomical disorders. Gynecologists in the 1970s popularized "band-aid" sterilization operations, performing same-day surgery through a small slit in the woman's abdomen near her bellybutton after injecting local anesthesia into the incision site. Outpatient surgical centers offering these and other simple surgeries flourished in the 1980s, partly due to a change in attitude among doctors and their patients.

Doctors are increasingly realizing that surgery doesn't necessarily mean the patient has to be hospitalized. Although most fertility specialists who perform surgery are hospital-based, more of them have begun adapting the concept of outpatient surgery in their practices.

Outpatient surgery also costs less then the same operation performed in the hospital. You don't have to pay for a hospital room or lose as much time from work, since you recover faster than from in-hospital surgery. Instead of being in the hospital for up to one week and out of work for six weeks, women who have major pelvic reconstructive surgery using outpatient methods are back home the same day and usually back to work within two weeks.

Most reconstructive operations for a woman's or a man's fertility problems can be performed safely and effectively on an outpatient basis. For the man, these procedures include testicular biopsy, microsurgical repair of varicoceles, surgical lowering of a testicle from the abdomen into the scrotum (orchidopexy) and microsurgical correction of blocked ducts.

Most gynecologic surgeons associate laparoscopy (surgery through the laparoscope) with minor, outpatient surgery, and laparotomy (surgery through an open incision) with major, in-hospital surgery.

But Dr. Berger's experience has shown that this simplified rule doesn't really apply. Even when he performs microsurgical repairs with the woman asleep under general anesthesia, he incorporates outpatient surgery techniques, such as employing local anesthesia and avoiding the use of traumatic instruments. This dramatically reduces the woman's pain and speeds her recovery.

Reproductive surgery is really a form of plastic surgery applied to the reproductive organs. Like plastic surgery on the face, the objective is to restore normal anatomy, in this case in the pelvic region. Dr. Berger knows he does better work through an open incision with good microsurgical control than when performing aggressive pelviscopy (advanced surgery through the laparoscope). As a result, patients feel better, heal faster, and have better surgical results in the outpatient setting, with no need for hospitalization at all.

In addition, he meticulously controls blood loss. Every time he cuts through tissue, he examines it under magnification to see if all bleeding has stopped. To feel confident about letting women go home the same day as surgery, he has to be certain that there is no bleeding inside the abdominal cavity.

To control post-operative pain, in addition to the general anesthesia he injects a long-lasting local anesthetic into the tissues being operated on. Immediately blocking the acute sensation of pain allows his patients to wake up pain-free, get dressed, and go home.

He backs this up with a take-home pain-killing machine, called a TENS, or Transcutaneous External Nerve Stimulation, unit. The TENS machine is a battery-operated box about the size of a Walkman. Instead of headphones, it has electrodes that attach to the skin near the incision.

When she's home, the woman controls the strength of the electrical stimulation to activate nerve endings in her skin, which in turn causes the nerve endings to release endorphins, the body's natural pain-killers. In more than three hundred outpatient open surgeries, most of Dr. Berger's patients have needed no narcotic medications after surgery. Instead, they use the TENS machine for a day or two, and then mail it back to him.

In addition, he avoids using traumatic "self-retaining" skin retractors and only exposes the site of surgery when he is operating on it. Each of these steps leads to less traumatic surgery and less postoperative pain than the more customary techniques used by most gynecologists.

Besides the many outpatient sterilization reversals he has performed, Dr. Berger treats other fertility problems using the same techniques. For salpingitis isthmica nodosa, he cuts out the damaged portion of tube as it exits from the uterus. He can remove adhesions from the bowel, fallopian tube, the area between the fallopian tube and ovary—virtually anywhere in the pelvis where there is scar tissue. He also performs tuboplasties to open up the end of a tube that has been closed due to PID; excises ovarian cysts, mostly due to endometriosis; performs uterine myomectomy, removing tumors from the surface of the uterus, the wall of the uterine muscle or inside the uterine cavity; and performs an ovarian wedge resection—surgically removing a section of the ovary to reduce it to normal size—to spark spontaneous ovulation.

To be successful, outpatient surgery requires coopera-
tive, reliable patients. If the woman has a fever after surgery, with a temperature that reaches 100 degrees F, she
must call the doctor immediately, since this may be a sign
of an infection. Dr. Berger maintains close contact with
anyone who has had major outpatient surgery to make sure
that her postoperative course is proceeding normally at
home. The woman should know what kinds of complications may occur and how to contact her doctor at any time
should a problem or question arise.

Laparoscopic Surgery

While microsurgery came into its own in the 1970s, the
1980s witnessed a surge in operations through the
laparoscope. In fact, laparoscopy has become the most frequently performed gynecological procedure in the United
States. Laparoscopy courses are taught all across the country, and procedures such as removing adhesions, endometriosis, and even ectopic pregnancies have become common
one-day, outpatient procedures using laparoscopy.

The main advantage of surgery through the laparoscope
is that the doctor can see into the abdomen without the
need for a wide incision, performing the surgery by passing
instruments through the thin telescope's operating channel. Before the laparoscope, a woman might have had to
undergo exploratory surgery if she felt acute abdominal
pain. Now she can have a laparoscopic exam that may reveal the nature of the problem and lead to an immediate,
less traumatic operation than standard laparotomy.

Laparoscopic surgery has its drawbacks, however, and
can't replace microsurgery through an open incision in every case. Although most women recover more rapidly from
surgery through the laparoscope, the potential for serious

complications is actually higher than for surgery through an open incision. For example, if the surgeon accidentally nicks a blood vessel during laparoscopic surgery, he may have problems controlling bleeding as the blood blocks his view through the laparoscope. For this reason, many fertility surgeons limit the extent of reconstructive operations through a laparoscope. Instead, they make a larger incision in the woman's abdomen and perform microsurgery for more difficult surgical procedures and for reconstructions requiring more delicate, precise techniques.

Through the laparoscope, an experienced doctor can see abnormalities of the size and shape of the uterus, fibroids, tumors, ovarian cysts, pelvic adhesions, and endometriosis (commonly found in front of or behind the uterus in the cul-de-sac) and any other abnormality involving the outside of the uterus, tubes, and ovaries.

Surgery through the laparoscope can remove scar tissue in a woman's pelvis or around her tubes or ovaries, or correct a narrowing at the tube's end. Forceps passed through the laparoscope's operating channel can be introduced into a partially blocked end of the tube and pulled out to reopen the end.

In general, the risks of an operation through the laparoscope—bleeding, infection, and anesthesia-related complications—are the same as for any other surgical procedure. Specific risks of laparoscopy include possibly injuring a woman's intestine or internal blood vessels. These are rare but potentially serious complications that may require immediate laparotomy to repair.

The most common problem a woman encounters after laparoscopy is abdominal, chest, or shoulder pain. Most often, this pain is due to the carbon dioxide gas used during laparoscopy, which irritates the respiratory system's diaphragm. The pain usually disappears in a day or two.

Hysteroscopic Surgery

When a radiologist read Judith's hysterosalpingogram, he thought the X-ray showed a normal uterus. But the fertility doctor saw a shadowing that didn't appear normal, and he recommended that she undergo a hysteroscopic exam for further evaluation.

The outpatient hysteroscopy showed that Judith, a thirty-year-old dentist, had a septum dividing her uterus. The doctor removed the septum through the hysteroscope's operative channel, avoiding the need for abdominal surgery. "I went out to dinner that night with my husband and was back to normal activities the next day," says Judith. She had a follow-up hysterosalpingogram a month later to ensure that the operation had worked. "The exam showed a real difference. My uterus looked normal," she says.

Just as your doctor uses the laparoscope as both a diagnostic and therapeutic tool inside the abdomen, the hysteroscope can be used to correct some abnormalities within the uterus as soon as they are found. By passing a tiny scissors through an operating channel in the scope, the doctor can treat such abnormalities as intrauterine adhesions; benign growths, such as polyps or small fibroid tumors growing into the uterine cavity; and abnormal development of the uterus, such as a uterine septum or growth of uterine muscle and connective tissue distorting the normal shape and volume of the uterus.

The operating hysteroscope allows removal of adhesions that may have formed in the uterus after a woman had a previous D&C, an abortion, from IUD use, or a uterine infection. Before hysteroscopy was available, it was difficult to recognize and treat uterine adhesions. Through the hysteroscope, fertility surgeons can now easily remove this scar tissue with no, or very infrequent, recurrence.

Although hysteroscopy is a minor operation, it's not always simple. It is often more technically difficult to perform than laparoscopy and requires an experienced doctor who will know what he is looking at as he peers into small spaces. As with other specialized techniques, proficiency requires experience and repeated use.

The potential complications of hysteroscopy include those general ones associated with any surgery, such as bleeding, infection, and anesthesia-related complications (such as a possible allergic reaction), as well as the specific risk of perforation of the uterus with the hysteroscope. (This is a rare complication and usually causes no harm.)

Endometriosis

Jane, aged thirty-four, had cysts on her ovaries from long-standing endometriosis. Her doctor suggested that she have the cysts removed laparoscopically under local anesthesia. The cysts were more extensive than the doctor thought, and it took him four hours of laparoscopic surgery to destroy them. After a rough post-op course, including two weeks of severe pain and discomfort, Jane's doctor suggested he do another laparoscopy to check his results. "No way I'm going to let you put another tube in me," Jane told him. Instead, she went to see a fertility specialist, who successfully performed microsurgery through an open incision to clear up some remaining minor adhesions. Jane went home the same day in little pain, and she was back at work by the end of the week.

Doctors have widely different ideas about how to treat endometriosis. Some doctors use medical treatment, often with the steroid drug Danazol (Danocrine) or similar drugs that cause the endometrium to shrink in size, which relieves the pain of endometriosis. Others prefer laparoscopic surgery, sending a small electrical probe or laser beam down a laparoscope to burn away the diseased tissue. Still others choose surgery through an open incision. No one is sure which treatment works best.

To try to find out, the Society of Reproductive Surgeons has started a registry of endometriosis cases so surgeons can report the results of various treatments. Comparing the common treatments for the various stages of endometriosis is analogous to what cancer experts have done: developed staging systems and compared treatments so that they could speak to each other in a common language.

Later on, the Society plans to organize randomized, controlled trials comparing the results of medical treatment, electrical coagulation, laser laparoscopy, or no treatment at all for early endometriosis. The study will document whether one treatment is superior to another, using the network of investigators gathered through the registry. This multicentered study will provide the opportunity to find out what's really happening to the thousands of women with endometriosis.

Most surgeons use either medical treatment or laparoscopic surgery for stage one (minimal) or stage two (mild) endometriosis, which includes implants on the woman's ovaries and other parts of the pelvic area, such as the bladder, but no obstructions in her fallopian tubes. One consideration in choosing a therapy is the timing. Since medical treatment suppresses a woman's ovulation and menstruation, she can't get pregnant during the months she's on the medication. After surgery to remove the implants, the couple can attempt a pregnancy as soon as the wife has recovered from the operation.

A woman may need a combination of medical and surgical treatments for stage three, or moderate, endometriosis, which causes endometrial cysts, tubal abnormalities, and a partial obliteration of the cul-de-sac from adhesions. To remove large endometrial "chocolate" cysts in the ovaries, some surgeons advocate draining the cysts and destroying them with a laser through the laparoscope. This can be potentially hazardous since some of the endometriosis may leak out and spread to other parts of the woman's abdominal cavity. Dr. Berger prefers to treat large endometrial cysts, tubal obstruction, and dense adhesions with microsurgery through an open incision in the abdomen.

Stage four, or extensive, endometriosis that has destroyed a large portion of the ovaries, obliterated the cul-de-sac, and left dense, vascular adhesions in the pelvic area often warrants treatment with both conservative reconstructive surgery and medication. In some cases, a woman has so much dense scar tissue from stage four endometriosis that even microsurgery can't repair the damage. In these severe cases, especially when a woman's pelvic pain can't be controlled with suppressive hormones, the only way to cure the disease is a total hysterectomy and removal of the ovaries. This aggressive approach can usually be avoided by an early diagnosis and treatment of endometriosis before it reaches this stage.

Unfortunately, many women with advanced endometriosis are given no choice but a hysterectomy by their gynecologist. In most (but not all) cases, endometriosis can be controlled through conservative surgery and medical treatment so that a woman can retain her ability to get pregnant. Endometriosis is a chronic disease, but if recognized, followed, and treated properly, it doesn't have to develop into an extensive condition. Instead of a hysterectomy, in vitro fertilization may be an option, particularly if a woman has obstructed tubes and extensive adhesions on her ovaries and fallopian tubes.

As with pelvic inflammatory disease, many times the only symptom of endometriosis is infertility. Most women with endometriosis, however, experience pain just before they get their period. If you begin to feel less pain while taking endometriosis medication, that's a good sign that the underlying endometriosis is resolving.

Endometriosis implants within the uterine muscle,

called adenomyosis, may also cause severe pain when a woman menstruates, as well as enlarge her uterus. The treatment, according to most medical textbooks, is a hysterectomy. But it, too, can often be treated by medication and conservative surgery.

Ectopic Pregnancies

Ectopic pregnancy also has several treatment options. The ability to diagnose ectopic pregnancy earlier has led to a trend toward more conservative surgery for the condition. Conservative surgery involves making an incision in the fallopian tube (salpingostomy) to remove the ectopic pregnancy or removing the portion of the fallopian tube containing the tubal pregnancy (partial salpingectomy).

Some gynecologists now advocate performing conservative surgery through an open incision to remove the growing fetus from the woman's fallopian tube. Others prefer surgery through a laparoscope with a laser. A few doctors advocate medical treatment with the cancer drug methotrexate, which causes the woman to abort the tubal pregnancy spontaneously. This chemical treatment, however, carries a risk of damaging the liver.

Treating the Man

Microsurgery has also benefited men greatly. Microsurgical techniques are now applied to repair varicose veins in the testicles, to open up blocked ducts along a man's reproductive tract, and to sew back together the ends of the vas deferens severed in a vasectomy.

Novel designs of penile implant devices and other innovative treatments have helped impotent and infertile men become fathers. And better sperm processing techniques combined with artificial insemination now allow couples to overcome sperm-mucus and antisperm antibody problems.

Varicocele Repair

Nathan and his wife Mary had no success in conceiving a child eight months into their marriage. A semen analysis showed that Nathan's sperm count was low, between 2 million and 3 million per milliliter. His motility was only 30 percent. His urologist put him on hormone therapy and suggested that Mary go for a fertility evaluation. Six months later, Mary, who tested normal, still wasn't pregnant. Together, they went to see Dr. Goldstein, who found varicoceles on each of Nathan's testicles, and suggested they be repaired microsurgically.

During Christmas week, Nathan checked into the hospital ambulatory unit the morning of his scheduled surgery. He took some painkilling medication one hour before Dr. Goldstein successfully repaired the varicoceles. "I had some pain when I woke up, and I was still a little uncomfortable when I went home that night," says Nathan, a twenty-nine-year-old accountant. He was up and around and back at work in three days. By the end of the week, he felt normal. He and Mary, aged twenty-six, went on vacation to Europe that summer, and just as they were returning, Mary noticed her period was about five days late. When they got home, Mary did a home pregnancy test; it was positive. Their daughter Clare is two years old.

Varicoceles—varicose veins in the scrotum—cause steady damage to the process of sperm formation starting from the time they appear. The majority of men with varicoceles are fertile when they are young, but their fertility gradually declines. As many as 90 percent of men with secondary infertility—that is, those who have previously fathered a child—have a varicocele. This suggests that varicoceles cause a progressive decline in fertility.

Fortunately, this most common cause of male infertility also is one of the most treatable. At least 80 percent of men will have improved sperm counts and better sperm motility after a varicocele repair, and can expect to increase their chance of fathering a child. An average of 20 to 40 percent of the wives of men who have had a varicocele repaired will become pregnant within two years of the repair. A successful varicocele repair virtually assures a halt to any further damage to the testicle, although it doesn't absolutely guarantee a pregnancy.

Both large and small varicoceles can be repaired equally well through surgery. A larger varicocele does more damage to the testicle than a smaller one. After repair, however, a man with a large varicocele generally shows a bigger increase in sperm count.

Three ways to repair varicoceles are available: conventional surgery, microsurgery, and balloon occlusion.

The conventional method of treating varicoceles involves making a three- to four-inch incision in the groin, under general anesthesia, and lifting the spermatic cord out of the scrotum. The spermatic cord is the lifeline to the testicle; it provides all nourishment through the blood vessels and contains the testicles' nerves and lymph glands, as well as the vas deferens. The surgeon looks for the bundle of enlarged veins attached to the cord, cuts them open, and ties them off with sutures, relieving the pressure on the swollen vein. After a few days in the hospital, the man goes home and returns to the doctor's office the next week to have the stitches removed. It may take a few weeks to recover fully from the surgery. Most urologic surgeons use this method to repair varicoceles. However, 10 to 25 percent of the men who have their varicoceles repaired in this fashion have recurrences and may need additional surgery.

One potential problem with this conventional operation is the formation of a hydrocele—a collection of fluid around the testicle. This occurs in 3 to 7 percent of men who undergo a conventional operation. If the tiny lymph ducts that run close to the veins also become tied off accidentally, then a hydrocele forms, and the temperature inside the testicle can remain high. This type of surgery may also damage the even tinier artery that runs into the testicle, which may cut off the blood supply to the testicle, causing it to waste away and lose its potency.

By performing the operation under magnification, experienced urologic microsurgeons can virtually eliminate the complications of recurrence, hydrocele, or injury to the testicle. Using an operating microscope, the surgeon can identify the lymph ducts and also find and isolate the tiny veins that, if left untied, can slowly enlarge and cause the varicocele to recur. In addition, he can more easily identify the testicular artery and avoid injuring it, and thereby prevent damage to the testicle from loss of its blood supply.

With a less than one-inch cut in the groin, the reproductive surgeon can bring the whole testicle out of the body, enabling him to identify and tie off the accessory veins that don't go into the spermatic cord. This markedly reduces the recurrence rate. Then, under microscope guidance, he cuts into the cord with a tiny knife, preserving the testicular artery and lymph ducts, and individually ties off the enlarged veins with ultrathin thread.

Microsurgery is gaining popularity because of its great success. In 525 cases, Dr. Goldstein has had but two varicocele recurrences. None of his patients have formed a hydrocele or have had their testicles injured.

Microsurgical varicocele repair also is less stressful on the patient than conventional surgery. The procedure only requires spinal anesthesia, or possibly light general anesthesia similar to the nitrous oxide given at the dentist's office. The patient can go to an ambulatory surgical center, have the operation, and go home the same day. What's more, there are no stitches to remove later since all the stitching is done beneath the skin and dissolves on its own.

About ten days after the operation, the man simply removes the tiny strips of bandages, called steri-strips, that hold the skin in place over the incision, and resumes his normal activities.

An even less traumatic, less painful varicocele repair uses small, silicone balloons to block off the veins. After making a half-inch incision in the groin, the operating surgeon or a radiologist snakes a tiny catheter into a large vein in the thigh under the guidance of a fluoroscope. A balloon is passed through the catheter, moved through the femoral vein into a kidney vein and finally the testicular vein. After checking an X-ray to make sure the balloon is in the right place, the surgeon inflates the balloon to the size of a jellybean and leaves it in place permanently to block off the vein. Occasionally, two balloons are needed to help block off the vein. This minor surgical approach requires only local anesthesia at the site of the incision, and is also performed on an outpatient basis.

But the potential complications of the balloon technique are more serious than those of the two other procedures. If the balloon gets lodged in the wrong place, such as the kidney vein, the man can lose a kidney. If it floats loose, it can lodge in a lung and produce a potentially life-threatening blood clot, called a pulmonary embolism. These complications are rare, but disasters can happen.

The balloon repair also takes longer to perform than surgery. Positioning the balloon takes about ninety minutes, so the entire procedure can last much longer than the thirty minutes required by the other methods. Varicoceles recur in about 10 to 15 percent of balloon repairs, slightly less than conventional surgery, but much more than microsurgical repairs.

In addition to improving sperm counts, a varicocele repair may have the added advantage of reducing or eliminating a man's sperm-bound antibodies. At Cornell, Dr.

Goldstein's team has found that microsurgical repair of varicoceles seems to eliminate sperm-bound antibodies and reduces the production of abnormally shaped sperm. He speculates that the varicocele may injure the lining of the sperm–making tubules, which promotes production of antibodies directed against sperm. Dr. Goldstein is currently following the patients he has operated upon to see whether a varicocele repair helps men with antisperm antibodies become more fertile.

A controversial issue regarding varicoceles involves repairing tiny ones that can't be seen or felt on examination, but can be detected with devices that measure blood flow. To detect these so-called subclinical varicoceles, some doctors use either a Doppler stethoscope, which magnifies the sound of the blood flowing through the testicle's veins, or a thermogram, a sophisticated thermometer that indicates pockets of heat in the testicles.

The Doppler device bounces sound waves off the blood vessels. The way the sound reflects indicates if there are any flow abnormalities inside the vessel, such as a varicocele. The thermogram measures the surface temperature of the scrotum, which reflects the temperature inside the testicle. This way the doctor can measure any heat buildup in the testicles, another indication of a varicocele.

Once detected, these subclinical varicoceles can be repaired like any other varicocele. But the results of repairing subclinical varicoceles are less dramatic than repairing varicoceles the doctor can feel. And subclinical varicoceles are extremely common even among fertile men, so they may have little or no importance in reducing fertility.

One problem in particular with the thermogram is that a single temperature measurement can't determine whether a varicocele is definitely present. To be reliable, a man should have multiple thermogram measurements taken at different times. If the doctor can't see or feel the varicocele, the diagnosis isn't certain; so varicocele surgery should not be scheduled based only on a single abnormal thermogram.

Although there is no specific medication for varicocele treatment, many fertility experts prescribe the drugs clomiphene citrate (Clomid, Serophene) or tamoxifen (Nolvadex) after surgery in an attempt to increase the sperm count. These drugs stimulate the production of follicle stimulating hormone (FSH) and luteinizing hormone (LH) to drive the testicles to work harder. Sometimes, a man receives repeated hormone injections of human chorionic gonadotropin. This stimulates maximal sperm output from the testicle. Combining varicocele surgery with drug therapy may slightly increase the sperm count, but may not improve a couple's chances for pregnancy any more than varicocele repair alone.

Impotence

When George married Marian she wanted to have children, and he agreed, though he already had two sons from a previous marriage. Ever since his divorce, however, George, fifty-six, had been impotent. A urologist found that "it wasn't all in my head," says George. Hardening of the arteries, which had caused a heart attack a few years earlier, had begun to narrow the blood vessels in his penis. Tests also showed that he had a reduced sperm count and motility, probably due to a varicocele.

George went to Dr. Goldstein to see what could be done for him. After conducting some tests, he suggested a penile prosthesis. George chose a flexible cable type "mainly because I had more control over it," he says. "It was painful for a few weeks after the surgery, but well worth it." Five months later, he went back to Dr. Goldstein to have the varicocele removed. After spending a few days in the hospital, he went home and began taking clomiphene. In three months, a semen analysis showed that his sperm count was four times higher and his sperm motility was much better. "Dr. Goldstein told me there's a good chance we can have children," George says.

About 10 percent of male infertility is due to impotence, or the inability of a man to ejaculate inside the vagina. An estimated 10 to 15 million American men are impotent. The majority of them have wives beyond their childbearing years, but impotence involves men of all ages. Impotence, as well as infertility, are generally signs of disease, not age. A careful search must be made to uncover the origins of the impotence if a man is to receive the proper treatment.

Most cases of impotence in the prime reproductive years are due to environmental factors. A man may take drugs such as cocaine, smoke marijuana, smoke cigarettes, or drink lots of coffee. All of these chemicals constrict blood vessels, including those in the penis, and therefore counteract a man's ability to open up his blood vessels and achieve an erection. Alcohol abuse can also lower a man's hormone levels and injure the nerves in the penis necessary to produce an erection.

A wide variety of medications have also been implicated in impotence. The most common offenders are high blood pressure medications, antidepressants, tranquilizers, narcotics, and estrogens. Going off medication for a month is a good test of medication-induced impotence. Substituting another drug with a different mechanism of action frequently restores potency. When drugs can't be withdrawn or substituted, and psychological factors have been ruled out, then a penile prosthesis may be the solution.

Increased secretion of the pituitary hormone prolactin, often due to a pituitary tumor, can cause impotence and a low sex drive. Men with kidney disease on chronic dialysis are often impotent due to high prolactin levels. The extra prolactin seems to decrease secretion of gonadotropin releasing hormone (GnRH) from the hypothalamus, resulting in lower levels of FSH and LH by the pituitary, which in turn reduces testosterone output. The best treatment is therapy with the drug bromocriptine (Parlodel) to lower prolactin levels and reduce the size of a tumor, if present, that's producing the excess prolactin.

About half of the impotent men taking bromocriptine become potent again. Surgery to remove pituitary tumors within the man's brain has been tried, but can be dangerous, and generally is no longer recommended.

As much as two-thirds of all impotence may be traced to physical problems. This includes diseases that reduce blood flow to the penis, such as hardening of the arteries, high blood pressure, diabetes, or Peyronie's disease (scar tissue in the penis); and diseases that interrupt the nerve supply to the penis, such as a stroke, spinal cord injury, kidney disease, diabetes, or pelvic surgery.

As recently as a few years ago, doctors commonly believed that 90 percent of impotence was psychological. But improved diagnostic methods, including monitoring for the normal night-time erections, measuring flow through the arteries of the penis and careful psychiatric evaluations, have helped to distinguish physical and psychological causes of impotence. Often, an impotent man has a combination of physical and psychological factors. He may require evaluation by both a urologist and a psychologist or psychiatrist, who must collaborate closely, to determine his best therapy.

For example, it may be difficult to tell the difference between an impotent man whose hormone cells in the testicles, called Leydig cells, don't function properly from a man who is clinically depressed. Both men feel like their energy has been sapped and have low sex drives.

Clinical depression seems to interrupt the brain's signals of chemical messengers, which can cause a man to lose sleep, feel irritable and lethargic, and lower his sex drive. Antidepressant medications can often correct the imbalanced signals in his brain, and restore a man's potency.

A man with another type of depression, situational depression, may show the same symptoms, including impotence. He is responding to stress—on the job, in his marriage—which in turn increases his anxiety over getting an erection. His potency usually improves following treatment with antidepressants or psychotherapy.

Performance anxiety, which arises in all men on occasion, can also cause impotence if it persists. Misinformation about sexuality can feed stress, performance anxiety, and impotence. Macho attitudes about how a "real man" should perform can backfire and contribute to impotence.

Reassurance, marital counseling, or both, are often all that men with psychological impotence need. Sex therapy results in a 75 to 80 percent cure rate for men impotent for less than one year due to a psychological cause.

Another similar syndrome—premature ejaculation—also can be treated with sex therapy. In this case, the problem isn't getting an erection, but maintaining one long enough to ejaculate in the vagina. If therapy fails, then the couple may be able to achieve a pregnancy through artificial insemination, as long as the man is capable of ejaculating. (Most men can ejaculate through masturbation even if they have a soft penis.) For artificial insemination, the doctor places a sperm sample inside the vagina and into the cervical canal through a syringe. Or the man can be taught how to draw the sperm up into a syringe and gently inject the sperm into his wife's vagina at home.

Men with combined causes of impotence should first try medical or sex therapy, or both. When all the treatable medical causes have been excluded, and when a man with psychological impotence doesn't respond to sex therapy, then he still has the option of a penile prosthesis. The Chinese implanted pieces of ivory into the penis more than three thousand years ago to treat impotence. More recently, doctors have successfully implanted a variety of prosthetic devices in thousands of impotent men.

There are two basic types of prostheses, the rigid or semirigid devices and the inflatable prostheses. The rigid or semirigid devices contain two silicone rods that are implanted under local anesthesia in a relatively easy operation requiring a two-day stay in the hospital. Earlier versions gave the man a permanent erection, which was a problem to conceal. More recent devices are either hinged or malleable, permitting easier concealment. A newer version of the malleable prosthesis has a silver wire core or a series of segments held together by a cable. These prostheses have several advantages: they are simple, inexpensive, reliable, always ready to use, and provide good erections. The disadvantages: the penis is always the erect size, although the prostheses do bend down for easier concealment.

The newest, more sophisticated prostheses are inflatable. One type, the self-inflatable prosthesis, consists of two hollow silicone tubes implanted in the penis with a pump reservoir near the tip. To achieve an erection, the man squeezes just behind the head of his penis. To deflate the device, he squeezes the release valve located just behind the reservoir. These devices can often be implanted with a local anesthetic, although postsurgery recovery takes longer than for a malleable prosthesis. These devices can also break or fail—the liquid filling the reservoir may leak out—and they require some skill and dexterity in inflating and deflating.

Fully inflatable prostheses also consist of two hollow silicone tubes connected to a reservoir containing fluid and a pump to inflate and deflate the tubes. The two cylinders are implanted in the penis, the reservoir is placed behind the bladder, and the pump is placed in the scrotum. A complex network of tubing connects the various parts.

To achieve an erection, the man gently squeezes the pump in the scrotum. This produces the most natural and hardest erection of all the prostheses. He presses the release valve on top of the pump to deflate the device. The shape and feel of this implant also best approximates the normal, nonerect state of the penis, which makes it the easiest to conceal. But because of the complexity of the device, it requires extensive surgery under general anesthesia, and also has a high failure rate. About 40 percent of men with fully inflatable devices will require another operation, usually to repair mechanical failure of the device, within five years.

Most of the physicians who perform implants tend to put in malleable prostheses. These prostheses have been around for more than twenty-five years and have a good track record. A man can move them up and down easily, and they give a good erection, particularly the cable-and-segment type prostheses. All of the inflatables have problems due to the complicated hydraulic systems that pump the fluid. Many surgeons tend to shy away from inflatables, particularly for younger men, to avoid having to do repeated replacement operations over the man's lifetime.

Another way to promote an erection for men with physical causes of impotence is self-injection of drugs directly into the penis. The drugs papaverine, a chemical derived from papaya, and prostaglandin E1, a chemical found throughout the body, cause blood vessels to dilate and increase blood flow to the penis. Some men with impotence due to a partial narrowing of blood vessels or nerve damage to blood vessels can inject one of these drugs directly into the penis before sex to stimulate an erection. The drugs bypass the damaged nerves and directly open up the blood vessels. The prostaglandin injection seems to produce less scarring inside the penis than papaverine.

The downside is that the man has to inject chemicals

into his penis every time he wants an erection. Also, these injections can result in serious complications, such as the development of scar tissue inside the penis from the constant injections. With severe scarring, these men may no longer be capable of erections, and the only treatment available to them is a prosthesis.

Since the late 1970s, surgeons have made attempts to reconnect or bypass damaged arteries to bring blood flow into the penis. To determine the integrity of the arteries in the penis, papaverine is injected directly into the spongy tissue of the penis. In the presence of normal blood vessels, a man will achieve a full erection within ten minutes. If he has no erection, the test may be repeated using an ultrasound scan to measure the arteries in his penis, which should double in diameter. The Doppler stethoscope can also measure changes in penile blood flow. To achieve an erection, the blood flow in a man's penis must increase six to eight times over the normal baseline blood flow.

If these tests reveal that the penile arteries are blocked or damaged, the man may need surgery to correct the damage. One surgical procedure brings arteries from the back of a muscle in his rectum and connects them to the penis. Another operation attaches arteries to veins to bring blood into the penis in a backwards fashion. The problem with these procedures is that the disease that causes impotence usually damages the small blood vessels of the penis as well as the large ones. So bringing new arterial blood to the penis may not increase local blood flow significantly. These operations work best in young, healthy men who have had trauma to the genital area that damaged the penile arteries. For these patients, about 40 percent have successful reconstructions, and they become potent again.

Some impotent men are able to get an erection, but lose it too quickly. They may have good blood flow into the penis, but are unable to obtain or maintain an erection because of a leaky vein inside the penis. Ten to twenty percent of impotence due to physical causes is due to these leaky veins.

To diagnose this type of impotence, the doctor first checks for blocked arteries in the penis with a papaverine injection. If a man has no erection, then saline is injected into his penis at a high infusion rate to determine how quickly it takes the saline to leak out. Normally, the saline will produce a full erection, just as if blood were filling the vessels in the penis. If the arteries dilate, but he doesn't get an erection, the veins may be leaking and failing to trap blood in the spongy tissue of his penis.

By injecting dye into the penis, a urologist can see where the leak is and perform an operation to tie off the abnormal veins causing the leak. For men with good blood flow into the penis, but a big leak going out, between 50 and 70 percent will have their potency restored.

Retrograde Ejaculation

A small number of men who have no sperm at all in their semen have backwards, or retrograde, ejaculation. About 10 percent of infertile men have zero sperm counts, and 10 percent of them have retrograde ejaculation. This condition, most commonly due to diabetes, is caused by nerve damage. Because of the nerve damage, the bladder sphincter doesn't close down at orgasm and ejaculation, as it normally would. The bulk of the semen takes the path of least resistance, which in this case is backwards into the bladder.

A simple way to test this is to examine a man's urine after he ejaculates. If there are sperm in the urine instead of his semen, then he has retrograde ejaculation. If a man has no sperm in his semen or a very low volume of sperm, the doctor should look for retrograde ejaculation.

Drugs similar to decongestants used to treat a head cold can minimize retrograde ejaculation by tightening the bladder neck. If drugs fail to work, then a man's sperm can be retrieved from his urine by putting a catheter into the bladder. The catheter contains a buffer solution to reverse the acidity of urine, which usually kills sperm. Or the man can alkalinize his urine by drinking bicarbonate of soda, and then urinate immediately after ejaculation. Recovered sperm are washed and artificially inseminated. Pregnancy rates, however, are low, only about 10 percent, because the sperm recovered are generally not of good quality.

Unblocking Ducts

Blocked ducts in a man's reproductive tract contribute to another 10 percent of male infertility. Half of these men are born with abnormal or missing ducts, such as an absent vas deferens or an abnormal epididymis. The other half have acquired blockages, most commonly due to scarring from infections with gonorrhea or chlamydia. If the epididymis becomes infected on both testicles, or if a man has only one healthy, functioning testicle and its epididymis becomes infected, this tiny tube may become blocked and the man may become completely sterile.

Microsurgery can unblock an infected epididymis, but subsequent pregnancy rates are low. Sperm reappear in the ejaculate in half of the men with infected ducts who have microsurgical corrections, but only 15 to 20 percent will father children. The reason for poor fertility probably has to do with how the epididymis functions. When sperm first enter the epididymis, they can't swim and won't penetrate an egg. As the sperm come out the other end of the epididymis, they can swim and penetrate an egg. If the epididymis is damaged and repaired microsurgically, it may still not allow sperm to mature fully and develop their full swimming and fertilizing abilities.

Another cause of blocked ducts includes injury to the vas deferens from a hernia repair. From 5 to 17 percent of boys who have a hernia repaired suffer a blocked vas. Fortunately, the blockage is usually only on one side. But if hernias are repaired on both sides, or a hernia on the side of the only functioning testicle is repaired, it could damage the vas deferens and cause infertility. These blocked tubes can be repaired microsurgically, and more than half of these men's wives become pregnant.

Vasectomy Reversal

"I thought I never wanted any more kids," recalls Roy, aged forty-six, who had a vasectomy at thirty after fathering three children. Then he divorced his first wife and married Dawn, aged thirty-seven, and after "spending a lot of time talking about having a child together, we decided to give it a try." A little apprehensive about the vasectomy reversal, Roy had the delicate surgery with no major trouble. He was in the hospital on a Wednesday, rested at home for a few days, and went back to his job at the phone company the next Monday.

Although Roy's reversal operation was a technical success—his tubes were open and healthy—his sperm count remained low a year later. "The doctor told me I had one strike against me since it had been so long since my vasectomy," he says. He and Dawn kept trying anyway, and she got pregnant about a year later, but lost the baby to a miscarriage. "I thought that was our one and only shot," says Dawn. Six months later, they went to Chapel Hill Fertility Center, where Roy was started on hormone treatments. His sperm count rose sharply, and within four months, Dawn was pregnant. Their son Andy is now two and a half years old.

"I'm experiencing more with Andy than when I watched my first three kids grow up," says Roy. "I can enjoy him more. I'm looking forward to being a Little League coach again."

A vasectomy causes sterility by blocking the vas deferens. Each year, about half a million American men choose vasectomy as their primary form of birth control. It can be safely performed as an outpatient procedure with minimal discomfort using local anesthesia. The doctor removes about a one-inch segment of the vas deferens and seals the cut ends of the vas with stitches, heat, or clips.

Inevitably some of the men who had vasectomies have reconsidered and regret their earlier decision. Most men who have had vasectomies and want them reversed are in their late thirties or early forties. These men had children, then divorced, and have now remarried, usually to younger women who do not have children of their own.

Another group of men who regret having undergone vasectomy are those in their early thirties who put off marriage and having children. Now these socially conscious men have married and they want children.

Still others want their fertility restored in response to improved financial status, allowing the couple to afford more children, or the improved health of either the man or the woman.

Urologic microsurgeons can perform the delicate sterilization reversal surgery. Before the introduction of microsurgery, less than 25 percent of the approximately three thousand men who had vasectomy reversals were able to impregnate their wives. Microsurgical repair of the vas has more than doubled the success rate. With recent publicity about greater successes, more of the 10 million men who have had vasectomies are seeking reversals.

The length of time since the vasectomy seems to affect the success of a reversal operation. If ten years or more have passed since vasectomy, even with microsurgical repair of the vas, less than 40 percent of these men father children. If the reversal is performed within a decade of vasectomy by an expert reproductive microsurgeon, about

90 percent of men have sperm return to their ejaculate. In the more than four hundred vasectomy reversals he has performed, Dr. Goldstein's reversal success rate is 50 percent for men who had vasectomies more than ten years ago and 70 percent for those who had the sterilization procedure less than five years ago. That doesn't mean that a man who had a vasectomy more than ten years ago shouldn't consider a reversal if he and his wife desire children, but he should know that his odds of success are lower.

To make a vasectomy more likely to be reversible, Dr. Goldstein and others leave one end of the vas open. This type of vasectomy should be reversible in at least 90 percent of men after a microsurgical repair of the vas, though it may not be as effective in sterilizing the man.

He also has imported a Chinese technique to do a quicker, less painful vasectomy without a scalpel that also is highly reversible. He makes a tiny puncture in the scrotum, pulls the vas deferens out, cuts it and seals both ends with heat, then slips the tube back in. There are no stitches and little blood. The no-scalpel vasectomy takes 10 minutes or less and the man can return to work the same day.

In contrast, a crudely performed vasectomy can damage the nerve supply of the vas deferens and possibly compromise its function, making a vasectomy reversal less successful. Also, if too much of the vas has been removed, a reversal attempt may not work.

In addition to blocking the vas deferens, a vasectomy may also inadvertently block the epididymis. Between 30 and 50 percent of vasectomies ultimately result in ruptures of the epididymis and a secondary obstruction in that tiny tube. In order to repair the obstruction, the urologic microsurgeon must open up the epididymis to allow a free flow of fluid and sperm through it and reconnect it to the vas deferens. This is a much more difficult procedure than the standard microsurgical vasectomy reversal because the epididymis is considerably thinner and more delicate than the muscular vas deferens. Nevertheless, in the hands of a skilled microsurgeon, the damaged epididymis can be repaired. Pregnancy rates, however, are in the 20 to 30 percent range, about half that of men who have a vasectomy reversal with no epididymis obstruction.

An open-ended vasectomy, leaving the testicular end of the vas open, can help prevent an epididymal "blowout." When the vas is cut, some sperm leak out of the open end of the vas, provoking an inflammatory reaction. The immune system responds by forming a ball of fluid, called a sperm granuloma, at the vasectomy site. The end of the vas forms a network of pockets and channels that trap the sperm. This small knot of tissue, from pea- to grape-size, relieves the pressure on the epididymis and protects that delicate tube.

Vasectomy may also lead to the production of anti-sperm antibodies, which play a significant role in those men who have reasonably good sperm counts after reversal surgery, yet can't get their wives pregnant. Up to two-thirds of vasectomized men develop antibodies that can interfere with sperm motility and fertilizing capability. This problem can sometimes be overcome by treatment with steroid medications to reduce antibody production, and sperm washing and separation procedures, followed by artificial insemination into the cervix, uterus, or fallopian tubes, depending on the total number of healthy sperm a man has in his ejaculate. The fewer the number of sperm, the closer they need to be placed to the fallopian tubes.

Sperm Processing and Artificial Insemination

Several methods for preparing sperm for artificial insemination are available to couples, the purpose being to select the most actively swimming sperm, the ones most likely to fertilize an egg.

The most popular form of sperm processing is sperm washing and "swim-up." Sperm washing involves placing sperm in a culture medium, similar to the fluid found in the female reproductive tract, and spinning the sperm slowly in a centrifuge to separate the sperm from the seminal fluid. The concentrated sperm are then resuspended in solutions appropriate for artificial insemination.

"Swim-up" involves placing either semen or washed sperm at the bottom of a tube of culture medium and allowing the best swimming sperm literally to "swim up" into the top layer, where they are recovered and used for insemination, leaving the poorer swimming sperm behind. Some "swim-up" media use different types of proteins, including albumin, to help enhance sperm motility. Most fertility clinics combine sperm washing and "swim-up" to allow motile sperm to migrate from a sperm pellet (spun down from the centrifuge) into fresh medium, which is then concentrated and used for insemination. Another method of isolating healthy sperm uses layers of silica, a sand-like material (such as Percoll gradient), or layers of fibers (such as glass wool filtration).

Doctors now believe that one method may work best for one man, and another method for another man. It doesn't appear possible to predict, based on a man's semen analysis, Penetrak, and sperm antibody tests, which method works best for a particular person. The optimal way to retrieve the most sperm may be to test a man's semen to select the best method for him before the couple goes through an insemination procedure.

Repeated washing, usually two or three times, removes dead sperm, white blood cells, and other debris from the seminal fluid. White blood cells in the seminal fluid can release toxins that adversely affect sperm. Washing removes these harmful substances from the seminal fluid.

Sperm washing also removes prostaglandins found in the seminal plasma. (These chemicals, found in practically all types of tissue, were first isolated from the prostate gland, and so were named prostaglandins.) In the past, before sperm were separated from seminal plasma, prostaglandins in the semen restricted the amount of semen that could be inseminated into a woman's uterus because the chemicals caused painful, intense uterine contractions at the time of insemination. Now, with sperm washing, doctors can eliminate the prostaglandins and gather as many motile sperm as possible for insemination.

Unfortunately, most men who have significant antisperm antibodies have the antibodies attached to their sperm—not just in the seminal fluid—which sperm washing can't remove. These sperm-bound antibodies often cause the sperm to clump together. If the sperm clump, they can't swim, and if they can't swim, they can't get to the egg to fertilize it.

Treating Sperm-Bound Antibodies

When the husband or wife, or both, have been diagnosed as having antisperm antibodies, several treatment options are available to them. If a wife's mucus is "hostile" to her husband's sperm, the woman can be treated with hormones to change the composition of the mucus, or she can use douches to change the mucus's acidity. If she has antibodies in her mucus, the doctor may recommend steroid treatments or condom therapy.

To reduce the immune reaction that produces antisperm antibodies, both the husband and wife may need to take steroid pills. These medications, such as prednisone and dexamethasone, can lower antisperm antibody levels and improve fertility in some men without altering their sperm count or percentage of normally shaped sperm. These potent drugs, which suppress the immune system, may produce serious complications, including raising the blood pressure, causing hip deterioration, and activating an already existing ulcer. In contrast to men, women usually take lower, continuous doses of steroids rather than high, intermittent doses. It's the high doses used for men that cause most of the complications.

If the wife, but not her husband, tests positive for antisperm antibodies, the couple can use condoms during intercourse to try to reduce the stimulation of her immune system. Treatment is often required for at least six months, always using condoms during intercourse except during the fertile time of her cycle.

Although sperm washing doesn't dislodge antibodies from the sperm, it does permit separation of the best swimming sperm. The couple can then have artificial insemination to deliver the healthy sperm high in the woman's reproductive tract. The fewer the number of healthy sperm, the closer the sperm must be placed to the egg.

The most common treatment for sperm antibodies is intrauterine insemination (IUI) with washed sperm. The sperm are injected directly into the uterus, bypassing the cervix and enabling more sperm to travel a shorter distance to the fallopian tubes. The pregnancy rate of IUI is about 20 to 25 percent after six to eight months of inseminations with washed sperm, if all other fertility conditions are normal. That's about one half the normal pregnancy rate for fertile women. If IUI is unsuccessful, then the couple can try intratubal insemination (ITI) or a new assisted reproductive technology such as Gamete Intra Fallopian Transfer (GIFT), or IVF. Each of these procedures in progression— IUI, ITI, GIFT, and IVF—requires fewer and fewer normal

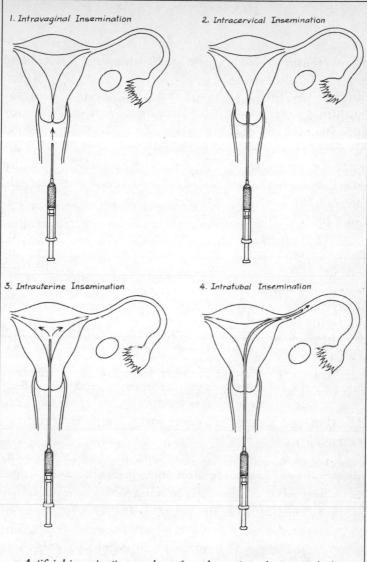

1. Intravaginal Insemination

2. Intracervical Insemination

3. Intrauterine Insemination

4. Intratubal Insemination

Artificial insemination can be performed a variety of ways, with the sperm injected into different parts of the woman's reproductive tract. Intravaginal insemination places sperm within the vagina (1). Intracervical insemination places sperm in the cervical canal (2). Intrauterine insemination places sperm in the uterine cavity (3). And intratubal insemination places sperm directly into the fallopian tubes (4).

sperm from the husband, and places his sperm increasingly close to his wife's egg.

The fertility specialist helps the couple time an intrauterine insemination around the wife's ovulation. In most cases, the couple uses an at-home test kit to detect the wife's surge of luteinizing hormone in mid-cycle, and the insemination takes place the day following the LH surge. The woman lies on an examining table with her hips slightly elevated. A speculum is placed into her vagina to allow the doctor to see her cervix, and then a narrow catheter is passed through her cervical canal and into the uterine cavity. The husband's sperm, prepared for insemination, are injected through the catheter into the uterus. After fifteen to forty-five minutes of rest, the woman may resume her normal activities.

IUI using washed sperm is also one of the most helpful treatments for a cervical mucus problem. If tests show that a husband's sperm can't survive in his wife's cervical mucus, an IUI can help the couple achieve a pregnancy simply by allowing sperm to bypass the mucus. After six cycles of IUI, about 60 percent of women with only cervical problems will become pregnant.

IUI is also an effective treatment for male factor infertility problems besides immunologic infertility, with about 20 to 30 percent of couples achieving a pregnancy after six months of inseminations.

Questions to Ask Your Doctor About Other Medical and Surgical Treatments for the Woman

Does my uterus have a normal or abnormal size and shape? If it's not healthy, what can I do to correct the problem?

Are my fallopian tubes open? Are both fimbria healthy?

Do you see any signs of infection? If so, what antibiotics do you recommend for us?

Are my ovaries and follicles normal-sized? Am I ovulating?

For women with endometriosis:

What stage of disease do I have?

What are my options for endometriosis treatments?

What is your experience with different treatments?

If you prefer certain types of treatment over others, please tell me why.

Do you ever refer women to other specialists for treatment? If so, under what circumstances?

For women who want sterilization reversal:

Do you perform sterilization reversal operations? If you do, based on your own experience what are my odds of becoming pregnant after a reversal? If not, can you refer me to someone who does?

Questions to Ask Your Doctor About Other Medical and Surgical Treatments for the Man

Do my ducts feel normal?

If my ducts are blocked, what are the chances that surgery will improve my sperm count? Will surgery help us achieve a pregnancy?

Do I have healthy vas deferens on both sides?

Do I have a varicocele on either side? If I do, how do you suggest I have it repaired?

Will my disease or its treatment affect my potency?

Do I have antibodies attached to my sperm, in my blood or in my semen?

Does my wife have antibodies to my sperm in her cervical mucus or in her blood?

Will sperm washing help us conceive?

Based on my sperm count, do you recommend we try an intrauterine insemination?

For impotent men:

Can we use artificial insemination to overcome an impotence problem?

What type of penile implants do you offer?

For men who want a vasectomy reversal:

Do you perform vasectomy reversals with a microscope? How many have you done? If you do, what are my chances of a successful reversal? What are our chances of having a baby after the reversal? If you don't, can you refer me to someone who does?

9

MORE
ADVANCED
TREATMENTS

If you and your partner have gone through fertility evaluations and your doctor has attempted standard medical and surgical treatments, all to no avail, then it may be time to consider the more advanced treatments now available to infertile couples. New, aggressive approaches are enabling three out of five infertile couples to fulfill their dreams of conceiving a child.

Most couples won't need these newer advanced treatments. Many of them are only available in select centers or through a handful of fertility specialists. Check the directory of fertility specialists in the back of the book to see which ones might provide the therapy you're looking for. To help you get a sense of which therapies might be more available, we begin with those that hold out the most promise for the greatest number of infertile couples.

Superovulation Plus Insemination

To improve the chances of couples with unexplained infertility, many fertility specialists give women hormones to produce more than one egg during a menstrual cycle, and then perform intrauterine insemination (IUI) timed to take place near ovulation. Superovulation improves the chances of pregnancy by producing more than one egg, and IUI brings concentrated numbers of motile sperm into close proximity with the greater number of eggs. The greater the number of sperm (up to a certain level) and eggs, and the closer they are brought together, the better the couple's chances of achieving a pregnancy.

Most doctors stimulate superovulation with Pergonal and human chorionic gonadotropin (hCG). Pure FSH (Metrodin) and hCG can also be used to induce the woman to produce and release more than one egg.

If a woman has poor cervical mucus and isn't ovulating, treating her with Pergonal or Metrodin usually stimulates her to ovulate and improves the quality of her cervical mucus. A postcoital test (PCT) performed during the stimulation cycle will determine whether intracervical insemination (ICI) or intrauterine insemination is necessary. If the couple has a good PCT, artificial insemination may not be necessary.

At Chapel Hill Fertility Center, the decision to attempt an ICI or IUI or to inseminate the sperm higher up the genital tract directly into the fallopian tubes (intratubal insemination) depends on the number of quality sperm available from the husband. That decision can be made as the time of ovulation approaches, based on the quality of the wife's mucus and husband's sperm at that time. Some couples want to know beforehand which type of insemination will likely be most successful, and Dr. Berger provides them his best estimate based on previous semen analyses and the wife's hormonal responses in previous induction cycles.

Some fertility specialists combine clomiphene, Pergonal, and FSH early in the cycle. Others also provide additional progesterone—in vaginal suppositories, oral tablets, or injections—later in the cycle to support the luteal phase. Follicle growth is usually monitored by ultrasound scans and a series of hormone measurements. Women who have ovulation induced with hCG will receive the insemination thirty-four to thirty-six hours after the hCG injection.

Many fertility specialists now believe that superovulation plus IUI is an effective treatment for couples with unexplained infertility. Some believe that women with ovulation problems and endometriosis are also good candidates. Others show good results for couples with antisperm antibodies carried by the wife, particularly if less than 50 percent of her husband's sperm are affected by the antibodies.

Before couples with unexplained infertility opt for the more invasive and costly Gamete Intra Fallopian Transfer (GIFT) or in vitro fertilization (IVF) procedures, IUI with superovulation is often recommended, since pregnancy rates with these procedures rival the 20 to 30 percent pregnancy rates of GIFT and 15 to 20 percent pregnancy rates of IVF. When a man's sperm concentration is under 10 million motile sperm per ml, the couple may be better off trying intratubal insemination. If that's unsuccessful, they can move on to GIFT or IVF procedures that mix the sperm and egg and then place them into the uterus or fallopian tubes. Instead of IUI, some fertility researchers have attempted to inseminate washed sperm directly into the peritoneal (abdominal and pelvic) cavity, which is called intraperitoneal insemination.

Couples with unexplained infertility who fail to conceive following repeated cycles of superovulation combined with IUI may still conceive with GIFT or IVF procedures.

Intratubal Insemination (ITI)

When Pam's pelvis was crushed in an auto accident, doctors told her she would never carry a baby to term. Even after reconstructive surgery, her cervix and uterus were blocking sperm from getting up into the reproductive tract. Pam, a thirty-three-year-old payroll clerk, tried to get pregnant for more than ten years before she saw Dr. Berger. He put her on fertility drugs to stimulate ovulation and tried one cycle of IUI, which did not result in a pregnancy. When that failed, he suggested that Pam and her homebuilder husband Don, also aged thirty-three, try an intratubal insemination. At Pam's most fertile time, Dr. Berger placed Don's washed sperm into her fallopian tubes.

"When I found out that Pam was pregnant, it floored me. I had already decided that nothing was going to work, that we were just wasting our time," says Don. "We were in Dr. Berger's waiting room, and he was on the phone behind a glass partition when he flashed a piece of paper at us that read, 'Congratulations, you're pregnant.' It took about a week before I believed it."

Intratubal insemination, a new technique, has successfully placed sperm within the fallopian tubes at the time of ovulation. Dr. Berger was the first to report performing ITI. He did so during spontaneous and induced ovulation cycles. Most cycles are induced with Pergonal, some with a combination of Pergonal and clomiphene, and others with clomiphene alone, depending on the woman's particular history. The timing of hCG injections to induce ovulation is based on ultrasound evaluation of ovarian follicle size, tests of blood levels of estradiol, progesterone and LH, and cervical mucus exams. Sperm washing and capacitation are performed just before the insemination since sperm normally become capacitated during their passage through the woman's reproductive tract, and placing sperm directly into the fallopian tube would bypass this essential step.

In order to collect the best swimming sperm, a fresh

semen sample is allowed to "swim up." Dr. Berger has inseminated from 100,000 to 1 million sperm per tube, depending on the amount available after "swim up."

About thirty-two to thirty-five hours after the hCG injection, he inseminates the husband's sperm into the wife, who has had only local anesthesia and an intravenous sedative. He places a laparoscope into her abdomen, inserts a blunt-tipped needle through a second site to help trace out her fallopian tube, and passes a catheter down through the needle just into the opening of the fimbrial end of her tube. Then Dr. Berger slowly injects sperm through the catheter —first into one, then into the other fallopian tube. About one hour after the procedure, the woman can go home. For women who have positive pregnancy tests ten to fourteen days later, he follows up with hCG assays and ultrasound exams until he documents a normal pregnancy.

Dr. Berger has performed ITI on approximately thirty women—those who have had unsuccessful standard infertility treatments (such as IUI) as well as those who were undergoing diagnostic laparoscopy for evaluation of infertility. He has performed the latter in hopes of achieving a pregnancy regardless of the underlying diagnosis.

So far, he has had moderate success with couples with longstanding infertility of more than five years, achieving an overall pregnancy rate of 20 percent, although the live birth rate has only been 7 percent.

Since it doesn't require an egg retrieval, or an egg laboratory with an embryologist, ITI can be provided by any gynecologist who administers infertility treatment, has experience with ovulation induction, sperm washing and capacitation, and has access to the operating room at the proper time of the woman's menstrual cycle.

ITI through the laparoscope does require a minor operation. But the advantage is that the doctor can place the sperm directly where they need to be for fertilization—in the fallopian tubes. Therefore, intratubal insemination requires fewer normal sperm than intracervical or intrauterine insemination. This is a particular advantage for a man with an extremely low sperm count or sperm that have a short life span or poor motility. ITI, however, only works for women who have at least one healthy, open fallopian tube.

The gynecologist can perform ITI through a narrow, flexible-tipped hysteroscope, which can be passed through the cervix and into the uterus. This enables the doctor to see the opening into the fallopian tube and insert the catheter into it. Applying this approach to ITI avoids the need for laparoscopy and, therefore, further simplifies the procedure for the woman.

Lasers Through the Laparoscope

The introduction of the laser has opened up the laparoscope to even more uses. The laser has many features that make it an ideal instrument to cut and remove tissue cleanly, with minimal bleeding.

Albert Einstein postulated the theory of laser energy in the early 1900s. The first working laser was developed in 1961 at Bell Laboratories, and was first used in gynecology in 1973 to treat cervical lesions. Doctors first put a laser through the laparoscope in 1979.

Laser light has greater energy focused in a smaller area than ordinary light. Just as a magnifying glass captures and focuses sunlight to make a fire, the surgeon focuses a laser beam to burn away tissues.

Each type of laser has a single specific wavelength that gives it unique properties. The types of lasers now in use include: the CO_2 laser, the most commonly used laser, which acts as a surgical knife to vaporize tissue; the Argon laser, whose red light is selectively absorbed by red pigment, such as endometriosis, and has the advantage of being able to move through flexible fibers; the Nd-YAG laser, which creates its beam from ordinary electrical power and has proven useful in hysteroscopy, particularly in endometriosis treatments; and an offshoot of the YAG, the KTP laser, which has properties much like those of the Argon laser but at a different wavelength.

The laser can be adjusted to destroy tissue just to a certain depth—as little as a millimeter thick—causing little or no damage to surrounding or underlying normal tissues. Because the laser beam seals off small blood and lymph vessels in the surgical area, there is minimal loss of blood and other body fluids. There is also less risk of infection since the heat of the laser light can sterilize the area, destroying infectious organisms.

Gynecological surgeons are using the intensely concentrated light beams from lasers to remove cervical lesions, including condyloma and precancerous conditions; to correct malformations of the uterus; to open up blocked fallopian tubes; to remove adhesions; and to reduce the size of polycystic ovaries.

Lasers and Endometriosis

Laser laparoscopists have led the way in tackling more severe endometriosis. The secret of the CO_2 laser for vaporizing endometriosis is that the surgeon can vary the depth of vaporization, depending on the amount of endometriosis and its location. The surgeon can remove endometriosis on thin tissues, such as the bladder and bowel wall, more safely with the laser than by electrocautery.

Because of the large amount of smoke created by laser vaporization of tissue, the laser laparoscope requires two operating channels, one to remove smoke that can block the surgeon's vision, the other to aim the laser beam. A small microchip camera can be attached to the laparoscope to provide a high-resolution view of the pelvic organs during surgery, a procedure called videolaserlaparoscopy.

In the hands of an experienced endoscopic laser surgeon who is comfortable operating while watching the video monitor, videolaserlaparoscopy is precise, safe, and fast. One advantage of combining the video camera with the laser is that the surgeon can apply the camera's magnification and zoom capabilities to operate on very small areas, according to Dr. Camran Nezhat of the Fertility and Endocrinology Center in Atlanta, Georgia, who has pioneered the use of videolaserlaparoscopy for the treatment of endometriosis and adhesions.

If the surgeon diagnoses endometriosis laparoscopically, he can treat it right away. By completely removing the endometriosis at that time, the surgeon avoids the need to treat the woman for months with medications that prevent her from ovulating and therefore delay the couple's attempts to conceive. The 40 to 65 percent pregnancy rates reported for laser laparoscopic surgery compare favorably with those for medical treatment and conservative microsurgery. Follow-up studies of women with endometriosis treated by laser so far haven't determined if these women have fewer recurrences than those treated with drugs or conventional surgery.

Although the benefits of lasers have been publicized over the past five years, the laser laparoscope isn't a panacea. In the presence of extensive adhesions and a large amount of ovarian disease, a surgeon may choose not to treat endometriosis at initial laparoscopy. These women may do better with medical pretreatment, followed by microsurgery. In addition, lasers can't replace microsurgery for dense adhesions between the fimbria of the fallopian tube and the ovary.

Laser surgery also has its disadvantages. Lasers can be dangerous if not used exactly correctly, and there have been reports of injuries to patients and medical staff during laser surgery. The equipment is expensive, from $50,000 to $100,000 or more for an operating room laser, and costly to maintain, and the cost of using the laser is of course passed on to the patient.

A surgeon accustomed to hands-on surgery with a scalpel or microsurgical instruments must have additional training before he feels comfortable with a laser. Just as a plastic ski boot doesn't transform a nonskier into a championship racer, owning a laser doesn't itself impart skill to a surgeon. The surgeon must gradually develop new laser skills by first performing simpler operations and then constantly practicing these newly learned skills.

Unblocking Fallopian Tubes

The same balloon treatment used to clear clogged arteries in the heart has been adapted by fertility specialists to open blocked fallopian tubes. The technique, called transcervical balloon tuboplasty, represents a safe way to achieve pregnancy for 20 percent of the estimated 10,000 women treated each year to clear obstructions within the fallopian tubes.

The procedure is attractive because it can be performed through a hysteroscope, making it a minor operation compared with open surgery, and it costs about as much as other minor, outpatient procedures. The surgeon guides a catheter with an internal guide wire and a balloon at the tip through the operating channel of the hysteroscope and into the fallopian tube. Once the tip of the catheter has reached the site of the obstruction, he inflates the balloon, stretching the fallopian tube and opening it up. Then he pushes the guide wire further into the fallopian tube to perforate an obstruction and advances the catheter over the guide wire, inflating the balloon again. Step by step, the surgeon opens up the tube along its entire length.

Unlike the heart technique, called coronary balloon angioplasty, transcervical balloon tuboplasty has much less risk of serious complications. A few women have had the guide wire perforate their fallopian tubes or uterus, but this hasn't caused any apparent harm. Chicago's Dr. Edmond Confino, who developed this technique, recently launched a clinical study with other researchers to help determine its pregnancy rate and the extent of ectopic pregnancies, as well as how many tubes close up after the procedure.

Of the few dozen women who have had the balloon procedure, several have become pregnant. The technique may well open new opportunities for the treatment of obstructed fallopian tubes. But it is not appropriate for women who have blocked tubes due to extensive scar tissue, or gaps in the tubes from tubal ligation.

Another balloon tuboplasty technique involves guiding the catheter into the tube under X-ray visualization rather than through a hysteroscope. With the aid of fluoroscopy, the doctor injects a radiopaque dye (which shows up on an X-ray) directly into the woman's fallopian tube. If the dye passes out the tube's other end, then there may have only been a temporary spasm in the tube or the dye may have flushed out a mucus plug or some menstrual debris that was blocking the tube. If the dye stops inside the tube, then the tube is still blocked and the doctor applies the balloon technique just as through a hysteroscope.

Nearly 90 percent of the women who have had the procedure at the University of Oregon, where it was developed, have had their tubes unblocked, sparing them major surgery, and about two dozen of nearly one hundred women who have had the procedure have conceived.

When the tube is blocked by scar tissue, the doctor may advance the guide wire beyond the obstruction and then advance a catheter over the guide wire to try to open up the blockage. Once the guide wire is withdrawn, a second dye flush confirms whether the tube has been cleared. This procedure causes only minor discomfort, including cramping and spotting over the next few days. The guide wire has perforated the tube in a few cases, but the tube heals without any apparent harm.

A few doctors use the transcervical catheterization technique experimentally to place embryos directly into the fallopian tubes through the uterus, thus avoiding the need for laparoscopic surgery.

Electroejaculation

Today's infertility technology has allowed scores of men who were told they would never father children to do just that. An electroejaculation technique to obtain sperm from men who can't ejaculate now offers renewed hope for some of the estimated 250,000 men in the United States with spinal cord injuries. In addition, it can help men with other problems that prevent ejaculation, such as multiple sclerosis (MS), diabetes, and testicular cancer treated by dissection of lymph nodes.

The best candidate for electroejaculation is a man who is healthy, exercises regularly, eats well, has normal-size testicles, and has had few urinary tract infections, according to Dr. Carol Bennett, assistant professor of urology at the University of Southern California, who probably has helped more men father children with electroejaculation than anyone else.

Electroejaculation is currently enjoying a renaissance. The earliest attempts at this procedure date back to 1948. The first reported births occurred in Australia and France in the 1970s. U.S. researchers began experimental programs in 1985. Now there are more than a dozen fertility clinics across the country that have combined electroejaculation with new advanced reproductive technologies such as IUI and GIFT to increase pregnancy rates.

The doctor inserts a probe into the man's rectum and attaches the probe to a box-like device that delivers mild electrical stimulation to the prostate in a gradually increasing fashion to induce an ejaculation. Stimulation starts at a low voltage and increases slowly; the man usually attains an erection and ejaculates within four minutes.

If the man has an adequate number of moving sperm, they are inseminated into his wife's cervix or her uterus. The electroejaculation procedure, therefore, must be timed around his wife's ovulation. Some of his sperm may be inseminated into her cervix on the day of her LH surge and more sperm inseminated into the uterus the next day after sperm washing and "swim-up."

Men with injured spinal cords have dysfunctional nerves running from the back down to the testicles and the epididymis. "Jump-starting" the nerves by electroejaculation in effect rewires the circuitry that disease, an accident, or surgery has short-circuited. The electric probe stimulates nerves that make it possible to obtain an ejaculate in about 70 percent of these men.

Most men with spinal cord injuries feel only a slight discomfort and a tightening in the testicles during treatment. If they feel pain, they receive anesthesia. Since they usually feel little pain, electroejaculation can be performed in an outpatient setting. Men without spinal cord injuries receive intravenous sedation or general anesthesia, since the large electric current can cause some pain.

Each year, an estimated eight thousand men under age thirty-five injure their spinal cords and another two thousand are diagnosed with testicular cancer. Fortunately, if testicular cancer is diagnosed early, chemotherapy and lymph node dissection can keep virtually 100 percent of these men alive. Between 45 percent and 70 percent of these men have their sperm counts return to normal within two years, but half of them fail to ejaculate after lymph node dissection, since nerve tissues are frequently affected by the surgery. Electroejaculation can help these men.

The overall pregnancy rates following insemination after electroejaculation are only about 10 percent, since the motility of electroejaculated sperm rarely exceeds 10 to 20 percent. Success depends on a well-coordinated medical team using the most up-to-date techniques developed to separate and harvest the best available sperm.

Since the quality of these men's sperm varies, some fertility clinics increase the chances of fertilizing at least one egg by superovulating the man's wife with hormones. About one-quarter of the men who undergo electroejaculation produce sperm of such compromised quality—less than 5 percent motility and less than 5 million sperm per milliter—that the realistic potential for pregnancy with IUI is extremely low. In this situation, ITI may be applicable. It's particularly important in the case of combined therapies that the reproductive urologist and reproductive gynecologist work together as a team.

If insemination by IUI or ITI doesn't produce a pregnancy, then GIFT or IVF can also be tried. In fact, men with sperm counts as low as 2 million sperm per ml have fathered children by these types of techniques.

Sperm recovered from the urine of men who have retrograde ejaculation (where ejaculation occurs into the bladder) has also been inseminated after electroejaculation. In fact, the first North American baby born following electroejaculation resulted from insemination of sperm recovered from retrograde ejaculation.

The potential damage of electroejaculation is injury to the rectum from excessive electrical stimulation, which is most likely to occur if an inexperienced operator attempts the procedure. As the success of electroejaculation grows, Dr. Bennett expects it will become a more widespread procedure, with trained surgeons available regionally.

Miscarriage Immunotherapy

Loretta, an office manager, and Harlan, a businessman, both aged twenty-five, never expected to face problems having a baby. But after Loretta's second miscarriage in a year, she sought Dr. Berger's advice. During a routine workup, he tested Loretta's and Harlan's blood, and discovered that she wasn't producing the blocking antibodies necessary to protect a pregnancy from her own immune system.

Three months after Loretta's last miscarriage, Dr. Berger gave her the option of being referred to an immunotherapy researcher in another state to receive white blood cell infusions or trying steroid and aspirin treatments under his care. She chose the steroid/aspirin treatments. Loretta came into Chapel Hill Fertility Center on the day of her LH surge, determined by a home test kit. After checking the hormone levels in her blood and performing an ultrasound scan to make sure that she was about to ovulate, Dr. Berger gave her an injection of hCG to ensure that she released her egg. That day Loretta and Harlan made love. Once ovulation was confirmed, Loretta began taking daily steroids, baby aspirin, and progesterone in separate tablets. She is now pregnant. "It feels different being pregnant this time," she says. "My uterus is expanded, I can feel pressure on it. I don't even mind the nausea in the morning."

Certain women, such as DES daughters, are at increased risk of miscarriage—signaled by bleeding or spotting, cramping, less breast tenderness, and the symptoms of premature labor, regular contractions of the uterus, a dull, low backache, menstrual-like cramps, and leaking fluid from the vagina due to rupture of membranes. Obstetrician-gynecologists have learned to treat these women from the beginning as having high-risk pregnancies.

Only in the early 1970s did doctors gain the ability to measure reproductive hormones that could detect a pregnancy as soon as (and even before) a woman's period was late. Now such routine hormone measurements allow doctors to know early on when a woman has miscarried. In addition, ultrasound scans can detect the normal growth and development of the fetus, and can see a fetal heartbeat, or the lack of one, as early as five weeks from the last menstrual period, or three weeks after conception.

Since one-half of the fetus's genes are from the father and can be recognized as "non-self" by the mother's immune system, in order to be successful the pregnancy must signal the mother's immune system to produce blocking antibodies that shield the fetus from her usual immune defenses. If a woman has repeated spontaneous abortions, she may lack these blocking antibodies.

Researchers at several centers are attempting to influence a mother's immune response to prevent her body from rejecting her fetus. A woman may receive injections of her husband's white blood cells, which helps enable her immune system to recognize early on the subtle differences between the fetus's antigens, or proteins coming from the father, thus inducing the formation of blocking antibodies. Or a woman may receive blood cells from a donor to produce a similar protective response.

Dr. D. Ware Branch of the University of Utah College of Medicine, one of the technique's pioneers, says that more than 70 percent of couples with unexplained recurrent spontaneous abortion have achieved a live birth after immunization with the husband's blood. Using donor cells is similar to using blood transfusions before transplanting a donor kidney to decrease the chance of rejection. The long-term survival of kidney grafts has been increased with both donor-specific and third-party blood.

The results of immunotherapy are impressive. But, in fact, half of the women who have recurrent abortions achieve successful pregnancies with no treatment at all. Doctors are beginning to use immunotherapy as a treatment of choice for recurrent spontaneous abortion, but universal acceptance awaits further evaluation of its effectiveness and safety. Dr. Branch has set up a trial to evaluate these treatments, but it may take up to five years to achieve enough pregnancies for his study either to prove or disprove the effectiveness of immunotherapy. Past experience with questionably effective treatments for threatened spontaneous abortion, such as with DES, should be a warning that the safety and effectiveness of any treatment must be carefully documented. In addition, long-term follow-up of mothers and their offspring is needed before immunologic therapy may be widely accepted.

Another immune system dysfunction that may lead to recurrent abortion is found among women with autoimmune disorders. In these diseases, such as rheumatoid arthritis and systemic lupus erythematosus, the body mistakenly redirects the immune system against itself. The antibodies made to fight off invaders such as infections get sent to destroy the body's own tissues and organs.

Autoantibodies may interfere with fertilization, implantation, and the normal progress of pregnancy. They have been found in greater numbers among women who have repeated miscarriages. They also have been found among women with unexplained infertility and have been associated with endometriosis as well. There seems to be a further correlation between autoantibodies and antibodies produced against sperm, which can prevent the sperm from ever reaching the egg or fertilizing it.

Having the mother take the steroid medication prednisone along with a baby aspirin daily may be a simple treatment for repeat miscarriages related to autoantibodies. A subtle blood-clotting disorder may induce miscarriage due to autoantibodies: vital nutrients can't reach the fetus because of blood clots in vessels that supply nutrients through the placenta. Blood tests can detect whether the mother has these antibodies, and if she does, she can take steroid and aspirin therapy.

The drug Danazol, the treatment of choice for mild endometriosis, may work not just because it suppresses hormones, as had previously been thought, but also because of its effects on the immune system. Dr. Norbert Gleicher, obstetrics-gynecology chairman at Chicago's Mount Sinai Medical Center, says Danazol removes autoantibodies from the blood, and that doctors may have treated endometriosis with the right drug, but for the wrong reasons.

Dr. Gleicher has proposed that a reproductive autoimmune failure syndrome exists. He believes that a variety of these autoantibodies may cause a woman to miscarry, and that this may well be the most frequent cause of repeated pregnancy losses. A considerable percentage of healthy women may have this syndrome lurking under the surface, that is, it has not caused them any problems until they try to get pregnant and then miscarry. He suggests that women who have repeated miscarriages should be tested for a wide variety of autoantibodies.

Other Miscarriage Therapies

A woman's first line of defense against miscarriage or premature delivery is bed rest. If bed rest doesn't help delay the premature opening of her cervix, then other treatments are available. One involves putting a stitch around the cervix to hold it closed. This technique, called cerclage, has become a common practice for women who have an "incompetent cervix," in which the cervix opens too early as the baby's weight increases. Cervical cerclage usually is reserved for women who already have lost a pregnancy, had a premature birth, or have signs of an incompetent cervix that can't remain closed for the required nine months of pregnancy. The stitch must be removed when labor begins in order to permit a normal vaginal delivery.

A woman can take the hormone progesterone during the first trimester to suppress her uterine contractions and reduce the risk of a miscarriage. When progesterone levels are low or falling early in pregnancy, the woman may receive progesterone to augment her ovaries' supply of the hormone to maintain the pregnancy until the placenta is large enough to manufacture a sufficient amount of progesterone on its own. Some fertility clinics and IVF centers also use hydroxyprogesterone caproate, a long-lasting synthetic version of progesterone, to prevent miscarriage.

Another group of drugs, called tocolytics (labor inhibitors), relax the body's smooth muscles, including the uterus, to stop the contractions of premature labor. Most commonly ritodrine and terbutaline, these drugs also increase the mother's heart rate, however, and may decrease her blood pressure. Pulse and blood pressure must be monitored carefully when a woman takes these drugs.

Unfortunately, we have limited knowledge of the short- and long-term effects of tocolytics on the fetus. They do reach the fetal circulation, and the fetal heart rate increases during treatment. Preliminary studies show that these drugs can delay premature births if used in time, but the data on their long-term safety isn't completely in yet.

Cancer Therapies

While some medications can help preserve fertility, other drug treatments, such as for cancer, can reduce fertility potential. A cancer with one of the best cure rates—Hodgkin's disease—has led cancer specialists to devise ways to preserve the fertility of both men and women who survive treatments. About 80 percent of Hodgkin's disease patients are cured. Most are still in their prime reproductive years once therapy ends, and they may want to have children.

Two methods are now in use to preserve the fertility of women who have had Hodgkin's disease. One involves surgically moving a woman's ovaries higher and more to the sides, away from the areas to be irradiated, and shielding the transposed ovaries with lead during radiation treatments. The second provides women with birth control pills during radiation and chemotherapy treatments. The pills suppress ovarian function and may minimize the damage to inactive follicles.

For a man who has had Hodgkin's disease, the amount of damage to his reproductive system depends on the amount and type of his treatment. Most men become sterile within ten weeks of either single or multiple drug treatments. Radiation also lowers a man's sperm count. The higher the radiation dose, the longer it takes a man to recover sperm production, if he recovers it at all.

To preserve a man's reproductive ability, researchers at the M. D. Anderson Hospital and Tumor Institute in Houston, Texas, have devised an effective and shorter, less intensive treatment for Hodgkin's disease than the standard six cycles of chemotherapy. The Texas team uses only two cycles followed by low-dose radiation, and when possible, they avoid radiation to the man's pelvis. Men treated in this way have been recovering their sperm counts, according to experimental radiologist Dr. Marvin Meistrich.

Other researchers have developed effective chemotherapies with different combinations of drugs that seem to protect the testicles from extensive injury.

In addition, most men with newly diagnosed Hodgkin's disease have a chance to freeze their sperm before starting therapy. The sperm can then be used later for artificial insemination in case the man doesn't recover his fertility. The physicians at M. D. Anderson also offer an experimental approach, treating men with testosterone before and during chemotherapy. The testosterone suppresses the man's sperm production and may protect his testicles from the toxic effects of chemotherapy by rendering them inactive. This is analogous to the use of birth control pills to inactivate a woman's ovaries before she undergoes treatment. In the future, a synthetic version of GnRH may also be used to suppress the function of both sexes' gonads during chemotherapy to preserve fertility.

Testicular Cooling

Heat can affect a man's sperm count. Excessive heat from tight pants or briefs, jogging suits that don't "breathe" (that is, that prevent the evaporation of sweat), saunas, hot tubs, overheated vehicles, and hot work environments—all can damage a man's sperm quality. In fact, Japanese men centuries ago took long, hot baths as a method of contraception.

The testicles are extremely sensitive to heat, and generally are several degrees cooler than the rest of the body. Tests of normal, fertile men show a range of testicle temperatures from 91.4 degrees Fahrenheit (33 degrees Centrigrade) to 92.3 degrees F (33.5 degrees C). In comparison, Dr. Goldstein has discovered that infertile men with varicoceles generally have scrotal skin surface temperatures and testicular temperatures two to three degrees Fahrenheit higher. This higher temperature impairs sperm quality.

For some men with impaired sperm production, avoiding adverse environmental factors can improve sperm quality—including the count, motility, and morphology. Avoiding hot tubs, saunas, and jacuzzis, and switching to loose-fitting, cotton underwear and pants may help.

New cooling devices, developed by two New York urologists, provide a non-invasive way to cool the testicles with the intention of improving semen quality and restoring fertility. The Testicular Hypothermia Device looks like a cotton athletic supporter. It cools the testicles by evaporating small amounts of water, controlled by a beeper-sized box worn around the waist. The device, designed by Dr. Adrian Zorgniotti, is worn all day long, except during sleep, and the water reservoir must be refilled every four to five hours.

The "Cool Jewels" device, developed by Dr. Goldstein, is similar to the cool packs used in picnic baskets, modified into a cup shape. The man wears the device all day long. He puts three cool packs in his freezer, and uses them one at a time for about four hours apiece. He wears them inside his jockey shorts, bathing suit, or athletic supporter.

These devices are generally reserved for infertile couples who have tried unsuccessfully to become pregnant with conventional therapies for two or more years and where the husband has poor sperm quality and scrotal temperatures of more than 93.2 degrees F (34 degrees C). To determine whether there is a true temperature elevation, the fertility specialist must take a minimum of three to six scrotal temperature readings at different times with a scrotal surface temperature probe.

Candidates for this treatment include men who have a varicocele but have refused surgery, or those with unexplained infertility. These devices lower the scrotal temperature down to normal ranges, but must be worn continuously for at least four months before the couple can be expected to achieve a pregnancy. In addition, the Testicular Hypothermia Device often makes a man's pants wet, which can be annoying and embarrassing. Wearing dark pants, however, makes this problem less noticeable. The "Cool Jewels" apparatus seems useful mostly for men who are infertile due to occupational exposure to heat, such as short-order cooks, foundry workers, pizza makers, and truck drivers. These devices rarely help men with low or no sperm counts to father children. They may help men with relatively normal sperm and otherwise unexplained infertility. At present, no well-controlled studies have proved their effectiveness.

Micromanipulation of Sperm and Eggs

One of the true wonders of today's infertility treatments is the way sperm and eggs can be handled with very fine tools called micromanipulators. The embryologist creates a small hole in the outer layer of the egg (the zona pellucida) to help allow weakened sperm to fertilize the egg. Either chemicals or a microneedle can create a hole through the outer coating so that there is no obstacle to sperm penetration. Instead of the sperm having to make their way through that outer layer, they can go straight through the opening to fertilize the egg. Or a microneedle can be loaded with a single sperm that is injected right into the egg to fertilize it.

These types of micromanipulation techniques are reserved for men with so few motile sperm that they can't otherwise fertilize their wives' eggs in the laboratory. Men with a minimum of 1.5 million motile sperm recovered after sperm washing and "swim-up" have a favorable outlook for IVF success. Those with a lower concentration of sperm with good motility, poor penetration of sperm into the egg, or lack of fusion of the sperm with the egg may fail to achieve a pregnancy in an IVF procedure. In these instances, micromanipulation of sperm and egg may be the couple's last chance to have their own biologic child and pass both sets of genes on to the baby.

Mechanical Drilling

By drilling a hole in an egg to allow a man's weak swimming sperm to enter it, researchers at Emory University in Atlanta have achieved pregnancies. The new microsurgical procedure, called partial zona dissection (PZD), has been tried on men with sperm counts under 10 million sperm per ml and less than 20 percent motility or a combination of under 20 million sperm per ml and less than 30 percent motility.

The PZD technique, pioneered by embryologist Dr. Jacques Cohen, is performed on eggs that don't fertilize through the university's IVF program. A woman's unaltered eggs and her dissected eggs are mixed in with her husband's sperm. The fertilized eggs, either PZD only or a mixture of PZD and controls, are implanted into the uterus to grow as they would in a natural pregnancy. The doctor transfers a maximum of three embryos into the uterus at one time. If more than three healthy embryos develop, they are frozen for possible implantation at a later date.

Nearly 60 percent of the PZD eggs have become fertilized. This compares favorably with the 70 percent fertilization rate for couples undergoing IVF with normal, fertile men. The IVF fertilization rate is between 30 and 40 percent overall for couples with a male factor problem.

So far, Dr. Cohen has performed partial zona dissection

on twenty-seven women, with eight becoming pregnant. Four have delivered babies, two giving birth to twins.

A drawback of PZD is that the outer layer of the egg is partially removed, and more than one sperm may enter the opening in the zona pellucida, increasing the incidence of fertilization by more than one sperm (polyspermy). Polyspermy occurs in 18 percent of PZD eggs compared with only 1 percent in natural pregnancies and about 5 percent of eggs fertilized in vitro. Virtually all eggs that are penetrated by more than one sperm don't survive, so abnormal babies due to polyspermia aren't expected to be born as a result of this technique. The PZD embryos appear to be as healthy as those formed from unaltered eggs.

Microinjection of Sperm

Yet another technique, microinjection of sperm, also shows promise for the future. This involves fertilizing an egg by injecting a single sperm through the zona pellucida. The doctor holds the egg on the end of a micromanipulator while placing a single sperm on the tip of an extremely thin needle. It takes a steady hand and powerful microscope to inject the sperm successfully through the zona into the egg.

Researchers at the Jones Institute in Norfolk, Virginia, have fertilized human eggs by microinjecting sperm, although this technique hasn't yet produced any live babies. In this experimental procedure, only donated, immature eggs and discarded sperm are used. Even with the lowest quality eggs and sperm, the eggs become fertilized, suggesting that microinjection may hold significant promise in the treatment of the most severe causes of male infertility.

Another microinjection technique, called subzonal insertion, involves placing sperm under the zona pellucida.

Human studies are just getting underway. A few pregnancies have been achieved.

All of these advanced fertility treatments are being evaluated to help infertile couples with the most severe problems achieve a pregnancy. While some of these treatments are in the experimental stage, the basic technique of in vitro fertilization has become an accepted clinical procedure throughout the world, and may be a viable option when conventional treatments fail.

Questions to Ask Your Doctor About the Newest Fertility Treatments

As for any medical treatment, the couple should ask questions about how appropriate the recommended procedure is for them. These questions may be even more important for a couple contemplating undergoing a new, and possibly experimental, fertility treatment.

Are we good candidates for this treatment?

What are our chances of achieving a pregnancy?

How many patients have you treated with our particular problem?

What is your success rate for couples like us using this treatment?

What other treatment options are available to us?

Why do you recommend this procedure over other available treatments?

How long will the treatment take? How much will it cost?

If surgery is required, can it be performed on an outpatient basis? What type of anesthesia will I need?

What are the potential side effects or complications? How likely are they?

Do you perform this new procedure and if not, can you refer us to someone who does? (The directory at the back of this book lists doctors who offer some of these advanced procedures.)

10

IVF
AND ITS
"COUSINS"

When Miriam and Roberto married six years ago, they wanted above all else to have a baby. They were heartbroken when they found out it wasn't going to be easy. Miriam, a thirty-five-year-old policewoman, had conceived while taking Pergonal, but the pregnancy was ectopic. The diagnosis did not come until after the fallopian tube ruptured, causing internal bleeding that required emergency surgery. By that time, the fallopian tube was severely damaged. With more fertility drugs, she conceived again and had another ectopic pregnancy. To avoid yet another ectopic pregnancy, Miriam had her remaining tube sealed off completely.

With her ovaries still functioning, but no healthy fallopian tube, Miriam became an ideal candidate for in vitro fertilization. She again took Pergonal to stimulate her ovaries, and had three eggs retrieved and fertilized with Roberto's sperm.

When her pregnancy test was positive, Miriam says, "We were ecstatic, overwhelmed." She went back to work as a detective, but took a leave of absence shortly afterward. Nine months later, with Roberto present, she gave birth to their son Omar. "I was happy to hear him cry so loud," says Roberto, a thirty-nine-year-old teacher. "I was happy but at the same time relieved that we had finished the whole thing."

Some day, Miriam and Roberto plan to tell their son the miraculous story of how he was conceived. "We plan to show him *the pictures taken through the microscope only forty-eight hours after the eggs were retrieved, and the ultrasound pictures taken at twenty-one days and at about fifteen weeks from the transfer into the uterus," says Roberto. "We will tell him exactly what happened, about the whole exciting process of seeing his total development."*

Somewhere in the world, a "test-tube" baby is born every day. The miracle of babies born through in vitro fertilization (IVF) no longer seems so miraculous. In fact, fertilization outside the human body is now available throughout the Western world. In North America, about two hundred centers perform IVF, and the best report pregnancy rates of 15 to 20 percent per cycle after embryo transfer. That's not too far off the 20 to 25 percent chance of natural pregnancy in any given month under ideal conditions.

What Is In Vitro Fertilization?

Simply stated, IVF involves removing eggs from a woman, fertilizing them in the laboratory (in a culture dish, actually, not a test tube) and then transferring the fertilized eggs, or "pre-embryos," into the uterus a few days later.

More specifically, after superovulation with hormones to produce multiple eggs, the IVF team places the retrieved eggs in sterile culture media along with washed sperm and keeps them at normal body temperature inside an incubator, where fertilization and early cell division take place. Then the team returns the pre-embryos to the uterus. From that point, if the embryos implant successfully, the pregnancy progresses as it would naturally.

What to Look For in an IVF Clinic

There are about two hundred IVF clinics in the United States and Canada, and finding the right one for you is just as important as your search for the right fertility specialist.

Inquire about the program's patient selection process, including any age limitations and the types of infertility patients it accepts. Most programs won't accept a woman over the age of forty. You should know the number of cycles the clinic is performing each week and how soon you can be seen. Waiting can be one year or longer in the busiest centers.

Ask straightforwardly about your chances of achieving a pregnancy at *that* clinic. How does this compare with your chances at other IVF centers? How does it compare with that of other couples with similar diagnoses at that particular clinic?

When you ask about the pregnancy rate, you should be aware that various IVF centers report results in different ways. Some include in their pregnancy rates both "chemical" pregnancies and "clinical" pregnancies.

Chemical pregnancy refers to a rise in hCG levels about ten to fourteen days after hCG administration, but many chemical pregnancies never make it to the more advanced stage at which the pregnancy can be seen with an ultrasound exam of the uterus.

The clinical pregnancy rate is a more important statistic. A clinical pregnancy continues at least until it can be documented with an ultrasound exam showing the presence of a fetus. But even pregnancies that reach this stage can miscarry, and—as after natural conception—up to one-third of all clinical pregnancies established through IVF don't progress to a live birth. By far the most important statistic you want is the clinic's live birth rate. The live birth rate should be calculated by taking into account *all* of the couples who have had treatment there over a specified length of time. Ask what your chances are of taking home a baby, based on the clinic's past experience.

The method of calculating the pregnancy rate varies from one clinic to the next. A program may report its pregnancy rate per patient, per cycle, per embryo transfer, per month, per year, or from its inception. Find out how many cycles were done before the clinic had its first pregnancy and what the success rate has been since then.

It may also help you evaluate a program to find out the "dropped cycle" rate. A "dropped cycle" means the woman began ovarian stimulation but never got to the stage of attempting egg retrieval. A high rate of dropped cycles (30 percent or more) may reflect a poor ovulation induction technique, or it may just mean that the clinic has stringent criteria before proceeding to egg retrieval.

Cost is obviously important. Does your health insurance policy cover any of the costs incurred during the IVF cycle? Many clinics now offer transvaginal ultrasound-guided egg retrieval instead of laparoscopy, which decreases the cost of the egg retrieval of by as much as 20 to 30 percent.

Other Options

Another way to assess a clinic's suitability for you is to examine the variety of services and support systems it offers. For example, some IVF clinics provide embryo freezing. The clinic may also provide adjuncts to IVF as well, such as egg freezing and embryo or egg donor programs.

Embryo freezing—actually freezing and storing fertilized eggs or pre-embryos—allows preservation for transfer in future spontaneous ovulation cycles. This is an advantage if many eggs are retrieved and fertilized, since most centers prefer to transfer back no more than four embryos per IVF cycle due to the increased risk of multiple pregnancy. If the center offers freezing, ask whether any basic research, using animal models, has been performed to assess the viability of the freezing and thawing technique.

There should be a clear-cut policy regarding any remaining frozen embryos that are left after a woman becomes pregnant. What happens to them? How long will they be kept in storage? Would you consent for them to be donated to other couples after you have your child?

IVF is an exceedingly difficult technique to perform with good results. Launching and maintaining an IVF program is an expensive, time-consuming process. Strict quality-control standards need to be established and met. A team of committed professionals, each with a specialized expertise, is essential. Besides a reproductive surgeon and reproductive endocrinologist, the team will probably include an embryologist, IVF lab technician(s), nurse-coordinator, and a counselor. Familiarize yourself with the qualifications and previous experience of the staff of the program. Its O.K. to ask about their credentials and experience.

Patient Education and Support

Before you decide to undergo treatment at any clinic, you should understand the entire IVF process, step-by-step, including when drug therapy begins, how often the woman needs blood tests and ultrasound monitoring, and when egg retrieval will likely take place. If you have traveled from out-of-town, the clinic should help arrange for a place for you to stay during the IVF treatment. Also, a doctor in your area should be contacted to assist in follow-up tests after you have returned home following embryo transfer.

Your first set of tests may duplicate the general fertility workup—blood tests for both partners to rule out immunological problems and to confirm that the woman is ovulating; a complete physical exam for the woman, including a measurement of her uterine cavity to determine how far to place the embryos into her uterus; and a semen analysis for the man. You should also receive instructions on how to administer the fertility drugs the wife will take to induce multiple egg production.

Ovulation Induction

"It was odd giving my wife the injections," says Sam, aged forty, a local councilman. He and his wife Jennifer, also forty, had tried to have a baby for nearly four years before they went to see Dr. Goldstein. He found that Sam had a low sperm count, probably due to a varicocele, which was repaired microsurgically. In the meantime, Jennifer's gynecologist could find nothing wrong with her after a fertility workup. Sam's post-op semen analysis showed that his sperm count was still low. He tried clomiphene for three months, but his sperm count did not rise, so he and Jennifer decided to try IVF.

At the start of their first IVF cycle, Sam gave Jennifer an injection of Pergonal in the buttock every night for a week. "I thought, 'I can't stick a needle in there.' But she said she hardly felt any pain."

The goal of any IVF program is to maximize the couple's chances of having a baby. To achieve pregnancy, there must be successful responses to ovulation medication, egg collection, fertilization, embryo replacement, and subsequent implantation. Failures can occur at any step along the way.

For example, of thirty women who start ovulation induction, six may have the cycle dropped because of inadequate stimulation. Of the remaining twenty-four women who undergo egg retrieval, only twenty-one may get to the point of embryo transfer, with three having eggs that didn't fertilize and divide. Of the twenty-one who have embryo transfers, only three might achieve a clinical pregnancy if the clinic's pregnancy rate is 15 percent per embryo transfer. One of those three is likely to miscarry, leaving only two couples that may have a live born infant. This means the live birth rate is 2/30 or 7 percent.

To maximize a couple's chances of pregnancy, all successful IVF programs use some combination of ovulation inducing agents to make multiple fertilizable eggs available at the time of scheduled egg retrieval.

The first attempts at IVF, a concept developed and made successful by the late British gynecologist Dr. Patrick Steptoe and his co-researcher, embryologist Robert Edwards, had little success because only one egg was recovered during a spontaneous ovulation cycle. These unstimulated cycles required the IVF team to detect the very beginning of the woman's LH surge, and then closely monitor her to find the best time to retrieve her egg. Following her spontaneous LH surge, Steptoe and Edwards would often have to perform egg retrievals very late at night or during early morning hours.

The success of IVF improved dramatically with the use of superovulation with Pergonal, first advocated by the Norfolk, Virginia, group headed by Drs. Georgianna and Howard Jones. Larger numbers of eggs could be recovered and, the IVF team could better time egg retrieval. Now, the use of superovulation has become routine with IVF. Recently, gonadotropin releasing hormone (GnRH) agonists have also been introduced prior to beginning controlled ovulation to prevent the woman from having her own spontaneous LH surge so that egg retrieval timing can be strictly controlled and the chance of a "dropped" cycle minimized.

Generally, the woman begins taking ovulation inducing drugs between the first and fifth days of her cycle to stimulate the development of multiple follicles. Several eggs are stimulated to develop at the same time so that a group of eggs will be available for fertilization. This "superovulation" is usually accomplished with combinations of the same hormone medications used to stimulate ovulation in other treatment cycles, such as for IUI: clomiphene citrate, Pergonal, pure follicle stimulating hormone (Metrodin), and human chorionic gonadotropin (hCG).

Many couples are already familiar with these medications since they may have used them in previous treatment cycles, before ever considering IVF. Usually, a member of the IVF team teaches the husband how to give his wife the daily injections so that she doesn't have to go to the doctor's office for her medication. Although this may be difficult to do at first, it gives the couple some control over their own treatment.

There are almost as many individual stimulation regimens as there are IVF programs. Most IVF clinics start providing high doses of hormones, either alone or in combinations, early in a woman's cycle—when more follicles can be recruited to progress and mature. The woman's response to stimulation is carefully monitored by estradiol levels, ultrasound exams, cervical mucus examination and, possibly, progesterone and LH levels to determine how the follicles containing the eggs are developing. Blood hormone levels may be obtained intermittently during the first week of stimulation, then daily, along with ultrasound exams and cervical mucus monitoring, as ovulation approaches. The doctor adjusts the stimulation schedule to maintain a steady growth in the size of ovarian follicles and a steady rise of estradiol levels. When the follicles reach maturity, usually after seven to ten days of medication, an hCG injection is administered to trigger egg maturation in anticipation of egg retrieval from the follicles.

At first, most IVF clinics had one standard way to induce ovulation. If a woman's follicles weren't stimulated sufficiently, she had no egg retrieval, and the cycle was canceled. Today most programs individualize ovulation induction, which has reduced IVF cancellation rates.

Since some women do better with larger amounts of hormones, and others with lesser amounts, hormone stimulation should be individualized as much as possible. Doctors often determine individual hormone doses based upon the woman's response to previous cycles of hormone therapy or to previous IVF cycles.

IVF researchers have learned that high amounts of gonadotropins can often disrupt and shorten a woman's luteal phase, making it difficult for implantation to occur or for her to carry the pregnancy to term. To help support the luteal phase, most IVF teams now provide progesterone daily from the day of egg retrieval until a pregnancy test is performed two weeks later. Others also provide repeated injections of hCG in the luteal phase of the cycle to keep the ovaries producing progesterone.

Unfortunately, between 10 and 20 percent of women attempting IVF have a poor ovarian response to ovulation-inducing drugs and never reach the stage of egg retrieval. Increasing the dose of gonadotropins in the early phase of the menstrual cycle may enhance egg recruitment for such poor responders.

Recently, several IVF teams have pretreated these poor responders using GnRH agonists such as leuprolide acetate (Lupron) to wipe the hormone slate clean, and then initiated gonadotropin ovulation induction. GnRH agonist pretreatment, followed by Pergonal, alone or with Metrodin, increases the number of eggs collected, the fertilization rate, the length of the luteal phase, and pregnancy rates. After pretreatment with a GnRH agonist, however, it usually takes larger amounts of Pergonal to produce ovulation than when no GnRH agonist is used.

This more controlled stimulation with GnRH and Pergonal has the advantage of fewer cancelled IVF cycles due to a spontaneous LH surge or premature luteinization of the follicles than with Pergonal alone. If a woman has an LH surge, most programs now cancel cycles because it's difficult to predict ovulation accurately, and retrieval of the eggs may be performed either too early or too late. Cycles may also be canceled due to a low number (less than three) of mature follicles, inadequate estradiol production, or poor follicle development.

Because of the improved ability to time a woman's egg retrieval to get mature eggs, many IVF teams now use GnRH routinely in IVF cycles. The disadvantages of pretreating the woman with GnRH agonist include a longer duration of treatment, more Pergonal injections, and an increased cost (for extra Pergonal and because Lupron itself is expensive). However, these disadvantages are counterbalanced by fewer canceled cycles.

A recent survey of U.S. IVF clinics by Serono, the manufacturer of Pergonal, reveals that 89 percent used GnRH agonists in at least some cycles in 1988, compared to only 2 percent in 1987. At present, to stimulate ovulation most U.S. IVF clinics only use GnRH in conjunction with Pergonal for those who respond poorly to Pergonal alone.

Egg Retrieval

Married for two years, Marilyn, aged thirty-six, and Edward, aged forty-six, wanted a baby. Since they had been unsuccessful after trying for a year, they each went to fertility specialists. Even though he had fathered two children in his first marriage, Edward showed a border-line low sperm count. Marilyn had intermittent high prolactin levels and elevated androgen levels. The following years were fraught with frustration as they both tried hormone treatments and numerous artificial inseminations without success. Their next alternative was an IVF procedure.

In their first IVF attempt, Marilyn had her eggs retrieved laparoscopically. "I didn't feel a thing when I was asleep, and I remember having a pleasant dream. In fact, I was annoyed that they had awakened me when it was over," says Marilyn. "Then my belly hurt where they had made the incision for the laparoscope, my hand hurt where the IV tube had been in place and I felt nauseous." Although three of her eggs were fertilized and transferred into her uterus, the attempt failed.

During her next IVF attempt, Marilyn had her eggs retrieved, with ultrasound guidance, through her vagina. "I felt a little uncomfortable when they were rinsing my ovaries, but it wasn't bad," she says. "I hardly felt when they stuck the needle into my follicles. After it was over, I didn't feel any pain."

If a woman doesn't take GnRH agonists, then as she nears the middle of her cycle she usually begins to monitor herself with a home test kit several times a day to check for her LH surge. The IVF team retrieves her eggs based on the prediction of when she will ovulate naturally after the LH surge, or after administering hCG, which is usually more accurate. In most cases, after taking Pergonal, the woman receives an hCG injection and the IVF team retrieves her eggs thirty-four to thirty-five hours later.

The team retrieves the woman's eggs either with a laparoscopic procedure or an ultrasound-guided needle placed through the vagina. She receives general anesthesia or local anesthesia with intravenous sedation and possibly takes mild analgesics.

With laparoscopy, the surgeon makes a small incision

in the woman's abdomen near the belly button for the laparoscope and two smaller incisions in the pubic hair line for egg retrieval instruments. He punctures the follicles with a thin needle inserted through the laparoscope or through a separate second puncture site in the abdomen. Then he withdraws fluid from each follicle and gives the fluid to an embryologist in the operating room or in an adjacent lab, who examines the follicular fluid under a microscope for eggs. The embryologist puts eggs found in the fluid into culture medium and incubates them. Meanwhile the surgeon irrigates the follicles with sterile solution and again collects the fluid to check for any additional eggs. Laparoscopy usually yields an egg from 60 to 80 percent of the follicles.

For ultrasound-guided retrieval, the IVF team covers an ultrasound probe, specifically designed for pelvic imaging, with a sterile condom or latex glove and inserts the probe into the woman's vagina. With the aid of a needle guide attached to the probe, the doctor harvests her eggs by puncturing the follicles and removing the follicular fluid. The embryologist immediately identifies and places the eggs in nutritive media in an incubator.

Ultrasound-guided egg retrieval has made the most physically demanding part of the IVF procedure less traumatic. In some centers, husbands can be with their wives during the egg retrieval. The procedure is usually easier on the woman than laparoscopy, and is equally effective in retrieving eggs. The quality and number of eggs, and the pregnancy rates, from ultrasound-guided egg retrieval compare favorably to those of laparoscopic retrieval. It is also usually less costly, faster, and leads to a quicker recovery than laparoscopic retrieval.

Because of these advantages, at many IVF clinics ultrasound-guided egg retrieval is more common than laparoscopic retrieval. Laparoscopy may be reserved for women who need a simultaneous assessment of pelvic anatomy through a diagnostic laparoscopy, but the best-equipped IVF clinics will have both retrieval methods available to pick the best method for a particular woman.

With either method, on average, the IVF team retrieves from six to eight eggs from the woman's follicles. Typically, three or four of the eggs are fully mature.

Semen Collection

"At first, it was embarrassing providing the sample because of all those people in the waiting room," recalls Sam. "They all knew what I was there for. But then I realized that all the guys were there for the same reason."

Before the start of the IVF cycle, the husband makes an appointment to give a semen sample for evaluation. In some cases, the husband's sperm can be frozen as a backup for the day of egg retrieval. As with a semen analysis, he is asked to refrain from ejaculation for two or three days beforehand to increase the number of sperm in the semen. On the day of egg retrieval, he provides a semen sample through masturbation, and the sample undergoes a standard semen analysis along with sperm washing and "swim up" to recover the healthiest sperm.

Egg Fertilization

For men with normal semen, about 50,000 of the most motile sperm are incubated with each of his wife's eggs. For a man with abnormally shaped sperm or a mild to moderately low sperm count or motility, as many as 500,000 sperm are mixed with each egg. An embryologist inspects the eggs, allows them to incubate in culture media, and then mixes the sperm with mature eggs. From two to twelve hours after egg retrieval, the embryologist places the mixture in an incubator overnight, and the following morning checks the eggs for fertilization.

There are four basic steps to fertilization: the egg's metabolism must be turned on, the sperm must be incorporated into the egg, a barrier must be erected to keep other sperm out, and the nuclei and chromosomes from the egg and the sperm must be united inside the egg.

Generally, about 80 percent of mature eggs become fertilized at this stage. Eggs penetrated by more than one sperm (polyspermy), which produces an abnormal embryo, are not transferred back to the wife's uterus.

In some IVF programs, the team allows immature eggs (about 50 percent of the retrieved eggs) to ripen in culture media for twelve hours or longer and then fertilizes them with the husband's sperm. A few IVF clinics even reinseminate eggs that haven't fertilized believing that the eggs were too immature at first and that incubating them in culture medium matures them enough for a second insemination. Usually, immature eggs don't often become fertilized and lead to a pregnancy.

By about thirty hours after fertilization, the sperm and egg have become a two-celled embryo. By forty-eight hours after fertilization, the embryo should have four cells, and by sixty hours it should have divided into eight cells. The embryo is usually transferred into the wife's uterus anywhere from the two-cell to the eight-cell stage.

If 80 percent of the retrieved eggs become fertilized, why do at best only 15 to 20 percent of women who go to IVF clinics become pregnant? The answer may lie with several factors. The uterus may not be properly prepared for implantation. A woman's hormonal support after embryo transfer may be inadequate. With IVF, embryos are transferred into the uterus much more quickly (after two days) than they would normally appear in the uterus in a natural cycle (five to seven days after ovulation). That is because after the first few days in incubation outside of the body, eggs won't keep dividing normally.

Embryo Transfer

Of the six eggs retrieved from Jennifer's follicles, three became fertilized by Sam's sperm and were transferred into her uterus. "We were ecstatic about the three fertilizations after spending a tense weekend waiting to hear about the results," Sam says. "We came in early Sunday morning for the embryo transfer. Two other couples were also in the office for the same thing, so we shared bagels and lox together. It was the most unusual Sunday brunch I have ever had."

When the fertilized eggs have divided, the woman returns to the IVF clinic for the transfer procedure. The reproductive surgeon threads a thin plastic catheter through the vagina, through the cervical canal, and into the uterus, and transfers the fertilized egg through the catheter. The patient's husband may be allowed to stay with his wife during the transfer process.

This ten-minute, outpatient procedure requires no anesthesia. The woman may experience some uterine cramping and discomfort, however, and possibly a small amount of bleeding. After resting for a few hours, she returns home and usually can resume normal activities in a day or two.

To enhance the embryo transfer rate, some IVF clinics now have the woman go through a mock embryo transfer using radiopaque dye in a pre-IVF cycle. A fluoroscope reveals where the dye (which is like the fluid that will contain the embryo) ends up. In certain body positions, such as with the woman on her back, the dye may run out of her vagina. She may be better off having her embryos transferred while she is in a knee-chest position (on her stomach, not her back). Others have devised equipment that holds the uterus tilted downward, hoping to use gravity to help the transferred embryos implant in the uterus.

The chances of having a child through IVF are also improved by transferring up to four embryos into the uterus. Transferring more than four embryos doesn't seem to improve the overall pregnancy rate, but does increase the likelihood of multiple pregnancy. Most IVF teams like to transfer three or four embryos during each IVF cycle. If more than four eggs are retrieved, all mature eggs are fertilized and the extra embryos may be frozen. If freezing is unavailable, the couple may be asked to donate the eggs to another infertile couple or to allow the IVF team to use them to refine culturing methods and embryo handling techniques.

Embryo Freezing

If an IVF procedure fails, the couple should wait at least one month while the wife recovers before undergoing superovulation and egg retrieval again. Saving eggs for future use by fertilizing them with sperm and then freezing them as embryos can be helpful. Frozen embryos can be transferred during subsequent spontaneous (natural) ovulation cycles without subjecting the wife to any additional medications and another egg retrieval.

At the right time to transfer the embryos during succeeding treatment cycles, the frozen embryos are thawed and transferred into the uterus as with any IVF attempt.

The ability to preserve embryos for future use lowers the total cost of repeated IVF treatments since the most costly first few stages (ovulation induction, egg retrieval, fertilization) don't have to be repeated. Another advantage is that the embryos can be transferred during a natural ovulation cycle when the woman's uterus is naturally ready for implantation.

About half of frozen embryos survive thawing, and 10 to 20 percent lead to pregnancies. From fifteen to twenty U.S. centers are now freezing embryos, and they have reported dozens of births. Improved freezing and thawing techniques are currently being developed and will almost certainly lead to more centers offering embryo freezing in the future.

If a couple has embryos frozen, they have to pay the IVF clinic a storage fee. After a certain length of time, the couple must decide what to do with any unused frozen embryos, such as whether to donate them to another infertile couple.

Some IVF clinics, such as the one at Cornell University, have the couple sign an agreement stating that the frozen embryos are the joint property of the couple. Upon the woman's forty-fifth birthday, the frozen embryos become the property of the Cornell IVF team. This ethical dilemma of survivorship gained worldwide attention when a wealthy California couple died in a plane crash without designating what to do with their frozen embryos left in Australia. After a lengthy court battle, the rights to the frozen embryos were transferred to the couple's estate.

Post-Embryo Transfer

"The first seven days after the embryo transfer were exciting," says Sam. "Jennifer's eggs were implanted in her womb and in a way she was pregnant. Everything was going well." As it got closer to two weeks and the pregnancy test, they spent more time together, nurturing each other. The pregnancy test result came back as borderline, and Sam and Jennifer had to wait another two days. In that time, her hCG levels crashed, and Jennifer got her period.

"That was hard for us to take. We started to think again that we would never have a baby," says Sam. "I told Jennifer that this was only our first IVF cycle, that she should keep her spirits up. Although they told us we only have a 20 percent chance, I reminded her that even though we have a male fertility problem, we had fertilizations. We're looking forward to the next attempt."

The two weeks of waiting after embryo transfer often become the most difficult part of the IVF treatment emotionally. After the embryo transfer, the woman may continue to take hCG or progesterone to help support the uterine lining built up in the first half of the cycle. During this period, various blood hormone levels are measured to track the wife's progress. If necessary, she receives more progesterone to help maintain the endometrial lining and prevent premature menstruation. Two weeks following embryo transfer, she returns for a pregnancy test.

If her pregnancy test is negative, the IVF team usually encourages the couple to schedule a follow-up visit with the clinic's doctor and a counselor, usually a social worker or psychologist, to ask any questions and to discuss their next step. The couple may decide to try another IVF attempt. A woman who goes through the IVF procedure four times has about a 50 percent chance of taking home a baby. After four attempts, the odds don't get any better.

If her pregnancy test is positive, the woman still has a 20 to 40 percent chance of miscarrying (women over forty tend to have a higher miscarriage rate, as high as 60 percent), which is slightly higher than the natural miscarriage rate, and about a 5 percent chance of an ectopic pregnancy, also higher than for the general population. Within two weeks after a positive pregnancy test, she returns for an ultrasound scan to confirm the presence of a fetal heartbeat and to see whether she is carrying more than one baby.

Since most IVF clinics now limit the number of transferred embryos to four, the incidence of multiple pregnancies isn't much higher than with superovulation without IVF.

In the more than fifteen thousand IVF births worldwide, so far there is no evidence of an increased risk of birth defects or premature births. Most IVF clinics don't consider IVF pregnancies high-risk pregnancies, except for the risk of miscarriage, for which many provide progesterone supplements to help maintain the pregnancy to term.

If the woman becomes pregnant, she will be referred back to her obstetrician. If she doesn't have an obstetrician, the clinic usually helps her find one. Genetic counseling and amniocentesis are usually recommended for any woman over thirty-five; a genetic abnormality, however, can occur at any age. Chorionic villus sampling is a newer alternative to diagnose a genetic disorder in the first trimester, but it carries a slightly higher risk of miscarriage than amniocentesis, which is performed in the second trimester. As always, you should discuss the need for and risks of genetic testing with your doctor.

Cancellation of a Cycle

Occasionally, an IVF team will decide not to attempt to retrieve a woman's eggs, but rather to cancel the treatment cycle. Sometimes the woman doesn't respond optimally to the medications and the blood tests and ultrasound exams don't reveal successful follicle growth. Her eggs may be immature, or too mature, to be fertilized. Or the eggs may fertilize, but not continue to divide, in which case they will not be transferred back into the uterus.

You have to realize that your chances for success in any one IVF cycle, even at the best clinics, is no higher than 20 percent once you have gotten to embryo transfer. Of all the couples who start IVF treatment, only 7 to 10 percent take home a baby. These percentages are likely to increase as fertility specialists gain more experience with IVF.

Who Are the Candidates for IVF?

The woman with the best chances for a successful IVF procedure is younger than thirty-five and has normal menstrual cycles, a good response to controlled ovarian hyperstimulation, and a husband with a good sperm count.

IVF can bypass most causes of infertility, including irreversibly blocked fallopian tubes, antisperm antibody problems, endometriosis, a cervical factor problem, very low sperm counts, and even unexplained causes of infertility. IVF is a particularly good alternative for a woman who produces mature eggs but can't conceive naturally because of blocked fallopian tubes, and for a woman with luteinized unruptured follicle syndrome, who develops but doesn't release mature eggs from her follicles.

The Age Factor

The chances of an IVF birth depend heavily on the wife's age. Younger women have higher pregnancy rates than older women. Women over age forty have only a rare chance of IVF success. Yet, even knowing the odds, many women over forty say they want to go through at least one IVF cycle before giving up their hopes of having a baby.

One way to determine whether a woman over forty has a strong chance of success may be to measure her estradiol and FSH levels on day three of the IVF cycle. At the Jones Institute, researchers have seen a trend toward higher pregnancy rates and fewer canceled cycles for women over forty when their FSH level is low on cycle day three.

The Male Factor

For four years, Diane and John tried to have a baby with no success, even after a dozen attempts at intrauterine insemination. A loan officer in a bank, John, aged forty-eight, had a borderline low sperm count, low sperm motility, and poor sperm morphology. When an IVF clinic opened near their home, their fertility specialist suggested they give it a try.

"Our first attempt, with all the injections I had to give her every night, brought us closer together," John says. Four of Diane's healthy eggs were fertilized and transferred, but the attempt failed. They decided to try again. "This time we knew the routine, but we were both feeling bad since we didn't expect to have to go through the procedure twice," he says. That attempt also failed. John and Diane, a thirty-eight-year-old school counselor, took some time off and came back for another attempt three months later.

This time, the test showed that Diane was pregnant. "We were scared because we thought it might be a false positive pregnancy test," she says. Then they had an ultrasound exam. "We actually saw a tiny, beating heart. It was a beautiful moment, so exciting to see the fruits of our labor," John says. Their daughter Doreen is fourteen months old.

Although IVF offers new hope to infertile couples, it's not the answer for all causes of infertility. Most IVF programs usually require a man to have a sperm concentration of more than 10 million sperm per ml with more than 20 percent normal sperm motility and at least 5 percent normally shaped sperm. Below these values, a couple rarely achieves a pregnancy without using donor sperm. Male factor patients already have a one-third less chance of fertilizing their wife's eggs in the lab than men with normal sperm counts.

Besides a semen analysis, the IVF clinic should also check the man and his wife for sperm antibodies, which reduce the chances of fertilization of both normal and oligospermic men. Many IVF clinics also test a man's sperm function using sperm penetration assays with zona-stripped hamster eggs. Although not totally reliable (some men score poorly and still fertilize their wife's eggs), the hamster test gives an indication of a man's fertilizing ability.

The most important determinant of IVF success for a male factor patient is his ability to fertilize his wife's eggs. After two cycles with no fertilization, most men will continue to fail to fertilize in subsequent cycles. If a couple with a male factor problem produces no fertilized eggs after two attempts, they should consider pursuing other alternatives, such as donor sperm or adoption.

Sperm from men with male factor infertility can have difficulty both in getting the sperm to the egg, and in penetrating the egg. Once the eggs become fertilized in the IVF lab, however, these couples with a male factor problem have pregnancy rates equal to infertile couples with no male factor problem. In other words, once a sperm fertilizes the egg, its mission has been accomplished and the outcome of pregnancy is just as good as for eggs fertilized by sperm from men with no known male factor problem. To improve the live birth rate of male factor patients, IVF researchers are looking for ways to improve the fertilizing ability of a man's sperm.

Competition

In their third IVF attempt, Marilyn and Edward had only one two-cell embryo that degenerated, and they never got to the embryo transfer stage. "We had gone to a big place that sent couples through like herds of cattle," Marilyn says. "They tried to tell us what was 'best' for us without stopping to understand our needs. They kept saying my eggs would never be fertilized with Edward's sperm, and that donor insemination was for us. But I told them that donor sperm was difficult for me to accept. I'm adopted, I don't know who my father was and I didn't want my baby not to know who his or her father was. They didn't bother to listen. I was so frustrated, that evening I went home and smashed several boxes of light bulbs, one at a time, in our backyard. It was very therapeutic."

As IVF has become one of the fastest-growing areas of infertility treatment, it has also become ripe for exploitation. Couples desperate for a baby may be lured by IVF clinics promising results they can't achieve.

Entrepreneurs are cashing in on a surging fertility industry, and the most controversial aspect of this commercialization of conception is IVF, which by some estimates is itself a $100 million industry.

Of the approximately two hundred U.S. and Canadian IVF clinics, about one-third are at university centers and the rest have private funding or are associated with for-profit hospitals. The most successful centers have long waiting lists, and new IVF clinics are opening all the time. Many programs have never had a live birth. Some programs that shut down after a year or more with no pregnancies are reopening after refining their techniques.

Yet, the bulk of IVF births comes from a small number of large programs. Those infertile couples who have gone through IVF treatment have found that IVF can cost them tens of thousands of dollars, with no money-back guarantees and stiff odds against success. Unfortunately, after all the expenses, heartache, poking, and prodding, most couples go home childless.

Doctors at the larger centers say that a high volume of patients is necessary to establish a track record, to perfect techniques, to maintain a level of competency, and to support the necessary staff specialists. They claim that a commitment of at least two years and an expenditure of $1 million is necessary for a new program to establish itself, and that physicians who dabble in IVF won't have comparable results if they don't make similar investments.

But large programs aren't trouble-free. Some couples at large clinics feel as if they are being put through an assembly line.

It's difficult to pinpoint the right balance. If a clinic performs too many cycles, it may be impersonal. Too few cycles, and the clinic staff may not have the experience to give couples the best chances of having a baby.

As the number of IVF clinics has grown, so has the professional and public pressure to regulate them. Exaggerated estimates of success have led doctors, insurance companies, members of Congress, and infertile couples to push for stronger regulation.

The American Fertility Society has an IVF registry, but in the past has divulged only cumulative data, not information about individual IVF clinics and their success rates. However, clinics that want to have their own data released can now do so through the registry.

A couple can check with the American Fertility Society to see whether an IVF clinic is listed in its registry. The more than a hundred official members of the Society for Assisted Reproductive Technology (SART) is restricted to IVF programs that can account for at least forty patients and three live births.

Scientists have also been urging the federal government to take a more active role in IVF research to improve a couple's odds. The government, which placed a moratorium in 1980 on federal funding for any research involving human embryos or fetuses, recently took a preliminary step toward allowing federal funding for IVF research. An ethics advisory board that was disbanded in 1980 has been resurrected and will take another look at the funding question.

IVF "Cousins"

Once considered a last-chance technology, IVF has spawned the development of other procedures that use variations of the same assisted reproductive techniques. These technologies offer couples the advantages of the years of experience that went into making IVF a viable infertility treatment. They carry IVF technology along to the next logical step in an attempt to help more infertile couples have babies.

Gamete Intra Fallopian Transfer (GIFT)

In addition to IVF as a treatment, most IVF clinics offer a more natural approach to fertilization, called Gamete (for egg and sperm) Intra Fallopian (within the fallopian tube) Transfer (GIFT). This combines eggs with sperm and then places the egg/sperm combination directly into the fallopian tubes, where conception occurs naturally.

The GIFT procedure requires a woman to have at least one normal fallopian tube. The ovulation induction and monitoring procedures for GIFT are basically the same as for IVF. After the surgeon retrieves the eggs, the embryologist draws up small amounts of sperm for each egg, and places up to two eggs plus 100,000 sperm into each fallopian tube. If the sperm fertilize the egg, it happens as it would naturally—inside the fallopian tube rather than in an incubator outside the body, as in IVF.

Except for women with two damaged fallopian tubes, candidates for IVF are also candidates for GIFT, which in many centers has a higher pregnancy rate (20 to 30 percent) than IVF. It is most suitable for couples with unexplained infertility, cervical or male factor problems, mild endometriosis, or luteinized unruptured follicle syndrome. GIFT also seems to offer women over forty a better chance at live birth than IVF.

GIFT has some disadvantages when compared to IVF. At present, GIFT usually requires laparoscopy to transfer the eggs and sperm into the fallopian tubes, making it a more major procedure than an IVF embryo transfer through the vagina and cervix into the uterus. (This difference in the two techniques may change with the use of hysteroscopes or ultrasound guidance to transfer sperm and eggs through the cervical canal into the tubes.) More important, if the GIFT procedure fails, there is no way of knowing whether the woman's eggs were fertilized, which is readily apparent with IVF.

IVF + GIFT = "ZIFT"

Because of this lack of knowledge about fertilization, some couples with a male factor problem now receive a combination of IVF and GIFT. The wife's eggs, retrieved with ultrasound guidance, are exposed to her husband's sperm in the lab. Within twenty-four hours, the fertilized egg (known as a zygote) is transferred to her fallopian tube, usually by laparoscopy.

Since this procedure uses the zygote, not the separate eggs and sperm, it's called Zygote Intra Fallopian Transfer (ZIFT). This has an advantage over a pure GIFT procedure, particularly for male factor couples, because the embryologist will know whether the wife's eggs have been fertilized by her husband's sperm. If his sperm don't fertilize her eggs, then the couple may decide at that point to accept donor insemination rather than pursue further efforts to achieve a pregnancy with the husband's sperm.

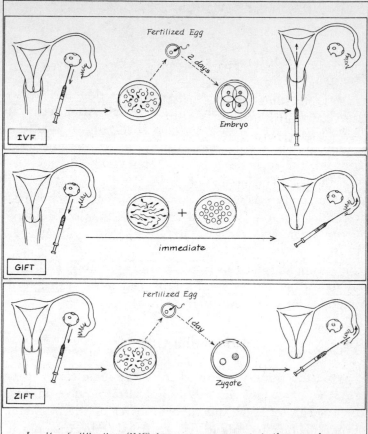

In vitro fertilization (IVF) has spawned several similar procedures, including Gamete Intra Fallopian Transfer (GIFT) and Zygote Intra Fallopian Transfer (ZIFT). All three procedures begin with eggs being retrieved from the woman's follicles. In IVF, the eggs are mixed with sperm in a culture dish in the lab, and two days later the doctor transfers the growing embryo into the woman's uterus. For GIFT, eggs are combined with sperm and immediately placed in the woman's fallopian tubes, where sperm fertilize the eggs. ZIFT is a combination of IVF and GIFT: the sperm and egg are mixed in a culture dish, and one day later the doctor places the developing zygote into the fallopian tube.

Intravaginal Culture (IVC)

Another technique that takes advantage of the body's own environment is intravaginal culture (IVC). After retrieval the eggs are placed with the husband's sperm in a culture medium inside a sterile, hermetically sealed container carried inside the vagina. A vaginal diaphragm holds the container in place. This maintains the egg and sperm at normal body temperature as well as, if not better than, any incubator in a laboratory. Two or so days later, the doctor opens the container and transfers any fertilized, dividing eggs into the uterus.

The simplicity of this procedure is appealing, and may lead to further reductions in costs and more widespread availability of treatment than classical IVF.

Ultrasound GIFT

To avoid the surgery involved in GIFT, some clinics perform the procedure entirely with ultrasound guidance, both for egg retrieval and tubal transfer of the eggs and sperm. This new technique, first reported from Australia, is gaining popularity in North America.

As IVF procedures multiply, researchers are learning more and more about the miracles of conception. By sampling the fluids and protein substances found inside the fallopian tube, they are getting a better understanding of the tube's normal environment.

If what's happening inside the fallopian tube and the conditions leading to successful implantation can be better understood, then more couples will have babies through IVF and related treatments. Some researchers believe that it may even be possible eventually to better the 20 to 25 percent natural conception rate per cycle.

For the moment, IVF, even at a 10 percent live birth rate, is an acceptable alternative for many couples. But even IVF isn't the last resort.

What Couples Should Ask When Looking for an IVF Clinic:

Do you have any limitations on the age or types of infertile couples you accept into your program?

What is your pregnancy rate per embryo transfer? Does this rate include only clinical pregnancies, or does it also include chemical pregnancies?

What is your pregnancy rate for couples our age with our particular problem?

What percentage of your couples initiating an IVF cycle don't make it to transfer?

What percentage of your IVF patients who have egg retrievals go on to embryo transfer?

What percentage of your couples have a male factor problem, and what is your success rate in treating them?

How many cycles does your program induce in a year?

How much does the procedure cost, including hormone treatments? (Costs generally range from about $6,000 to $7,000, including the drugs.)

Do you freeze embryos?

What happens to frozen embryos after we achieve a pregnancy?

Do you offer egg freezing, embryo donation, or egg donation programs?

Do you offer GIFT or other advanced procedures involving assisted reproductive technology?

What is your live birth rate among all couples who have started an IVF cycle in your program?

Part Three

ALTERNATIVES

11

DONATING SPERM, EGGS, EMBRYOS

When you have struggled through fertility treatments, possibly even in vitro fertilization or other assisted reproductive technologies, and still have not had a baby, you may become increasingly frustrated and desperate. By this time, you have to come to grips with the idea that you may never have a child together.

But that doesn't mean that one or the other partner can't contribute to the birth of a baby that carries his or her genes by donating sperm, eggs, or embryos.

Donor Insemination

If a thorough physical evaluation reveals that a man has an untreatable fertility problem and that his wife has no known fertility problems, then the couple should consider donor insemination. It has become an increasingly important method of infertility treatment due to male factors and is far and away the most popular and successful method for treating severe male factor problems. More than thirty thousand babies are conceived by donor insemination each year in the United States.

In most cases, donor insemination simply involves placing donor sperm in the wife's cervical mucus at the fertile time of her cycle. If the wife also has fertility problems, more advanced methods, using donor sperm, may be necessary. If her cervical mucus is hostile to the donor sperm, the donor sperm can be washed, concentrated, placed inside a narrow catheter and safely inserted through the cervical canal into the uterus (IUI) or fallopian tubes (ITI) at the time of ovulation. Donor sperm can also replace the husband's sperm in any of the assisted reproductive technologies, including IVF or its "cousins."

Finding a Donor

If you are considering donor insemination, your fertility specialist can help you find a suitable donor. The donor should be carefully screened and selected to resemble the husband as closely as possible, including his age, education, race, height and weight, hair and eye color, blood group and type, occupation, religion, and nationality.

Because of the widespread availability of frozen donor sperm from a number of sperm banks throughout the country, a suitable donor match can be found for most men. At some fertility centers, couples can examine lists of donor characteristics and themselves make the selection of the sperm donor.

When a doctor orders donor sperm from a sperm bank, he requests that the donor have particular characteristics. Often, the characteristics of several donors closely resemble those of the husband. Your doctor should give you information about the available donors so that you can select the most appropriate one. The donor's identification by a code number will be kept as a part of your permanent record.

In the recent past, many practitioners of donor insemination did little to protect couples from genetic disorders and infectious diseases, such as acquired immune deficiency syndrome (AIDS), that might be passed through donor semen. Even now, some doctors who perform donor insemination with fresh sperm still may not routinely test donors for antibodies to the AIDS virus or for infections with syphilis, gonorrhea, hepatitis, and chlamydia.

Less than half of the physicians who regularly perform donor insemination test donors for antibodies to the AIDS virus, according to a 1988 government survey of nearly four hundred physicians. Also shocking is that less than half of the responding physicians require genetic screening for donors and only three-quarters inquire about the proven fertility of donors. About 10 percent of the doctors who responded to the survey said they rely on commercial sperm banks to perform the screening for them.

The 1988 report by the Office of Technology Assessment will probably lead couples to make more use of commercial sperm banks, since they are more likely than individual physicians to screen donors effectively for the AIDS virus, other STDs, and genetic defects. Still, don't take it for granted that these safeguards are being used without asking for, and obtaining, written information about the screening of potential donors.

How Good Are the Sperm?

Rhonda, aged thirty-seven, and Owen, aged thirty-eight, chose their frozen semen from a large national sperm bank. Their first attempt at donor insemination failed because Rhonda's cervical mucus was hostile to the donor's sperm, killing off most of them very rapidly. The doctor suggested they try an intrauterine insemination the next month. The day following her urine LH surge, Rhonda came in for an IUI. But upon thawing, the donor sperm showed a very low motile sperm count, "so low that the doctor didn't want to use that sperm sample. But I felt close to the donor. He sounded so much like Owen," says Rhonda. The frozen donor sperm were washed and inseminated into her uterus.

You should ask your doctor whether the donated sperm came from a commercial sperm bank that is a member of the American Association of Tissue Banks, which has set criteria and professional standards for screening donors. If possible, try to find out the sperm bank's success rate. This is often hard to obtain, since many sperm banks often don't collect information from their physician-clients regarding the number of pregnancies achieved. Ask the doctor how many pregnancies he has had from this bank and how successful donor insemination has been, in his experience, for couples with similar fertility problems.

You should know how many motile sperm per ml are contained in the donor samples received by your doctor. The success of donor insemination correlates with the number of motile sperm inseminated. A quality sperm bank will provide straws or vials containing at least 20 million motile sperm or more per ml. The doctor should check the sperm count and the rapidly progressive forward motility upon thawing the sample and preparing it for insemination.

The Medical Aspects of Donor Insemination

"At our second attempt, Owen and I were both really excited," Rhonda says. "The ultrasound exam showed that I had four follicles. Everything felt right." An IUI was performed on the day of the LH surge. The following day, Rhonda came back for an insemination of more sperm into her uterus and, after lying on her back with her hips elevated for about forty-five minutes, she and Owen went home. Four days after the inseminations, she felt sick to her stomach, and "I knew I was pregnant," Rhonda says. A few days later, Owen suggested she

take a home pregnancy test, which was positive. She went to the doctor's office the next day, and he confirmed the pregnancy by checking her blood hormone levels. A week later, a vaginal ultrasound examination showed that her pregnancy was developing normally. She and Owen plan to name their baby girl Terri.

If you have chosen donor insemination to overcome a male factor problem, your chances for a pregnancy will correlate with the number of fertility problems the wife has. Women who have two healthy fallopian tubes, no endometriosis, need no medication to stimulate ovulatory cycles, and are under age thirty-five have an excellent chance of becoming pregnant within three to six cycles. Women with no apparent fertility problems have approximately a 90 percent chance of pregnancy, if they continue with donor insemination for up to twelve cycles. Women with ovulation problems during donor insemination cycles may take longer to conceive. If a woman hasn't conceived within four to six well-timed donor insemination cycles, she should consider another donor and have further fertility evaluation.

A combination of basal body temperature monitoring, cervical mucus monitoring, and detection of the luteinizing hormone surge leads to the best timing for insemination. Most doctors inseminate sperm either once or twice each cycle near the time of ovulation.

Before performing donor insemination, Dr. Berger obtains cervical cultures to check for infection or bacteria in the wife's reproductive tract, and the couple goes through the basic screening blood tests. Some couples prefer donor insemination without any further fertility evaluation; others will have a hysterosalpingogram and ovulation monitoring to check that the wife has open tubes and normal hormone levels and follicle development.

The donated sperm can cost the couple from $125 to $250 per sample. Unfortunately, most insurance companies will not reimburse for donated sperm. They maintain that this isn't a treatment for an infertile man.

Fresh versus Frozen Semen

Since the ever-growing epidemic of AIDS, more couples undergoing donor insemination have been opting for frozen semen. (Donor insemination has also been called artificial insemination by donor, or AID, in the past. To avoid confusion with the disease AIDS, most fertility specialists now use the terms "Therapeutic Donor Insemination" or "Donor Insemination" instead.) Before being used, frozen donor semen should be quarantined for at least six months to ensure that the donor hasn't developed antibodies to the AIDS virus during that time.

To prevent the possible transmission of the AIDS virus (as well as other infectious conditions such as gonorrhea, chlamydia, and hepatitis) through donated semen, the American Fertility Society, the Food and Drug Administration, and the Centers for Disease Control have collaborated on revised guidelines for donor insemination. The guidelines call for a potential donor to be interviewed to determine whether he has a history of risk factors for infection with the AIDS virus; to have a physical exam to document any obvious signs of AIDS infection; and to have a blood test for infection with the AIDS virus or the development of antibodies to the virus—both when he donates semen and six months later before the frozen semen is released for use. The federal government may institute a mandatory system to ensure that all semen used for donor insemination is adequately screened and tested and that standards are enforced.

Frozen semen has the advantage of being able to be shipped anywhere, be stored in a liquid nitrogen tank, and be immediately available at the fertile time of the woman's cycle. The major disadvantage of a frozen semen sample is that it reduces the number of motile sperm so that it takes, on average, more inseminations to achieve a pregnancy than with fresh semen. It may take six or more inseminations with frozen semen for a woman to become pregnant, compared with only three or four tries using fresh semen.

Taking into account lower sperm motility, some fertility specialists perform intrauterine insemination with thawed frozen semen. Dr. Berger performs an intracervical insemination on the day of the wife's LH surge, if she has fertile mucus that day. The following day, he can also perform an IUI with a second thawed sample, which has been washed, allowed to "swim up" and concentrated into a small volume. He has found that more women become pregnant with both inseminations in a single cycle than with an intracervical insemination alone.

Tracking Down a Donor's Identity

Typically, your doctor receives a code number along with the donor semen from the sperm bank. The sperm bank usually has no information about you. At least two sperm banks holding so-called "extraordinary" sperm from intellectually or athletically outstanding donors now screen the couple, but in a manner that still keeps the identities of the sperm donor and the couple from each other.

Most doctors who keep records that could lead to identification of the donor will not release this information, unless the couple or a court order instructs them to do so. This may be necessary if, for example, the child needs to know about his or her chances of having a hereditary disease.

Emotional Factors

"The most difficult thing for me was the way I was informed that I had a low sperm count," recalls Phil, a forty-four-year-old government employee who lives in New York. *"One of the urologist's staff came out to the waiting room, and in front of everyone there, said, 'You have practically no sperm.' That attacked my foundations as a man."* Once Phil and his wife, Ann, a thirty-eight-year-old tennis pro, decided to try donor insemination, Phil says, *"I didn't feel so humiliated as when I first got the semen analysis results. Once the decision was made, it felt okay."*

Even though his family's blood line faced extinction, Phil had no problem accepting donor insemination. *"It all depends on how crucial it is to have a genetic link to the future,"* he says. *"Neither my sister nor I could have our own biological children, but I felt that a child was a child."*

Over a three-year period, Phil and Ann tried donor inseminations, with all the ups and downs of starting a new cycle of treatment over and over again. During that time, they took a break for six months while Ann took medication for endometriosis. Then their fertility specialist found that she had sperm antibodies in her mucus, and Phil began wearing condoms during sex. Meanwhile, they tried more donor inseminations without success. When they finally concluded that donor insemination would not work for them, they decided to stop trying to have a baby.

Donor insemination is readily accepted by many couples, but it can be stressful for them. How well you may feel depends on you and your spouse's individual personalities and attitudes. Studies of couples who attempt donor insemination have found them to be as well adjusted psychologically and sexually as "normal" fertile couples, whether or not they achieve a pregnancy. Most couples who have gone through donor insemination say that they are satisfied with their marriages and that the procedure even helped bring them closer together. Yet, for some couples the experience of uncorrected infertility adds such a strain to the relationship that their marriage may not survive.

Being conceived through donor insemination doesn't appear to affect the child's emotional development. The children conceived through donor insemination most often are well adjusted, do well in school, and don't seem to have identity crises. The majority of couples don't tell their children that they were conceived using a donor's sperm.

Social and Ethical Issues

Donor insemination raises many complex issues for the couple. You may wonder whether the decision to let friends and family know may some day cause your child to ask about his biological father. You also have to consider insensitive things family and friends might say to you and the child. Essentially, you have to address the question, "If we let people know now, are we likely to regret it later?"

Your decision to use donor insemination carries implications that reach far into the future. Some other questions you must consider: What if our child is born with a birth defect? Will we regret our decision? Can our marriage stand the strain?

There are no pat answers to such questions. Certainly, there are no answers applicable to everyone. Each couple must be able to explore these questions freely with each other, and answer them as best they can. If you are having difficulty, a professional counselor may be able to help.

Some people compare children born through donor insemination to children who were adopted. But the experience a couple goes through in conceiving a child, and the actual nine months of pregnancy with donor insemination offspring, is quite different than that of an adoptive couple, who don't experience the process of pregnancy. And if you adopt, you can't keep it a secret from family and friends, as you can with donor insemination.

Legal Issues

If you choose donor insemination, clearly, you want the maximum protection under the law for you and your child. Yet, only a few states require that donors be screened for disease, and twenty states have no laws at all regulating donor insemination.

The legal issue of paternity is much more clearly defined. Thirty states have laws covering paternity with donor insemination, and provide that the offspring is the legal child of the birth mother and her husband. Many laws specifically state that a man who provides his semen to a doctor for use in donor insemination isn't the child's legal father. In all states, the husband of the woman who delivers the child is presumed to be the child's legal father. This legally makes donor insemination a much more straightforward procedure than surrogate motherhood.

Egg Donation

Egg donation, analogous to sperm donation, is the process by which the doctor uses the husband's sperm to fertilize an egg donated by a woman other than his wife—usually through an assisted reproduction technique, such as IVF or one of its "cousins." In the case of IVF, the doctor transfers the fertilized egg into the wife's uterus, which has been primed with hormones to accept the developing embryo.

This technique is particularly useful for women who don't produce eggs, such as after premature menopause, or women who have had their ovaries removed or have had radiation therapy for cancer that destroyed their ovarian function. It also has become an alternative for women who want to avoid passing along a genetically defective trait in the wife's family, such as hemophilia.

More than 150,000 women in the United States can't bear children because of ovarian problems. Premature menopause has become more of a problem in recent years with many women deferring pregnancy until their thirties. In some cases, women with premature menopause can be treated hormonally and ovulate again. For those who don't ovulate, even after hormone treatments, fertility specialists can now offer the egg donation alternative.

Donor egg programs, once on the outer edge of infertility research, are growing in popularity and availability. The Cleveland Clinic fielded hundreds of phone calls after it advertised that it was opening a donor egg bank. Now the clinic has a pool of potential egg donors from healthy young women aged eighteen to thirty-five who have no known genetic or sexually transmitted diseases and have normal menstrual cycles, enabling doctors to match the physical characteristics of recipients with those of carefully selected donors. About a half-dozen IVF programs now have established similar egg donation programs.

The donor eggs can be retrieved by laparoscopy or by using a transvaginal ultrasound guided approach. While the egg donors take superovulatory hormones for about a week to increase their egg production, the recipient also receives hormones—first to synchronize her cycle with that of the donor and then to prepare her uterus for pregnancy. These hormones include estrogen, which can be taken orally or administered in patches that attach to the skin, and progesterone administered by pills, vaginal suppositories, or injections.

Fertilization of the donor eggs with the husband's sperm usually takes place in the IVF lab. As with IVF, up to four fertilized eggs may be transferred to increase the couple's chances of pregnancy. At present, only fresh donor eggs are used because unfertilized eggs are too fragile to withstand freezing. A couple's chances of pregnancy are about the same as if they were using the wife's own eggs.

Donor eggs can also be fertilized in the recipient woman's fallopian tubes via Gamete Intra Fallopian Transfer (GIFT). Also, fertilized eggs or zygotes have been transferred to a recipient's fallopian tubes via laparoscopy, known as Zygote Intra Fallopian Transfer (ZIFT).

Finding Egg Donors

The usual sources of donated eggs have included women undergoing an IVF or GIFT procedure who have an overabundance of eggs, the wife's sister, other relatives, or a woman having a tubal ligation.

Some egg donation programs accommodate only recipients who provide their own donors. Others rely on women who are having tubal ligations—during which eggs can be retrieved without additional surgery. Most egg donation programs offer donors from $500 to $1,200 for their time and inconvenience, which usually includes undergoing psychological screening, blood tests, and ultrasound exams, as well as superovulation and egg retrieval.

Embryo freezing allows the doctor to synchronize the donor and recipient cycles more easily. If the recipient's uterus isn't ready to receive the fertilized eggs, the donated eggs can be fertilized and then frozen and transferred at a more appropriate time. The extra eggs retrieved from IVF and GIFT cycles are now often fertilized and the embryos frozen for later use by the infertile couple, who may decide, after they have had their own successful treatment, to donate their embryos to another infertile couple.

In this era of new reproductive technology, if you are seeking an egg donor, you must know your state laws. For example, Louisiana law forbids payment for eggs or embryos recovered through IVF. Some states—Illinois, Florida, Louisiana—specifically forbid freezing embryos even if it's for clinical treatment and not for research purposes.

Emotional Issues

Most egg donation programs accept only married couples in good mental and physical health who have a stable marriage. You will undergo a psychological evaluation that usually includes a screening interview and psychological testing. If you provide your own donor, then the psychological evaluation looks at the possible effects on a child who grows up in a family where an aunt or a friend is the child's genetic mother.

Like sperm donation, egg donation from an anonymous donor offers you the possibility of concealing the fact of the egg donation from friends and relatives as well as the child. You should openly discuss with each other your feelings about what to tell others before undertaking egg donation, and then stick to your decision, revealing as much information as you wish in whatever way suits you best.

The Couple's Concerns

If you are seeking an egg donor, you probably have a long history of infertility and have tried a wide range of fertility treatments. You may choose egg donation over adoption or surrogate motherhood to give the wife the opportunity to become pregnant and deliver the baby.

There are no uniform standards for screening egg donors. Just as with sperm donors, you should be informed about various characteristics of the donor to determine how closely she matches the wife's characteristics, that she is in good health and has no known family history of genetically transmitted physical or mental illnesses. You may ask a donor for an AIDS antibody test before allowing her eggs to be fertilized with the husband's sperm. You should also consider whether you agree as a couple about egg donation and have the personal and financial resources to cope with the stresses of the treatment.

If you receive eggs from a known donor, you should have a consent form signed by the donor stipulating that she would never pursue any court action seeking access to any child resulting from the egg donation. If the egg donor is anonymous, as with sperm donation, neither the donor nor the recipient knows each other's identity. This probably provides the best protection for the child against the possibility of a custody dispute later on.

Egg Donors and Their Concerns

Egg donors, often recruited through announcements in the media, generally are younger, less affluent, and less well-educated than egg recipients. They may volunteer to donate eggs to help another couple have a child. Some egg donors also use the experience as a way of dealing with their own unresolved fertility issues; they previously may have had an induced abortion, which also is a reason why some women volunteer to become surrogate mothers.

The primary concern of most potential donors is whether you can provide a good home environment for a baby. Donors want assurance that the recipients of their eggs are physically healthy and psychologically well-adjusted, that their marriages are stable, and that the husband and wife are committed to being good, supportive parents.

Ethical Principles

Some people fear that compensating egg donors will lead to commercialization, and tempt women to sell their eggs, as is often the case with sperm donors. (Some sperm banks, however, don't pay donors for their samples.) Others, including the Catholic Church, contend that egg donation and sperm donation violate the sanctity of marriage by bringing a third party into the conjugal relationship.

A great deal of debate has arisen about third-party collaboration in reproduction. The ethical and legal ramifications become murky when the collaboration breaks down and the donor wants to claim "rights" to the child. There's more confusion regarding egg donation than sperm donation, although the two situations are analogous and future laws will probably specify that an egg donor, like a sperm donor, is not the legal parent of any offspring conceived.

Embryo Transplant

Another donor technique involves using a husband's sperm to artificially inseminate a woman other than his wife. The resulting embryo is then flushed out of the other woman's uterus and placed into his wife's uterus. The couple may pay a fee of up to $5,000 to the surrogate for her part in conceiving and nurturing the early development of the embryo. Recruits for embryo donors are carefully screened for genetic diseases and emotional problems.

The embryo transplant technique can only be used when the woman has a uterus and therefore can carry a fetus. It enables a woman with ovarian failure or one who might risk passing on a genetic disease to be the birth mother, although not the genetic mother, of her child.

In this situation, the woman who will donate the embryo receives inseminated sperm from the recipient's husband. Five days after fertilization, the doctor flushes the embryo out of the pregnant donor's uterus and transfers it to the uterus of the infertile wife to carry to birth, if the embryo implants successfully.

If the husband is also infertile, the couple can use donor sperm to inseminate the donor egg. In this case, neither partner of the infertile couple contributes genes, since both the sperm and egg come from donors. But the wife carries and gives birth to the child, and her husband is the legal father, so they do not have to adopt the child, as in the case of surrogate motherhood.

One of the keys to embryo transplantation is synchronizing the recipient woman's menstrual cycle with the donor's cycle by using hormone treatments. The development of the wife's endometrium must be synchronized with the embryo's stage of development. If the endometrium isn't ready, the embryo won't implant.

Some embryo transplant programs rely on "superovulated" women as their egg donors. Others use fertile volunteers who receive compensation each cycle to cover their own expense and inconvenience. The procedure carries the potential risks of an infection and an ectopic pregnancy, but these risks are small. The donor's risk of exposure to a sexually transmitted infection from the recipient's husband is minimized or eliminated with proper medical screening and testing of the involved parties beforehand.

Potential Legal Problems

In most states, "baby bartering" is illegal, and might be interpreted to include paid egg donors who bear a child for someone else. Anti-slavery laws also prohibit the buying or selling of people, including newborns. Sixteen states now prohibit payment for embryos.

You should also be concerned about the donor's behavior both before and during the conception cycle. Specifically, the donor should agree to refrain from sex, and not use any drugs or consume alcohol during the treatment cycle. You should obtain a signed consent agreement with the donor stating these conditions, although like any contract, simply signing an agreement doesn't always guarantee that the parties involved will live up to it.

Egg Freezing

Egg freezing unquestionably presents fewer legal, moral, and ethical problems than freezing, and then transferring, embryos. It holds potential for young women going through early menopause or women prone to other ovarian disorders that severely impair their fertility. Fertility researchers have encountered numerous technical problems associated with freezing and thawing eggs, however.

One freezing method holds the egg in suspended animation by slowing down its metabolism. But during the cooling down process, ice crystals tend to form on the membrane surrounding the egg. These crystals can pierce and disrupt the egg's membranes so that when the egg is thawed it may not be viable. Some researchers also worry that the trauma of freezing and thawing may genetically damage eggs.

Sperm, much smaller than eggs, are less prone to ice

crystal formation, and have survival rates of about 40 percent after freezing and thawing. The survival rate of thawed frozen eggs is 15 percent, at best. So far, a dozen or more children have been born from thawed frozen eggs.

Another freezing method, which quickly moves an egg into an antifreeze-like chemical, leads to few or no ice crystals. But this experimental technique is all-or-nothing: either the egg survives the thawing, or it dies.

An egg, like a sperm, is a single cell, not a human being or even a potential person yet. But some people have argued against embryo freezing because they believe life begins precisely when sperm meets egg. Freezing eggs for future use would avoid this ethical problem. If researchers can get more eggs to survive freezing and thawing, then more couples might opt for egg freezing over embryo freezing.

Host Uterus

The host uterus enables you to have your own genetic offspring even though the wife may be unable to carry a child to term. Her eggs can be fertilized by her husband's sperm in the IVF laboratory and the embryo transferred into another woman's uterus, where it is carried until birth.

This may provide a solution for women without a uterus, those who can't risk pregnancy because of a health problem, and those with conditions that would put a fetus at severe risk, such as Rh incompatibility with a mother who has high levels of anti-Rh antibodies.

The Host Uterus Contract

At the outset, you sign a contract with a carefully screened woman to be the life-support system for your growing embryo. Since this other woman is carrying the husband's and wife's baby, there is a reduced risk of her refusing to hand the child over to the true biologic parents—one of the dangers of surrogate motherhood. Even though you are the genetic parents, you will likely have to adopt the baby legally from the woman who carries and delivers it. In most states, the woman who gives birth is legally presumed to be the child's mother and, if she is married, her husband is considered the child's legal father.

The "host uterus" gives a woman who has ovaries but is incapable of carrying her own baby a chance to have a child that is genetically her own and her husband's by having another woman carry the pregnancy. This differs from surrogate motherhood, in which the wife is neither the genetic nor the birth mother.

The host uterus concept carries fewer ethical and legal problems than surrogate motherhood, where the woman who is inseminated by the husband's sperm contributes half of the genes to the baby, which she then carries to birth. While the host may form an emotional bond with the baby she has carried for nine months, she is likely to feel less of a loss than a surrogate mother, who has to give up her own genetic baby for adoption to the infertile couple.

Naturally, any woman who carries a baby to term for you is likely to develop a close relationship with the baby. A woman who provides a host uterus, and changes her mind and wants to keep the child, could argue that her contribution was just as vital to the child's development, and birth, as you and your mate's sperm and egg. The contract between you and the woman providing the host uterus should address this issue. But if either party broke the contract, you probably would be embroiled in legal confusion.

A woman offering to carry another couple's pregnancy

may be placing herself at physical and psychological risk. It's important for you that she receive counseling to ensure that she fully understands the risks and voluntarily consents. This will help avoid the potential of her being exploited by others.

With the uncertain legal situation across the country regarding these new varieties of third-party reproduction, including the host uterus technique, you should think carefully about this type of "frontier" baby and seek professional and legal counseling before entering into a relationship with a woman who is willing to serve as a host uterus or surrogate mother.

Surrogate Motherhood

One of the most controversial areas of the new reproductive technology is surrogate motherhood. Dozens of brokers across the country have established surrogate counseling centers offering infertile couples a "womb for rent." Despite the highly publicized Baby M case, most surrogate motherhood arrangements go smoothly when the parties involved take the proper precautions and have the surrogate mother thoroughly evaluated.

A surrogate mother is inseminated with the sperm of a man whose wife can't conceive or carry a child to term. Once the baby is born, the surrogate allows the biological father and his infertile wife to adopt the baby.

Who Are the Candidates?

Surrogate motherhood is usually reserved for rare circumstances. For some couples, it represents the last hope of having a child who's genetically related to at least one spouse. In particular, surrogate motherhood may be suitable for women who don't produce eggs, whose eggs aren't fertilized by their husband's healthy sperm because of an egg problem, who are afraid of passing on a genetic defect, who have been advised not to get pregnant because of a medical condition, or who have had a hysterectomy.

How to Find a Surrogate

You can explore various avenues to find an appropriate surrogate. One way is to ask family members or friends if they are willing to become a surrogate. Remember the case of the mother who carried a triplet pregnancy conceived via IVF with her daughter's eggs and her son-in-law's sperm. She ended up giving birth to her own grandchildren! Some couples advertise in the newspaper for surrogates; others go to their fertility expert or a lawyer or a center that specializes in finding surrogates.

Surrogate agencies look for physically and psychologically healthy women who would like to serve as a surrogate for an infertile couple. These agencies put the potential surrogate through a battery of psychological and medical tests, match her with a prospective couple, negotiate a contract, acquire informed, legal consent of the surrogate and the infertile couple, and work with the doctors who will perform the insemination.

Who Becomes a Surrogate?

A typical surrogate mother is twenty-eight years old, married with two children, has a high school education, and a full-time job. These women usually become surrogates because they empathize with an infertile couple and want to help them have a child. Being a surrogate may provide some women with a sense of accomplishment. Some do it because they had a previous abortion and believe that creating a child for someone else may help them resolve their own feelings. Others may be motivated by financial considerations, since the surrogate may receive $10,000 to $25,000 for her involvement. Yet, most women decide to become surrogates for altruistic reasons.

Meeting the Surrogate

Whether you meet the surrogate depends on your individual choice. Some couples feel that keeping the surrogate anonymous or distant puts them in a better frame of mind to develop a strong relationship with the newborn, with less likelihood of interference by the surrogate. They feel better about communicating with the surrogate only through their doctor, lawyer, or surrogate center. Others want to have frequent contact with the surrogate before, during, and after the pregnancy and birth. If the surrogate is a friend or family member, you already have a very close relationship with her.

You should ascertain whether the potential surrogate can cope with carrying the baby and giving it up. Even if she does have her family's and friends' support, the surrogate should have counseling arranged for her after the baby is born (as well as before she becomes a surrogate and during the pregnancy). Once they have given the baby to the adoptive couple, most surrogates say they feel fulfilled and more satisfied about themselves.

Both the surrogate and the adoptive couple usually say that they perceive the child as the couple's, not the surrogate's. But this isn't always the case, and various disputes have arisen over who should be the legal guardians of the child born through surrogate motherhood.

The Surrogate Motherhood Contract

The rights of the genetic father, his infertile wife, the surrogate, and the surrogate's husband should be agreed-upon in writing beforehand.

The clear, detailed surrogacy agreement should specify that the child will become the legitimate, adopted child of the infertile couple, the intended parents. Despite this safeguard, late changes of mind occasionally occur. Some legal experts have suggested that after the child is born, the surrogate should be given a limited grace period, similar to those provided in many adoption laws, in which she can give notice that she has changed her mind. If there is a dispute between the surrogate and the intended parents, then legal proceedings will probably determine who keeps the child. That decision should be guided by the child's best interests.

Legal Issues

The highly publicized Baby M case set the legal precedent in New Jersey. Other states may follow suit or decide the issue on their own. Most state laws view a woman who bears a child as the mother, and the baby born by a surrogate must be given up willingly by the surrogate mother (and her husband, if she is married) for adoption to the infertile couple, even though the infertile woman's husband is the true biological father.

Other laws that have been applied to surrogate motherhood cases include those concerning artificial insemination, private adoption, family laws, step-parent laws, even anti-slavery laws. It's now possible for couples to skirt some state laws by choosing a surrogate from a state with a more favorable legal climate.

The legal waters of surrogate motherhood will continue

to be murky. More than half the states in the country are considering legislation to legalize, regulate, or ban surrogate motherhood. Among the pending laws, some states would ban surrogacy altogether, while others would ban only paid surrogacy—allowing unpaid surrogacy, but regulating the practice.

When problems arise, the courts will have to decide upon the appropriateness of the various aspects of the surrogacy contract. The competing rights of the biological father (the sperm provider) and the biological mother (the surrogate), their spouses, and the child must be sorted out. Surrogate motherhood court cases have had mixed results, some ruling in favor of the surrogate, others for the biological father and his wife.

Counseling the surrogate mother beforehand may help to avoid subsequent custody disputes. Surrogate screening should provide the surrogate with information about her own health status and the risks of surrogacy. The counseling should ensure that both the surrogate mother and the intended parents know what they are getting into. The directors of surrogate motherhood centers are attempting to develop some standards, including criteria for the screening and testing of couples and surrogates.

Surrogate Publicity

In the United States about a hundred babies are born to surrogate mothers each year. Although the publicity surrounding the Baby M decision has caused some couples to reconsider surrogate motherhood, others still consider it their best option. There was a similar heated reaction—and publicity—years ago about donating sperm. Despite the adverse publicity surrounding surrogate motherhood, infertile couples are still calling surrogacy centers. There is also a growing underground market aimed at infertile couples wishing to hire surrogate mothers.

There remain many questions and issues—legal, ethical, medical, religious—that need clarification. Surrogate motherhood and other reproductive technologies invite doctors, lawyers, and legislators to intrude on the private, intimate experience of conception and birth. Advocates of women's rights have had to confront whether the cost of gaining this fertility option may cause women to lose reproductive control. Some fear that motherhood will be denigrated by separating a woman's genetic and birth functions, and that this may make it more difficult for a woman to retain control over her body.

Many are concerned about the possibility that a poor woman might be coerced into carrying a rich man's child. They think commercial arrangements reduce surrogates to paid baby-carriers. Yet, if sperm donors are paid and surrogates aren't, this might be considered another example of women doing more work for less money than men.

Surrogate motherhood is a dramatic example of how medical technology has outrun society's established definitions and laws. We currently have a crazy quilt of state laws concerning who controls decisions about the family, how to deal with surrogates who have second thoughts, and what is best for the children produced by these technologies. New hybrid family relationships, often the last hope of infertile couples, deserve your careful consideration, but also require close scrutiny.

Questions to Ask Your Doctor About Artificial Insemination by Donor

How do you screen potential semen donors? (Such screening should include tests for the AIDS virus, hepatitis

virus, and other sexually transmitted diseases and genetic disorders.)

What choice of sperm banks do we have? Are the sperm
banks members of the American Association of Tissue
Banks?

How many motile sperm does the donor sample contain?

What are our chances of a pregnancy, given our fertility
problems?

How many attempts do you expect it will take us to
achieve a pregnancy?

Do you use frozen or fresh semen? (Accept only frozen
semen from a donor that has been tested for the AIDS
virus or antibodies to the AIDS virus and the semen
quarantined for at least six months until the donor has
been retested.)

How much will the donor semen cost us?

Will we be able to track down the identity of the sperm
donor if necessary for medical reasons?

What is the medical and genetic history of the donor?

What is the law in our state regarding donor insemination?

Questions to Ask Your Doctor
About Egg Donation

Can you provide us with donor eggs, or refer us to an IVF
program that can?

Can we bring in our own egg donor?

How will the donor be screened?

What hormones will I (the wife) have to take, and how will they be administered?

What are our chances of achieving a pregnancy, given our particular fertility problems?

Does our state have any laws prohibiting egg donation?

How much will we have to pay for donor eggs?

Do you have a contract for us to sign with the egg donor?

Questions to Ask Your Doctor About Embryo Transplant, Host Uterus, or Surrogate Motherhood

Are we good candidates for this procedure?

Will you perform this procedure or refer us to a specialist who will?

How do you recruit potential donors or surrogates? How are they screened?

What is the donor's or surrogate's fee?

What are the laws in our state regarding this procedure?

Do you have a contract for us and the donor or surrogate to sign?

12

COPING WITH INFERTILITY, AND ALTERNATIVES TO FURTHER TREATMENT

"I really believed that if I was a good person and took care of myself, didn't abuse drugs, wasn't too fat or too thin, then my body would work the way it was supposed to. I was truly surprised when I didn't get pregnant," says Robin, a twenty-nine-year-old biologist.

Most infertile couples believe that if they understand the causes of their fertility problem, dedicate themselves to treating it, and persevere in their pursuit of pregnancy, they will eventually have a baby. Unfortunately, this isn't always true. Frequently, there are factors beyond your or your fertility doctor's control that determine the outcome of fertility treatments. When things don't work out, your frustrations and fears of not having a child can become intensified.

You will have to cope with the emotional impact of infertility before, during, and after your treatment. If you are fortunate enough to have a baby, dealing with the emotional crises of infertility may be easier than if you have made heroic efforts but failed to produce a child.

If fertility treatments do not succeed, you have to be able to work through your feelings, and either choose to end fertility treatment and accept life without a child, or pursue other options, such as adoption. At some point, you must be able to resolve the emotional issues involved so that your unfulfilled struggle to have a baby will not remain your life's main focus.

Infertility and Your Emotions

The emotional challenges of infertility change during the different phases of recognition, evaluation, treatment, and resolution of your problem. Many factors may influence your emotional responses, including the causes of your infertility, the types of treatment you have been receiving, how long you have been dealing with infertility, and how well you and your spouse cope with the usual stresses of life.

You may feel anxious before and during your initial interview with a fertility specialist and whenever the specialist makes a specific diagnosis of your fertility problem. This is especially true for the partner who may feel guilty or angry about being identified as the source of the problem. If both you and your mate contribute to your fertility problem, as is often the case, then one won't be as quick to take blame for causing the infertility.

Don't be surprised if you feel emotionally unsettled at the beginning of your fertility evaluation. The workup is foreign and intrusive, and may be uncomfortable both physically and emotionally. During your treatment, you will likely become more accustomed to the rigors of therapy. But if the treatment drags on, you may find that your stress level increases as you become increasingly aware of the possibility that your treatment may not be successful.

Losing Control

Pam, aged twenty-eight, and her husband Jeff, aged thirty-four, went to see a fertility specialist after three years of trying unsuccessfully to have a baby. Her ovulation monitoring showed an ovulation and luteal phase defect, which was treated with hormones. After several months, she and Jeff, who had a low sperm count and poor sperm morphology, also tried artificial insemination, but without success.

Then Pam got a new job for a pharmaceutical company, and they stopped treatment for several months while she was traveling out of town. "It was a great career opportunity, but I had to quit after six months because it was so stressful. Being on the road, visiting doctors' offices full of pregnant women—all this grief that I had been pushing down came up again."

Although she's a go-getter and has worked all of her life, Pam is trying to slow down and not put so much pressure on herself. "When I got to the point where I felt like I was losing control, it scared me. I felt like a lost soul, as if I had died and was just floating." Through counseling, she came to realize that "the worst thing was that I kept saying to myself, 'Be thankful you have a house, your health, a good husband.' I kept belittling my infertility, trying to convince myself that it wasn't as bad as I thought. But it's all right to feel bad. It's normal to feel that way."

One of the most important emotional issues of fertility treatment is loss of control. You may often feel as if you have lost control over your bodies and your lives. You may never before have been confronted with a problem that not only challenges your concept of your own health and integrity, but also makes you dependent on your doctor and the medical care system.

You may sleep, drink, and think infertility all day long, from the minute the wife wakes up to take her basal body temperature until the husband and wife go to bed knowing that "tonight's the night" to make love. The constant intrusion into your lives of fertility drugs that require repeated ultrasound scans, blood tests, and examinations also puts daily pressure on your relationship.

In addition, infertility can strike at the very core of your identities. Children were supposed to be a part of life's plan. Marriage and family are a universal dream. But the dream may seem more like a nightmare to the infertile couple who hasn't been able to conceive.

Regaining Control

One way you can regain control is to understand your particular fertility problem. You need detailed information about the infertility workup, reasonable treatment options, and your chances of success. Only then can you make well-informed decisions regarding the course of your treatment.

Both partners should think about and discuss the extent to which they want to pursue fertility treatment. How far are you willing to go in achieving a pregnancy, knowing that no treatment is guaranteed to be successful? Would you consider adoption, and if so, how quickly? How do you feel about the prospect of living without your own biologic child, or any child at all?

Once the evaluation begins, the fertility team should provide you with as much information as you need to make these decisions. If you fail to achieve a pregnancy or carry a pregnancy, the doctor and his staff should also help you understand and accept what has happened. This means spending adequate time with you to talk about what you have gone through and its impact, and making himself available to answer any questions that you may have.

Each time a treatment fails, you may experience a period of mourning, which includes sadness accompanied by grief, anger, and jealousy. After many failed treatment cycles, you may experience numbness and disbelief, often replaced by a period of questioning, as you look for more answers, more treatments. Because of the significant recent advances in infertility treatment, most infertile couples believe that fertility specialists can work wonders. But medical science doesn't have the solution to every fertility problem. Of all couples who experience infertility, about 50 percent will eventually have their own biological child.

Emotions Through Assisted Reproduction

Stuart, a forty-year-old printer and his computer programmer wife, Jane, thirty-two, are now going for their second IVF attempt to try to compensate for his very low sperm count. "I feel like I'm depriving her of the experience of being pregnant," he says. "We've thought about adoption, but we want to keep trying IVF. We're lucky we don't have to worry about the money.

"Sometimes, it's hard to deal with all the emotions. We stopped visiting with old friends who had a child because it was just too painful for us to see them," Stuart says. "It's also hard for us to see people playing with their children in the park, or even just walking with them on the street."

Of all fertility treatments, in vitro fertilization (IVF) and other assisted reproductive techniques tend to be the most intense emotional experiences for husbands and wives. Almost all couples fear these highly involved procedures, not only for what they have to go through, but also because they are afraid that they will fail. They know this may be their last chance to achieve a pregnancy.

Despite the low probability of success, most couples are overly optimistic about the likelihood of achieving a pregnancy via IVF. Although they may intellectually acknowledge that they have less than a 20 percent chance of success, most couples undergoing IVF believe that they will be the ones to beat the odds. In some ways, they may need to have these positive beliefs in order to endure the treatment.

If the treatment fails, your immediate reaction may include depression and anger. But many couples work through these emotions, becoming more optimistic again and ready to try another cycle. IVF patients seem to be the self-selected infertility "survivors," according to Dr. William Keye, chief of reproductive endocrinology and infertility at the University of Utah in Salt Lake City. They seem to have the emotional, physical, and financial resources to tolerate the treatment procedures and keep trying.

Following unsuccessful treatment cycles, many wives feel a period of intense anguish, accompanied by tears and a wish to be alone. They feel sad, empty, hopeless. Husbands report similar feelings, although they may demonstrate them less graphically.

The husband often feels separated from his wife during the treatment process. His wife may be the one most involved in treatment, even if the diagnosis is male factor infertility. He can be more involved by participating in her treatment: giving his wife her hormone injections, and going with her for blood tests and ultrasound scans. This enhances his sense of involvement, and he may be better able to explore his feelings if the treatment fails. His presence and support also help his wife get through the treatment process.

Some infertile couples become closer as they prepare for assisted reproduction. They may support and nurture each other through the arduous treatment, sharing what the procedure means to them and what they will do if they fail to conceive. Most IVF teams provide counseling before as well as during an IVF cycle. You should be forewarned about stressful events in the cycle, such as those two weeks after embryo transfer while you wait to hear the results of the pregnancy test.

Your fertility specialist and his or her team usually bring up the possibility of your not having your own child, and should encourage you to think about alternatives. The team may discuss adoption as an option, including information and contacts at agencies, or not having children at all. Because an assisted reproduction procedure is often the last treatment option, if you fail to achieve a pregnancy the team's counselor may be able to help you accept your loss and talk about your feelings and future options.

Emotions Through a Miscarriage

Abby had had several miscarriages before she saw a fertility doctor, who found that she wasn't ovulating regularly and wasn't producing enough progesterone after ovulation to support a pregnancy. He treated the thirty-three-year-old financial analyst with clomiphene and Pergonal to induce ovulation and supplemental progesterone in the luteal phase of the cycle. "Just when I got to the point when I couldn't take the hormone treatments any more, that's when something came through for me," Abby says. "I ran into a friend who had heard that I had miscarried, and she told me she had been through the same thing last year, and now was pregnant. She told me it was a matter of keeping up the treatments. I'm glad I didn't give up."

Women who have miscarried are caught in an emotional gray area between the ongoing frustration of infertility and the pain of losing an unborn child. Many people believe that a miscarriage isn't as important as the death of a newborn or older child. But the death of an unborn child has a similar emotional impact on the couple who experiences the loss. Grieving and mourning are the normal psychological reactions to any loss. If you minimize or deny these emotions, it may be harder for you to come to terms with your experience and eventually resolve your feelings about the miscarriage.

Miscarriage can throw a couple's emotions into turmoil. Individuals typically feel sad, depressed, angry, or even helpless and hopeless. For some, the fear of yet another disaster can turn off the sex drive, while others increase their sexual contact in their desire for another pregnancy.

Recognizing the intense emotional pain an infertile couple goes through after a miscarriage, some hospitals have changed their attitudes about how best to help the couple. In the past, the couple would have been automatically "protected" from seeing their unborn child. Now, some hospitals provide pictures or a lock of hair as something tangible for the infertile couple to take with them. Many couples have burials or memorial services for the unborn child.

Seeing the miscarried fetus helps many people to substantiate the reality of their loss, which in turn helps them grieve for the lost child, according to Sister Jane Marie Lamb, founder of Source of Help in Airing and Resolving Experiences (SHARE), a support group for couples who have experienced miscarriage, with two hundred chapters nationwide.

Infertility: Like (and Not Like) a Death in the Family

In many ways, infertility is like a chronic illness that uses up a great deal of the couple's resources, demanding the expenditure of time, money, and physical and psychological energy. Even when you achieve a pregnancy and have a child, you may still feel that you are infertile. (This often arises when you attempt another pregnancy.) The infertility has been such a major component of your lives that it is not easily forgotten.

Infertility may be felt as an invisible stigma: the emotional scars are usually more significant than the physical manifestations of infertility. Although a childless marriage is obvious to your family and friends, you may choose not to reveal exactly why you haven't had children. But you can never escape your own knowledge of the facts.

When someone dies, the death usually brings family and friends together to grieve the loss. In contrast, infertility leads to a very private form of grief. There is no service each month when the woman starts her period. No one sends cards or flowers. Family and friends often feel uncomfortable and may be reluctant to broach the subject, and as a result, you often grieve without the same type of support that sustains the family grieving a death.

Infertility and Stress

Through two years of marriage, Helen and Arnie had failed to achieve a pregnancy due to infrequent ovulation, manifested by her irregular menstrual periods. Helen, a thirty-seven-year-old sculptor, feels her infertility as a private, personal loss. "I have a sense of failing my husband because I'm the one with the fertility problem," says Helen. "I was in the 'Y' exercising when I saw a woman breastfeeding. Her baby was making loud sucking noises. I had to get out, get away from that very graphic, sensual sound. I cried in the locker room, thinking that I would never feel a baby at my breast."

Trying to live with infertility while still attempting to become pregnant can put you on an emotional roller coaster. Psychotherapists who specialize in grief say that it's emotionally easier finally to lay someone to rest after a death than it is to grieve and simultaneously maintain hope, as most infertile couples do month after month. At some point, if you remain infertile despite the best treatments available, you have to learn how to let go of the baby you never had.

The frequent visits to the doctor's office, daily temperature charts, and sex on schedule can tax any couple. The costs and time involved can be emotionally and financially draining. Getting time off from work and making excuses to your employers and family may add to your burden. Besides the daily stresses and physical demands of medical treatment, infertile couples must adjust emotionally to their constantly thwarted hope for a child. The emotional frustration you feel isn't necessarily accompanied by depression or physical symptoms, but it's there nonetheless.

Minimizing Stress

"Sometimes it feels as if all the burden falls on me. I'm the one who goes to the doctor to get tested, who had the surgery, and who drives forty miles each night to see a nurse friend for hormone injections during a treatment cycle," says Helen. During her last cycle, Helen didn't have to carry the burden alone. "Arnie charted my temperature, he ran the LH urine kits to help time the insemination, and he called the doctor's office for the pregnancy test result, which unfortunately was negative."

"The most important thing has been recognizing the need to keep living our lives," Helen says. Even though it means they will lose a few cycles of treatment, she and Arnie, a thirty-eight-year-old television producer, are going on vacation for six weeks. "You set yourself up for a fall if the only thing that's important is achieving a pregnancy," she says. "A lot of things in my life are exciting, including my marriage. If we don't have a child, then we will still have a great marriage. There are lots of friends' and relatives' children to love, or we may consider adoption."

Arnie adds, "I think it's important not to drive yourself crazy trying everything under the sun. Also, you have to either support each other or get support from someone else."

The couple involved in the evaluation and treatment of infertility can help support each other through the process. The husband can record his wife's temperature on a BBT chart, learn how to give his wife hormone injections, or be with her during inseminations. His participation helps his wife avoid feeling alone and isolated.

You should arrange to have someone available who can help answer your questions, show sensitivity to your feelings, and address your "lack of control" during fertility treatment. Some couples express a need to know if their thoughts and feelings about infertility are normal, and want to share their questions and fears with other couples. The husband or wife may also want to talk to someone other than each other. For these couples, either a counselor on the fertility specialist's staff or an infertility self-help group, such as those under the umbrella of Resolve, may help fill these needs.

Men and Women and How They Cope

Clara and her husband Carl each had children in previous marriages, but have been unable to have a child together. Clara, aged forty-two, the owner of a bake shop, had several miscarriages before visiting a fertility specialist. The doctor diagnosed an ovulatory problem and, after considering her age, treated her with Pergonal. After three treatment cycles without pregnancy, Clara and Carl, a thirty-nine-year-old plumber, have decided to take a break from treatment for a few months. "I really got tired of being poked and prodded," she says. "I feel drained after three tries and no success."

Clara has told Carl that "sometimes I want a baby so bad I can't stand it," she says. "But it's hard for me to get him to talk about our

*therapy. The most I can get out of him is, 'Don't worry. If we don't
have children, it's okay.'"*

Men and women tend to react differently to their infertility. A man's infertility may affect his sense of self-esteem
and self-image, his feelings of adequacy and masculinity.
He may feel that he has a damaged body, that he is biologically incompetent to carry on the species. Women tend to
focus more on being pregnant and giving birth; men want
their bloodline carried on.

It's probably easier for a man to block out or minimize
some of his feelings because he doesn't have to go through
a monthly menstrual cycle and doesn't have to feel all the
changes in his body. Part of the difference in this response
also relates to the fact that many men have been educated
to keep a stiff upper lip, to hold their feelings inside.

Also, the husband doesn't feel all the physical and psychological changes that accompany pregnancy. Men may
feel sad and disappointed about not achieving a pregnancy
or losing one through miscarriage, but they don't experience it in the same way as their wives.

Some infertile men compensate by treating themselves
as their only child, getting intensely involved in activities
such as body building, health foods, and macho sexuality.
Some have casual extramarital affairs, according to Emory
University psychologist Dr. John Snarey. Others become
more socially involved in such child-rearing activities as
leading a youth group, teaching Sunday school, or coaching a Little League team. Most infertile men deal with their
inability to father children by lavishing parent-like devotion on their homes, pets, gardens, or cars, often going so
far as to refer to them as "my baby."

Auburn University psychologist Dr. Annette Stanton
observes that women generally seem to believe that infer-

tility can harm more areas of their lives than men do. Women who remain infertile often say that they originally had intended to make motherhood their primary occupation, but subsequently returned to school or devoted more energy to their careers as a result of infertility.

If the "motherhood mandate" remains intact, women may believe that they are somehow inadequate as women if they can't have children, and may feel bad about themselves because of their infertility. Perhaps men simply are less willing to admit to negative emotions, or infertility may on average be more distressing for women than for men.

Each partner copes with the stresses of infertility by using those mechanisms that have been honed in the past by life's other traumas and crises. It's important that you listen to each other and understand your differences. Too often, partners blame one another or take their anger out on their spouse. A couple should be able to approach their fertility problem as a team, not as adversaries.

The Dreaded Bed

The impact of infertility inevitably reaches the infertile couple's deepest intimacy. One or both partners may feel less attracted to the other. With the initial reactions of shock, grief, anger, denial, and depression, the sex drive diminishes. When this happens, sex becomes a chore associated with attempts to get pregnant rather than the spontaneous expression of love that was experienced previously.

The feeling of inadequacy can extend to other areas, including the husband's and/or wife's job performance and relationships with others. Infertile men and women who experience sexual dissatisfaction and who already have low self-esteem are most vulnerable to emotional problems such as persisting anxiety and depression that spread to other parts of their lives. The "go-getter" types may also feel bad about themselves because they thought everything was possible if they worked hard enough. Having a baby may be the first time they have experienced "failure," finding that no matter how diligently they try, there are forces at work beyond their control.

Family and Friends

Robin, twenty-nine, and her husband Leon, thirty-nine, went to a specialist after one year of a barren marriage. The routine fertility workup found that Robin had endometriosis. After Robin had undergone surgery and medical treatment to remove her endometriosis, Robin and Leon wrote letters to their parents and siblings explaining their infertility problems. "We couldn't keep saying that Robin needed minor surgery. We had to give them some explanation," says Leon, the manager of a sportswear outlet. "We thought we had to clue them in."

"Once they knew what we were going through, they were sympathetic, but I don't believe they really understood," says Robin. "My sister Beth has three children, the third one conceived when she wasn't trying to become pregnant. We had just been through a GIFT procedure and found out I didn't get pregnant. Beth delayed telling us about her third pregnancy because she knew it would be difficult for us. As the years have passed, our families know we've come to accept our infertility, and they, too, have become more comfortable with that."

Family and friends often unintentionally add to your sense of inadequacy or isolation. You may be reluctant to talk about or even reveal your problem, not just out of shame, but because others might not take your situation seriously and may offer false reassurances or bad advice.

You have to realize that your family and close friends may not know exactly how to support you when it comes to dealing with infertility, and they may make insensitive and unhelpful remarks. That's not to say that family and friends don't want to help, or that they don't care or aren't interested in you. It may mean that they are uninformed about infertility and they don't know how to help, or that their own feelings about your infertility (denial and anxiety) interfere with their ability to help. It may be too painful for them to face the pain of infertility in someone they love.

Family, friends, and even strangers may respond inappropriately due, in part, to the stress they feel being around someone else who is suffering. Your potential supporters may also feel angry about the way infertility has disrupted their usual ways of relating to you. Even when your friends know what they want to say, they may feel awkward saying it.

So sharing your infertility with family and close friends can yield mixed results. They may give you support, but your interactions may still be awkward and constrained. Once you feel you are ready and have gotten over the initial shock of infertility, you have to figure out whom to tell and what to tell them.

You can help your family and friends be more supportive. Talk to them openly about how you feel and what you are going through. Tell them what you need from them. Saying, "Be supportive" may not be clear enough. You may need to define this better, by saying, for example, "Be aware of sensitive topics of conversation, like baby showers" or "Let me cry when I'm upset."

Common Myths About Infertility

"Before learning that we were infertile, we enjoyed getting together with my family for Mother's Day and attending church," says Robin.

> *"In my parents' church on Mother's Day, the mothers in the congregation wear corsages and the sermon is usually related to motherhood. One year, the message I received from the sermon was that you're worthless unless you're a mother. I remember looking around the congregation for other women not wearing corsages and wondering how they were feeling. Leon and I then decided that we preferred not to attend church on Mother's Day. That was our way of coping."*

When they find out that you have a fertility problem, many people, even loved ones, may blithely toss off a comment or crude remark that has no factual basis. They may be covering up their own discomfort in dealing with infertility, or they may not know any better. You may have to educate them about the common myths of infertility.

Give them specific feedback, such as, "I feel frustrated when you say I should just relax and I'll get pregnant." Ask them not to judge your emotions by saying things like, "You ought to feel better by now" or "It's just Nature's way." Don't be afraid to tell others what you *don't* need from them or what *isn't* helpful.

Here are some of the common infertility myths you may hear from others, and why they are false:

- "Infertility is all in your head." Infertility is due to disorders of the reproductive system, and while emotions can affect all body functions, one or more physical causes are identified in 95 percent or more of infertile couples.

- "You're thinking about it too much. Why don't you go on a vacation." Getting away from it all is important for everyone, but while it may soothe your jangled nerves, it won't help you treat a physiologic or anatomic disorder.

- "Go to another doctor and you're sure to get pregnant." A second opinion may be a good idea, especially if both partners have not had appropriate fertility workups or if communicating with your doctor is a problem. But just switching doctors doesn't guarantee success.

- "If you work at it and want it enough, you'll get pregnant." Unlike many other parts of your lives, infertility may be beyond your control. While new methods of diagnosing and treating infertility have improved most couples' chances of having a baby, there's no guarantee, and some problems remain unsolvable.

- "Just pray and have faith." Believing in your treatment can help you get through often demanding fertility procedures and help you maintain a positive outlook, even when all hope seems lost. But sheer will and blind faith won't overcome a physical problem, such as blocked tubes.

- "There are plenty of children for adoption." While this may be true for black and hispanic couples, there are fewer white children being put up for adoption relative to the number of white couples who want to adopt children. Your chances of adopting a newborn baby are no better than the chances of achieving a pregnancy through IVF or other assisted reproductive techniques.

- "Adopt a child, and you'll get pregnant." Besides being increasingly difficult to adopt these days, those couples who do adopt later become pregnant in only about 5 percent of cases, a similar percentage to those who don't adopt and who become pregnant.

Statements like these indicate a certain amount of ignorance about infertility, and are counterproductive. To help dispel these myths, ask your family and friends what they experience as they try to be supportive. Do they feel sad, anxious, helpless? What is it like for the friend or relative?

You can educate those close to you about what it's like to go through infertility, the emotional roller coaster, the demands on your time and money. Tell them not to be afraid of hurting your feelings by asking questions. Answering questions and telling your story may be painful, but in the process your relationship may grow stronger.

Pay attention to what you feel when a friend or sister tells you she is pregnant. Some feelings like jealousy and resentment are hard to accept. You may be feeling that you deserve a child more than she does, or that, if you had children, you would be a better parent. Admitting those feelings even to yourself may be hard to do. You may feel at a loss of what to say. Work together, learn how to deal with each other. Explain which situations are painful, and avoid them or at least be aware of them. Holiday times, when the family all gathers together to exchange gifts, may be among the most difficult.

Infertility Support Groups

"I was sleeping a lot, I felt on edge," says Clara. "My family doctor put me on an antidepressant for a month. He and his wife had gone through fertility treatments, so he knew what was going on with me. His wife shared some of her feelings, and told me about a local Resolve group. I sent them my money right away, and they told me about their monthly meetings and newsletter. Now I have other infertile people to talk to. I tell my fertile friends what's going on with my treatment, but they can't empathize. They haven't experienced infertility firsthand."

You may find that some of your emotional needs can best be met by other infertile couples. No one really understands better what it feels like to be unable to bear a child. You may find it helpful to participate in an infertility support group where you can talk about your experiences and feelings in a sympathetic, understanding atmosphere. Then you can begin to feel that you aren't so alone. Having the group listen to you and accept you for who you are may help you to accept yourselves, and stop feeling so isolated.

The national self-help group for infertile couples, Resolve, based in Massachusetts, now has 15,000 members in forty-nine chapters across the country. By becoming a basic member (for $25), you become part of a national network of members with similar problems, including a twenty-four-hour hotline that puts you in touch with volunteers who provide support and answer questions. You also receive a national newsletter, journal articles, and up-to-date fact sheets. Local Resolve chapters have regular programs on medical and emotional issues, newsletters, information on local services (including adoption), and support groups.

Many fertility clinics also offer their own support groups to facilitate sharing, or newsletters with articles and letters from infertile couples. These groups and newsletters provide information and emotional support for infertile couples who are going through, or have gone through, fertility treatments. They also address coping strategies and specific needs of the doctor's patients.

It's natural, if you have had no success in achieving a pregnancy, to seek out other infertile couples. Infertile couples can't avoid interacting with fertile people if they are to maintain family relationships or friendships. Support groups may help you ease your way back into social networks where you can feel comfortable living your lives without children, either temporarily or permanently.

When to Stop Treatment

"Nothing we had done had worked, and the only thing left was IVF," says Leon. *"Robin and I had already spent thousands of dollars, and we were looking at spending much more, which would have been a financial burden. With the information we had, given what we had been through, we felt our chances of success were minimal, and no better with IVF than the other treatments we had pursued.*

"We discussed adoption, but my age was a consideration. I was concerned that I'd be over sixty by the time my child was out of high school. Besides, the public adoption agency had a long waiting list for a baby of the same race and an age cutoff at thirty-eight. We decided not to consider a foreign or private adoption, and didn't want to risk adopting through a 'baby broker.'

"The decision not to have children was almost inevitable," Leon continues. *"We had been staring at the possibility for a long while. Once you can't achieve a pregnancy easily, there's always the possibility that you never will. Robin and I weren't willing to subject our bodies, emotions, and pocketbooks to the endless varieties of treatment once we believed that treatment wasn't likely to succeed."*

"Leading up to the time to stop, we began thinking about it a little at a time," recalls Robin. *"We needed a new car, and had to choose between a two-seat sports car or a sedan with a back seat. We really wanted the sports car, and so we bought it, telling ourselves that if we had a child, we'd sell it. We were already thinking that the treatment wouldn't work. Earlier in our treatment, we wouldn't have done that.*

"I'm competitive. I don't remember quitting anything. It was hard for me to say, 'Let's stop,' " Robin says. *"But the treatment becomes such a routine that it controls your life. When we first quit, I didn't know what else to do with my time. But quitting also changes your life. Either it makes you closer or drives you further apart. It can't be the way it was before. Leon and I definitely feel closer and enjoy our time together. A few years before, I would have thought of ourselves as being lonely without children. Occasionally, I think about what would happen if Leon was gone, but you get through that, too. You feel the grief. It's like burying a dream. You have to lay it to rest and get on with your life, put it behind you."*

One of the most difficult times is when treatment hasn't worked. Your doctor may tell you, "The treatment has failed. I can't offer you any other medical treatments that are more likely to work." (More often, there is always something else to try, even if that means repeating the same treatment.) But it's not up to the doctor to say, "It's time for you to stop." *You* have to make that decision. It should be a well thought out decision that you make freely and feel comfortable with.

Your fertility specialist may feel that he has failed you. Doctors don't like to admit they can't help everyone who comes into their office. This may make it difficult for him to advise you when you should consider stopping treatment. A sensitive physician, however, can help make you aware of the signals you may be sending that indicate perhaps one or both partners is ready to stop trying. One partner may appear emotionally drained or exhausted. One or both partners may seem immobilized, unable to function normally or to make clear decisions. You may become obsessed with your goal of achieving a pregnancy, or have unrealistic expectations about treatment, falling prey to the seduction of every new technology.

Other signals that you are not coping effectively may include repetitive calls to ask the same questions, complaints of anxiety, depression, sleeplessness, and marital conflict. Or you may demonstrate your ambivalence about fertility treatment by missing appointments or not adhering to the treatment regimen.

The financial toll of prolonged, unsuccessful fertility treatments can be heavy as well. You must also take this into consideration when you discuss how much longer you will keep trying to have a baby.

When to stop treatment is a major decision for any couple. Once the decision is made, it's usually made for good, and it is rarely a sudden decision. Infertile couples tend to think about stopping throughout their treatment.

Sometimes the decision not to pursue further treatment is made passively for an infertile couple who has exhausted all treatment options. As each successive treatment fails, another option is lost. One by one, the doors close until the only one open is not to have children.

When appropriate therapies have been tried for a sufficient duration of time, and have failed, your fertility treatment will come to an end. If and when this happens, you will have to adopt or live without children. You may not feel that you are able to accept either of the two choices. Feelings of vulnerability and desperation may make you unable to assess your situation clearly. This is the time for you to rely on all the support you have—family, friends, local support groups—to help you work through your emotions to reach a sound decision.

Ultimately, you must make a very personal assessment about what's best for you. You may need to wrestle with the idea of not having children for a long time before you come to accept the inevitable. Each partner has to face it alone, but you also have to deal with it together if you are to remain a couple. Some marriages can't withstand the strain, but many couples draw closer together. They have been through a lot together, and somehow the struggle and self-examination make them more intimate.

If and when you decide to stop treatment, it's important for you really to give up infertility treatment and get on with your lives. There are alternative solutions to fertility problems, but they can't really be developed while you are still counting on getting pregnant.

Fertility specialists like to quote their pregnancy rates— the "bottom line" for fertility treatments. But pregnancy isn't the only way to measure success. Couples who don't conceive after treatment are not failures as human beings.

You needn't denigrate your self-worth by defining a successful life as having children.

Adoption

Society's values have fostered the idea that infertile couples are somehow not complete because they can't conceive. Implicit in this message is the idea that blood is thicker than water, that biological babies are "better," and that adoption is second-best. You probably have received perplexing messages about creating families. The challenge is to sort out the messages and to make some sense of them for your own lives and the family you seek to create.

For every hundred American couples seeking adoption, only two or three children are available. This illustrates the practical obstacles to the adoption option. These statistics are no better than continuing treatment after several unsuccessful IVF cycles!

Fewer young women, particularly white women, are putting babies up for adoption. There are, however, other options, including adopting an older child waiting in an institution or foster home, or a nonwhite or foreign-born baby. Many couples bypass traditional adoption agencies in favor of an independent adoption.

About 2 million Americans are competing each year to adopt 50,000 domestic infants and about 6,000 foreign-born babies, according to the National Adoption Committee. That makes for poor odds for the couple who want to adopt. About half of domestic adoptions are arranged through agencies, the rest independently. The couples most likely to adopt successfully are middle-class, between the ages of thirty-three and thirty-seven, earning incomes of $25,000 to $50,000, the committee says.

Although there are no good records about the number

of adoptions of older American children, the best estimates, based on annual placement rates from the largest
U.S. agencies, suggest that 5,000 to 10,000 older children
are adopted each year. Check the resources in the back of
this book for agencies that help couples with various types
of adoptions.

When you do decide to adopt, let people know. Contact
as many people as you possibly can, and put your name on
as many agency waiting lists as possible. Also, find out
about an adoptive parent group in your area to help you
through the adoption process.

Private Agency Adoption

*Last fall, Pam and Jeff applied to a private adoption agency. After they
were accepted, the social worker told them it would probably take two
years before they had their adopted baby. "I'm glad we decided to
adopt," says Pam. "I want to have a baby, but I was ready to stop
treatment. I couldn't go on forever. I didn't think I could ever stop
trying to have a baby. But after I had to give up my dream job because
of the stresses of fertility treatments, I knew I had had enough. I'm
happy to relax and wait for the agency to come through for us."*

Licensed private adoption agencies usually seek homes for
American or foreign infants and toddlers. They screen and
counsel pregnant women who contact them about giving
up their babies for adoption. The agency frequently provides for medical care to the mother during the pregnancy,
and gives the couple a complete social and medical history
of the baby. The identity of the birth mother is ordinarily
kept confidential from the adoptive parents.

The agency also has social workers who screen the potential adoptive couple with visits to the couple at home.
These agencies often reject adoptive parents who are over

age forty or under age twenty-five, who have their own biological children, or who have no proof of infertility.

Waiting lists for private adoption are generally two to five years for a white baby, less than a year for a black baby. There are more white couples who want to adopt and, although these agencies generally have more black babies available, they generally do not allow white couples to adopt black babies.

Public Agency Adoption

Run by counties or states, public adoption agencies seek parents for children who have been removed from the custody of their biological parents. Public agencies have newborns, but most of their children are school-aged or teen-aged. They may have a physical or emotional handicap.

Adoptions through public agencies are inexpensive, but the process is arduous. If either you or your spouse has been divorced, if you are of different religions or are over age forty, you are likely to be rejected. The wait for a healthy white baby can take up to ten years, and by then you may be too old to adopt!

Independent Adoption

For independent adoption, a couple contacts an attorney, doctor, clergyman, or "baby broker" who works directly with a pregnant woman. While most adoption agencies prohibit direct contact between the birth mother and adoptive parents, an independent adoption may give the infertile couple a chance to contact the birth mother before delivery.

A baby broker typically places classified ads in newspapers across the country, locates a pregnant woman willing to give up the baby at birth, and sends her to a state with lenient adoption laws, where the woman delivers and surrenders her newborn. For his work, the broker receives a nonrefundable fee of about $10,000. Some states permit reimbursement to the birth mother for reasonable expenses, and the adoptive couple frequently pays for her lost wages, counseling, food, rent, and medical care during the pregnancy. Some birth mothers have demanded cars, tuition, and trust funds in exchange for babies.

Independent adoption is the speediest route, from three months to two years for a healthy white baby. But it's also the most vulnerable to ethical, legal, and emotional risks. Many brokers have no training in social work or psychology. Adoption experts express concern that some prospective parents aren't properly screened and that birth mothers may not receive adequate counseling. You also run the risk that an unscrupulous baby broker may raise the price just before the couple adopts the baby. Problems may arise if the birth mother wants further contact with the child and the couple opposes it.

The birth mother should be free of any pressure from the couple or the intermediary, and usually doesn't sign any binding adoption agreement until at least three days after she gives birth. Independent adoption is now illegal in six states, and others are tightening their laws.

Foreign Adoption

For some couples, the best option is to adopt a foreign child. They may have been shut out of American adoption agencies because of their age or due to the reluctance of agencies to allow white couples to adopt a minority baby. (There is no shortage of black and American-born Hispanic babies for minority couples to adopt.) The infertile couple may not feel capable of accepting an older or handicapped child, or they may not want to risk an independent adoption.

Rather than wait years for a white American baby, more and more infertile white couples are looking into foreign adoption. To meet this demand, government licensed adoption agencies have proliferated and made foreign adoption more available. American couples adopt about 10,000 foreign babies each year, with 6,000 currently coming from South Korea alone, and most of the rest from South America. It usually takes a couple about one year to adopt a foreign baby after they have applied to an agency.

The rules of foreign adoption vary from country to country. In South Korea, for example, agencies stipulate that couples can't be more than forty years older than their adopted children. In India, agencies discourage previously divorced couples from adopting. Brazilian agencies require that prospective parents be married at least five years and that either the adopting husband or wife be at least thirty years old.

Foreign adoption begins with a home study by a licensed social worker, just as in domestic adoptions. Once the couple has been approved by the agency, they can start their search for a foreign baby. The simplest approach is to locate an adoption agency that has overseas contacts. Or the couple may want to use an intermediary, such as an attorney who specializes in foreign adoptions. The couple should choose an agency or attorney that can demonstrate experience in foreign adoptions. If possible, they should try to speak to people who have adopted babies from the agency or through the attorney.

Adoption Costs

Agency and independent adoptions range from $1,500 to $15,000. Foreign adoptions range from $5,000 to $20,000. So adopting a child isn't necessarily less expensive than going through infertility treatment. The money goes toward paying for social worker fees, medical care and counseling for the birth mother, legal fees, and travel for foreign children.

Some insurance companies offer adoption benefits, such as time off from work and a limited reimbursement of expenses. But a foreign-born baby may not be covered under medical benefits until the child is legally adopted, which can take up to a year after arriving in America. Most adoptions aren't finalized until six to twelve months after a couple takes custody of the child. Check with your insurance carrier about whether you have any benefits and, if so, when they begin.

What Agencies Look for in a Couple

Whatever route you go in search of an adopted child, the adoption agencies, brokers, or birth mothers look for certain characteristics in the adoptive couple. In general, they like to see a stable marriage and a couple who can afford to take care of the child. Also, they want to know if you have come to terms with your problem—that, for example, one partner doesn't blame the other for the couple's infertility.

Some agencies have taken to interviewing prospective adoptive parents in groups. This gives them the opportunity to see how you interact with other people. The adoption study by a social worker in your home also weighs heavily in an agency's decision to accept a couple. You can use this home study with the social worker to express your feelings about your infertility and why you want to adopt.

It may even help you work out any uncertain feelings about adoption.

Making Use of Waiting Time

Once you have made the commitment to adopt, you may want to use your time to think about and prepare for the arrival of your new family member. This parallels the preparation time couples have during pregnancy, although it may last longer than nine months. Like the couples who have a natural child, adoptive couples aren't innately endowed with child care skills, and must also go through a learning phase. If you have applied for adoption, you need to consult baby books and seek out friends and relatives just as other expectant parents do.

Questions may run through your minds about preparing for the child: "What can we do to prepare emotionally for the instantaneous transformation from a twosome to a threesome?" If you are adopting a foreign baby, you may wonder, "What can we do to make the baby feel welcome in a strange environment?" Or if you are adopting a toddler or older child, "What kind of transition problems can we expect when our child arrives?"

The waiting period may be difficult and frustrating, but you should cherish your moments together. Being alone together will someday be a precious commodity. This may be the time to take a vacation or second honeymoon; it could be your last chance for a long time.

Answering Questions About Adoption

You can also think about what to say when strangers ask questions about the adoption. This may be a good time to open up with your relatives, who may still be having trouble accepting either your infertility or your decision to adopt.

You may decide to learn as much as you can about the baby's background. For newborns, the mother's state of health during pregnancy is important since her habits and health affect the baby's condition. Any information about the birth mother's and father's family histories may be important to the child later.

In addition, you can decide how, and when, to tell the infant or young child about the adoption. Sooner or later, someone is bound to bring up the subject. Since the 1960s, most parents have heeded expert advice and have told children early in life that they were adopted. But parents almost universally overestimate their child's ability to comprehend his or her own adoption. Adopted children need to be retold more fully as they get older. You may later have to decide whether to aid the adopted child in a search for his or her natural parents.

Whether you choose to adopt or not, you should feel satisfied that you have done all you could about your fertility problem. After the adversity of infertility, you probably know yourself better, you may feel like a stronger person, and your marriage may be stronger, too.

Once you have resolved your feelings about your infertility, you can realize that it's not, in and of itself, a major part of your life. Infertility doesn't loom nearly so large any more. You can accept that your personality and identity do not revolve around your ability to have children.

Still, like most infertile couples, somewhere in the back of your minds you may think of yourselves as "infertile," even if you have a baby. Once you have a child, he or she is a constant reminder of your infertility. And you may treat your child as "precious" since you know how hard it can be to have a baby.

You will probably remember when everything seemed

to be a crisis while you were going through fertility treatments. Like any other life crisis, you can gradually put it into better perspective as time goes by. Whether you have a baby or not, you will have learned that there is life after infertility.

Questions for the Infertile Couple to Ask Themselves About Their Fertility Treatments

How far are we willing to go in order to have a baby?

Do we have to have our own biologic child?

Would we accept adopting a baby? How quickly would we want to adopt?

Would we consider living without children?

What should we tell our family and friends about our infertility?

What can we do to make it easier for them to accept?

What should we tell them about what is and what isn't helpful to us?

Questions for Each Partner Undergoing Infertility Treatment

Am I willing to talk to my spouse about how I really feel about our infertility and the treatments we're going through?

Am I willing to talk to my fertility specialist or one of his team members about how I really feel?

How can I help my spouse get through fertility treatments?

Questions for the Infertile Couple to Ask Their Doctor

(In general)

Do you know of any local patient support groups? How can I contact them?

How do we know when it may be time to stop fertility treatments?

Are there any of the signs that it may be time to stop? (Emotional exhaustion, obsession with achieving a pregnancy, wanting indiscriminately to try any new treatment)

(After a miscarriage)

Can we see the baby we've lost or take home his or her picture or lock of hair?

Can you help us arrange for a burial or memorial service?

Questions for the Infertile Couple to Ask Themselves About Adoption

Can we afford to adopt a baby?

Will the child come between us or interfere with our relationship?

Are we talking openly to each other about how we feel about adoption?

Do we want to apply to a public or private adoption agency, or opt for an independent or foreign adoption?

What should we tell our friends and relatives about the adopted baby?

Can we find out about the birth mother's or father's medical history?

What was the birth mother's health during her pregnancy and delivery?

When, and how, should we tell the child that he or she was adopted?

Should we aid the child in the search for his or her natural parents?

Sue's Story

For four years, Sue and her husband, Frank, both age thirty-five, have had a strong interest in adopting a Korean child. They had a son, Grant, now age five, after antibiotic treatments cleared up a genital infection. Yet, after nearly two years of various surgeries to remove scar tissue and endometriosis, Sue still hadn't conceived again, so they put themselves on a waiting list to adopt a foreign baby.

"A year ago, the most important thing in my life was having a baby," says Sue. "Every time I got my period, it was a major catastrophe." Now Frank, an insurance executive, and Sue have decided to take a few years off from fertility treatments, and she has decided not to work as a respiratory therapist. Instead, Sue says, "I'm going into 'baby-raising mode,' loving my toddler, taking him to pre-school. And if we adopt, I'll have another one on my hands.

"I have blind faith that I will get pregnant again," she says. "Three of my friends had kids after age forty, so I know it's doable. I'll be patient and persevere. Grant keeps asking, 'Mommy, when are we going to get pregnant?' He knows I never gave away his crib. One way or another, we're going to use that crib again."

DIRECTORY
OF U.S. FERTILITY
SPECIALISTS

The following Directory of Fertility Specialists derives from a questionnaire sent to all members of three subsocieties of the American Fertility Society—the Society of Reproductive Endocrinologists, the Society of Reproductive Surgeons and the Society for Assisted Reproductive Technology—plus the American Society of Andrology.

The information included in the directory was provided by those physicians who responded to our questionnaire. Only those who responded to our mailings are included here. Other qualified fertility specialists may have been omitted. While this directory can help you find a nearby fertility specialist, or one who has a particular clinical interest, it is not an endorsement of any physician. In all cases, you should use the same careful deliberation that you normally would employ when choosing a physician.

NS: Not specified or not sufficient information.

ALABAMA

Birmingham

Richard E. Blackwell, M.D., Ph.D.
Univ. of Alabama, Ob/Gyn Dept.
Birmingham, AL 35294
(205) 934-3697
Board Certifications Ob/Gyn,
Reproductive Endocrinology
Member Society of Reproductive
Endocrinologists
Practice Setting academic
Clinical Interests reproductive
endocrine/infertility, IVF, GIFT,
cryopreservation of both oocytes and
embryos, sperm banking, AID

D. Erskine Carmichael, M.D.
2700 Tenth Ave. S.
Birmingham, AL 35205

(205) 933-1192
Board Certification Ob/Gyn
Member Society of Reproductive
Surgeons
Practice Setting private
Clinical Interests NS

Kathryn L. Honea, M.D.
2006 Brookwood Medical Center Dr.
Suite 508
Birmingham, AL 35209
(205) 870-9784
Board Certification Ob/Gyn
Member Society for Assisted
Reproductive Technology
Practice Setting private
Clinical Interests infertility, IVF, pelvic
surgery including pelvoscopy and
laser laparoscopy

J. Benjamin Younger, M.D.
Univ. of Alabama, Ob/Gyn Dept.
Old Hillman Bldg., Room 547
Birmingham, AL 35294
(205) 934-5631
Board Certification Ob/Gyn
Member Society of Reproductive
Surgeons
Practice Setting academic
Clinical Interests ovulation induction,
IVF and related procedures,
endoscopic surgery

Mobile

Sezer Aksel, M.D.
Univ. of S. Alabama, Ob/Gyn Dept.
CC/CB Div. Reproductive
Endocrinology
Mobile, AL 36688
(205) 460-7173
Board Certifications Ob/Gyn,
Reproductive Endocrinology
Member Society of Reproductive
Endocrinologists
Practice Setting academic/HMO
Clinical Interests ovulation induction,
luteal defects, hirsutism, estrogen
replacement, IVF-ET and GIFT

ARIZONA

Glendale

Paul M. Block, M.D.
5757 W. Thunderbird Rd., #W200
Glendale, AZ 85306
(602) 843-1777
Board Certification Urology
Member American Society of
Andrology
Practice Setting private/HMO
Clinical Interests male infertility,
vasectomy reversals (microsurgical),
sperm aspiration (in conjunction with
IVF)

Phoenix

Tawfik H. Rizkallah, M.D.
Phoenix Fertility Institute, P.C.
1300 N. Twelfth St., Suite 522
Phoenix, AZ 85006
(602) 252-8628
Board Certifications Ob/Gyn,

Reproductive Endocrinology
Member Society of Reproductive
Endocrinologists
Practice Setting private
Clinical Interests reproductive
endocrinology

ARKANSAS

Little Rock

Amer Z. Al-Juburi, M.D.
UAMS
4301 W. Markham, Slot 540
Little Rock, AR 72205-7199
(501) 661-5240
Board Certifications NS
Member American Society of
Andrology
Practice Setting academic
Clinical Interests male reproduction,
infertility, andrology

John F. Redman, M.D.
Univ. of Arkansas, College of
Medicine, Urology Dept.
4301 W. Markham, Slot 540
Little Rock, AR 72205-7199
(501) 686-5242
Board Certification Urology
Member American Society of
Andrology
Practice Setting academic
Clinical Interests techniques of
vasovasostomy, varicocelectomy

CALIFORNIA

Berkeley

Ferdinand J. Beernink, M.D.
2999 Regent St.
Berkeley, CA 94705
(415) 843-7722
Board Certification Ob/Gyn
Member Society of Reproductive
Surgeons
Practice Setting private
Clinical Interests office IVF, infertility
surgery, ovulation induction,
oligospermia, AID, laser laparoscopy,
GIFT

Ryszard J. Chetkowski, M.D.
3001 Colby St.
Alta Bates Hospital

Berkeley, CA 94705
(415) 540-1416
Board Certification Ob/Gyn
Member American Society of
Andrology
Practice Setting private
Clinical Interests IVF, GIFT, ovulation
induction, microsurgery, laser
laparoscopy, reproductive
endocrinology

Beverly Hills

Mark Wayne Surrey, M.D.
450 N. Bedford Dr., #110
Beverly Hills, CA 90210
(213) 277-2393
Board Certification Ob/Gyn
Member Society of Reproductive
Surgeons
Practice Setting academic/private
Clinical Interests infertility diagnosis and
treatment

Castro Valley

Alan I. Shapiro, M.D.
20130 Lake Chabot Rd., Suite 303
Castro Valley, CA 94546
(415) 581-6884
Board Certifications Ob/Gyn,
Reproductive Endocrinology
Member Society of Reproductive
Endocrinologists
Practice Setting private
Clinical Interests reproductive
endocrinology, infertility, gynecology,
microsurgery, IVF

Davis

Stephen P. Boyers, M.D.
Univ. of California at Davis School of
Medicine
Div. of Reproductive Biology and
Medicine
Suber House
Davis, CA 95616
(916) 752-3303
Board Certifications Ob/Gyn,
Reproductive Endocrinology
Member Society of Reproductive
Endocrinologists
Practice Setting academic

Clinical Interests reproductive surgery,
IVF-ET, GIFT, artificial insemination

Garden Grove

Ricardo H. Asch, M.D.
12555 Garden Grove Blvd., Suite 203
Garden Grove, CA 92668
(714) 638-1500
Board Certifications Ob/Gyn,
Reproductive Endocrinology
Member Society of Reproductive
Endocrinologists
Practice Setting private
Clinical Interests IVF, endoscopic surgery

Jose P. Balmaceda, M.D.
12555 Garden Grove Blvd., Suite 203
Garden Grove, CA 92668
(714) 638-1500
Board Certifications Ob/Gyn,
Reproductive Endocrinology
Member Society of Reproductive
Endocrinologists
Practice Setting private
Clinical Interests IVF, endoscopic surgery

Glendale

Charles M. March, M.D.
1560 E. Chevy Chase Dr.
Glendale, CA 91206
(818) 242-9933
Board Certification Ob/Gyn
Member Society of Reproductive
Surgeons
Practice Setting academic/private
Clinical Interests intrauterine surgery,
pelvic surgery, ovulation induction

La Jolla

Jeffrey S. Rakoff, M.D.
Scripps Clinic and Research
Foundation
10666 N. Torrey Pines Rd.
La Jolla, CA 92037
(619) 457-8680
Board Certification Ob/Gyn
Member Society of Reproductive
Surgeons
Practice Setting private
Clinical Interests infertility surgery, IVF

Loma Linda

Bert J. Davidson, M.D., Ph.D.
11370 Anderson St., Suite 3900
Loma Linda, CA 92354
(714) 796-4806
Board Certifications Ob/Gyn,
Reproductive Endocrinology
Member Society of Reproductive
Endocrinologists
Practice Setting academic/private
Clinical Interests infertility,
microsurgery, laser surgery, operative
laparoscopy, ovulation induction, IVF,
GIFT, insemination

William C. Patton, M.D.
25455 Barton Rd., A204
Loma Linda, CA 92354
(714) 370-0170
Board Certifications Ob/Gyn,
Reproductive Endocrinology
Member Society of Reproductive
Endocrinologists
Practice Setting private
Clinical Interests infertility and
endocrinology, ovulation induction,
microsurgery, artificial insemination

Clifford A. Walters, M.D.
25455 Barton Rd., A208
Loma Linda, CA 92354
(714) 824-0888
Board Certifications Ob/Gyn,
Reproductive Endocrinology
Member Society of Reproductive
Endocrinologists
Practice Setting private
Clinical Interests sperm banking for
insemination, tubal surgery, ovulation
induction, Pergonal-intrauterine
insemination

Long Beach

Bill Yee, M.D.
2880 Atlantic Ave., Suite 220
Long Beach, CA 90806
(213) 595-2229
Board Certification Ob/Gyn
Member American Society of
Andrology
Practice Setting academic/private
Clinical Interests IVF/GIFT

Los Angeles

Carol J. Bennett, M.D.
USC Med. Ctr., Urology Dept.
1200 N. State St., GH5900
Los Angeles, CA
(213) 227-6126
Board Certification Urology
Member American Society of
Andrology
Practice Setting academic
Clinical Interests male infertility

Stanley Friedman, M.D.
921 Westwood Blvd.
Los Angeles, CA 90049
(213) 208-6765
Board Certification Ob/Gyn
Member Society of Reproductive
Surgeons
Practice Setting private
Clinical Interests infertility, all aspects

J.C. Gambone, M.D.
Department of Ob/Gyn
University of California-Los Angeles
Med. Ctr.
Los Angeles, CA 90024
(213) 825-7755
Board Certifications Ob/Gyn,
Reproductive Endocrinology
Member Society of Reproductive
Endocrinologists
Practice Setting academic
Clinical Interests infertility, IVF

Flor L. Geola, M.D.
11600 Wilshire Blvd., #210
Los Angeles, CA 90025
(213) 477-0501
Board Certifications Internal Medicine,
Endocrinology
Member American Society of
Andrology
Practice Setting private
Clinical Interests endocrinology

Jouko K. Halme, M.D.
Univ. of California
UCLA Med. Ctr.
Los Angeles, CA 90024
(213) 825-7755
Board Certifications Ob/Gyn,
Reproductive Endocrinology
Member Society of Reproductive
Endocrinologists
Practice Setting academic

Clinical Interests general infertility, operative laparoscopy, microsurgery, endometriosis, IVF-ET

Robert Israel, M.D.
637 S. Lucas Ave., Suite 7
Los Angeles, CA 90017
(213) 977-2388
Board Certification Ob/Gyn
Member Society of Reproductive Surgeons
Practice Setting academic/private
Clinical Interests infertility, endometriosis, hysteroscopy

Roger A. Lobo, M.D.
LAC-USC Med. Ctr.
1240 N. Mission Rd.
Los Angeles, CA 90033
(213) 226-3026
Board Certifications Ob/Gyn, Reproductive Endocrinology
Member Society of Reproductive Endocrinologists
Practice Setting academic/private
Clinical Interests reproductive endocrinology, infertility, menopause, androgen metabolism, induction of ovulation, IVF

Jaroslav Jan Marik, M.D.
Tyler Med. Clinic
921 Westwood Blvd.
Los Angeles, CA 90024
(213) 208-6765
Board Certification Ob/Gyn
Member Society of Reproductive Surgeons
Practice Setting private
Clinical Interests general infertility, surgical correction of female genitalia, endometriosis, IVF

Richard P. Marrs, M.D.
1245 Wilshire Blvd., Suite 905
Los Angeles, CA 90017
(213) 482-4552
Board Certifications Ob/Gyn, Reproductive Endocrinology
Member Society of Reproductive Endocrinologists
Practice Setting private
Clinical Interests GIFT, IVF, reproductive endocrinology, infertility

Ronald M. Nelson, M.D.
White Memorial Med. Ctr.
1710 Brooklyn Ave.

Los Angeles, CA 90033
(213) 263-4186
Board Certifications Ob/Gyn, Reproductive Endocrinology
Member Society of Reproductive Surgeons
Practice Setting private
Clinical Interests reproductive surgery, endocrinology and infertility, including AID and intrauterine insemination

Richard J. Paulson, M.D.
1240 N. Mission Rd., Suite L1022
Los Angeles, CA 90033
(213) 226-3421
Board Certifications Ob/Gyn, Reproductive Endocrinology
Member Society of Reproductive Endocrinologists
Practice Setting academic
Clinical Interests IVF, reproductive surgery

Jacob Rajfer, M.D.
UCLA Med. Ctr., Urology Div.
Los Angeles, CA 90024
(213) 206-8164
Board Certification Urology
Member American Society of Andrology
Practice Setting academic/private
Clinical Interests NS

Cappy M. Rothman, M.D.
2080 Century Park E., Suite 907
Los Angeles, CA 90067
(213) 277-2873
Board Certification Urology
Member American Society of Andrology
Practice Setting private
Clinical Interests andrology, microsurgery

Mark V. Sauer, M.D.
Women's Hospital
1240 N. Mission Rd., Room L946
Los Angeles, CA 90033
(213) 226-3445
Board Certifications Ob/Gyn, Reproductive Endocrinology
Member Society of Reproductive Endocrinologists
Practice Setting academic
Clinical Interests IVF and general infertility, embryo donation

Los Gatos

Carmelo S. Sgarlata, M.D.
  15151 National Ave.
  Los Gatos, CA 95032
  (408) 356-0431
  Board Certifications Ob/Gyn,
  Reproductive Endocrinology
  Member Society of Reproductive
  Endocrinologists
  Practice Setting private
  Clinical Interests reproductive
  endocrinology, IVF/ET

Menlo Park

Henry Ritter, Jr., M.D.
  888 Oak Grove Ave.
  Menlo Park, CA 94025
  (415) 326-5495
  Board Certification Urology
  Member American Society of
  Andrology
  Practice Setting private/HMO
  Clinical Interests andrology

Newport Beach

John F. Farrer, M.D.
  307 Placentia Ave.
  Newport Beach, CA 92663
  (714) 646-5073
  Board Certification Urology
  Member American Society of
  Andrology
  Practice Setting private
  Clinical Interests male infertility

Oakland

Stephen C. Pruyn, M.D.
  280 W. MacArthur Blvd.
  Ob/Gyn Dept., Fertility Division
  Kaiser Permanente Med. Ctr.
  Oakland, CA 94611
  (415) 956-1080
  Board Certification Ob/Gyn
  Member Society of Reproductive
  Surgeons
  Practice Setting HMO
  Clinical Interests infertility, particularly
  reproductive surgery

Orange

Sergio C. Stone, M.D.
  Univ. of California at Irvine
  101 City Dr., Bldg. 41
  Orange, CA 92668
  (714) 634-5617
  Board Certifications Ob/Gyn,
  Reproductive Endocrinology
  Member Society of Reproductive
  Endocrinologists
  Practice Setting academic/private
  Clinical Interests microtuboplasty, laser
  surgery, IVF/GIFT, ovulation, sperm
  factor, artificial insemination

Palo Alto

G. David Adamson, M.D.
  540 University Ave., Suite 200
  Palo Alto, CA 94301
  (415) 322-1900
  Board Certifications Ob/Gyn,
  Reproductive Endocrinology
  Member Society of Reproductive
  Endocrinologists
  Practice Setting private
  Clinical Interests reconstructive surgery,
  laser laparoscopy and pelviscopy,
  endometriosis, IVF/GIFT, donor
  insemination

Pasadena

William Blank, M.D.
  Huntington Reproductive Ctr.
  39 Congress St.
  Pasadena, CA 91105
  (818) 440-9161
  Board Certification Urology
  Member American Society of
  Andrology
  Practice Setting private
  Clinical Interests male infertility,
  electroejaculation

Gordon P. Griggs, M.D.
  10 Congress, #400
  Pasadena, CA 91105
  (818) 449-6223
  Board Certification Ob/Gyn
  Member Society of Reproductive
  Surgeons
  Practice Setting private

Clinical Interests infertility, gynecology, endocrinology

Redondo Beach

David R. Meldrum, M.D.
AMI S. Bay Hospital, IVF Ctr.
514 N. Prospect Ave.
Redondo Beach, CA 90277
(213) 318-4741
Board Certifications Ob/Gyn,
Reproductive Endocrinology
Member Society of Reproductive
Endocrinologists
Practice Setting private
Clinical Interests IVF, endometriosis,
laser laparoscopy, tubal microsurgery

San Diego

Ana A. Murphy, M.D.
Univ. of California, San Diego Med.
Ctr.
225 Dickinson St.
San Diego, CA 92103
(619) 543-2384
Board Certification Ob/Gyn
Member Society of Reproductive
Surgeons
Practice Setting academic
Clinical Interests operative laparoscopy/
infertility surgery, medical and
surgical therapy for endometriosis

Benito Villanueva, M.D.
9339 Genesee Ave., Suite 220
San Diego, CA 92121
(619) 455-7520
Board Certification Ob/Gyn
Member Society of Reproductive
Surgeons
Practice Setting private
Clinical Interests gynecology and
infertility

San Francisco

Robert Glass, M.D.
Univ. of California at San Francisco
Ob/Gyn Dept., M1489
San Francisco, CA 94143
(415) 476-1824
Board Certification Ob/Gyn
Member Society for Assisted
Reproductive Technology

Practice Setting academic
Clinical Interests IVF

Simon R. Henderson, M.D.
3838 California St., Suite 808
San Francisco, CA 94118
(415) 668-2124
Board Certifications Ob/Gyn,
Reproductive Endocrinology
Member Society of Reproductive
Endocrinologists
Practice Setting private
Clinical Interests tubal microsurgery,
video laser laparoscopy, pelviscopy,
conservative gynecological surgery,
ovulation induction

Carl J. Levinson, M.D.
3838 California St., #103
San Francisco, CA 94118
(415) 750-6400
Board Certification Ob/Gyn
Member Society of Reproductive
Surgeons
Practice Setting private
Clinical Interests endometriosis,
microsurgery, advanced laparoscopic
surgery

Mary C. Martin, M.D.
Univ. of California, Ob/Gyn Dept.
Room M-1489
San Francisco, CA 94143-0132
(415) 476-2224
Board Certifications Ob/Gyn,
Reproductive Endocrinology
Member Society of Reproductive
Endocrinologists
Practice Setting academic
Clinical Interests reproductive
endocrine/infertility practice, IVF

R. Dale McClure, M.D.
Urology Dept.
400 Parnassus Ave., Room 610
San Francisco, CA 94143
(415) 476-8800
Board Certification Urology
Member American Society of
Andrology
Practice Setting academic
Clinical Interests epididymal aspiration
for IVF, semen manipulation
techniques for IVF and IUI, sperm
antibodies

Robert D. Nachtigall, M.D.
390 Laurel St., #205

San Francisco, CA 94118
(415) 921-6100
Board Certifications Ob/Gyn,
Reproductive Endocrinology
Member Society of Reproductive
Endocrinologists
Practice Setting private
Clinical Interests AID, intrauterine
insemination, Pergonal, PMS, ERT

Ira D. Sharlip, M.D.
2100 Webster St., #309
San Francisco, CA 94115
(415) 923-3080
Board Certification Urology
Member Society of Reproductive
Surgeons
Practice Setting private
Clinical Interests male infertility,
urologic microsurgery, vasectomy
reversal

Geoffrey Sher, M.D.
Pacific Fertility Ctr.
2100 Webster St., Suite 220
San Francisco, CA 94115
(415) 923-3344
Board Certifications Ob/Gyn, Maternal
and Fetal Medicine
Member Society for Assisted
Reproductive Technology
Practice Setting private
Clinical Interests IVF, GIFT,
inseminations

San Mateo

Francis Polansky, M.D.
101 S. San Mateo Dr.
San Mateo, CA 94401
(415) 340-0500
Board Certifications Ob/Gyn,
Reproductive Endocrinology
Member Society of Reproductive
Endocrinologists
Practice Setting private
Clinical Interests IVF

Stanford

Emmet J. Lamb, M.D.
Stanford Univ. School of Medicine,
Ob/Gyn Dept.
Stanford, CA 94305
(415) 723-5251
Board Certifications Ob/Gyn,

Reproductive Endocrinology
Member Society of Reproductive
Endocrinologists
Practice Setting academic
Clinical Interests tubal disease, IVF,
amenorrhea

Tarzana

Sheldon L. Schein, M.D.
18370 Burbank Blvd., #301
Tarzana, CA 91356
(818) 996-5550
Board Certification Ob/Gyn
Member Society for Assisted
Reproductive Technology
Practice Setting private
Clinical Interests infertility, all phases

Torrance

Oscar A. Kletzky, M.D.
Harbor–UCLA Med. Ctr.
1000 W. Carson St., Bldg. D3
Torrance, CA 90509
(213) 533-3867
Board Certification Reproductive
Endocrinology
Member Society of Reproductive
Endocrinologists
Practice Setting academic/private
Clinical Interests gyn endocrinology and
infertility

Ronald S. Swerdloff, M.D.
Harbor–UCLA Med. Ctr.
1000 W. Carson St.
Torrance, CA 90509
(213) 212-1867
Board Certifications Internal Medicine,
Endocrinology
Member American Society of
Andrology
Practice Setting academic
Clinical Interests infertility, sexual
dysfunction, hypogonadism, hirsutism

Frederick N. Wolk, M.D.
23451 Madison St., #340
Torrance, CA 90505
(213) 373-9451
Board Certification Urology
Member American Society of
Andrology
Practice Setting private
Clinical Interests male infertility

Walnut Creek

Donald I. Galen, M.D.
1855 San Miguel Dr., Suite 4
Walnut Creek, CA 94596
(415) 937-6166
Board Certification Ob/Gyn
Member Society of Reproductive
Surgeons
Practice Setting private
Clinical Interests microsurgery,
reconstructive pelvic surgery, laser,
IVF, reproductive endocrinology

COLORADO

Aurora

J. Joshua Kopelman, M.D.
1550 S. Potomac, Suite 330
Aurora, CO 80012
(303) 369-1050
Board Certification Ob/Gyn
Member Society of Reproductive
Surgeons
Practice Setting private
Clinical Interests infertility surgery,
especially endometriosis

Denver

Bruce H. Albrecht, M.D.
455 S. Hudson St.
Denver, CO 80222
(303) 333-3378
Board Certifications Ob/Gyn,
Reproductive Endocrinology
Member Society of Reproductive
Endocrinologists
Practice Setting private
Clinical Interests ovulation induction,
laparoscopic laser tubal surgery,
recurrent pregnancy losses

Fred Grossman, M.D.
4200 W. Conejos Pl., #536
Denver, CO 80204
(303) 571-1355
Board Certification Urology
Member American Society of
Andrology
Practice Setting private
Clinical Interests male infertility,
diagnostic and therapeutic

vasovasostomy, testis biopsy,
varicocele

George P. Henry, M.D.
Reproductive Genetics, In Vitro
455 S. Hudson St., Level 3
Denver, CO 80220
(303) 399-1464
Board Certification Ob/Gyn
Member Society for Assisted
Reproductive Technology
Practice Setting private
Clinical Interests IVF, prenatal diagnosis,
amniocentesis, genetic counseling

Michael L. Moore, M.D.
4545 E. Ninth Ave., Suite 210
Denver, CO 80220
(303) 399-6515
Board Certifications NS
Member American Society of
Andrology
Practice Setting private
Clinical Interests GIFT, laparoscopic
surgery, andrology

Richard J. Worley, M.D.
455 S. Hudson St., Level 1
Denver, CO 80222
(303) 333-3378
Board Certifications Ob/Gyn,
Reproductive Endocrinology
Member Society of Reproductive
Endocrinologists
Practice Setting private
Clinical Interests endocrinology,
infertility, reproductive surgery, IVF

CONNECTICUT

Bridgeport

Karol J. Chacho, M.D.
4699 Main St.
Bridgeport, CT 06606
(203) 372-5282
Board Certifications Ob/Gyn,
Reproductive Endocrinology
Member Society of Reproductive
Endocrinologists
Practice Setting private/academic
Clinical Interests infertility,
endometriosis

Anthony G. Santomauro, M.D.
Infertility Institute and Fertility
Selections

4639 Main St.
Bridgeport, CT 06606
(203) 371-9947
Board Certification Ob/Gyn
Member Society of Reproductive
Surgeons
Practice Setting private
Clinical Interests reproductive surgery
with laser and laparoscopy, ovulation
induction, GIFT, AID, gender
preselection

Brookfield

John J. McGrade, M.D.
300 Federal Rd.
Brookfield, CT 06804
(203) 775-1217
Board Certifications Ob/Gyn,
Reproductive Endocrinology
Member Society of Reproductive
Endocrinologists
Practice Setting private
Clinical Interests general infertility, laser,
IVF

Farmington

Anthony A. Luciano, M.D.
Univ. of Connecticut Health Ctr.,
Ob/Gyn Dept.
263 Farmington Ave.
Farmington, CT 06032
(203) 679-2193
Board Certifications Ob/Gyn,
Reproductive Endocrinology
Member Society of Reproductive
Endocrinologists
Practice Setting academic
Clinical Interests laser, endoscopy, IVF,
GIFT, TID, IUI

Donald Maier, M.D.
Univ. of Connecticut Health Ctr.,
Ob/Gyn Dept., L2076
Farmington, CT 06032
(203) 679-4580
Board Certifications Reproductive
Endocrinology
Member Society of Reproductive
Endocrinologists
Practice Setting academic
Clinical Interests repeated pregnancy
losses, laser surgery

Narendra Tohan, M.D.
3 Wildwood Rd.
Farmington, CT 06032
(203) 677-5066
Board Certification Reproductive
Endocrinology
Member American Society of
Andrology
Practice Setting academic/private
Clinical Interests endometriosis, male/
female infertility, induction of
ovulation

Hartford

Augusto P. Chong, M.D.
675 Tower Ave.
Hartford, CT 06112
(203) 242-6201
Board Certifications Ob/Gyn,
Reproductive Endocrinology
Member Society of Reproductive
Endocrinologists
Practice Setting academic/private
Clinical Interests IVF-ET, ovulation
induction, laser surgery, surgery,
ovulation induction

Manocher Lashgari, M.D.
675 Tower Ave.
Hartford, CT 06112
(203) 243-2554
Board Certification Ob/Gyn
Member Society of Reproductive
Surgeons
Practice Setting Private
Clinical Interests NS

New Haven

Alan H. DeCherney, M.D.
Yale Univ. School of Medicine
333 Cedar St.
New Haven, CT 06510
(203) 785-4708
Board Certifications Ob/Gyn,
Reproductive Endocrinology
Member Society of Reproductive
Endocrinologists
Practice Setting academic
Clinical Interests infertility

Gabor B. Huszar, M.D.
Yale Univ. School of Medicine,
Ob/Gyn Dept.
333 Cedar St.

New Haven, CT 06510
(203) 785-4010
Board Certifications NS
Member American Society of
Andrology
Practice Setting academic
Clinical Interests male factor infertility,
intrauterine insemination, donor
insemination

Mary Lake Polan, M.D.
Yale Univ. School of Medicine,
Ob/Gyn Dept.
333 Cedar St.
New Haven, CT 06510
(203) 785-4708
Board Certifications Ob/Gyn,
Reproductive Endocrinology
Member Society of Reproductive
Endocrinologists
Practice Setting academic
Clinical Interests infertility,
endocrinology, peri- and
postmenopausal women

Stamford

Frances W. Ginsburg, M.D.
The Stamford Hospital
P.O. Box 9317
Stamford, CT 06904
(203) 325-7000
Board Certifications Ob/Gyn,
Reproductive Endocrinology
Member Society of Reproductive
Endocrinologists
Practice Setting private
Clinical Interests all aspects of infertility
except for IVF

DISTRICT OF COLUMBIA

Richard E. Blake, M.D.
6323 Georgia Ave., NW, 3rd Floor
Washington, DC 20011
(202) 291-2005
Board Certifications NS
Member Society of Reproductive
Endocrinologists
Practice Setting academic/private
Clinical Interests fertility assessment and
treatment, laser surgery, ovulation
induction

Richard J. Falk, M.D.
2440 Main St., NW

Washington, DC 20037
(202) 293-6567
Board Certifications Ob/Gyn,
Reproductive Endocrinology
Member Society of Reproductive
Endocrinologists
Practice Setting private
Clinical Interests microsurgery, operative
laparoscopy, laser, IVF, GIFT, ZIFT

Thomas A. Klein, M.D.
Walter Reed Army Med. Ctr.,
Ob/Gyn Dept.
Washington, DC 20307
(202) 576-1201
Board Certifications Ob/Gyn,
Reproductive Endocrinology
Member Society of Reproductive
Endocrinologists
Practice Setting other
Clinical Interests infertility, tubal disease

Christos Mastroyannis, M.D.
1160 Varnum St. NE, Suite 300
Washington, DC
(202) 269-7121
Board Certifications Ob/Gyn,
Reproductive Endocrinology
Member Society of Reproductive
Endocrinologists
Practice Setting academic/private
Clinical Interests GIFT, endometriosis,
menopause, endocrinology,
hyperprolactinemia, infertility

Safa M. Rifka, M.D.
Columbia Hospital
2440 Main St. NW, #401
Washington, DC 20037
(202) 293-6567
Board Certifications Ob/Gyn,
Reproductive Endocrinology
Member Society of Reproductive
Endocrinologists
Practice Setting private
Clinical Interests infertility

Irwin Shuman, M.D.
1145 19th St. NW, Suite 800
Washington, DC 20036
(202) 223-1024
Board Certification Urology
Member American Society of
Andrology
Practice Setting private
Clinical Interests male infertility,
vasectomy reversal

James A. Simon, M.D.
Georgetown Univ. School of Medicine
3800 Reservoir Rd. NW
Washington, DC 20007
(202) 687-8283
Board Certifications Ob/Gyn,
Reproductive Endocrinology
Member Society of Reproductive
Endocrinologists
Practice Setting academic
Clinical Interests infertility, tubal
disease, menopause

Robert J. Stillman, M.D.
2150 Pennsylvania Ave. NW
Washington, DC 20037
(202) 994-5060
Board Certifications Ob/Gyn,
Reproductive Endocrinology
Member Society of Reproductive
Endocrinologists
Practice Setting academic
Clinical Interests IVF, DES,
endometriosis, smoking and
reproduction

Robert A. Vigersky, M.D.
3800 Reservoir Rd. NW
Washington, DC 20012
(202) 784-3780
Board Certifications Internal Medicine,
Endocrinology and Metabolism
Member American Society of
Andrology
Practice Setting private
Clinical Interests male infertility,
weight-related amenorrhea (anorexia,
exercise)

Michael J. Zinaman, M.D.
Georgetown Univ. Med. Ctr.,
Ob/Gyn Dept.
3800 Reservoir Rd. NW
Washington, DC 20007
(202) 687-8283
Board Certification Ob/Gyn
Member American Society of
Andrology
Practice Setting academic
Clinical Interests endometriosis

FLORIDA

Clearwater

Edward A. Zbella, M.D.
Fertility Institute of W. Florida

2454 McMullen Booth Rd., Suite 502
Clearwater, FL 34619
(813) 796-7705
Board Certifications Ob/Gyn,
Reproductive Endocrinology
Member Society of Reproductive
Endocrinologists
Practice Setting private
Clinical Interests infertility, laparoscopic
laser surgery, IVF, GIFT, ZIFT,
embryo cryopreservation

Fort Lauderdale

Jerome J. Hoffman, M.D.
10 Compass Lane
Fort Lauderdale, FL 33308
(305) 491-1111
Board Certification Ob/Gyn
Member Society of Reproductive
Surgeons
Practice Setting academic
Clinical Interests NS

Jeffrey C. Seiler, M.D.
3000 West Cypress Rd.
Fort Lauderdale, FL 33309
(304) 978-5216
Board Certification Ob/Gyn
Member Society of Reproductive
Surgeons
Practice Setting other
Clinical Interests infertility, laser and
microsurgery, treatment of
endometriosis, tubal disease and
uterine malformation, sterilization
reversal, ovulation induction

Jacksonville

Ronald W. Skowsky, M.D.
Univ. Hospital of Jacksonville,
Medicine Dept.
655 W. Eighth St.
Jacksonville, FL 32209
(904) 350-6899
Board Certifications Internal Medicine,
Endocrinology and Metabolism
Member American Society of
Andrology
Practice Setting academic
Clinical Interests neuroendocrinology,
general endocrinology, reproductive
endocrinology

Lauderdale Lakes

Eliezer J. Livnat, M.D.
3001 N.W. 49th Ave., #203
Lauderdale Lakes, FL 33313
(305) 739-3750
Board Certification Ob/Gyn
Member Society of Reproductive
Surgeons
Practice Setting private
Clinical Interests laser microsurgery,
ovulation induction, GIFT, IVF

Margate

Wayne S. Maxson, M.D.
5800 Colonial Dr., Suite 200
Margate, FL 33063
(305) 972-5001
Board Certification Reproductive
Endocrinology
Member Society of Reproductive
Endocrinologists
Practice Setting private
Clinical Interests IVF, microsurgery,
operative and laser laparoscopy and
ovulation induction

Miami

Bernard Cantor, M.D.
85 N.W. 168 St., Suite B
Miami, FL 33169
(305) 651-5995
Board Certifications Ob/Gyn,
Reproductive Endocrinology
Member Society of Reproductive
Endocrinologists
Practice Setting private
Clinical Interests reconstructive surgery
and microsurgery, endometriosis, laser
endoscopy, ovulatory dysfunction,
habitual abortion

Terry T. Hung, M.D., Ph.D.
Univ. of Miami School of Medicine,
Ob/Gyn Dept.
P.O. Box 016960
Miami, FL 33101
(305) 547-5818
Board Certifications Ob/Gyn,
Reproductive Endocrinology
Member Society for Assisted
Reproductive Technology
Practice Setting academic/private

Clinical Interests microsurgery, IVF,
GIFT

Orlando

Gary W. DeVane, M.D.
85 W. Miller St., Suite 301
Orlando, FL 32806
(407) 843-0587
Board Certifications Ob/Gyn,
Reproductive Endocrinology
Member Society of Reproductive
Endocrinologists
Practice Setting private
Clinical Interests infertility, reproductive
surgery, IVF, artificial insemination,
endocrinology

Plantation

Joseph V. Raziano, M.D.
201 N.W. 82nd Ave., Suite 104
Plantation, FL 33324
(305) 472-2201
Board Certifications Ob/Gyn,
Reproductive Endocrinology
Member Society of Reproductive
Endocrinologists
Practice Setting private
Clinical Interests female endocrinology,
infertility, laser surgery

Tampa

Marc A. Bernhisel, M.D.
2919 Swann Ave., Suite 305
Tampa, FL 33609
(813) 870-3553
Board Certifications Ob/Gyn,
Reproductive Endocrinology
Member Society of Reproductive
Endocrinologists
Practice Setting private
Clinical Interests endoscopic surgery,
microsurgery, laser, IVF/GIFT,
ovulation induction, menstrual
irregularities, hirsutism

George B. Maroulis, M.D.
Univ. of S. Florida, Ob/Gyn Dept.
1 Davis Blvd., Suite 307
Tampa, FL 33606
(813) 251-7269
Board Certifications Ob/Gyn,
Reproductive Endocrinology

Member Society of Reproductive
Endocrinologists
Practice Setting academic
Clinical Interests IVF-GIFT, induction of
ovulation, hysteroscopic surgery

Robert E. McCammon, M.D.
829 W. Buffalo Ave., #215
Tampa, FL 33603
(813) 238-6445
Board Certification Ob/Gyn
Member Society of Reproductive
Surgeons
Practice Setting private
Clinical Interests surgical, IVF

Barry S. Verkauf, M.D.
2919 Swann Ave., Suite 305
Tampa, FL 33609
(813) 870-3553
Board Certification Reproductive
Endocrinology
Member Society of Reproductive
Endocrinologists
Practice Setting private
Clinical Interests infertility, reproductive
endocrinology

Stephen W. Welden, M.D.
2817 W. Virginia Ave.
Tampa, FL 33617
(813) 876-4731
Board Certification Ob/Gyn
Member Society of Reproductive
Surgeons
Practice Setting private
Clinical Interests laser and reproductive
microsurgery, gynecologic
endocrinology

GEORGIA

Atlanta

Hilton I. Kort, M.D.
993-D Johnson Ferry Rd., Suite 330
Atlanta, GA 30342
(404) 257-1900
Board Certification Ob/Gyn
Member Society of Reproductive
Surgeons
Practice Setting private
Clinical Interests infertility, IVF, laser
surgery

Joe B. Massey, M.D.
993-D Johnson Ferry Rd., Suite 330

Atlanta, GA 30342
(404) 257-1900
Board Certification Ob/Gyn
Member Society of Reproductive
Surgeons
Practice Setting private
Clinical Interests NS

Dorothy E. Mitchell-Leef, M.D.
Emory Univ. Clinic
1365 Clifton Rd., N.E.
Atlanta, GA 30322
(404) 321-0111 ext. 3408
Board Certification Ob/Gyn
Member Society of Reproductive
Surgeons
Practice Setting academic
Clinical Interests infertility evaluation
and treatment, surgical and hormonal
therapy of endometriosis

Camran Nezhat, M.D.
5555 Peachtree Dunwoody Rd., Suite
276
Atlanta, GA 30342
(404) 255-8778
Board Certification Ob/Gyn
Member Society of Reproductive
Surgeons
Practice Setting private
Clinical Interests videolaseroscopy for
the treatment of endometriosis

Andrew A. Toledo, M.D.
Emory Univ., Ob/Gyn Dept.
69 Butler Street, S.E.
Atlanta, GA 30303
(404) 589-3354
Board Certifications Ob/Gyn,
Reproductive Endocrinology
Member Society of Reproductive
Endocrinologists
Practice Setting academic
Clinical Interests ovulation induction,
tubal surgery, reproductive
endocrinopathies, IVF-ET

Augusta

R. Don Gambrell, Jr., M.D.
903 Fifteenth St.
Augusta, GA 30912
(404) 724-8878
Board Certifications Ob/Gyn,
Reproductive Endocrinology
Member Society of Reproductive
Endocrinologists

Practice Setting private
Clinical Interests all aspects of infertility
and endocrinology

Paul G. McDonough, M.D.
Med. College of Georgia,
Ob/Gyn Dept.
Augusta, GA 30912
(404) 721-3832
Board Certifications Ob/Gyn,
Reproductive Endocrinology
Member Society of Reproductive
Endocrinologists
Practice Setting academic
Clinical Interests infertility and genetics,
molecular biology of sexual
differentiation

Edward J. Servy, M.D.
812 Chafee Ave.
Augusta, GA 30904
(404) 724-0228
Board Certification Ob/Gyn
Member American Society of
Andrology
Practice Setting private
Clinical Interests reproduction
endocrinology

Sandra P. T. Tho, M.D.
Med. College of Georgia,
Ob/Gyn Dept.
Augusta, GA 30912
(404) 721-4095
Board Certifications Ob/Gyn,
Reproductive Endocrinology
Member Society of Reproductive
Endocrinologists
Practice Setting academic
Clinical Interests recurrent pregnancy
loss, azoospermia, delayed puberty,
precocious puberty

Macon

T. J. Lin, M.D.
777 Hemlock
Macon, GA 31208
(912) 744-1056
Board Certifications Ob/Gyn,
Reproductive Endocrinology
Member Society of Reproductive
Endocrinologists
Practice Setting academic/private
Clinical Interests gynecologic
endocrinopathy and infertility

Douglas E. Ott, M.D.
420 Charter Blvd., Suite 208
Macon, GA 31210
(912) 477-8996
Board Certifications NS
Member Society of Reproductive
Surgeons
Practice Setting private
Clinical Interests infertility, operative
endoscopy

Marietta

Joseph K. Wheatley, M.D.
660 Cherokee St.
Marietta, GA 30060
(404) 428-4475
Board Certification Urology
Member Society of Reproductive
Surgeons
Practice Setting private
Clinical Interests microsurgery,
varicocele

ILLINOIS

Chicago

Melvin R. Cohen, M.D.
900 N. Michigan Ave. Annex
Chicago, IL 60611
(312) 440-5180
Board Certification NS
Member Society of Reproductive
Surgeons
Practice Setting academic
Clinical Interests NS

M. Yusoff Dawood, M.D.
Univ. of Illinois College of Medicine,
Ob/Gyn Dept.
840 S. Wood St.
Chicago, IL 60612
(312) 996-7430
Board Certifications Ob/Gyn,
Reproductive Endocrinology
Member Society of Reproductive
Endocrinologists
Practice Setting academic
Clinical Interests female infertility,
endometriosis, ovulation induction,
tubal reconstruction

Jan Friberg, M.D., Ph.D.
750 N. Orleans
Chicago, IL 60610

(312) 649-9686
Board Certifications Ob/Gyn,
Reproductive Endocrinology
Member Society of Reproductive
Endocrinologists
Practice Setting academic/private/HMO
Clinical Interests reproductive
immunology, male infertility,
ovulation induction, IVF, tubal
surgery

David I. Hoffman, M.D.
680 N. Lake Shore Dr., Suite 810
Chicago, IL 60611
(312) 908-7270
Board Certifications Ob/Gyn,
Reproductive Endocrinology
Member Society of Reproductive
Endocrinologists
Practice Setting academic
Clinical Interests assisted reproduction,
ovulation induction, reconstructive
surgery, menopause, POF

Vivian Lewis, M.D.
Univ. of Illinois, Ob/Gyn Dept.
Chicago, IL 60612
(312) 996-7430
Board Certifications Ob/Gyn,
Reproductive Endocrinology
Member Society of Reproductive
Endocrinologists
Practice Setting academic
Clinical Interests menopause, infertility

Aaron S. Lifchez, M.D.
836 W. Wellington
Chicago, IL 60657
(312) 883-7090
Board Certification Ob/Gyn
Member Society of Reproductive
Surgeons
Practice Setting private
Clinical Interests ovulatory dysfunction,
reconstructive tubal surgery, assisted
reproductive technologies (IVF-ET,
GIFT, ZIFT)

Edward L. Marut, M.D.
Michael Reese Hospital and Med.
Ctr., Ob/Gyn Dept.
Chicago, IL 60616
(312) 791-4000
Board Certifications Ob/Gyn,
Reproductive Endocrinology
Member Society of Reproductive
Endocrinologists

Practice Setting academic/private
Clinical Interests IVF-ET, GIFT, ZIFT,
ovulation induction, microsurgery,
endometriosis, fibroid treatment and
surgery

Mariano Perez-Pelaez, M.D.
Institute of Reproductive Medicine
111 N. Wabash Ave.
Chicago, IL 60602
Telephone NS
Board Certification Ob/Gyn
Member American Society of
Andrology
Practice Setting private
Clinical Interests infertility and other
reproductive disorders

Ewa M. Radwanska, M.D.
Rush Med. College, Ob/Gyn Dept.
1653 W. Congress Parkway
Chicago, IL 60612
(312) 942-6609
Board Certifications Ob/Gyn,
Reproductive Endocrinology
Member Society of Reproductive
Endocrinologists
Practice Setting academic
Clinical Interests ovulation induction,
IVF, GIFT

Parto Rezai, M.D.
467 W. Deming Pl., Suite 806
Chicago, IL 60614
(312) 883-8544
Board Certifications Ob/Gyn,
Reproductive Endocrinology
Member Society of Reproductive
Endocrinologists
Practice Setting private
Clinical Interests infertility, reproductive
endocrinopathies

Lawrence S. Ross, M.D.
Michael Reese Hospital, Urology
Dept.
31st St. and Lake Shore Dr.
Chicago, IL 60616
(312) 791-5590
Board Certification Urology
Member American Society of
Andrology
Practice Setting academic/private
Clinical Interests male infertility,
microsurgery

James R. Schreiber, M.D.
5841 S. Maryland Ave.
Univ. of Chicago
Chicago, IL 60637
(312) 703-6642
Board Certifications Ob/Gyn,
Reproductive Endocrinology
Member Society of Reproductive
Endocrinologists
Practice Setting academic
Clinical Interests female reproductive
endocrinology, infertility

John J. Sciarra, M.D.
Prentice Women's Hospital
333 E. Superior St.
Chicago, IL 60611
(312) 908-7504
Board Certification Ob/Gyn
Member Society of Reproductive
Surgeons
Practice Setting academic
Clinical Interests hysteroscopy,
laparoscopy, gynecologic surgery

Antonio Scommegna, M.D.
Michael Reese Hospital, Ob/Gyn
Dept.
31st St. and Lake Shore Dr.
Chicago, IL 60616
(312) 791-4004
Board Certifications Ob/Gyn,
Reproductive Endocrinology
Member Society of Reproductive
Endocrinologists
Practice Setting academic
Clinical Interests reproductive
endocrinology and infertility, IVF/ET,
GIFT, laser laparoscopy and YAG laser

Gary A. Shangold, M.D.
Univ. of Chicago, Ob/Gyn Dept.
5841 S. Maryland Ave.
Chicago, IL 60637
(312) 702-6124
Board Certifications Ob/Gyn,
Reproductive Endocrinology
Member Society of Reproductive
Endocrinologists
Practice Setting academic
Clinical Interests infertility,
endometriosis, hysteroscopy and
mullerian anomalies, operative
laparoscopy, laser, IVF, GIFT

Aquiles J. Sobrero, M.D.
2800 N. Sheridan Rd., Suite 304

Chicago, IL 60611
(312) 281-1871
Board Certification Ob/Gyn
Member Society of Reproductive
Surgeons
Practice Setting academic/private
Clinical Interests reproductive
endocrinology, disorders of ovulation,
cervical and tubal factors,
endometriosis, male factor

Jorge A. Valle, M.D.
Illinois Masonic Med. Ctr.
836 W. Wellington Ave.
Chicago, IL 60657
(312) 883-7090
Board Certification Ob/Gyn
Member Society of Reproductive
Surgeons
Practice Setting private
Clinical Interests infertility, IVF, gyn-
endocrinology

Rafael F. Valle, M.D.
333 E. Superior St., #1152
Chicago, IL 60611
(312) 908-0651
Board Certification Ob/Gyn
Member Society of Reproductive
Surgeons
Practice Setting academic
Clinical Interests gynecology, infertility,
reproductive surgery

Earl F. Wendel, M.D.
707 N. Fairbanks Court
Chicago, IL 60611
(312) 908-8146
Board Certification Urology
Member American Society of
Andrology
Practice Setting academic
Clinical Interests male infertility

Downers Grove

W. Paul Dmowski, M.D., Ph.D.
4333 Main St.
Downers Grove, IL 60515
(312) 810-0212
Board Certifications Ob/Gyn,
Reproductive Endocrinology
Member Society of Reproductive
Endocrinologists
Practice Setting academic/private/HMO
Clinical Interests endometriosis, IVF,
GIFT, sex preselection

Amos Madanes, M.D.
  Midwest Infertility Ctr.
  4333 Main St.
  Downers Grove, IL 60515
  (312) 810-0212
  Board Certification Reproductive
  Endocrinology
  Member Society of Reproductive
  Endocrinologists
  Practice Setting private
  Clinical Interests NS

Elmhurst

Firdausi F. Mazda, M.D.
  172 Schiller
  Elmhurst, IL 60126
  (312) 941-2646
  Board Certification Urology
  Member American Society of
  Andrology
  Practice Setting private
  Clinical Interests male infertility

Hoffman Estates

Reena Jabamoni, M.D.
  990 Grand Canyon Parkway, Suite
  114
  Hoffman Estates, IL 60194
  (312) 843-7090
  Board Certification Ob/Gyn
  Member American Society of
  Andrology
  Practice Setting private
  Clinical Interests treatment of
  endometriosis, insemination, ovulatory
  disorders, intraabdominal laser surgery

Palos Heights

Charles O. Turk, D.O.
  7340 W. College Dr.
  Palos Heights, IL 60463
  (312) 361-3233
  Board Certification NS
  Member American Society of
  Andrology
  Practice Setting private
  Clinical Interests microsurgical
  vasectomy reversal, male infertility

Park Ridge

Charles E. Miller, M.D.
  1875 Dempster St., Suite 665
  Park Ridge, IL 60068
  (312) 696-8217
  Board Certification Ob/Gyn
  Member Society of Reproductive
  Surgeons
  Practice Setting academic/private/HMO
  Clinical Interests endoscopic laser
  surgery, microsurgery, medical and
  surgical treatment of endometriosis

Springfield

Phillip C. Galle, M.D.
  SIU School of Medicine,
  Ob/Gyn Dept.
  P.O. Box 19230
  Springfield, IL 62794-9230
  (217) 782-8241
  Board Certifications Ob/Gyn,
  Reproductive Endocrinology
  Member Society of Reproductive
  Endocrinologists
  Practice Setting academic
  Clinical Interests infertility, ovulatory
  disorders, tubal surgery, laser surgery,
  hirsutism

INDIANA

Elkhart

Ervin W. Heiser, M.D.
  1400 Hudson St.
  Elkhart, IN 46516
  (219) 295-8805
  Board Certification Ob/Gyn
  Member Society of Reproductive
  Surgeons
  Practice Setting private
  Clinical Interests AID, IUI, GIFT,
  gynecologic endocrinology, laser
  laparoscopy

Indianapolis

Leo M. Bonaventura, M.D.
  8091 Township Line Rd., Suite 108
  Indianapolis, IN 46260
  (317) 875-5978
  Board Certifications Ob/Gyn,

Reproductive Endocrinology
Member Society of Reproductive
Endocrinologists
Practice Setting private
Clinical Interests microscopic laser
surgery, tubal surgery, IVF, GIFT

Robert E. Cleary, M.D.
8091 Township Line Rd., Suite 109
Indianapolis, IN 46260
(317) 872-0582
Board Certification Reproductive
Endocrinology
Member Society of Reproductive
Endocrinologists
Practice Setting private
Clinical Interests infertility and
gynecology

Donald L. Cline, M.D.
2010 W. 86th St.
Indianapolis, IN 46260
(317) 872-1515
Board Certification Ob/Gyn
Member Society of Reproductive
Surgeons
Practice Setting private
Clinical Interests laser and microsurgery,
ovulation induction

John C. Jarrett, II, M.D.
8091 Township Line Rd., Suite 110
Indianapolis, IN 46260
(317) 876 0539
Board Certifications Ob/Gyn,
Reproductive Endocrinology
Member Society of Reproductive
Endocrinologists
Practice Setting private
Clinical Interests IVF, GIFT, operative
pelviscopy, microsurgery,
endometriosis

David S. McLaughlin, M.D.
Indianapolis Fertility Ctr.
8091 Township Line Rd., Suite 108
Indianapolis, IN 46260
(317) 875-5978
Board Certification Ob/Gyn
Member Society of Reproductive
Surgeons
Practice Setting private
Clinical Interests gynecologic,
reproductive laser surgery, GIFT, IVF,
tubal ovum transfer

Merrillville

Srbislav N. Brasovan, M.D.
8585 Broadway, Suite 670
Merrillville, IN 46410
(219) 738-2742
Board Certification Ob/Gyn
Member Society of Reproductive
Surgeons
Practice Setting private
Clinical Interests reproductive surgery,
infertility, gender selection, laser
surgery

IOWA

Iowa City

Frederick Keith Chapler, M.D.
Univ. of Iowa Hospital, Ob/Gyn
Dept.
Iowa City, IA 52242
(319) 356-2638
Board Certifications Ob/Gyn,
Reproductive Endocrinology
Member Society of Reproductive
Endocrinologists
Practice Setting academic
Clinical Interests hyperprolactinemia,
polycystic ovarian disease, Mullerian
anomalies, reparative surgery

Waterloo

Lane A. Reeves, M.D.
Medical Arts Ctr., Suite 355
2055 Kimball Ave.
Waterloo, IA 50702
(319) 291-2000
Board Certification Ob/Gyn
Member Society of Reproductive
Surgeons
Practice Setting private
Clinical Interests reproductive endocrine-
infertility, reproductive surgery,
therapeutic insemination, GnRH,
hMG

KANSAS

Wichita

B. W. Webster, M.D.
Ctr. for Reproductive Medicine

2903 E. Central
Wichita, KS 67214
(316) 687-2112
Board Certifications Ob/Gyn,
Reproductive Endocrinology
Member Society of Reproductive
Endocrinologists
Practice Setting academic
Clinical Interests IVF/GIFT, tubal
reconstruction, operative laparoscopy/
hysteroscopy, ovulation induction

KENTUCKY

Louisville

Arnold M. Belker, M.D.
250 E. Liberty St., Suite 602
Louisville, KY 40202
(502) 584-0651
Board Certification Urology
Member American Society of
Andrology
Practice Setting private
Clinical Interests microsurgical
vasectomy reversal, microsurgical
correction of male ductal obstruction

Christine L. Cook, M.D.
Univ. of Louisville School of
Medicine, Ob/Gyn Dept.
550 S. Jackson St.
Louisville, KY 40292
(502) 588-7906
Board Certification Ob/Gyn
Member American Society of
Andrology
Practice Setting academic/private
Clinical Interests male factor infertility,
IVF, ovulation induction

Marvin A. Yussman, M.D.
601 S. Floyd St.
Louisville, KY 40292
(502) 583-3845
Board Certification Ob/Gyn
Member Society of Reproductive
Surgeons
Practice Setting academic
Clinical Interests microsurgery,
pelviscopic surgery

LOUISIANA

Baton Rouge

Edwin A. Bowman, M.D.
Fertility Clinic of Baton Rouge
8742 Goodwood Blvd.
Baton Rouge, LA 70806
(504) 927-6061
Board Certification Ob/Gyn
Member Society of Reproductive
Surgeons
Practice Setting academic/private
Clinical Interests infertility surgery, laser
surgery, microsurgery, treatment of
endometriosis

Kenner

Heber E. Dunaway, Jr., M.D.
200 W. Esplanade Ave., Suite 210
Kenner, LA 70065
(504) 464-8622
Board Certification Ob/Gyn
Member Society of Reproductive
Surgeons
Practice Setting private
Clinical Interests IVF, GIFT, ZIFT, laser
microsurgery techniques, ovulation
induction, antisperm antibodies

Joseph A. LaNasa, Jr., M.D.
200 W. Esplanade Ave., Suite 305
Kenner, LA 70065
(504) 469-4459
Board Certification Urology
Member American Society of
Andrology
Practice Setting private
Clinical Interests andrology,
microsurgical genital tract
reconstruction and varicocele ligation,
vasovasostomy

Lafayette

William D. Pelletier, M.D.
4540 Ambassador Caffery, Suite
A-220
Lafayette, LA 70508
(318) 981-4706
Board Certification Ob/Gyn
Member Society of Reproductive
Surgeons

Practice Setting private
Clinical Interests infertility, endocrine

James L. Zehnder, M.D.
4540 Ambassador Caffery, Suite
A-220
Lafayette, LA 70508
(318) 981-4706
Board Certification Ob/Gyn
Member Society of Reproductive
Surgeons
Practice Setting private
Clinical Interests general infertility, laser
laparoscopy, microsurgery, abdominal
laser surgery

Metairie

Joseph H. Bellina, M.D., Ph.D.
3850 N. Causeway Blvd.
Suite 900
Metairie, LA 70002
(504) 832-4200
Board Certification Ob/Gyn
Member American Society of
Andrology
Practice Setting private
Clinical Interests laser reconstructive
surgery of pelvic and reproductive
organs

Robert W. Kelly, M.D.
3850 N. Causeway Blvd., Suite 900
Metairie, LA 70002
(504) 832-4200
Board Certifications Ob/Gyn,
Reproductive Endocrinology
Member Society of Reproductive
Endocrinologists
Practice Setting private
Clinical Interests reproductive
endocrinology, reconstructive fertility
surgery

Myron E. Moorehead, M.D.
4720 I-10 Service Rd., Suite 100
Metairie, LA 70001
(504) 888-1526
Board Certification Ob/Gyn
Member Society of Reproductive
Surgeons
Practice Setting private
Clinical Interests reproductive surgery/
infertility

New Orleans

Rodney A. Appell, M.D.
4400 General Meyer Ave.
New Orleans, LA 70131
(504) 368-0425
Board Certification Urology
Member American Society of
Andrology
Practice Setting academic/private
Clinical Interests infertility (male),
impotence, incontinence

David N. Curole, M.D.
Fertility Institute of New Orleans
6020 Bullard Ave.
New Orleans, LA 70128
(504) 246-8971
Board Certification Ob/Gyn
Member Society of Reproductive
Surgeons
Practice Setting private
Clinical Interests GIFT/IVF, ovulation
induction, sex selection,
endometriosis, laser surgery, donor/
husband insemination

Richard P. Dickey, M.D., Ph.D.
Fertility Institute of New Orleans
6020 Bullard Ave.
New Orleans, LA 70128
(504) 246-8971
Board Certifications Ob/Gyn,
Reproductive Endocrinology
Member Society of Reproductive
Endocrinologists
Practice Setting private
Clinical Interests GIFT, IVF, ovulation
induction, endometriosis, laser
surgery, donor/husband insemination,
sex selection

Wayne J. G. Hellstrom, M.D.
Tulane Univ. School of Medicine,
Urology Dept.
1430 Tulane Ave.
New Orleans, LA 70112
(504) 588-5271
Board Certification Urology
Member American Society of
Andrology
Practice Setting academic
Clinical Interests male infertility,
microsurgical reanastomosis, erectile
dysfunction

George T. Schneider, M.D.
Ochsner Clinic
1514 Jefferson Highway
New Orleans, LA 70121
(504) 838-4031
Board Certification Ob/Gyn
Member Society of Reproductive
Surgeons
Practice Setting private
Clinical Interests general infertility

Steven N. Taylor, M.D.
Fertility Institute of New Orleans
6020 Bullard Ave.
New Orleans, LA 70128
(504) 246-8971
Board Certification Ob/Gyn
Member Society of Reproductive
Surgeons
Practice Setting private
Clinical Interests GIFT, IVF, ovulation
induction, endometriosis, laser
surgery, donor/husband insemination,
sex selection

Ian H. Thorneycroft, M.D., Ph.D.
Tulane Univ. Med. School, Ob/Gyn
Dept.
1430 Tulane Ave.
New Orleans, LA 70112
(504) 587-2147
Board Certifications Ob/Gyn,
Reproductive Endocrinology
Member Society of Reproductive
Endocrinologists
Practice Setting academic
Clinical Interests reproductive
endocrinology, infertility, menopause

John C. Weed, M.D.
1525 Dafossat St.
New Orleans, LA 70115
(204) 899-7832
Board Certification Ob/Gyn
Member Society of Reproductive
Surgeons
Practice Setting academic
Clinical Interests endometriosis,
infertility

MAINE

Portland

James O. Pringle, M.D.
19 West St.
Portland, ME 04102

(207) 774-4269
Board Certification Urology
Member American Society of
Andrology
Practice Setting private
Clinical Interests male infertility

MARYLAND

Baltimore

Theodore A. Baramki, M.D.
Physicians Pavilion, Suite 203
6701 N. Charles St.
Greater Baltimore Medical Ctr.
Baltimore, MD 21204
(301) 828-2753
Board Certifications Ob/Gyn,
Reproductive Endocrinology
Member Society of Reproductive
Endocrinologists
Practice Setting private
Clinical Interests infertility,
microsurgery, repeated miscarriages,
prenatal genetic diagnosis

Marian D. Damewood, M.D.
The Johns Hopkins Hospital, Ob/Gyn
Dept.
600 N. Wolfe St.
Baltimore, MD 21205
(301) 955-2016
Board Certifications Ob/Gyn,
Reproductive Endocrinology
Member Society of Reproductive
Endocrinologists
Practice Setting academic
Clinical Interests infertility surgery,
reproductive endocrinology

Jairo E. Garcia, M.D.
6701 N. Charles St.
GBMC Physicians Pavilion, Suite 207
Baltimore, MD 21204
(301) 828-2484
Board Certification Ob/Gyn
Member Society of Reproductive
Surgeons
Practice Setting private
Clinical Interests IVF, infertility

Rafael C. Haciski, M.D.
201 E. University Parkway
Baltimore, MD 21218
(301) 554-2942
Board Certification Ob/Gyn

Member Society of Reproductive
Surgeons
Practice Setting academic/private
Clinical Interests infertility, tubal disease

George R. Huggins, M.D.
Francis Scott Key Med. Ctr.
4940 Eastern Ave.
Baltimore, MD 21224
(301) 550-0335
Board Certification Ob/Gyn
Member Society of Reproductive
Surgeons
Practice Setting academic/private
Clinical Interests microsurgery,
endometriosis

Santiago L. Padilla, M.D.
GBMC Pavilion, Suite 207
6701 N. Charles St.
Baltimore, MD 21204
(301) 828-2484
Board Certifications Ob/Gyn,
Reproductive Endocrinology
Member Society of Reproductive
Endocrinologists
Practice Setting private
Clinical Interests IVF, microsurgery, laser
laparoscopic surgery

John A. Rock, M.D.
Div. of Reproductive Endocrinology,
Houck 247
The Johns Hopkins Med. Institute
600 N. Wolfe St.
Baltimore, MD 21205
(301) 955-3355
Board Certifications Ob/Gyn,
Reproductive Endocrinology
Member Society of Reproductive
Endocrinologists
Practice Setting academic/private
Clinical Interests reparative and
constructive surgery, infertility,
endometriosis, repeated pregnancy
wastage, tubal disorders

William D. Schlaff, M.D.
The Johns Hopkins Hospital, Houck
249
Baltimore, MD 21205
(301) 955-6883
Board Certifications Ob/Gyn,
Reproductive Endocrinology
Member Society of Reproductive
Endocrinologists
Practice Setting academic

Clinical Interests andrology, ovulatory
dysfunction, reproductive surgery

Peter N. Schlegel, M.D.
James B. Brady Urologic Institute
The Johns Hopkins Hospital
600 N. Wolfe St.
Baltimore, MD 21205
(301) 955-5100
Board Certification NS
Member American Society of
Andrology
Practice Setting academic
Clinical Interest male factor infertility

J. Walter Smyth, M.D.
5601 Loch Raven Blvd.
Baltimore, MD 21239
(301) 433-7300
Board Certification Urology
Member American Society of
Andrology
Practice Setting private
Clinical Interests general practice of
urology and subfertility

Donald B. Spangler, M.D.
9105 Franklin Square Dr.
Baltimore, MD 21237
(301) 682-7800
Board Certification Ob/Gyn
Member Society of Reproductive
Surgeons
Practice Setting academic/private
Clinical Interests infertility and
reproductive endocrinology

Edward E. Wallach, M.D.
600 N. Wolfe St., Houck 264
Baltimore, MD 21205
(301) 955-7800
Board Certifications Ob/Gyn,
Reproductive Endocrinology
Member Society of Reproductive
Endocrinologists
Practice Setting academic/private
Clinical Interest infertility

Howard Zacur, M.D., Ph.D.
Department of Gynecology and
Obstetrics
The Johns Hopkins Univ. School of
Medicine
Park B-2-202 A
600 North Wolfe St.
Baltimore, MD 21218
Telephone NS
Board Certifications Ob/Gyn,

Reproductive Endocrinology
Member Society of Reproductive
Endocrinologists
Practice Setting academic
Clinical Interests prolactin disorders

Bethesda

Frank E. Chang, M.D.
10215 Fernwood Rd., Suite 303
Bethesda, MD 20854
(301) 897-8850
Board Certifications Ob/Gyn,
Reproductive Endocrinology
Member Society of Reproductive
Endocrinologists
Practice Setting private
Clinical Interests IVF, GIFT, laser
surgery

Jay M. Grodin, M.D.
10215 Fernwood Rd. #303
Bethesda, MD 20817
(301) 897-8850
Board Certifications Ob/Gyn,
Reproductive Endocrinology
Member Society of Reproductive
Endocrinologists
Practice Setting private/HMO
Clinical Interests infertility—medical,
surgical, IVF

Chevy Chase

Frederick J. Frensilli, M.D.
5530 Wisconsin Ave., #950
Chevy Chase, MD 20815
(301) 652-7872
Board Certification Urology
Member American Society of
Andrology
Practice Setting private
Clinical Interests male infertility,
microsurgery, sperm banking, sperm
enhancement techniques

Rockville

Burt A. Littman, M.D.
9711 Med. Ctr. Dr., Suite 214
Rockville, MD 20850
(301) 424-1904
Board Certifications Ob/Gyn,
Reproductive Endocrinology
Member Society of Reproductive

Endocrinologists
Practice Setting private
Clinical Interests ovulation induction,
microsurgery, endometriosis,
menopause, GnRH agonists

Linda Liu, M.D.
6246 Montrose Rd.
Rockville, MD 20852
(301) 468-1451
Board Certifications Internal Medicine,
Endocrinology and Metabolism
Member American Society of
Andrology
Practice Setting academic/private
Clinical Interests male reproductive
disorders, delayed puberty, hormonal
deficiencies, oligospermia,
gonadotropin and GnRH treatments

Timonium

Janet L. Kennedy, M.D.
2405 York Rd., Suite 304
Timonium, MD 21093
(301) 252-6633
Board Certifications Ob/Gyn,
Reproductive Endocrinology
Member Society of Reproductive
Endocrinologists
Practice Setting private
Clinical Interests surgical therapy, pelvic
factor infertility, male factor infertility
including antisperm antibodies

MASSACHUSETTS

Boston

Susan T. Haas, M.D.
333 Longwood Ave., Suite 520
Boston, MA 02115
(617) 566-1066
Board Certification Ob/Gyn
Member American Society of
Andrology
Practice Setting academic
Clinical Interests laparoscopic and
hysteroscopic surgery, microsurgery,
endocrinology

Florina Haimovici, M.D.
Harvard Med. School
250 Longwood Ave., SGMB 230
Boston, MA 02115
(617) 732-2194

Board Certifications NS
Member American Society of
Andrology
Practice Setting academic
Clinical Interests NS

Joseph A. Hill, M.D.
Brigham and Women's Hospital
Harvard Med. School
75 Francis St.
Boston, MA 02115
(617) 566-1066
Board Certifications Ob/Gyn,
Reproductive Endocrinology
Member American Society of
Andrology
Practice Setting academic
Clinical Interests recurrent spontaneous
abortion, endometriosis, immunologic
infertility

Robert B. Hunt, M.D.
319 Longwood Ave.
Boston, MA 02115
(617) 731-6111
Board Certification Ob/Gyn
Member Society of Reproductive
Surgeons
Practice Setting private
Clinical Interests reconstructive pelvic
surgery for female infertility

Robert Davis Oates, M.D.
720 Harrison Ave., DOB 606
Boston, MA 02118
(617) 638-8485
Board Certification NS
Member American Society of
Andrology
Practice Setting academic
Clinical Interests all areas of male
infertility, especially surgery and
electroejaculation

Veronica A. Ravnikar, M.D.
Brigham and Women's Hospital
Ob/Gyn Dept., Room 3-069
75 Francis St.
Boston, MA 02115
(617) 732-4455
Board Certifications Ob/Gyn,
Reproductive Endocrinology
Member Society of Reproductive
Endocrinologists
Practice Setting academic
Clinical Interests infertility, tubal

surgery, IVF, GIFT, reproductive
endocrinology, menopause

Isaac Schiff, M.D.
Massachusetts General Hospital,
Vincent I
Boston, MA 02114
(617) 726-5290
Board Certifications Ob/Gyn,
Reproductive Endocrinology
Member Society of Reproductive
Endocrinologists
Practice Setting academic
Clinical Interests infertility, menopause

Machelle M. Seibel, M.D.
Beth Israel Hospital, Ob/Gyn Dept.
330 Brookline Ave.
Boston, MA 02215
(617) 735-2360
Board Certifications Ob/Gyn,
Reproductive Endocrinology
Member Society of Reproductive
Endocrinologists
Practice Setting academic/private
Clinical Interests ovulatory dysfunction,
PCO, IVF, endometriosis

Brighton

H. David Mitcheson, M.D.
Baystate Urologists
697 Cambridge St.
Brighton, MA 02135
(617) 782-1200
Board Certification Urology
Member American Society of
Andrology
Practice Setting private
Clinical Interests urology, infertility,
incontinence, impotence, urodynamics

Brookline

Melvin L. Taymor, M.D.
1 Brookline Place, Suite 421
Brookline, MA 02146
(617) 731-8000
Board Certifications NS
Member Society of Reproductive
Surgeons
Practice Setting private
Clinical Interests general infertility,
specializing in ovulation induction,
IVF, GIFT

Malden

Dan Tulchinsky, M.D.
The Malden Hospital
Malden, MA 02148
(617) 397-6540
Board Certifications Ob/Gyn,
Reproductive Endocrinology
Member Society of Reproductive
Endocrinologists
Practice Setting private
Clinical Interests infertility and
endocrinology

Pittsfield

Sandor H. Wax, M.D.
217 South St.
Pittsfield, MA 01201
(413) 499-8575
Board Certification Urology
Member American Society of
Andrology
Practice Setting private
Clinical Interest male infertility

Springfield

Ronald K. Burke, M.D.
Fertility Institute of Western
Massachusetts
130 Maple St.
Springfield, MA 01103
(413) 781-8220
Board Certification Ob/Gyn
Member Society of Reproductive
Surgeons
Practice Setting private
Clinical Interests reproductive medicine
and surgery, operative laparoscopy,
pelvic laser surgery, andrology

Waltham

Patricia McShane, M.D.
20 Hope Ave.
Waltham, MA 02254
(617) 647-6263
Board Certification Reproductive
Endocrinology
Member Society of Reproductive
Endocrinologists
Practice Setting private
Clinical Interests infertility, IVF

Worcester

Stephen M. Cohen, M.D.
Univ. Massachusetts Med. Ctr.,
Ob/Gyn Dept.
55 Lake Ave. N.
Worcester, MA 01655
(508) 856-3107
Board Certification Ob/Gyn
Member Society of Reproductive
Surgeons
Practice Setting academic/private
Clinical Interests infertility surgery, laser
surgery, infertility, operative
laparoscopy

MICHIGAN

Ann Arbor

Rudi Ansbacher, M.D., M.S.
Univ. of Michigan Med. Ctr.,
Ob/Gyn Dept.
Med. Professional Bldg., Room
D-2206
Ann Arbor, MI 48109-0718
(313) 763-4344
Board Certification Ob/Gyn
Member Society of Reproductive
Surgeons
Practice Setting academic
Clinical Interests infertility, repetitive
miscarriages

Birmingham

S. Jan Behrman, M.D.
122 E. Brown St.
Birmingham, MI 48011
(313) 644-4006
Board Certifications Ob/Gyn,
Reproductive Endocrinology
Member Society of Reproductive
Surgeons
Practice Setting academic/private
Clinical Interests IVF, uterine anomalies

David A. Brinton, M.D.
122 E. Brown St.
Birmingham, MI 48011
(313) 644-4006
Board Certification Ob/Gyn
Member Society of Reproductive
Surgeons
Practice Setting NS

Clinical Interests pelviscopy, laser laparoscopy, uterine anomalies, IVF

John R. Musich, M.D.
Beaumont Fertility Ctr.
122 E. Brown St.
Birmingham, MI 48011
(313) 644-4006
Board Certifications Ob/Gyn,
Reproductive Endocrinology
Member Society of Reproductive
Endocrinologists
Practice Setting private
Clinical Interests infertility, gynecologic
endocrinology

Willis H. Stephens, Jr., M.D.
Michigan Infertility Ctr.
189 Townsend St.
Birmingham, MI 48009
(313) 647-5565
Board Certification Ob/Gyn
Member American Society of
Andrology
Practice Setting private
Clinical Interests infertility, reproductive
endocrinology, reproductive
microsurgery, therapeutic donor
insemination

Dearborn

Maria F. Hayes, M.D.
Ctr. for Reproductive Medicine
Oakwood Med. Bldg.
18181 Oakwood Blvd., Suite 100G
Dearborn, MI 48124
(313) 593-5880
Board Certifications Ob/Gyn,
Reproductive Endocrinology
Member Society of Reproductive
Endocrinologists
Practice Setting private
Clinical Interests IVF, microsurgery, laser
surgery

David M. Magyar, D.O.
Ctr. for Reproductive Medicine
Oakwood Med. Bldg.
18181 Oakwood Blvd., Suite 100G
Dearborn, MI 48124
(313) 593-5880
Board Certifications Ob/Gyn,
Reproductive Endocrinology
Member Society of Reproductive
Endocrinologists

Practice Setting private
Clinical Interests IVF, microsurgery, laser
surgery

Detroit

Khalid M. Ataya, M.D.
Wayne State Univ.
275 E. Hancock Ave.
Detroit, MI 48201
(313) 745-0499
Board Certification Reproductive
Endocrinology
Member Society of Reproductive
Endocrinologists
Practice Setting academic
Clinical Interests NS

C. B. Dhabuwala, M.D.
4160 John R., Suite 1021
Detroit, MI 48201
(313) 833-3320
Board Certification Urology
Member American Society of
Andrology
Practice Setting academic
Clinical Interests male infertility and
impotence

Kenneth A. Ginsburg, M.D.
Wayne State Univ., Ob/Gyn Dept.
4707 St. Antoine
Detroit, MI 48201
(313) 745-7693
Board Certification NS
Member American Society of
Andrology
Practice Setting academic
Clinical Interests all aspects of male and
female infertility, AID, IVF,
microsurgery

Kamran S. Moghissi, M.D.
Wayne State Univ./Hutzel Hospital,
Ob/Gyn Dept.
4707 St. Antoine
Detroit, MI 48201
(313) 745-7285
Board Certification Reproductive
Endocrinology
Member Society of Reproductive
Endocrinologists
Practice Setting academic
Clinical Interests infertility, IVF,
reproductive endocrinology

Flint

Minoo B. Chinoy, M.D.
1402 W. Court St.
Flint, MI 48503
(313) 767-3220
Board Certification Ob/Gyn
Member Society of Reproductive
Surgeons
Practice Setting private
Clinical Interests infertility,
microsurgery, operative laparoscopy,
laser surgery, endometriosis

Lansing

Farrah Fahimi, M.D.
1322 E. Michigan Ave., Suite 314
Lansing, MI 48912
(517) 489-4900
Board Certifications Ob/Gyn,
Reproductive Endocrinology
Member Society of Reproductive
Endocrinologists
Practice Setting private
Clinical Interests infertility, IVF, GIFT,
microsurgery

Mohammed Mohsenian, M.D.
1322 E. Michigan Ave., Suite 314
Lansing, MI 48912
(517) 484-4900
Board Certifications Ob/Gyn,
Reproductive Endocrinology
Member Society of Reproductive
Endocrinologists
Practice Setting private
Clinical Interests IVF, laser surgery,
endometriosis, all aspects of infertility

Grand Rapids

R. Donald Eward, M.D.
885 Forest Hill Ave., S.E.
Grand Rapids, MI 49506
(616) 942-5180
Board Certification Ob/Gyn
Member American Society of
Andrology
Practice Setting private
Clinical Interests microsurgery,
andrology, endometriosis

Robert D. Visscher, M.D.
1900 Wealthy, S.E.

Grand Rapids, MI 49506
(616) 774-0700
Board Certification Reproductive
Endocrinology
Member Society of Reproductive
Endocrinologists
Practice Setting academic/private
Clinical Interests reproductive
endocrinology, IVF

Grosse Pointe Farms

Alexander M. Dlugi, M.D.
Henry Ford Med. Ctr.
Pierson Clinic
131 Kercheval Ave.
Grosse Pointe Farms, MI 48236
(313) 343-5900
Board Certifications Ob/Gyn,
Reproductive Endocrinology
Member Society of Reproductive
Endocrinologists
Practice Setting Other
Clinical Interests endoscopic surgery,
ovulation induction, IVF

Ypsilanti

Jonathan W. T. Ayers, M.D.
Ann Arbor Reproductive Medicine
Assoc.
4990 Clark Rd., Suite 100
Ypsilanti, MI 48197
(313) 434-4766
Board Certifications Ob/Gyn,
Reproductive Endocrinology
Member Society of Reproductive
Endocrinologists
Practice Setting Other
Clinical Interests ovulation induction,
infertility surgery, operative
laparoscopy with laser, artificial
insemination, IVF

Edwin P. Peterson, M.D.
Ann Arbor Reproductive Medicine
Assoc.
4990 Clark Rd., Suite 100
Ypsilanti, MI 48197
(313) 434-4766
Board Certifications Ob/Gyn,
Reproductive Endocrinology
Member Society of Reproductive
Endocrinologists
Practice Setting Other
Clinical Interests ovulation induction,

infertility surgery, operative laparoscopy with laser, artificial insemination, IVF

MINNESOTA

Minneapolis

George E. Tagatz, M.D.
Univ. of Minnesota, Ob/Gyn Dept.
Box 395, Mayo Bldg.
Minneapolis, MN 55455
(612) 626-3232
Board Certifications Ob/Gyn,
Reproductive Endocrinology
Member Society of Reproductive
Endocrinologists
Practice Setting academic
Clinical Interests medical and surgical
reproductive endocrinology, IVF, tubal
microsurgery, AID

Rochester

Paul C. Carpenter, M.D.
200 First St., S.W.
Rochester, MN 55901
(507) 284-3781
Board Certifications Internal Medicine,
Endocrinology
Member American Society of
Andrology
Practice Setting academic/private
Clinical Interests male infertility,
pituitary/gonad/adrenal diseases

Robert C. Northcutt, M.D.
Mayo Clinic, W18
200 First St., S.W.
Rochester, MN 55902
(507) 284-0051
Board Certifications Internal Medicine,
Endocrinology and Metabolism
Member American Society of
Andrology
Practice Setting private
Clinical Interests male factor infertility,
pituitary dysfunction

Steven J. Ory, M.D.
Mayo Clinic, W10
200 First Street, S.W.
Rochester, MN 55905
(507) 284-4520
Board Certifications Ob/Gyn,
Reproductive Endocrinology

Member Society of Reproductive
Endocrinologists
Practice Setting academic
Clinical Interests ovulation induction,
endometriosis, reproductive surgery,
IVF

Charles C. Rife, M.D.
Mayo Clinic
200 First Street, S.W.
Rochester, MN 55901
(507) 284-3981
Board Certification Urology
Member American Society of
Andrology
Practice Setting academic/private
Clinical Interests male aspects of
infertility, both medical and surgical

Tiffany J. Williams, M.D.
Mayo Clinic
200 First Street, S.W.
Rochester, MN 55905
(507) 284-2425
Board Certification Ob/Gyn
Member Society of Reproductive
Surgeons
Practice Setting academic
Clinical Interests pelvic microsurgery

St. Paul

Stanley John Antolak, Jr., M.D.
280 N. Smith Ave.
658 Doctors Professional Bldg.
St. Paul, MN 55102
(612) 227-9518
Board Certification Urology
Member American Society of
Andrology
Practice Setting private
Clinical Interests andrology, male
infertility, general urology

MISSISSIPPI

Jackson

Bryan D. Cowan, M.D.
Univ. Mississippi Med. Ctr.,
Ob/Gyn Dept.
2500 N. State St.
Jackson, MS 39216
(601) 984-5330
Board Certifications Ob/Gyn,
Reproductive Endocrinology

Member Society of Reproductive
Endocrinologists
Practice Setting academic
Clinical Interests IVF, ovulation, tubal
surgery, laser surgery, endoscopic
surgery, microsurgery

G. Rodney Meeks, M.D.
2500 N. State St.
Jackson, MS 39216
(601) 984-5314
Board Certification Ob/Gyn
Member American Society of
Andrology
Practice Setting academic
Clinical Interests gynecology, infertility,
artificial insemination

MISSOURI

Columbia

L. L. Penney, M.D.
1 Hospital Dr., Ob/Gyn Dept.
Columbia, MO 65212
(314) 882-7938
Board Certifications Ob/Gyn,
Reproductive Endocrinology
Member Society of Reproductive
Surgeons
Practice Setting academic/private
Clinical Interests NS
Research Interests NS

Dana J. Weaver, M.D.
N510 Health Science Ctr., Urology
Dept.
Columbia, MO 65212
(314) 882-1151
Board Certification Urology
Member American Society of
Andrology
Practice Setting academic
Clinical Interests infertility, sperm
banking, microsurgery

Kansas City

John W. Betts, M.D.
4400 Broadway, Suite 309
Kansas City, MO 64111
(816) 756-0277
Board Certification Ob/Gyn
Member Society of Reproductive
Surgeons
Practice Setting private

Clinical Interests infertility, reproductive
endocrinology, IVF, GIFT

Gregory C. Starks, M.D.
6400 Prospect Ave., T107
Kansas City, MO 64132
(816) 361-3640
Board Certification Ob/Gyn
Member Society of Reproductive
Surgeons
Practice Setting academic/private
Clinical Interests GnRH agonist, laser
surgery in infertility

Nezaam M. Zamah, M.D.
3101 Broadway, Suite 650B
Kansas City, MO 64111
(816) 931-2733
Board Certification Ob/Gyn
Member Society of Reproductive
Surgeons
Practice Setting academic/private
Clinical Interests endometriosis,
infertility, pelvic reconstructive
surgery, laser surgery, IVF, GIFT,
tubal reanastomosis

St. Louis

Ernst R. Friedrich, M.D.
4911 Barnes Hospital Plaza
St. Louis, MO 63110
(314) 362-1019
Board Certification Ob/Gyn
Member Society of Reproductive
Surgeons
Practice Setting academic
Clinical Interests hysteroscopy,
laparoscopy, laser, microsurgery,
urogynecology, endoscopy under local
anesthesia

Donald J. Mehan, M.D.
1035 Bellevue Ave.
St. Louis, MO 63117
(314) 644-6767
Board Certification Urology
Member American Society of
Andrology
Practice Setting academic/private
Clinical Interests male hypofertility and
hypogonadism

Ronald C. Strickler, M.D.
Jewish Hospital at Washington Univ.
Med. Ctr.
216 S. Kings Highway

St. Louis, MO 63110
(314) 454-8920
Board Certifications Ob/Gyn,
Reproductive Endocrinology
Member Society of Reproductive
Endocrinologists
Practice Setting academic
Clinical Interests general infertility and
endocrinology

Barry I. Witten, M.D.
621 S. New Ballas Rd.
St. Louis, MO 63141
(314) 569-6880
Board Certifications Ob/Gyn,
Reproductive Endocrinology
Member Society of Reproductive
Endocrinologists
Practice Setting academic/private
Clinical Interests reproductive
endocrinology, infertility, GIFT, laser,
microsurgery

NEBRASKA

Omaha

Jeffrey P. Buch, M.D.
Univ. of Nebraska Med. Ctr.
Urologic Surgery Div.
42nd St. and Dewey Ave.
Omaha, NE 68105
(402) 559-6354
Board Certification Urology
Member American Society of
Andrology
Practice Setting academic
Clinical Interests male infertility (all
aspects), microsurgery

NEVADA

Reno

Carlos Soto-Albors, M.D.
Northern Nevada Fertility Ctr.
350 W. Sixth St.
Reno, NV 89503
(702) 322-4521
Board Certifications Ob/Gyn,
Reproductive Endocrinology
Member Society of Reproductive
Endocrinologists
Practice Setting private
Clinical Interests IVF/GIFT, sterilization

reversal, tubal microsurgery, laser
surgery, hysteroscopy

Sparks

Harold C. Chotiner, M.D.
2385 E. Prater
Sparks, NV
(702) 355-5550
Board Certification Ob/Gyn
Member Society of Reproductive
Surgeons
Practice Setting private
Clinical Interests all aspects of infertility,
DES uterus

NEW HAMPSHIRE

Hanover

Paul D. Manganiello, M.D.
Dartmouth–Hitchcock Med. Ctr.
2 Maynard St.
Hanover, NH 03756
(603) 646-8162
Board Certifications Ob/Gyn,
Reproductive Endocrinology
Member Society of Reproductive
Endocrinologists
Practice Setting academic
Clinical Interests IVF, embryo transfer,
treatment of menstrual disorders

NEW JERSEY

Cherry Hill

Thomas J. DeBenedictis, M.D.
1301 N. Kings Highway
Cherry Hill, NJ 08034
(609) 795-3556
Board Certification Urology
Member American Society of
Andrology
Practice Setting academic/private
Clinical Interests male infertility

Joel L. Marmar, M.D.
1301 N. Kings Highway
Cherry Hill, NJ 08034
(215) 923-6225
Board Certification Urology
Member American Society of
Andrology
Practice Setting academic/private

Clinical Interests male infertility, microsurgery, vasectomy reversals

East Orange

Leonard M. Pogach, M.D.
East Orange V.A. Med. Ctr.
East Orange, NJ 07039
(201) 676-1000
Board Certifications Internal Medicine,
Endocrinology and Metabolism
Member American Society of
Andrology
Practice Setting academic
Clinical Interests impotence, male
infertility

Marlton

Robert A. Skaf, M.D.
Pavilion at Greentree, Suite 405
Marlton, NJ 28053
(609) 596-2233
Board Certifications Ob/Gyn,
Reproductive Endocrinology
Member Society of Reproductive
Endocrinologists
Practice Setting private
Clinical Interests ovulation induction,
endometriosis

Montclair

Herbert A. Goldfarb, M.D.
29 The Crescent
Montclair, NJ 07042
(201) 744-7470
Board Certification Ob/Gyn
Member Society of Reproductive
Surgeons
Practice Setting private
Clinical Interests CO_2 laser
(endometriosis), YAG laser (in lieu of
hysterectomy)

Neptune

Paul G. Stumpf, M.D.
The Jersey Shore Med. Ctr.
1945 Corlies Ave.
Neptune, NJ 07753
(201) 776-4128
Board Certifications Ob/Gyn,
Reproductive Endocrinology

Member Society of Reproductive
Endocrinologists
Practice Setting academic/private
Clinical Interests microsurgery, repair of
sterilization, laparoscopy, ovulation
induction

New Brunswick

Ekkehard Kemmann, M.D.
UMD–RW Johnson Med. School
Academic Health Science Ctr., CN19
New Brunswick, NJ 08903
(201) 937-7627
Board Certification Reproductive
Endocrinology
Member Society of Reproductive
Endocrinologists
Practice Setting academic
Clinical Interests female infertility

Newark

Eli F. Lizza, M.D.
UMDNJ–New Jersey Med. School,
Surgery/Urology Dept.
185 S. Orange Ave.,
Room G-536
Newark, NJ 07103-2757
(201) 456-4465
Board Certification Urology
Member American Society of
Andrology
Practice Setting academic/private
Clinical Interests male infertility and
microsurgery

Cecilia L. Schmidt, M.D.
UMDNJ New Jersey Med. School
100 Bergen St.
Newark, NJ 07103-2757
(201) 456-6029
Board Certifications Ob/Gyn,
Reproductive Endocrinology
Member Society of Reproductive
Endocrinologists
Practice Setting other
Clinical Interests IVF, endometriosis,
reproductive endocrinology

Gerson Weiss, M.D.
UMDNJ–New Jersey Med. School
185 S. Orange Ave., E506
Newark, NJ 07103-2757
(201) 456-5266
Board Certifications Ob/Gyn,

Reproductive Endocrinology
Member Society of Reproductive
Endocrinologists
Practice Setting academic
Clinical Interests infertility

River Edge

Stuart H. Levey, M.D.
117 Kinderkamack Rd.
River Edge, NJ 07661
(201) 342-6600
Board Certification Urology
Member American Society of
Andrology
Practice Setting private/academic
Clinical Interests general male infertility
problems, microsurgical (vas and
epididymal)

Short Hills

Thomas Annos, M.D.
40 Farley Pl.
Short Hills, NJ 07078
(201) 467-0099
Board Certifications Ob/Gyn,
Reproductive Endocrinology
Member Society of Reproductive
Endocrinologists
Practice Setting private
Clinical Interests infertility surgery,
operative laparoscopy, video laser
laparoscopy

Springfield

Morey Wosnitzer, M.D.
420 Morris Ave.
Springfield, NJ 07081
(201) 379-6949
Board Certification Urology
Member Society of Reproductive
Surgeons
Practice Setting private
Clinical Interests male infertility,
vasovasostomy, azoospermia
investigation, AI with frozen sperm
specimens

West Orange

Eugene A. Stulberger, M.D.
769 Northfield Ave., Suite 220

West Orange, NJ 07052
(201) 325-2440
Board Certification Urology
Member American Society of
Andrology
Practice Setting private
Clinical Interests male infertility

NEW YORK

Albany

Alan H. Bennett, M.D.
K209 Albany Med. Ctr. Hospital
Albany, NY 12208
(518) 445-3341
Board Certification Urology
Member American Society of
Andrology
Practice Setting academic
Clinical Interests sexual dysfunction/
male infertility

William J. Butler, M.D.
Albany Med. Ctr., Ob/Gyn Dept.
Albany, NY 12208
(518) 445-5902
Board Certifications Ob/Gyn,
Reproductive Endocrinology
Member Society of Reproductive
Endocrinologists
Practice Setting academic
Clinical Interests endocrinology and
infertility, prenatal diagnosis and
genetic counseling, IVF

Bronx

David H. Barad, M.D.
Albert Einstein College of Medicine,
Ob/Gyn Dept.
Ullmann Bldg., Rm. 123,
1300 Morris Park Ave.
Bronx, NY 10461
(212) 430-3152
Board Certifications Ob/Gyn,
Reproductive Endocrinology
Member Society of Reproductive
Endocrinologists
Practice Setting academic
Clinical Interests laparoscopic surgery,
hysteroscopic surgery, microsurgery,
assisted reproductive medicine (IVF,
GIFT, ZIFT donor ovum)

Ruth Freeman, M.D.
Albert Einstein College of Medicine
1300 Morris Park Ave.-123, Ullmann
Bldg.
Bronx, NY 10461
(212) 655-7723
Board Certifications Internal Medicine,
Endocrinology and Metabolism
Member American Society of
Andrology
Practice Setting academic
Clinical Interests patients with possible
hormonal problems with infertility

Brooklyn

George D. Kofinas, M.D.
121 Dekalb Ave.
Brooklyn, NY 11201
(718) 643-6307
Board Certifications Ob/Gyn,
Reproductive Endocrinology
Member Society of Reproductive
Endocrinologists
Practice Setting academic/private
Clinical Interests endoscopic treatment
of infertility, ovulation induction,
hirsutism

Francisco I. Reyes, M.D.
Suny HSC at Brooklyn
450 Clarkson Ave., Box 24
Brooklyn, NY 11203
(718) 270-2101
Board Certifications Ob/Gyn,
Reproductive Endocrinology
Member Society of Reproductive
Endocrinologists
Practice Setting academic
Clinical Interests endocrine dysfunction,
microsurgery

Alvin M. Siegler, M.D.
One Hanson Place
Brooklyn, NY 11243
(718) 638-1104
Board Certification Ob/Gyn
Member Society of Reproductive
Surgeons
Practice Setting private
Clinical Interests gynecologic endoscopy

Flushing

Chun Fu Wang, M.D.
146-01 45th Ave., Suite 208

Flushing, NY 11355
(718) 670-5792
Board Certifications Ob/Gyn,
Reproductive Endocrinology
Member Society of Reproductive
Endocrinologists
Practice Setting private/academic
Clinical Interests induction of ovulation,
infertility surgery, hyperandrogenic
syndrome

Forest Hills

Maxwell Roland, M.D.
109-33 71st Rd.
Forest Hills, NY 11375
(718) 268-6800
Board Certication Ob/Gyn
Member Society of Reproductive
Surgeons
Practice Setting private
Clinical Interests evaluation of problems
of infertility, including associated
menstrual disorders

Great Neck

Bruce R. Gilbert, M.D., Ph.D.
1010 Northern Blvd., Suite 126
Great Neck, NY 11021
(516) 487-2700
Board Certification NS
Member American Society of
Andrology
Practice Setting academic/private
Clinical Interests male infertility

Bernard L. Lieberman, M.D.
233 E. Shore Rd.
Great Neck, NY 11023
(516) 466-9595
Board Certification Ob/Gyn
Member Society of Reproductive
Surgeons
Practice Setting private
Clinical Interests microsurgery, laser
surgery, laparoscopy, ovulation
induction, intrauterine insemination

Huntington

John R. De Filippi, M.D.
181 Main St.
Huntington, NY 11743
(516) 423-4775

Board Certification Urology
Member American Society of Andrology
Practice Setting private
Clinical Interests urology, kidney stones, male infertility, impotence, endourology, prosthetics

Manhasset

Ehud J. Margalioth, M.D.
North Shore Univ. Hospital, Ob/Gyn Dept.
300 Community Dr.
Manhasset, NY 11030
(516) 562-4470
Board Certification Ob/Gyn
Member American Society of Andrology
Practice Setting academic
Clinical Interests andrology, IVF, reproductive immunology (antisperm antibodies), general infertility

George W. Miner, M.D.
1380 Northern Blvd.
Manhasset, NY 11030
(516) 627-4838
Board Certification Urology
Member American Society of Andrology
Practice Setting NS
Clinical Interests male infertility

David L. Rosenfeld, M.D.
300 Community Dr.
North Shore Univ. Hospital
Manhasset, NY 11030
(516) 562-4470
Board Certification Reproductive Endocrinology
Member Society of Reproductive Endocrinologists
Practice Setting academic
Clinical Interests infertility, microsurgery, laparoscopic surgery, laser surgery

Gerald M. Scholl, M.D.
North Shore Univ. Hospital
300 Community Dr.
Manhasset, NY 11030
(516) 562-4470
Board Certifications Ob/Gyn, Reproductive Endocrinology
Member Society of Reproductive Endocrinologists

Practice Setting academic
Clinical Interests full range of infertility services

New Hyde Park

Brett C. Mellinger, M.D.
Long Island Jewish Med. Ctr., Urology Dept.
270–05 76th Ave.
New Hyde Park, NY 11042
(718) 470-4556
Board Certification NS
Member American Society of Andrology
Practice Setting academic
Clinical Interests all aspects of male infertility and sexual dysfunction, urologic microsurgery

New York City

Richard D. Amelar, M.D.
137 E. 36th St.
New York, NY 10016
(212) 532-0635
Board Certification Urology
Member Society of Reproductive Surgeons
Practice Setting private
Clinical Interests medical and surgical aspects of male infertility

Hussein K. Amin, M.D.
St. Luke's Roosevelt Hospital, Ob/Gyn Dept.
1111 Amsterdam Ave.
New York, NY 10025
(212) 222-4500
Board Certifications Ob/Gyn, Reproductive Endocrinology
Member Society of Reproductive Endocrinologists
Practice Setting academic/private
Clinical Interests microsurgery, ovulation stimulation, IVF/ET, GIFT

Alan S. Berkeley, M.D.
530 E. 70th St., M-035
New York, NY 10021
(212) 628-0545
Board Certification Ob/Gyn
Member Society of Reproductive Surgeons
Practice Setting academic
Clinical Interests IVF, abdominal and

laparoscopic laser surgery, ovulation induction, GnRH analogues

Ina Cholst, M.D.
525 E. 68th St.
New York, NY 10021
(212) 472-4885
Board Certifications Ob/Gyn,
Reproductive Endocrinology
Member Society of Reproductive
Endocrinologists
Practice Setting academic
Clinical Interests infertility,
endometriosis, laser surgery

Joseph E. Davis, M.D.
595 Madison Ave.
New York, NY 10022
(212) 421-8143
Board Certification Urology
Member American Society of
Andrology
Practice Setting private
Clinical Interests male infertility,
vasectomy, reversal of vasectomy

Lawrence Dubin, M.D.
137 E. 36th St.
New York, NY 10016
(212) 532-0635
Board Certification Urology
Member American Society of
Andrology
Practice Setting private
Clinical Interests medical and surgical
aspects of male infertility

Mitchell N. Essig, M.D.
88 University Pl.
New York, NY 10003
(212) 243-4050
Board Certifications Ob/Gyn,
Reproductive Endocrinology
Member Society of Reproductive
Endocrinologists
Practice Setting private
Clinical Interests ovulation induction,
GIFT, IVF

Walter Futterweit, M.D.
1172 Park Ave.
New York, NY 10128
(212) 861-7442
Board Certifications Internal Medicine,
Endocrinology and Metabolism
Member American Society of
Andrology
Practice Setting private

Clinical Interests hirsutism, infertility,
neuroendocrinology

Marc Goldstein, M.D.
525 E. 68th St.
New York, NY 10021
(212) 746-5470
Board Certification Urology
Member Society of Reproductive
Surgeons
Practice Setting academic/private
Clinical Interests male infertility,
microsurgical repair of obstruction,
microsurgical varicocelectomy and
vasectomy reversal

Raphael Jewelewicz, M.D.
Columbia Presbyterian Med. Ctr.,
Ob/Gyn Dept.
630 W. 168 Street
New York, NY 10032
(212) 305-5265
Board Certifications Ob/Gyn,
Reproductive Endocrinology
Member Society of Reproductive
Endocrinologists
Practice Setting private
Clinical Interests all aspects of infertility
including IVF and GIFT

Trishit Kumar Mukherjee, M.D., Ph.D.
133 E. 73rd St.
New York, NY 10021
(212) 861-9000
Board Certifications Ob/Gyn,
Reproductive Endocrinology
Member Society of Reproductive
Endocrinologists
Practice Setting private
Clinical Interests IVF, tuboplastic
surgery

Harris M. Nagler, M.D.
Department of Urology
Beth Israel Med. Ctr.
First Ave. at 16th St.
New York, NY 10003
(212) 420-3900
Board Certification Urology
Member American Society of
Andrology
Practice Setting academic
Clinical Interests microsurgical
reconstruction, varicocele

John R. Quagliarello, M.D.
530 First Ave., Suite 5G
New York, NY 10016

(212) 340-6356
Board Certifications Ob/Gyn,
Reproductive Endocrinology
Member Society of Reproductive
Endocrinologists
Practice Setting private
Clinical Interests ovulation induction,
artificial insemination—donor,
intrauterine

J. Victor Reyniak, M.D.
1107 Fifth Ave.
New York, NY 10128
(212) 410-4080
Board Certifications Ob/Gyn,
Reproductive Endocrinology
Member Society of Reproductive
Endocrinologists
Practice Setting private
Clinical Interests reconstructive utero-
tubal surgery, operative laparoscopy

Zev Rosenwaks, M.D.
New York Hospital–Cornell Med. Ctr.,
Ob/Gyn Dept.
530 E. 70th St., Room M036
New York, NY 10021
(212) 472-5003
Board Certifications Ob/Gyn,
Reproductive Endocrinology
Member Society of Reproductive
Endocrinologists
Practice Setting academic
Clinical Interests infertility, IVF,
androgen excess, adrenal hyperplasia,
hyperprolactinemia, hirsutism,
dysmenorrhea

Peter J. Sarosi, M.D.
88 University Pl.
New York, NY 10003
(212) 243-4050
Board Certifications Ob/Gyn,
Reproductive Endocrinology
Member Society of Reproductive
Endocrinologists
Practice Setting private
Clinical Interests infertility, IVF/GIFT

Irving M. Spitz, M.D.
Ctr. for Biomedical Research
Population Council
1230 York Ave.
New York, NY 10021
(212) 570-8734
Board Certifications Internal Medicine,
Endocrinology and Metabolism

Member American Society of
Andrology
Practice Setting academic
Clinical Interests reproductive
endocrinology

Attila Toth, M.D.
New York Hospital–Cornell Univ.
Med. College
530 E. 70th St., Room M0026
New York, NY 10021
(212) 472-6410
Board Certification Ob/Gyn
Member American Society of
Andrology
Practice Setting academic/private
Clinical Interests luteal phase defect,
PMS

Stanley T. West, M.D.
1049 Park Ave.
New York, NY 10028
(212) 860-2900
Board Certifications Ob/Gyn,
Reproductive Endocrinology
Member Society of Reproductive
Surgeons
Practice Setting private
Clinical Interests infertility and
microsurgery

Port Jefferson

Daniel Kenigsberg, M.D.
60 N. Country Rd., Suite 102
Port Jefferson, NY 11777
(516) 331-7575
Board Certifications Ob/Gyn,
Reproductive Endocrinology
Member Society of Reproductive
Endocrinologists
Practice Setting private
Clinical Interests IVF, infertility,
endocrinology

Rochester

John H. Mattox, M.D.
Univ. of Rochester Med. Ctr.
601 Elmwood Ave., Box 668
Rochester, NY 14642
(716) 275-7981
Board Certifications Ob/Gyn,
Reproductive Endocrinology
Member Society of Reproductive
Endocrinologists

Practice Setting academic
Clinical Interests ovulatory dysfunction, fertility surgery including laser and microsurgery, andrology

Eberhard K. Muechler, M.D.
1561 Long Pond Rd.
Rochester, NY 14626
(716) 723-7470
Board Certifications Ob/Gyn, Reproductive Endocrinology
Member Society of Reproductive Endocrinologists
Practice Setting private
Clinical Interests ovulation induction, ovarian failure, IVF, GIFT, virilization

Rye

John J. Stangel, M.D.
70 Maple Ave.
Rye, NY 10580
(914) 967-6800
Board Certifications Ob/Gyn, Reproductive Endocrinology
Member Society of Reproductive Endocrinologists
Practice Setting private
Clinical Interests Reproductive endocrinology and infertility, endometriosis, habitual spontaneous abortion, tubal function, assisted reproductive technologies

Stony Brook

Magdalen E. Hull, M.D.
SUNY at Stony Brook, Ob/Gyn Dept.
HSC9T, Room 060
Stony Brook, NY 11794
(516) 444-2737
Board Certifications Ob/Gyn, Reproductive Endocrinology
Member Society of Reproductive Endocrinologists
Practice Setting academic
Clinical Interests GnRH analogs, endometriosis, IVF, ovarian cysts, fibroids, transvaginal tuboplasty

Syracuse

Shawky Z. A. Badawy, M.D.
Health Science Ctr.

750 E. Adams St.
Syracuse, NY 13224
(315) 470-7905
Board Certifications Ob/Gyn, Reproductive Endocrinology
Member Society of Reproductive Endocrinologists
Practice Setting academic
Clinical Interests microsurgery, laser surgery, operative laparoscopy, operative hysteroscopy, IVF

Jung K. Choe, M.D.
SUNY Health Science Ctr.,
Ob/Gyn Dept.
750 E. Adams St.
Syracuse, NY 13210
(315) 470-7905
Board Certifications Ob/Gyn, Reproductive Endocrinology
Member Society of Reproductive Endocrinologists
Practice Setting academic
Clinical Interests infertility, IVF-ET, GIFT, menopause

Utica

Murray L. Nusbaum, M.D.
1656 Champlin Rd.
Utica, NY 13502
(315) 797-3665
Board Certification Ob/Gyn
Member Society of Reproductive Surgeons
Practice Setting private
Clinical Interests full spectrum of couple, male and female, fertility

Valhalla

Stanley J. Kogan, M.D.
Westchester County Med. Ctr.
Macy 1
Valhalla, NY 10595
(914) 285-8628
Board Certification Urology
Member American Society of Andrology
Practice Setting private
Clinical Interests cryptorchidism, varicocele, penile disorders in adolescence and childhood, ambiguous genitalia

Williamsville

Ronald E. Batt, M.D.
1000 Youngs Rd.
Williamsville, NY 14221
(716) 688-1500
Board Certification Ob/Gyn
Member Society of Reproductive
Surgeons
Practice Setting private
Clinical Interests endometriosis,
infertility

John D. Naples, M.D.
1000 Youngs Rd.
Williamsville, NY 14221
(716) 688-1500
Board Certification Ob/Gyn
Member Society of Reproductive
Surgeons
Practice Setting private
Clinical Interests microsurgery, laser
surgery, ovulatory induction, IUI,
GIFT

Mark F. Severino, M.D.
1000 Youngs Rd.
Williamsville, NY 14221
(716) 688-1500
Board Certification Ob/Gyn
Member Society of Reproductive
Surgeons
Practice Setting private
Clinical Interests infertility,
endometriosis

NORTH CAROLINA

Chapel Hill

Gary S. Berger, M.D.
Chapel Hill Fertility Ctr.
109 Conner Dr., Suite 2104
Chapel Hill, NC 27514
(919) 968-4656
Board Certifications Ob/Gyn, Preventive
Medicine
Member Society of Reproductive
Surgeons
Practice Setting private
Clinical Interests all aspects of infertility,
outpatient reconstructive surgery,
microsurgery, laser surgery,
sterilization reversal, endometriosis,
PID, uterine anomalies, habitual

spontaneous abortion, assisted
reproductive technologies

Mary G. Hammond, M.D.
Univ. of North Carolina,
Ob/Gyn Dept.
Old Clinic Bldg., CB7570
Chapel Hill, NC 27599-7570
(919) 966-4459
Board Certifications Ob/Gyn,
Reproductive Endocrinology
Member Society of Reproductive
Endocrinologists
Practice Setting academic
Clinical Interests ovulation induction,
artificial insemination, IVF

Jaroslav F. Hulka, M.D.
Univ. of North Carolina,
Ob/Gyn Dept.
Old Clinic Bldg., CB 7570
Chapel Hill, NC 27599-7570
(919) 966-5287
Board Certification Reproductive
Endocrinology
Member Society of Reproductive
Surgeons
Practice Setting academic
Clinical Interests obstetrics and
gynecology, reproductive
endocrinology

Stephen F. Shaban, M.D.
Chapel Hill Fertility Ctr.
109 Conner Dr., Suite 2104
Chapel Hill, NC 27514
(919) 968-4656
Board Certifications NS
Member American Society of
Andrology
Practice Setting private
Clinical Interests unexplained infertility,
idiopathic oligospermia, abnormalities
of ejaculation, laser surgery,
electroejaculation

Luther M. Talbert, M.D.
Dept. of Ob-Gyn, Box 7570
Univ. of North Carolina School of
Med.
Chapel Hill, NC 27599-7570
(919) 966-4459
Board Certifications Ob/Gyn,
Reproductive Endocrinology
Member Society of Reproductive
Endocrinologists
Practice Setting academic

Clinical Interests assisted reproductive technologies—IVF, GIFT

Charlotte

Jack L. Crain, M.D.
1901 Brunswick Ave.
Charlotte, NC 28207
(704) 343-3400
Board Certifications Ob/Gyn,
Reproductive Endocrinology
Member Society of Reproductive
Endocrinologists
Practice Setting private
Clinical Interests video laser laparoscopy,
tubal microsurgery, GIFT/IVF

George L. Gaunt, M.D., Ph.D.
Ctr. for Reproductive Medicine
2034 Randolph Rd.
Charlotte, NC 28207
(704) 372-4600
Board Certifications NS
Member American Society of
Andrology
Practice Setting private
Clinical Interests male and female
infertility, hormonal abnormalities,
IVF, patient education, emotional
aspects of infertility

Durham

William C. Dodson, M.D.
Duke Univ. Med. Ctr.
Box 3527
Durham, NC 27710
(919) 684-5327
Board Certification Ob/Gyn
Member Society for Assisted
Reproductive Technology
Practice Setting academic
Clinical Interests IVF, GIFT,
superovulation and intrauterine
insemination

Charles B. Hammond, M.D.
Duke Univ. Med. Ctr., Ob/Gyn Dept.
Box 3853
Durham, NC 27710
(919) 684-3008
Board Certifications Ob/Gyn,
Reproductive Endocrinology
Member Society of Reproductive
Endocrinologists
Practice Setting academic

Clinical Interests infertility and
reproductive endocrinologic disorders,
menopause, general gynecology

Arthur F. Haney, M.D.
Duke Univ. Med. Ctr.
Box 2971
Durham, NC 27710
(919) 684-6160
Board Certifications Ob/Gyn,
Reproductive Endocrinology
Member Society of Reproductive
Endocrinologists
Practice Setting academic
Clinical Interests endometriosis, general
reproductive endocrinology

Claude L. Hughes, Jr., M.D., Ph.D.
Duke Univ. Med. Ctr.
Box 3143
Durham, NC 27710
(919) 684-5327
Board Certifications Ob/Gyn,
Reproductive Endocrinology
Member Society of Reproductive
Endocrinologists
Practice Setting academic
Clinical Interests reproductive
endocrinology & infertility

Wilmington

William H. Cooper IV, M.D.
1500 Medical Center Dr.
Wilmington, NC 28401
(919) 763-9509
Board Certification Ob/Gyn
Member Society of Reproductive
Surgeons
Practice Setting private
Clinical Interests laser surgery, tubal
reanastomosis, pergonal and
intrauterine inseminations,
hysteroscopic metroplasty,
hysteroscopic recannualization of
fallopian tubes, ovulation induction
for IVF

Winston-Salem

Jamil A. Fayez, M.D.
Bowman Gray School of Medicine,
Ob/Gyn Dept.
300 S. Hawthorne Rd.
Winston-Salem, NC 27103
(919) 748-2368
Board Certifications Ob/Gyn,

Reproductive Endocrinology
Member Society of Reproductive
Endocrinologists
Practice Setting academic
Clinical Interests NS

Jonathan P. Jarow, M.D.
Bowman Gray School of Medicine,
Urology Dept.
300 S. Hawthorne Rd.
Winston-Salem, NC 27103
(919) 748-4131
Board Certification NS
Member American Society of
Andrology
Practice Setting academic
Clinical Interests male reproductive and
sexual function

Donald E. Pittaway, M.D., Ph.D.
Bowman Gray School of Medicine,
Ob/Gyn Dept.
300 S. Hawthorne Rd.
Winston-Salem, NC 27103
(919) 748-4141
Board Certifications Ob/Gyn,
Reproductive Endocrinology
Member Society of Reproductive
Endocrinologists
Practice Setting academic
Clinical Interests infertility, laser and
microsurgery, laparoscopic surgery,
IVF/GIFT, endometriosis, AID

OHIO

Akron

Nicholas J. Spirtos, D.O.
Akron City Hospital
525 E. Market St.
Akron, OH 44309
(216) 375-3585
Board Certifications Ob/Gyn,
Reproductive Endocrinology
Member Society of Reproductive
Surgeons
Practice Setting other
Clinical Interests IVF, GIFT,
microsurgery

Thomas L. Stover, M.D.
1611 C Akron Peninsula Rd.
Akron, OH 44313
(216) 928-0595
Board Certification Ob/Gyn
Member Society of Reproductive

Surgeons
Practice Setting private
Clinical Interests reproductive surgery,
microtubal surgery, operative
laparoscopy/laser surgery

Cincinnati

James H. Liu, M.D.
231 Bethesda Ave., ML 526
Cincinnati, OH 45267-0526
(513) 558-8440
Board Certifications Ob/Gyn,
Reproductive Endocrinology
Member Society of Reproductive
Endocrinologists
Practice Setting academic
Clinical Interests ovulation induction,
microsurgical reconstruction

Sanford S. Osher, M.D.
10495 Montgomery Rd., Suite 14
Cincinnati, OH 45242
(513) 984-9878
Board Certification Ob/Gyn
Member Society of Reproductive
Surgeons
Practice Setting private
Clinical Interests operative laparoscopy,
reproductive surgery, laser surgery
Research Interests NS

Robert W. Rebar, M.D.
Univ. of Cincinnati, Ob/Gyn Dept.
231 Bethesda Ave., ML 526
Cincinnati, OH 45267-0526
(513) 558-8440
Board Certifications Ob/Gyn,
Reproductive Endocrinology
Member Society of Reproductive
Endocrinologists
Practice Setting academic
Clinical Interests reproductive
endocrinology

Jennifer L. Thie, M.D.
Bethesda Professional Bldg.
629 Oak St., Suite 601
Cincinnati, OH 45206
(513) 861-7334
Board Certification Ob/Gyn
Member American Society of
Andrology
Practice Setting private
Clinical Interests infertility,
endometriosis, donor program (frozen
donor bank)

Cleveland

Robert L. Collins, M.D.
Cleveland Clinic Foundation,
Gynecology Dept.
9500 Euclid Ave.
Cleveland, OH 44195-5307
(216) 444-1758
Board Certifications Ob/Gyn,
Reproductive Endocrinology
Member Society of Reproductive
Endocrinologists
Practice Setting other
Clinical Interests ovulation induction—
GnRH, GnRH analogs, myomas,
endometriosis, laser surgery,
microsurgery and IVF

James M. Goldfarb, M.D.
Mount Sinai Med. Ctr., Ob/Gyn
Dept.
1 Mount Sinai Dr.
Cleveland, OH 44106
(216) 421-4870
Board Certifications Ob/Gyn,
Reproductive Endocrinology
Member Society of Reproductive
Endocrinologists
Practice Setting academic/private
Clinical Interests infertility, ovulation
induction, IVF

Kalish R. Kedia, M.D.
2609 Franklin Blvd.
Cleveland, OH 44113
(216) 363-2425
Board Certification Urology
Member American Society of
Andrology
Practice Setting academic/private
Clinical Interests male infertility,
microsurgery, male contraception

Steven M. Klein, M.D.
21125 Shelburne Rd.
Cleveland, OH 44122
(216) 464-4494
Board Certification Ob/Gyn
Member Society of Reproductive
Surgeons
Practice Setting private
Clinical Interests infertility—uterine
factor, endocrinology—hirsutism

Martin M. Quigley, M.D.
Cleveland Clinic
9500 Euclid Ave.

Cleveland, OH 44195
(216) 444-2240
Board Certifications Ob/Gyn,
Reproductive Endocrinology
Member Society of Reproductive
Endocrinologists
Practice Setting other
Clinical Interests infertility, female
endocrinology, laser laparoscopy,
donor eggs

Laszlo Sogor, M.D., Ph.D.
Univ. Hospitals, Ob/Gyn Dept.
2074 Abington Rd.
Cleveland, OH 44106
(216) 844-1692
Board Certification Ob/Gyn
Member American Society of
Andrology
Practice Setting academic
Clinical Interests donor insemination,
cryopreservation

Leon Speroff, M.D.
MacDonald Hospital for Women
2105 Adelbert Rd.
Cleveland, OH 44106
(216) 844-3334
Board Certifications Ob/Gyn,
Reproductive Endocrinology
Member Society of Reproductive
Endocrinologists
Practice Setting academic
Clinical Interests endocrinology and
infertility

Columbus

Moon H. Kim, M.D.
Univ. Reproductive Ctr.
1654 Upham Dr., MH 535
Columbus, OH 43210
(614) 293-8511
Board Certifications Ob/Gyn,
Reproductive Endocrinology
Member Society of Reproductive
Endocrinologists
Practice Setting academic
Clinical Interests induction of ovulation,
microsurgery and laser surgery of
tubes, IVF, GIFT

Paul W. Musselman, M.D.
3555 Olentangy River Rd., Suite 3010
Columbus, OH 43214
(614) 267-5427
Board Certification Urology

Member American Society of
Andrology
Practice Setting private
Clinical Interests male infertility,
vasovasostomy, vasoepididymostomy,
medical treatment of infertility

James H. Nelson, III, M.D.
1492 E. Broad St., Suite 1601
Columbus, OH 43205
(614) 253-8529
Board Certification Urology
Member American Society of
Andrology
Practice Setting private
Clinical Interests andrology

John A. Nesbitt, M.D.
456 W. Tenth Ave., Room 4833
Columbus, OH 43210
(614) 293-5264
Board Certification Urology
Member American Society of
Andrology
Practice Setting academic
Clinical Interests infertility surgery, male
infertility

Jeffrey P. York, M.D.
456 W. Tenth Ave.
Columbus, OH
(614) 293-8157
Board Certification Urology
Member American Society of
Andrology
Practice Setting academic/private
Clinical Interests infertility, impotence,
rehabilitative medicine

Dayton

Ahmad Hamidinia, M.D.
30 Apple St., Suite 6255
Dayton, OH 45409
(513) 220-2680
Board Certification Urology
Member American Society of
Andrology
Practice Setting private
Clinical Interests microsurgery,
vasovasostomy, male infertility,
obstructive azoospermia

Lyndhurst

Wulf H. Utian, M.D., Ph.D.
Infertility Ctr. of N.E. Ohio
29001 Cedar Rd., Suite 600
Lyndhurst, OH 44124
(216) 442-4747
Board Certifications Ob/Gyn,
Reproductive Endocrinology
Member Society of Reproductive
Endocrinologists
Practice Setting academic/private
Clinical Interests microsurgery, IVF,
surrogate IVF, sperm banking, embryo
freezing

Toledo

Jagadish S. Jhunjhunwala, M.D.
Med. College of Ohio
Division of Urology, CS10008
Toledo, OH 43699
(419) 381-3578
Board Certification Urology
Member American Society of
Andrology
Practice Setting academic
Clinical Interests male infertility

Najib G. Wakim, M.D.
Med. College of Ohio, CS10008
Toledo, OH 43699
(419) 381-4537
Board Certification Ob/Gyn
Member American Society of
Andrology
Practice Setting academic
Clinical Interests NS

Warrensville Heights

Julian A. Gordon, M.D.
Suburban Hospital Med. Office Bldg.
4200 Warrensville Ctr. Rd.
Warrensville Heights, OH 44122
(216) 295-1010
Board Certification Urology
Member American Society of
Andrology
Practice Setting private
Clinical Interests male factor infertility,
male sexual dysfunction

Wright Patterson A.F.B.

Marc A. Fritz, M.D.
U.S.A.F. Med. Ctr., Ob/Gyn Dept.
Wright Patterson AFB, OH 45433
(513) 257-1970
Board Certifications Ob/Gyn,
Reproductive Endocrinology
Member Society of Reproductive
Endocrinologists
Practice Setting academic (military)
Clinical Interests infertility, tubal
reconstructive surgery, ectopic
pregnancy, luteal phase deficiency

OKLAHOMA

Oklahoma City

Gilbert G. Haas, Jr., M.D.
P.O. Box 26901, 4SP 720
Oklahoma City, OK 73190
(405) 271-8700
Board Certifications Ob/Gyn,
Reproductive Endocrinology
Member Society of Reproductive
Endocrinologists
Practice Setting academic
Clinical Interests antisperm antibodies,
male factor infertility, cervical factor
infertility, IVF, reparative pelvic
surgery

David A. Kallenberger, M.D.
3433 N.W. 56th St., Suite 210 N.
Oklahoma City, OK 73112
(405) 945-4701
Board Certification Ob/Gyn
Member Society for Assisted
Reproductive Technology
Practice Setting private
Clinical Interests IVF, GIFT, cryo-
preservation, reconstructive infertility
surgery, laser and nonlaser techniques

Johnny B. Roy, M.D.
P.O. Box 26901, 5SP330
Oklahoma City, OK 73190
(405) 271-6966
Board Certification Urology
Member American Society of
Andrology
Practice Setting academic
Clinical Interests male factor infertility

Tulsa

John M. Shane, M.D.
6465 S. Yale Ave., Suite 304
Tulsa, OK 74136
(918) 492-5511
Board Certifications Ob/Gyn,
Reproductive Endocrinology
Member Society of Reproductive
Endocrinologists
Practice Setting private
Clinical Interests ovulation induction,
endometriosis including laser standby,
GIFT, AID

Donald R. Tredway, M.D., Ph.D.
1145 S. Utica, Suite 1209
Tulsa, OK 74104
(918) 584-2870
Board Certifications Ob/Gyn,
Reproductive Endocrinology
Member Society of Reproductive
Endocrinologists
Practice Setting private
Clinical Interests induction of ovulation,
infertility surgery, luteal insufficiency,
IVF, premenstrual syndrome

OREGON

Portland

Kenneth A. Burry, M.D.
3181 S.W. Sam Jackson Parkway
Ob/Gyn Dept., L466
Portland, OR 97201
(503) 279-7513
Board Certifications Ob/Gyn,
Reproductive Endocrinology
Member Society of Reproductive
Endocrinologists
Practice Setting academic
Clinical Interests IVF

Michael J. Kaempf, M.D.
2332 N.W. Irving St.
Portland, OR 97210-3284
(503) 224-5681
Board Certification Urology
Member American Society of
Andrology
Practice Setting private
Clinical Interests male infertility

Phillip Edward Patton, M.D.
3110 S.W. Sam Jackson Parkway

Portland, OR
(503) 279-7513
Board Certifications Ob/Gyn,
Reproductive Endocrinology
Practice Setting academic/private
Member Society of Reproductive
Endocrinologists
Clinical Interests reproductive surgery,
recurrent pregnancy loss, IVF

PENNSYLVANIA

Abington

Jay S. Schinfeld, M.D.
1245 Highland Ave., Suite 601
Abington, PA 19001
(215) 887-2010
Board Certifications Ob/Gyn,
Reproductive Endocrinology
Member Society of Reproductive
Endocrinologists
Practice Setting private
Clinical Interests laser, IVF, male factor
infertility, endometriosis, chronic
pelvic pain

Elkins Park

Michael D. Birnbaum, M.D.
8118 Old York Rd.
Elkins Park, PA 19117
(215) 635-0545
Board Certification Ob/Gyn
Member Society of Reproductive
Surgeons
Practice Setting academic/private
Clinical Interests endometriosis, laser
surgery, androgen disorders in women

Hershey

Bruce I. Rose, M.D., Ph.D.
Milton S. Hershey Med. Ctr.
Ob/Gyn Dept.
Pennsylvania State Univ.,
P.O. Box 850
Hershey, PA 17033
Telephone NS
Board Certification Ob/Gyn
Member American Society of
Andrology
Practice Setting academic
Clinical Interests microsurgery, infertility

complicated by sperm problems,
donor insemination, sperm banking

Richard J. Santen, M.D.
Milton S. Hershey Med. Ctr.
Pennsylvania State Univ.
Hershey, PA 17033
(717) 531-8395
Board Certifications Internal Medicine,
Metabolism and Endocrinology
Member American Society of
Andrology
Practice Setting academic
Clinical Interests andrology

Robert A. Wild, M.D.
Milton S. Hershey Med. Ctr.
C310, Box 850
Hershey, PA 17033
(717) 531-8521
Board Certifications Ob/Gyn,
Reproductive Endocrinology
Member Society of Reproductive
Endocrinologists
Practice Setting academic
Clinical Interests PCOS, surgery,
endometriosis

Kingston

Harry Reich, M.D.
480 Pierce St.
Kingston, PA 18704
(717) 283-0502
Board Certification Ob/Gyn
Member Society of Reproductive
Surgeons
Practice Setting private
Clinical Interests laparoscopic treatment,
endometriosis, adhesions, ectopic
pregnancy, oophorectomy

Philadelphia

Frances R. Batzer, M.D.
Philadelphia Fertility Institute
330 S. Ninth St.
Philadelphia, PA 19107-6096
(215) 829-5030
Board Certifications Ob/Gyn,
Reproductive Endocrinology
Member Society of Reproductive
Endocrinologists
Practice Setting private
Clinical Interests IVF, GIFT, tubal
surgery, reproductive tract surgery to

augment fertility, intrauterine
insemination

Luis Blasco, M.D.
Hospital of the Univ. of Pennsylvania
3400 Spruce St., Suite 106, Dulles
Philadelphia, PA 19104
(215) 662-2960
Board Certification Reproductive
Endocrinology
Member Society of Reproductive
Endocrinologists
Practice Setting academic/private
Clinical Interests NS

Jerome H. Check, M.D.
1015 Chestnut St., Suite 1020
Philadelphia, PA 19107
(215) 925-6306
Board Certifications Internal Medicine,
Endocrinology and Metabolism
Member American Society of
Andrology
Practice Setting academic/private
Clinical Interests all facets, especially
ovulation disorders

Stephen L. Corson, M.D.
Philadelphia Fertility Institute
330 S. Ninth St.
Philadelphia, PA 19107-6096
(215) 829-5030
Board Certifications Ob/Gyn,
Reproductive Endocrinology
Member Society of Reproductive
Endocrinologists
Practice Setting private
Clinical Interests IVF, GIFT, tubal
surgery, reproductive tract surgery to
augment fertility, intrauterine
insemination

Douglas C. Daly, M.D.
330 S. Ninth St.
Philadelphia, PA 19107-6096
(215) 829-5030
Board Certifications Ob/Gyn,
Reproductive Endocrinology
Member Society of Reproductive
Endocrinologists
Practice Setting private
Clinical Interests ovulation induction,
microsurgery and hysteroscopic
surgery, IVF

Esther Eisenberg, M.D.
Pennsylvania Hospital, Ob/Gyn Dept.
Eighth and Spruce Sts.

Philadelphia, PA 19107
(215) 829-6385
Board Certifications Ob/Gyn,
Reproductive Endocrinology
Member Society of Reproductive
Endocrinologists
Practice Setting academic
Clinical Interests infertility, IVF

Martin F. Freedman, M.D.
Albert Einstein Med. Ctr.
Klein Building, Suite 400
Philadelphia, PA 19141
(215) 456-7990
Board Certifications Ob/Gyn,
Reproductive Endocrinology
Member Society of Reproductive
Endocrinologists
Practice Setting private
Clinical Interests IVF, ovulation
induction, microsurgery, habitual
abortion

Celso-Ramon Garcia, M.D.
3400 Spruce St., Room 106, Dulles
Bldg.
Philadelphia, PA 19104
(215) 662-2974
Board Certification Ob/Gyn
Member Society of Reproductive
Surgeons
Practice Setting academic
Clinical Interests infertility and
reproductive surgery

Walter L. Gerber, M.D.
Temple Univ. Hospital, Urology Dept.
3401 N. Broad St.
Philadelphia, PA 19140
(215) 221-3375
Board Certification Urology
Member American Society of
Andrology
Practice Setting academic/private
Clinical Interests male infertility and
vasectomy reversal

Irvin H. Hirsch, M.D.
Thomas Jefferson Univ. Hospital
111 S. Eleventh St., Suite 6128
Philadelphia, PA 19107
Telephone NS
Board Certification Urology
Member American Society of
Andrology
Practice Setting academic
Clinical Interests male factor evaluation,

treatment & surgery; sperm banking;
intrauterine insemination

David A. Iddenden, M.D.
Dept. Ob/Gyn
Presbyterian Medical Ctr. of
Philadelphia
39th & Market Sts.
Philadelphia, PA 19104
(215) 662-8798
Board Certification Ob/Gyn
Member Society of Reproductive
Surgeons
Practice Setting academic
Clinical Interests endometriosis,
menopause

Luigi Mastroianni, Jr., M.D.
Hospital of the Univ. of Pennsylvania
3400 Spruce St., Room 106, Dulles
Bldg.
Philadelphia, PA 19104-4283
(215) 662-2951
Board Certifications Ob/Gyn,
Reproductive Endocrinology
Member Society of Reproductive
Endocrinologists
Practice Setting academic
Clinical Interests reproductive
endocrinology and infertility

William H. Pfeffer, M.D.
563 Lankenau Med. Bldg. East
Philadelphia, PA 19151
(215) 645-3575
Board Certifications Ob/Gyn,
Reproductive Endocrinology
Member Society of Reproductive
Endocrinologists
Practice Setting private
Clinical Interests endometriosis, laser,
reconstructive surgery, GIFT

Steven J. Sondheimer, M.D.
Hospital of the Univ. of Pennsylvania
Philadelphia, PA 19104
(215) 662-2978
Board Certifications Ob/Gyn,
Reproductive Endocrinology
Member Society of Reproductive
Endocrinologists
Practice Setting academic/private
Clinical Interests infertility,
endometriosis, pelvic pain

Richard W. Tureck, M.D.
Hospital of the Univ. of Pennsylvania
Philadelphia, PA 19104

(215) 662-2952
Board Certification Ob/Gyn
Member Society of Reproductive
Surgeons
Practice Setting academic
Clinical Interests general infertility, IVF

Keith N. Van Arsdalen, M.D.
Hospital of the Univ. of Pennsylvania,
Urology Div.
3400 Spruce St., 5 Silverstein
Philadelphia, PA 19104
(215) 662-2891
Board Certification Urology
Member American Society of
Andrology
Practice Setting academic
Clinical Interests urology, male infertility

Jaime M. Vasquez, M.D.
1025 Walnut St., Ob/Gyn Dept.
Philadelphia, PA 19107
(215) 928-7873
Board Certification Ob/Gyn
Member Society of Reproductive
Surgeons
Practice Setting academic
Clinical Interests conservative pelvic
surgery, microsurgery, IVF, GIFT

Craig A. Winkel, M.D.
Jefferson Med. College of Thomas
Jefferson Univ.
1025 Walnut St., Room 300
Philadelphia, PA 19107
(215) 928-8461
Board Certifications Ob/Gyn,
Reproductive Endocrinology
Member Society of Reproductive
Endocrinologists
Practice Setting academic
Clinical Interests IVF/embryo transfer,
pelviscopy, microsurgery, ovulation
induction

Pittsburgh

Amir H. Ansari, M.D.
510 S. Aiken Ave., Suite 312
Pittsburgh, PA 15232
(412) 622-1720
Board Certification Ob/Gyn
Member Society of Reproductive
Surgeons
Practice Setting academic/private
Clinical Interests all causes of infertility,
IVF/ET, GIFT

Philip Troen, M.D.
  Montefiore Hospital
  3459 Fifth Ave.
  Pittsburgh, PA 15213
  (412) 648-6401
  Board Certifications Internal Medicine,
  Endocrinology and Metabolism
  Member American Society of
  Andrology
  Practice Setting academic
  Clinical Interests endocrinology, internal
  medicine, andrology

Stephen J. Winters, M.D.
  Montefiore Hospital
  3459 Fifth Ave.
  Pittsburgh, PA 15213
  (412) 648-6423
  Board Certifications Internal Medicine,
  Endocrinology and Metabolism
  Member American Society of
  Andrology
  Practice Setting academic
  Clinical Interests reproductive
  endocrinology, hypogonadism, male
  infertility

Springfield

Sherman W. Everlof, M.D.
  24 E. Springfield Rd.
  Springfield, PA 19064
  (215) 544-7171
  Board Certification Ob/Gyn
  Member Society of Reproductive
  Surgeons
  Practice Setting academic/private
  Clinical Interests reproductive surgery—
  micro and laser surgery, ovulation
  induction, laser endoscopy

West Reading

Vincent A. Pellegrini, M.D.
  301 S. Seventh Ave.
  West Reading, PA 19611
  (215) 374-2214
  Board Certification Ob/Gyn
  Member Society of Reproductive
  Surgeons
  Practice Setting private
  Clinical Interests office-based IVF,
  vaginal ultrasound, microsurgery,
  Pergonal therapy, washed
  inseminations

RHODE ISLAND

Cumberland

Bruce J. Nadjmi, M.D.
  175 Nate Whipple Highway
  Cumberland, RI 02864
  (401) 765-4442
  Board Certification Urology
  Member American Society of
  Andrology
  Practice Setting academic/private
  Clinical Interests bladder tumor and
  infertility

Providence

Ray V. Haning Jr., M.D.
  Women and Infants' Hospital,
  Ob/Gyn Dept.
  101 Dudley St.
  Providence, RI 02905
  (401) 274-1100 ext. 1564
  Board Certifications Ob/Gyn,
  Reproductive Endocrinology
  Member Society of Reproductive
  Endocrinologists
  Practice Setting academic
  Clinical Interests induction of ovulation,
  microsurgery, hysteroscopy,
  laparoscopy, IVF

Barry S. Stein, M.D.
  90 Plain St.
  Providence, RI 02903
  (401) 421-0710
  Board Certification Urology
  Member American Society of
  Andrology
  Practice Setting academic
  Clinical Interests fertility, oncology

Woonsocket

Naeem M. Siddiqi, M.D.
  12 Cumberland Hill Rd.
  Woonsocket, RI 02895
  (401) 769-9170
  Board Certification Urology
  Member American Society of
  Andrology
  Practice Setting private
  Clinical Interests infertility, impotence

SOUTH CAROLINA

Charleston

Fletcher C. Derrick, Jr., M.D.
216 Calhoun St.
Charleston, SC 29401
(803) 577-7371
Board Certification Urology
Member American Society of
Andrology
Practice Setting private
Clinical Interests male fertility,
microsurgery, semen lab, artificial
insemination—husband and donor,
sexual dysfunction

Charles C. Tsai, M.D.
Medical Univ. of South Carolina,
Ob/Gyn Dept.
171 Ashley Ave.
Charleston, SC 29425
(803) 792-8351
Board Certifications Ob/Gyn,
Reproductive Endocrinology
Member Society of Reproductive
Endocrinologists
Practice Setting academic
Clinical Interests IVF and embryo
transfer, vaginal physiology in
menopausal women

H. Oliver Williamson, M.D.
Medical Univ. of South Carolina,
Ob/Gyn Dept.
171 Ashley Ave.
Charleston, SC 29425
(803) 792-2861
Board Certifications Ob/Gyn,
Reproductive Endocrinology
Member Society of Reproductive
Endocrinologists
Practice Setting academic/private
Clinical Interests reproductive
immunology (sperm antibodies),
genital anomalies, habitual abortion

Columbia

Elizabeth R. Baker, M.D.
2 Richland Med. Park, Suite 211
Columbia, SC 29203
(803) 765-7732
Board Certifications Ob/Gyn,
Reproductive Endocrinology
Member Society of Reproductive

Endocrinologists
Practice Setting academic
Clinical Interests infertility, reproductive
endocrinology, endometriosis,
ovulation induction, athletic
amenorrhea, menopause

Edward E. Moore, M.D.
Carolina Ctr. for Fertility and
Endocrinology
1818 Henderson St.
Columbia, SC 29201
(803) 779-6320
Board Certification Ob/Gyn
Member Society of Reproductive
Surgeons
Practice Setting private
Clinical Interests infertility surgery (laser
surgery, operative laparoscopy),
endometriosis treatment, ovulation
induction, hysteroscopy

Mount Pleasant

Gary Holtz, M.D.
900 Bowman Rd., Suite 108
Mount Pleasant, SC 29464
(803) 881-3900
Board Certifications Ob/Gyn,
Reproductive Endocrinology
Member Society of Reproductive
Endocrinologists
Practice Setting private
Clinical Interests reconstructive surgery

Grant W. Patton, Jr., M.D.
Southeastern Fertility Ctr.
900 Bowman Rd., Suite 108
Mount Pleasant, SC 29464
(803) 881-3900
Board Certification Ob/Gyn
Member Society of Reproductive
Surgeons
Practice Setting private
Clinical Interests NS

SOUTH DAKOTA

Sioux Falls

John H. Hoskins, M.D.
1200 S. Euclid
Sioux Falls, SD 57105
(605) 336-0635
Board Certification Urology
Member American Society of

Andrology
Practice Setting academic/private
Clinical Interests NS

Si G. Lee, M.D.
2701 S. Spring Ave.
Sioux Falls, SD 57105
(605) 331-5555
Board Certifications Ob/Gyn,
Reproductive Endocrinology
Member Society of Reproductive
Endocrinologists
Practice Setting private
Clinical Interests laser microsurgery,
endocrine disorders, use of ovulatory
agents including Pergonal

Milton G. Mutch, Jr., M.D.
1201 S. Euclid, Suite 204
Sioux Falls, SD 57105
(605) 336-3873
Board Certification Ob/Gyn
Member Society of Reproductive
Surgeons
Practice Setting private
Clinical Interests infertility, gynecologic
surgery

TENNESSEE

Bristol

Pickens Gantt, M.D.
225 Midway St.
Bristol, TN 37620
(615) 968-4800
Board Certifications Ob/Gyn,
Reproductive Endocrinology
Member Society of Reproductive
Endocrinologists
Practice Setting academic/private
Clinical Interests IVF/ET, GIFT, AID,
IUI, infertility, laser surgery,
hysteroscopy, endometrial ablation,
laparoscopic surgery

Chattanooga

John A. Lucas, III, M.D.
931 Spring Creek Rd., Suite 200
Chattanooga, TN 37412
(615) 899-4113
Board Certifications Ob/Gyn,
Reproductive Endocrinology
Member Society of Reproductive
Endocrinologists

Practice Setting private
Clinical Interests ovulation induction,
reconstructive pelvic surgery, IVF/
GIFT

Memphis

Daniel C. Martin, M.D.
910 Madison Ave., Suite 805
Memphis, TN 38103
(901) 529-0674
Board Certification Ob/Gyn
Member Society of Reproductive
Surgeons
Practice Setting private
Clinical Interests reproductive surgery

Nashville

James F. Daniell, M.D.
2222 State St.
Nashville, TN 37203
(615) 321-0513
Board Certification Ob/Gyn
Member Society of Reproductive
Surgeons
Practice Setting private
Clinical Interests female surgical
infertility, microsurgery, laparoscopic
and hysteroscopic surgery

Carl M. Herbert, M.D.
Vanderbilt Univ. Med. Ctr., Ob/Gyn
Dept.
Nashville, TN 37232
(615) 322-6957
Board Certification Ob/Gyn
Member American Society of
Andrology
Practice Setting academic/private
Clinical Interests reproductive surgery,
lasers, adolescent endocrinology, IVF,
new reproductive technologies, male
factor infertility

George A. Hill, M.D.
Vanderbilt Univ. Med. Ctr., Ob/Gyn
Dept.
D-3223-MCN
Nashville, TN 37232
(615) 322-6574
Board Certifications Ob/Gyn,
Reproductive Endocrinology
Member Society of Reproductive
Endocrinologists
Practice Setting academic

Clinical Interests laser surgery, ovulation induction, IVF

Spyros N. Pavlou, M.D.
Vanderbilt Univ., Endocrinology Div.
AA-4206 Med. Ctr. N.
Twenty-first and Garland
Nashville, TN 37232
(615) 322-4871
Board Certifications Internal Medicine,
Endocrinology and Metabolism
Member American Society of
Andrology
Practice Setting academic
Clinical Interests disorders of male
reproduction—infertility

Anne Colston Wentz, M.D.
Vanderbilt Univ. Med. Ctr., Ob/Gyn
Dept.
Nashville, TN 37232
(615) 322-6576
Board Certification Reproductive
Endocrinology
Member Society of Reproductive
Endocrinologists
Practice Setting academic
Clinical Interests luteal phase
inadequacy, ovulation induction, male
infertility, IVF/GIFT, everything non-
surgical, recurrent abortion

TEXAS

Austin

Joe S. McIlhaney, Jr., M.D.
811 E. 32nd St.
Austin, TX 78705
(512) 476-7766
Board Certification Ob/Gyn
Member Society of Reproductive
Surgeons
Practice Setting private
Clinical Interests IVF/GIFT

Thomas C. Vaughn, M.D.
3705 Medical Parkway, Suite 230
Austin, TX 78705
(512) 451-0149
Board Certifications Ob/Gyn,
Reproductive Endocrinology
Member Society of Reproductive
Endocrinologists
Practice Setting private
Clinical Interests infertility, IVF, GIFT

Beaumont

Frank Anthony Giglio, M.D.
3560 Delaware, Suite 402
Beaumont, TX 77706
(409) 898-7115
Board Certification Ob/Gyn
Member Society of Reproductive
Surgeons
Practice Setting private
Clinical Interests infertility, gynecology,
surgery—gross, microsurgery,
laparoscopic

Carrollton

H. Jane Chihal, M.D., Ph.D.
Texas Endocrine and Fertility Institute
4333 N. Josey Lane, Suite 200
Carrollton, TX 75010
(214) 394-0114
Board Certifications Ob/Gyn,
Reproductive Endocrinology
Member Society of Reproductive
Endocrinologists
Practice Setting private
Clinical Interests IVF, microsurgery,
infertility (all phases), hormonal
disorders

Dallas

Bruce R. Carr, M.D.
Univ. of Texas S.W. Med. Ctr.,
Ob/Gyn Dept.
5323 Harry Hines Blvd.
Dallas, TX 75235
(214) 688-4747
Board Certifications Ob/Gyn,
Reproductive Endocrinology
Member Society of Reproductive
Endocrinologists
Practice Setting academic
Clinical Interests ovulation induction,
tubal microsurgery, intrauterine
insemination, habitual abortion

Brian M. Cohen, M.D.
8160 Walnut Hill Lane, Suite 104
Dallas, TX 75231
(214) 369-0528
Board Certifications Ob/Gyn,
Reproductive Endocrinology
Member Society of Reproductive
Endocrinologists

Practice Setting private
Clinical Interests operative and laser laparoscopy, microsurgery, ovulation induction

John D. McConnell, M.D.
 Univ. of Texas S.W. Med. Ctr.
 5323 Harry Hines Blvd.
 Dallas, TX 75235
 (214) 688-4765
 Board Certification Urology
 Member American Society of Andrology
 Practice Setting academic
 Clinical Interests male infertility and microsurgery

J. Michael Putman, M.D.
 3707 Gaston, Suite 410
 Dallas, TX 75246
 (214) 823-2692
 Board Certification Ob/Gyn
 Member Society of Reproductive Surgeons
 Practice Setting private
 Clinical Interests reproductive surgery—microsurgery, laser, ovulation induction, endometriosis, IUI, DI, IVF-GIFT

El Paso

Neal L. Ross, M.D.
 1700 Curie Dr., #5000
 El Paso, TX 79907
 (915) 532-3906
 Board Certification Ob/Gyn
 Member Society of Reproductive Surgeons
 Practice Setting private
 Clinical Interests infertility surgery

Galveston

C. James Chuong, M.D.
 Univ. of Texas Med. Branch, Ob/Gyn Dept.
 Galveston, TX 77550
 (409) 761-7023
 Board Certifications Ob/Gyn, Reproductive Endocrinology
 Member Society of Reproductive Endocrinologists
 Practice Setting academic
 Clinical Interests reproductive endocrinology and infertility, IVF,

microsurgical tuboplasty, premenstrual syndrome, neuroendocrinology

Manubai Nagamani, M.D.
 Univ. of Texas Med. Branch, Ob/Gyn Dept.
 Galveston, TX 77059
 (409) 761-3985
 Board Certifications Ob/Gyn, Reproductive Endocrinology
 Member Society of Reproductive Endocrinologists
 Practice Setting academic/private
 Clinical Interests microsurgery, IVF and GIFT, menopause

Houston

John E. Bertini, Jr., M.D.
 St. Joseph Med. Place 1
 1315 Calhoun, Suite 1502
 Houston, TX 77002-8232
 (713) 650-1502
 Board Certification NS
 Member American Society of Andrology
 Practice Setting private
 Clinical Interests male infertility

Veasy C. Buttram, Jr., M.D.
 Women's Ctr. of Texas
 7550 Fannin, Suite 104
 Houston, TX 77054
 (713) 797-9123, ext. 150
 Board Certifications Ob/Gyn, Reproductive Endocrinology
 Member Society of Reproductive Surgeons
 Practice Setting academic
 Clinical Interests endometriosis, uterine leiomyomata, uterine anomalies, pelvic adhesive disease, anovulatory disorders

Glenn R. Cunningham, M.D.
 6565 Fannin, Suite 817
 Houston, TX 77030
 (713) 795-7484
 Board Certifications Internal Medicine, Endocrinology and Metabolism
 Member American Society of Andrology
 Practice Setting academic
 Clinical Interests male reproduction, prostatic diseases

Joseph R. Feste, M.D.
2530 Fannin
Houston, TX 77054
(713) 797-9123
Board Certification Ob/Gyn
Member Society of Reproductive
Surgeons
Practice Setting private
Clinical Interests advanced operative
laparoscopy and microsurgery utilizing
laser energy

Robert Ray Franklin, M.D.
7550 Fannin
Houston, TX 77054-1989
(713) 797-9123
Board Certification Ob/Gyn
Member Society of Reproductive
Surgeons
Practice Setting academic/private
Clinical Interests infertility

William E. Gibbons, M.D.
Baylor College of Medicine, Ob/Gyn
Dept.
1 Baylor Plaza
Houston, TX 77030
(713) 798-7500
Board Certifications Ob/Gyn,
Reproductive Endocrinology
Member Society of Reproductive
Surgeons
Practice Setting academic
Clinical Interests IVF/GIFT,
microsurgery (laser), endocrinology,
menopause

George M. Grunert, M.D.
7550 Fannin
Houston, TX 77054
(713) 797-9123
Board Certifications Ob/Gyn,
Reproductive Endocrinology
Member Society of Reproductive
Surgeons
Practice Setting private
Clinical Interests IVF, GIFT,
microsurgery, laser surgery, general
reproductive endocrine

Barry Jacobs, M.D.
1200 Binz, #1200
Houston, TX 77004
(713) 528-0060
Board Certification Ob/Gyn
Member Society of Reproductive
Surgeons

Practice Setting private
Clinical Interests gynecology, infertility,
reproductive endocrinology

Larry I. Lipshultz, M.D.
6560 Fannin, #1003
Houston, TX 77030
(713) 798-4001
Board Certification Urology
Member Society of Reproductive
Surgeons
Practice Setting academic/private
Clinical Interests evaluation and
treatment of the infertile and
impotent male

Eberhard C. Lotze, M.D.
7550 Fannin
Houston, TX 77054
(713) 797-9123
Board Certification Ob/Gyn
Member Society of Reproductive
Surgeons
Practice Setting private
Clinical Interests endoscopic surgery,
reconstructive microsurgery

Luis J. Rodriguez-Rigau, M.D.
Texas Institute for Reproductive
Medicine and Endocrinology
7800 Fannin, Suite 500
Houston, TX 77054
(713) 791-1874
Board Certifications NS
Member American Society of
Andrology
Practice Setting private
Clinical Interests reproductive
endocrinology (male and female)

Stanley F. Rogers, M.D.
7550 Fannin, Suite 107
Houston, TX 77054
(713) 797-9123
Board Certification Ob/Gyn
Member Society of Reproductive
Surgeons
Practice Setting private
Clinical Interests infertility, especially
surgical approaches

Ivor Lawrence Safro, M.D.
380 Piney Point Rd.
Houston, TX 77024
(713) 464-6922
Board Certifications NS
Member Society of Reproductive
Surgeons

Practice Setting academic/private
Clinical Interests IVF, microsurgery

Keith D. Smith, M.D.
7800 Fannin, Suite 500
Houston, TX 77054
(713) 791-1874
Board Certifications Internal Medicine,
Endocrinology and Metabolism
Member American Society of
Andrology
Practice Setting private
Clinical Interests reproductive
endocrinology of the male and female

Ronald L. Young, M.D.
Dept. Ob/Gyn
Baylor College of Medicine
1 Baylor Plaza
Houston, TX 77030
Telephone NS
Board Certification Ob/Gyn
Member Society of Reproductive
Surgeons
Practice Setting academic/private
Clinical Interests reproductive
endocrinology, infertility, menopause

Lackland A.F.B.

Daniel M. Strickland, M.D.
Wilford Hall U.S.A.F. Med. Ctr.
Lackland A.F.B., TX 78236-5300
(512) 670-6143
Board Certifications Ob/Gyn,
Reproductive Endocrinology
Member Society of Reproductive
Endocrinologists
Practice Setting other
Clinical Interests general infertility,
infertility surgery, laser, hysteroscopy

Lubbock

Frank DeLeon, M.D.
Texas Tech Univ.
Department of Ob/Gyn
3601 Fourth St.
Lubbock, TX 79430
(806) 743-2357
Board Certifications Ob/Gyn,
Reproductive Endocrinology
Member Society of Reproductive
Endocrinologists
Practice Setting academic

Clinical Interests reproductive
endocrinology and infertility, IVF

Odessa

Carol A. Bergquist, M.D.
800 W. Fourth St.
Odessa, TX 79760
(915) 335-5200
Board Certification Ob/Gyn
Member Society of Reproductive
Surgeons
Practice Setting academic
Clinical Interests infertility, reproductive
surgery, hormonal imbalance, repeated
pregnancy loss

San Antonio

Richard M. Lackritz, M.D.
1303 McCullough St., Suite 272
San Antonio, TX 78212
(512) 225-1501
Board Certifications Ob/Gyn,
Reproductive Endocrinology
Member Society of Reproductive
Endocrinologists
Practice Setting private
Clinical Interests all aspects of infertility
with obstetric follow-up

Carlos E. Menendez, M.D.
7950 Floyd Curl Dr., #602
San Antonio, TX 78229
(512) 692-7684
Board Certifications Internal Medicine,
Endocrinology and Metabolism
Member American Society of
Andrology
Practice Setting private
Clinical Interests infertility, impotence,
hirsutism, prolactin and pituitary
problems

David Leon Olive, M.D.
7703 Floyd Curl Dr.
San Antonio, TX 78284
(512) 567-4938
Board Certifications Ob/Gyn,
Reproductive Endocrinology
Member Society of Reproductive
Endocrinologists
Practice Setting academic/private
Clinical Interests endometriosis, IVF,
male infertility

Robert S. Schenken, M.D.
  Univ. of Texas, Health Science Ctr. at
  San Antonio, Ob/Gyn Dept.
  7703 Floyd Curl Dr.
  San Antonio, TX 78284
  (512) 567-4930
  Board Certification Reproductive
  Endocrinology
  Member Society of Reproductive
  Endocrinologists
  Practice Setting academic
  Clinical Interests IVF, GIFT, ovulation
  induction, endometriosis, recurrent
  abortion, artificial insemination,
  infertility

Tyler

Joe Bill Belue, M.D.
  120 E. Charnwood
  Tyler, TX 75701
  (214) 597-8371
  Board Certification Ob/Gyn
  Member Society of Reproductive
  Surgeons
  Practice Setting private
  Clinical Interests laparoscopic diagnosis
  and treatment with laser as indicated,
  GIFT

Webster

Henry R. Wagner, M.D.
  Bay Area Urology
  8 Professional Park
  Webster, TX 77598
  (713) 332-9502
  Board Certification Urology
  Member American Society of
  Andrology
  Practice Setting private
  Clinical Interests male infertility,
  vasectomy reversals

UTAH

Provo

Richard Hatch, M.D.
  930 N. 500 W.
  Provo, UT 84604
  (801) 373-1818
  Board Certifications Ob/Gyn,
  Reproductive Endocrinology
  Member Society of Reproductive

Endocrinologists
  Practice Setting private
  Clinical Interests all aspects of infertility,
  particularly male infertility

Salt Lake City

Kirtly Parker Jones, M.D.
  Univ. of Utah Med. Ctr., Ob/Gyn
  Dept.
  Salt Lake City, UT 84132
  (801) 581-3834
  Board Certifications Ob/Gyn,
  Reproductive Endocrinology
  Member Society of Reproductive
  Endocrinologists
  Practice Setting academic
  Clinical Interests menopause, ovulation
  induction, IVF

William R. Keye, M.D.
  50 N. Medical Dr.
  Salt Lake City, UT 84132
  (801) 581-4172
  Board Certifications Ob/Gyn,
  Reproductive Endocrinology
  Member Society of Reproductive
  Endocrinologists
  Practice Setting academic
  Clinical Interests endometriosis, laser
  surgery

A. Marsh Poulson, Jr., M.D.
  2B200 Univ. of Utah
  50 N. Medical Dr.
  Salt Lake City, UT 84137
  (801) 581-3834
  Board Certification Ob/Gyn
  Member Society of Reproductive
  Surgeons
  Practice Setting academic
  Clinical Interests infertility—especially
  tubal reconstructive surgery, laser
  surgery, IVF

Ronald L. Urry, M.D.
  Univ. of Utah School of Med.
  50 N. Medical Drive, 3B208
  Salt Lake City, UT 84132
  (801) 581-3740
  Board Certification NS
  Member American Society of
  Andrology
  Practice Setting academic
  Clinical Interests andrology, general
  infertility, sperm banking, IVF

VERMONT

Burlington

Mark Gibson, M.D.
Univ. of Vermont School of Medicine,
Ob/Gyn Dept.
Burlington, VT 05401
(802) 656-1235
Board Certifications Ob/Gyn,
Reproductive Endocrinology
Member Society of Reproductive
Endocrinologists
Practice Setting academic
Clinical Interests ovulation induction,
laser surgery, AID frozen, GIFT, IVF

Daniel H. Riddick, M.D.
Med. Ctr. Hospital of Vermont,
Ob/Gyn Dept.
Burlington, VT 05401
(802) 656-1235
Board Certifications Ob/Gyn,
Reproductive Endocrinology
Member Society of Reproductive
Endocrinologists
Practice Setting academic
Clinical Interests all aspects of
reproductive endocrinology and
infertility

VIRGINIA

Arlington

Michael Dimattina, M.D.
46 S. Glebe Rd., #301
Arlington, VA 22204
(703) 920-3890
Board Certifications Ob/Gyn,
Reproductive Endocrinology
Member Society of Reproductive
Endocrinologists
Practice Setting private
Clinical Interests infertility, GIFT,
endometriosis, male factors

Charlottesville

Bruce G. Bateman, M.D.
Ob/Gyn Dept., Box 387
Univ. of Virginia Hospital
Charlottesville, VA 22908
(804) 924-0312
Board Certifications Ob/Gyn,

Reproductive Endocrinology
Member Society of Reproductive
Endocrinologists
Practice Setting academic
Clinical Interests IVF

James D. Kitchin, III, M.D.
Univ. of Virginia Hospital, Ob/Gyn
Dept.
Charlottesville, VA 22908
(804) 924-0312
Board Certifications Ob/Gyn,
Reproductive Endocrinology
Member Society of Reproductive
Endocrinologists
Practice Setting academic
Clinical Interests operative gynecology,
reproductive endocrinology and
infertility

Wallace C. Nunley, Jr., M.D.
Univ. of Virginia Hospital
Box 387, Ob/Gyn Dept.
Charlottesville, VA 22908
(804) 924-0312
Board Certifications Ob/Gyn,
Reproductive Endocrinology
Member Society of Reproductive
Endocrinologists
Practice Setting academic
Clinical Interests gynecologic
reconstructive surgery, pituitary,
adrenal, ovarian endocrinologic
disorders

Fairfax

Maria Bustillo, M.D.
Genetics and IVF Institute
3020 Javier Rd.
Fairfax, VA 22031
(703) 698-7355
Board Certifications Ob/Gyn,
Reproductive Endocrinology
Member Society of Reproductive
Endocrinologists
Practice Setting private
Clinical Interests infertility,
hypothalamic amenorrhea

Norfolk

Anibal A. Acosta, M.D.
Hofheimer Hall, Sixth Floor
825 Fairfax Avenue
Norfolk, VA 23507

(804) 446-8919
Board Certifications Ob/Gyn,
Reproductive Endocrinology
Member American Society of
Andrology
Practice Setting academic
Clinical Interests reproductive medicine

William C. Andrews, M.D.
880 Kempsville Rd., Suite 2200
Norfolk, VA 23502
(804) 466-6350
Board Certification Ob/Gyn
Member Society of Reproductive
Surgeons
Practice Setting private
Clinical Interests NS

Charles C. Coddington III, M.D.
Ob/Gyn Dept., Hofheimer Hall
825 Fairfax Ave.
Norfolk, VA 23507
(804) 446-8940
Board Certifications Ob/Gyn,
Reproductive Endocrinology
Member Society of Reproductive
Endocrinologists
Practice Setting academic
Clinical Interests reproductive surgery
including laser, andrology, IVF

Suheil J. Muasher, M.D.
825 Fairfax Ave.
Norfolk, VA 23507
(804) 446-8916
Board Certifications Ob/Gyn,
Reproductive Endocrinology
Member Society of Reproductive
Endocrinologists
Practice Setting academic
Clinical Interests infertility, surgical
therapy for infertility, assisted
reproduction (IVF, GIFT)

Sergio Oehninger, M.D.
825 Fairfax Ave., Sixth Floor,
Hofheimer Hall
Jones Institute for Reproductive
Medicine
Norfolk, VA 23507
(804) 446-8940
Board Certification Ob/Gyn
Member American Society of
Andrology
Practice Setting academic
Clinical Interests andrology, assisted
reproductive technology

Richmond

Robert J. Fierro, M.D.
7605 Forest Ave., Suite 411
Richmond, VA 23229
(804) 285-7553
Board Certifications Ob/Gyn,
Reproductive Endocrinology
Member Society of Reproductive
Surgeons
Practice Setting private
Clinical Interests reproductive
endocrinology, prolactin, IVF, GIFT,
microlaser surgery

Joseph G. Gianfortoni, M.D.
113 Forest Ave., Suite 411
Lifesource Institute for Fertility and
Endocrinology
Richmond, VA 23229
(804) 285-7553
Board Certifications Ob/Gyn,
Reproductive Endocrinology
Member Society of Reproductive
Endocrinologists
Practice Setting private
Clinical Interests micro and laser
surgery, laparoscopic surgery, IVF,
GIFT, ovulation induction,
endometriosis, female hormonal
imbalance

Sanford M. Rosenberg, M.D.
Richmond Ctr. for Fertility and
Endocrinology
7605 Forest Ave., #207
Richmond, VA 23229
(804) 285-9700
Board Certifications Ob/Gyn,
Reproductive Endocrinology
Member Society of Reproductive
Endocrinologists
Practice Setting private
Clinical Interests laser laparoscopy,
microsurgery, IVF/GIFT

Winchester

Alessandro G. Basso, M.D.
Winchester Surgical Clinic,
Urology Div.
20 S. Stewart St.
Winchester, VA 22601
(703) 662-0377
Board Certification Urology
Member American Society of

Andrology
Practice Setting private
Clinical Interests male infertility,
impotence

WASHINGTON

Seattle

Richard Eugene Berger, M.D.
Reproductive and Sexual Med. Clinic
1120 Cherry, Suite 403
Seattle, WA 98104
(206) 223-3121
Board Certification Urology
Member American Society of
Andrology
Practice Setting academic/private/HMO
Clinical Interests male infertility and
impotence

Lori Marshall, M.D.
Virginia Mason Clinic
1100 Ninth Ave.
Seattle, WA 98111
(206) 223-1232
Board Certifications Ob/Gyn,
Reproductive Endocrinology
Member Society of Reproductive
Endocrinologists
Practice Setting other
Clinical Interests infertility, especially
ovulation induction, endometriosis,
premature ovarian failure

Donald Earl Moore, M.D.
Univ. of Washington, School of
Medicine
RH-20, Ob/Gyn Dept.
Seattle, WA 98195
(206) 543-6137
Board Certifications Ob/Gyn,
Reproductive Endocrinology
Member Society of Reproductive
Endocrinologists
Practice Setting academic
Clinical Interests general infertility, IVF

C. Alvin Paulsen, M.D.
1200 Twelfth Ave. S.
Seattle, WA 98144
(206) 326-4060
Board Certifications NS
Practice Setting academic
Member American Society of
Andrology
Clinical Interests internal medicine

Donald C. Smith, M.D.
1229 Madison, #1050
Seattle, WA 98104
(206) 587-0585
Board Certification Ob/Gyn
Member Society of Reproductive
Surgeons
Practice Setting private/academic
Clinical Interests general infertility, IVF,
GIFT, microsurgical techniques

Leon R. Spadoni, M.D.
BB619 Univ. Hospital, RH-20
Seattle, WA 98195
(206) 543-9626
Board Certification Ob/Gyn
Member Society of Reproductive
Surgeons
Practice Setting academic
Clinical Interests ovulation induction,
tubal microsurgery, male factor

Wayne D. Weissman, M.D.
1221 Madison, Suite 1210
Seattle, WA 98104
(206) 292-6488
Board Certification Urology
Member American Society of
Andrology
Practice Setting private
Clinical Interests male infertility,
microsurgery, sperm aspiration, sperm
enhancement

Paul W. Zarutskie, M.D.
Univ. of Washington
Ob/Gyn Dept., RH-20
Seattle, WA 98195
(206) 543-0670
Board Certifications Ob/Gyn,
Reproductive Endocrinology
Member Society of Reproductive
Endocrinologists
Practice Setting academic
Clinical Interests IVF, male factor,
microinjection

Tacoma

Stephen R. Plymate, M.D.
Box 454, Madigan Army Med. Ctr.
Tacoma, WA 98431
(206) 967-6646
Board Certifications Internal Medicine,
Endocrinology & Metabolism
Member American Society of
Andrology

Practice Setting academic
Clinical Interests male infertility

WEST VIRGINIA

Morgantown

Roger C. Toffle, M.D.
4601 Health Sciences North
Med. Ctr., Dept. Ob/Gyn, WVU
Morgantown, WV 26506
(304) 293-3840
Board Certifications Ob/Gyn,
Reproductive Endocrinology
Member Society of Reproductive
Endocrinologists
Practice Setting academic
Clinical Interests ovulation induction,
reproductive surgery

WISCONSIN

Madison

Sander S. Shapiro, M.D.
Univ. Hospital
Madison, WI
(608) 263-1217
Board Certification Reproductive
Endocrinology
Member Society of Reproductive
Endocrinologists
Practice Setting academic
Clinical Interests reproductive
endocrinology

Milwaukee

Richard B. Bourne, M.D.
2600 N. Mayfair Rd., Suite 545

Milwaukee, WI 53226
(414) 476-0430
Board Certification Urology
Member American Society of
Andrology
Practice Setting private
Clinical Interests male infertility, all
aspects

Frederick G. Dettman, M.D.
5589 North Bay Ridge Ave.
Milwaukee, WI 53217
(414) 961-1191
Board Certification Ob/Gyn
Member Society of Reproductive
Surgeons
Practice Setting private
Clinical Interests tubal reconstruction,
endometriosis

K. Paul Katayama, M.D., Ph.D.
Advanced Institute of Fertility
Sinai–Samaritan Med. Ctr.
2000 W. Kilbourn Ave.
Milwaukee, WI 53233
(414) 937-5437
Board Certification Reproductive
Endocrinology
Member Society of Reproductive
Endocrinologists
Practice Setting private
Clinical Interests IVF, GIFT,
microsurgery (tubal repair),
endocrinology (PCO, anovulation),
ovulation induction

CANADIAN INFERTILITY CENTERS

The following list comes from the membership directory of the Canadian Fertility and Andrology Society. That directory also includes a list of all individual members of the society, as well as listing therapeutic donor insemination clinics and sexually transmitted disease clinics. It is available from the Canadian Fertility and Andrology Society, 2065 Alexandre de Seve, Suite 409, Montreal, Quebec, Canada, H2L 2W5, (514) 521-6812.

Again, the authors do not intend to imply endorsement of the centers listed in this book. In all cases, you should use the same careful deliberation that you normally would employ when choosing a physician or medical clinic.

ALBERTA

Calgary

Infertility Clinic
Foothills Hospital
3330 Hospital Dr., N.W.
Calgary, Alta.
T2N 2T9
(403) 270-1110

Edmonton

Dr. David C. Cumming
Health Science Centre
1D1 W. MacKenzie
Edmonton, Alta.
T6J 2R7
(403) 432-6636

Infertility Clinic
Univ. of Alberta Hospital
8440-112 St.
Edmonton, Alta.
T6G 2B7
(403) 432-8822

Dr. W. B. Schulze
318 Medical Arts Bldg.

11010 Jasper Ave.
Edmonton, Alta.
T5K 0K5
(403) 426-1920

University of Alberta
5–108 Clinical Sciences Bldg.
Edmonton, Alta.
T6G 2G6
Telephone NS

BRITISH COLUMBIA

Vancouver

Dr. V. Gomel
IVF and GIFT Programs
Room 2J40
Grace Hospital
4490 Oak St.
Vancouver, B.C.
V6H 3V5
(604) 875-2337

Dr. T. Rowe
Infertility Clinic
St. Paul's Hospital
1081 Burrard St.
Vancouver, B.C.

V6Z 1Y6
(604) 682-2344

MANITOBA

Winnipeg

Dr. E. Cowden, Dr. R. Livingstone
Reproductive Endocrine and Fertility
Clinic
St. Boniface General Hospital
409 Tache Ave.
Winnipeg, Man.
R2H 2A6
(204) 233-8563

Dr. C. Faiman
Reproductive Endocrine Clinic
Health Sciences Centre
700 William Ave.
Winnipeg, Man.
R3E 0Z3
(204) 774-6511

Dr. J. Kredentser
Infertility Clinic
Univ. of Manitoba
59 Emily St.
Winnipeg, Man.
R3E 0W3
Telephone NS

NOVA SCOTIA

Halifax

Endocrine Infertility Centre
5821 University Ave.
Halifax, N S
B3H 1W3
(902) 420-6655

ONTARIO

Burlington

Dr. L. D. Komer
Infertility Clinic
2015 Lakeshore Rd.
Burlington, Ont.
L7R 1A1
(416) 639-2571

Hamilton

Infertility Clinic
McMaster Univ. Med. Centre
1200 Main St. W.
Hamilton, Ont.
(416) 521-2100

Dr. R. G. Stopps
262 James St. S.
Hamilton, Ont.
L8P 3B5
(416) 523-0626

Kingston

Dr. R. H. Hudson, Dr. R. Perez-Marrero
Andrology Clinic
Kingston General Hospital
76 Stuart St.
Kingston, Ont.
K7L 2V7
Dr. Hudson: (613) 549-4070
Dr. Perez-Marrero: (613) 542-0137

Dr. R. Reid, Dr. H. Gorwill
Female Reproduction Clinic
Kingston General Hospital
76 Stuart St.
Kingston, Ont.
K7L 2V7
Dr. Reid: (613) 542-9473
Dr. Gorwill: (613) 544-1777

London

Dr. A. A. Yuzpe
University Hospital
339 Windermere Rd.
London, Ont.
N6A 5A5
(519) 663-2903

Ottawa

Dr. E. Jolly, Dr. A. Leader
Fertility Centre
Ottawa Civic Hospital
1053 Carling Ave.
Ottawa, Ont.
K1Y 4E9
Dr. Jolly: (613) 737-8556
Dr. Leader: (613) 737-8559

Ottawa General Hospital, Ob/Gyn Dept.
  501 Smythe Rd.
  Ottawa, Ont.
  K1H 8L6
  Telephone NS

Toronto

Dr. Murray N. Kroach
  Male Fertility Clinic
  Toronto E. General Hospital
  825 Coxwell Ave.
  Toronto, Ont.
  M4C 3E7
  (416) 425-0112

Reproductive Biology and Infertility Unit
  St. Michael's Hospital
  30 Bond St.
  Toronto, Ont.
  M5B 1W8
  (416) 360-4000

Reproductive Biology Unit
  Toronto General Hospital
  200 Elizabeth St.
  Toronto, Ont.
  M5G 2C4
  (416) 595-3111

Dr. Alan B. Shewchuk
  700 Bay St., Suite 604
  Toronto, Ont.
  M5G 1N3
  (416) 595-1521

Dr. J. Shuber, Dr. Eisen Abraham
  Reproductive Biology and Infertility Unit
  Mount Sinai Hospital
  600 University Ave.
  Toronto, Ont.
  M5B 1X5
  Dr. Shuber: (416) 586-4626
  Dr. Abraham: (416) 586-4628

QUÉBEC

Chicoutimi

Hôpital de Chicoutimi
  C.P. 5006
  Chicoutimi, Qué.
  G7H 5H6
  (418) 549-2195

Jonquiere

Centre Hospitalier de Jonquiere
  C.P. 1200
  Jonquiere, Qué.
  G7X 7X2
  (418) 547-3651

Montréal

Clinique de Fertilité
  Hôpital Maisonneuve–Rosemont
  5415 l'Assomption
  Montréal, Qué.
  (514) 252-3400

Clinique de Fertilité
  Hôpital Notre-Dame
  1560 Sherbrooke E.
  Montréal, Qué.
  H2L 4M1
  (514) 876-7232

Dr. J. Lorrain
  Clinique de Fertilité
  Hôpital du Sacre Coeur
  5400 W., boul. Gouin
  Montréal, Qué.
  H4J 1C5
  (514) 333-2121

Clinique de Fertilité
  Hôpital St. Luc
  264 Dorchester E.
  Montréal, Qué.
  H2X 1P1
  (514) 281-2141

Hôtel-Dieu de Montréal
  3840 rue de St. Urbain
  Montréal, Qué.
  H2W 1T8
  (514) 844-0161

Infertility Clinic
  Royal Victoria Hospital
  687 Pine Ave. W.
  Montréal, Qué.
  H3A 1A1
  (514) 842-1231

Montréal General Hospital
  1650 ave. Cedar
  Montréal, Qué.
  H3G 1A4
  (514) 937-6011

Pierrefonds

Dr. Vito Cardone
4940 boul. Lalande
Pierrefonds, Qué.
H8Y 1V7
(514) 324-1048

Québec

Centre d'Endocrinologie de la
Reproduction
et d'Infertilité du Couple
Hôpital St. François d'Assise
10 rue de l'Espinay
Québec, Qué.
G1S 3L5
(418) 525-4307

Hôpital du St. Sacrement
1050 chemin Ste.-Foy
Québec, Qué.
G1S 4L8
(418) 688-7211

Rimouski

Clinique de Planning
Centre Régional de Rimouski
150 Rouleau
Rimouski, Qué.
G5L 5T1
(418) 723-7851

Sherbrooke

Centre Hospitalier de l'Univ. de
Sherbrooke

3001, 12e ave. Nord
Sherbrooke, Qué.
J1J 3H5
(819) 563-5555

Ste.-Foy

Dr. J. E. Rioux, Dr. R. Tremblay
Le Centre Hospitalier de l'Univ. de
Laval
2705 boul. Laurier
Ste.-Foy, Qué.
G1V 4G2
(418) 654-2295

Westmount

Dr. Brian Morris
5025 Sherbrooke W., #310
Westmount, Qué.
H4A 1S9
(514) 485-1333

SASKATCHEWAN

Saskatoon

Dr. C. Simpson
University Hospital, Ob/Gyn Dept.
Saskatoon, Sask.
S7N 0X0
(306) 244-2323

RESOURCES

Infertility Services

American Association of Tissue Banks

1350 Beverly Road, Suite 220A
McLean, VA 22101
(703) 827-9582
Supplies a list of AATB-associated sperm banks in the United States and Canada. Send a stamped, self-addressed envelope.

American College of Obstetricians and Gynecologists Resource Center

409 12th Street, SW
Washington, DC 20024-2188
(202) 638-5577

This national organization of ob-gyns has a resource center that can provide patient education pamphlets, lists of ob-gyns in certain areas of the country, and answers to basic questions about infertility and women's health.

American Fertility Society

2140 Eleventh Avenue South
Suite 200
Birmingham, AL 35205-2800
(205) 933-8494

This national organization of fertility specialists provides general information about infertility and pamphlets for patients.

American Society of Andrology

309 West Clark Street
Champaigne, IL 61820
(217) 356-3182

Refers patients to andrologists across the country.

American Urological Association, Inc.

1120 North Charles Street
Baltimore, MD 21201
(301) 727-1100

Provides patient information pamphlets and the names of physicians/officers of the association who can supply information about specific questions and possible referral to a local urologist.

DES Action USA (East Coast Office)

Long Island Jewish Medical
  Center
New Hyde Park, NY 11040
(516) 775-3450

**DES Action USA (West Coast
Office)**
2845 24th Street
San Francisco, CA 94110
(415) 826-5060

Provides education and
  support to mothers,
  daughters, and sons exposed
  to the drug
  diethylstilbestrol (DES).

Endometriosis Association
8585 North 76th Place
Milwaukee, WI 53223
1-800-992-3636 (in the United
  States)
1-800-426-2363 (in Canada)

Furnishes information on local
  support groups, crisis call
  assistance, and education
  and research programs
  regarding endometriosis.

**National Society of Genetic
  Counselors**
233 Canterbury Drive
Wallingford, PA 19086
(215) 872-7608

Provides information on
  genetic counseling services
  and referrals.

**Planned Parenthood
  Federation of America**

810 Seventh Avenue
New York, NY 10019
(212) 541-7800

Provides referral to local
  Planned Parenthood
  affiliates that may supply
  infertility diagnosis and
  counseling.

Resolve, Inc.
5 Water Street
Arlington, MA 02174
(617) 643-2424
1-800-225-5185

This national self-help group
  for infertile couples
  provides physician and IVF
  referrals, literature about
  many aspects of infertility,
  a newsletter, and telephone
  counseling. It has support
  groups across the country.

SHARE
(Source of Help in Airing and
  Resolving Experiences)
St. Elizabeth's Hospital
211 South Third Street
Belleville, IL 62222
(618) 234-2415

Supplies information packets
  on miscarriage, stillbirth,
  ectopic pregnancy, and
  neonatal (near birth) death;
  a bibliographic listing of
  books, articles, and audio-
  visual material on grieving;
  a bimonthly newsletter; a
  listing of parents in

outreach groups; and a
support group referral list.

Adoption Services

*Child Welfare League of
America*
Suite 310, 440 First Street,
NW
Washington, DC 20001
(202) 638-2952

Publishes *The National Adoption
Resource Directory,* listing
adoption agencies across the
country.

*Latin American Parent
Association*
P.O. Box 72
Seaford, NY 11783
(718) 236-8689

Provides information about
adopting babies from Latin
America.

National Adoption Center
1218 Chestnut Street
Philadelphia, PA 19107
1-800-TOADOPT (except in
Pennsylvania)
(215) 925-0200 (in
Pennsylvania and
elsewhere)

Promotes adoption
opportunities for children
throughout the country,
particularly those with
special needs.

*National Adoption
Information Clearinghouse*
Suite 600, 1400 Eye Street,
NW
Washington, DC 20005
(202) 842-1919

Provides fact sheets, articles,
films, and videotapes about
adoption; a computerized
list of books and written
materials on adoption; a
directory of adoption
agencies and other adoption
resources; and information
on state and federal laws on
adoption.

*National Committee for
Adoption*
1930 17th Street, NW
Washington, DC 20009-6207
(202) 328-1200

An association of private
adoption agencies that
provides information,
publications, and resource
listings on adoption.

North American Council on Adoptable Children
1821 University Avenue
Suite S-275
St. Paul, MN 55104
(612) 644-3036

A national support group for adoptive parents that specializes in placing older, handicapped, and minority children.

OURS, Inc.
3307 Highway 100 North,
Suite 203
Minneapolis, MN 55422
(612) 535-4829

This national support group provides information about licensed adoption agencies with a focus on foreign adoptions.

If you would like to receive further information, including a newsletter from Chapel Hill Fertility Center, please contact: Sandy Pratt, Patient Care Coordinator, Chapel Hill Fertility Center, 109 Conner Drive, Suite 2104, Chapel Hill, NC 27514.

GLOSSARY

Abortion premature termination of a pregnancy; may be induced or spontaneous (miscarriage)

Acquired immune deficiency syndrome (AIDS) a usually fatal disease caused by a virus that destroys the immune system's ability to fight off infection

Acrosome the packet of enzymes in a sperm's head that allows the sperm to dissolve a hole in the coating around the egg, which allows the sperm to penetrate and fertilize the egg

Acrosome reaction chemical change that enables a sperm to penetrate an egg

Adhesion a union of adjacent organs by scar tissue

Adrenal glands the endocrine gland on top of each kidney

Aerobic bacteria bacterial organisms that require relatively high concentrations of oxygen to survive and reproduce

Agglutination clumping together, as of sperm, often due to infection, inflammation, or antibodies

Amenorrhea absence of menstruation

Amniocentesis aspiration of amniotic fluid from the uterus, usually performed at three to three and a half months of pregnancy, to test the fetus for genetic abnormalities

Anaerobic bacteria bacterial organisms that survive in relatively low oxygen concentrations

Androgens male sex hormones

Andrologist a specialist who treats sperm problems

Anovulation absence of ovulation

Antibody a protective agent produced by the body's immune system in response to a foreign substance

Antigen any substance that induces the formation of an antibody

Antisperm antibodies antibodies that can attach to sperm and inhibit movement of sperm or fertilization

Artificial insemination (AI) placement of a sperm sample inside the female reproductive tract (See also intracervical insemination, intrauterine insemination, intratubal insemination)

Aspiration suctioning of fluid, as from a follicle

Asymptomatic without any symptoms

Autoantibodies antibodies formed against one's own tissues

Autoimmunity an immune reaction against one's own tissues

Azoospermia absence of sperm

Bacteria microscopic, single-celled organisms that can cause infections of the genital tract

Basal body temperature (BBT) the temperature taken at its lowest point in the day, usually in the morning before getting out of bed

Biopsy a fragment of tissue removed for study under the microscope

Blood-testis barrier barrier that separates sperm from the bloodstream

Bromocryptine (Parlodel) a drug that reduces levels of the pituitary hormone prolactin

Cannula a hollow tube used, for example, to inseminate sperm artificially

Capacitation process by which sperm become capable of fertilizing an egg

Catheter a flexible tube used for aspirating or injecting fluids

Cauterize to destroy tissue with heat, cold, or caustic substances usually to seal off blood vessels or ducts

Cervix the lower portion of the uterus that opens into the vagina

Cervicitis inflammation of the cervix

Chlamydia a type of bacteria that is frequently transmitted sexually between partners or from an infected mother to her newborn child; the most common sexually transmitted bacterial disease

Chorionic villus sampling (CVS) taking a biopsy of the placenta, usually at the end of the second month of pregnancy, to test the fetus for genetic abnormalities

Chromosome threads of DNA in a cell's nucleus that transmit hereditary information

Clomiphene citrate (Clomid, Serophene) a fertility pill that stimulates ovulation through release of gonadotropins from the pituitary gland

Colposcopy examination of the cervix through a magnifying telescope to detect abnormal cells

Condom a latex (rubber) device that fits over the penis to prevent pregnancy and sexually transmitted infections.

Congenital defect a birth defect

Conization surgical removal of a cone-shaped portion of the cervix, usually as treatment for a precancerous condition

Contraindication a reason not to use a particular drug or treatment

Corpus luteum ("yellow body") formed in the ovary following ovulation, it produces progesterone

Cryocautery cautery by freezing

Cryptorchidism failure of one or both testicles to descend into the scrotum

Cul-de-sac pouch located at the bottom of the abdominal cavity between the uterus and rectum

Culdoscopy examination of the internal female pelvic organs through an incision in the vagina

Cyst a sac filled with fluid

Danazol (Danocrine) a synthetic androgen frequently prescribed for endometriosis

Deoxyribonucleic acid (DNA) the combination of amino acids in the cell's nucleus that make up the chromosomes, which transmit hereditary characteristics

Diethylstilbestrol (DES) a synthetic estrogen (originally prescribed to prevent miscarriage) that caused malformations of the reproductive organs in some who were exposed to the drug during fetal development

Dilatation and curettage (D&C) an operation that involves stretching the cervical opening to scrape out the uterus

DINKS an acronym for couples with Double *I*ncome, No Kids

Donor insemination artificial insemination with donor sperm

Dysfunction abnormal function

Ectopic pregnancy pregnancy located outside of the uterus, most commonly in a fallopian tube

Egg (ovum) the female reproductive cell

Egg donation donation of an egg by one woman to another who attempts to become pregnant by in vitro fertilization

Ejaculate the sperm-containing fluid released at orgasm

Ejaculatory ducts the male ducts that contract with orgasm to cause ejaculation

Electrocautery cauterization using electrical current

Electroejaculation controlled electrical stimulation to induce ejaculation in a man with damage to the nerves that control ejaculation

Embryo the developing baby from implantation to the second month of pregnancy

Embryologist a specialist in embryo development

Embryo transfer placing a laboratory-fertilized egg into the uterus

Embryo transplant a procedure that involves flushing an embryo from the uterus and placing it into another woman's uterus

Endocrine gland an organ that produces hormones

Endometrial biopsy removal of a fragment of the lining of the uterus for study under the microscope

Endometriosis growth of endometrial tissue outside of its normal location in the uterus

Endometritis inflammation of the endometrium

Endometrium the inner lining of the uterus

Epididymis the tightly coiled, thin-walled tube that conducts sperm from the testicles to the vas deferens

Epididymitis inflammation of the epididymis

Estradiol the principal estrogen produced by the ovary

Estrogens female sex hormones

Fallopian tubes ducts that pick up the egg from the ovary; where a sperm normally meets the egg to fertilize it

Fecundability the ability to become pregnant

Fetus the developing baby from the second month of pregnancy until birth

Fertilization union of the male gamete (sperm) with the female gamete (egg)

Fibroid (myoma or leiomyoma) a benign tumor of the uterine muscle and connective tissue.

Fimbria the finger-like projections at the end of the fallopian tube nearest the ovary that capture the egg and deliver it into the tube

Fimbrioplasty plastic surgery on the fimbria of a damaged or blocked fallopian tube

Follicle a fluid-filled sac in the ovary that releases an egg at ovulation

Follicle stimulating hormone (FSH) the pituitary hormone that stimulates follicle growth in women and sperm formation in men

Follicular phase the pre-ovulatory phase of a woman's cycle during which the follicle grows and high estrogen levels cause the uterine lining to proliferate

Fluoroscope an imaging device that uses X-rays to view internal body structures on a screen

Fructose produced by the seminal vesicles, the sugar that sperm use for energy

Gamete a reproductive cell; the sperm in men, the egg in women

Gamete Intra Fallopian Transfer (GIFT) combining eggs and sperm outside of the body and immediately placing them into the fallopian tubes to achieve fertilization

Gardnerella a bacteria that may cause a vaginal infection

Gene the unit of heredity, composed

of DNA; the building block of chromosomes

Gestation sac the fluid-filled sac in which the fetus develops, visible by an ultrasound exam

GIFT see Gamete Intra Fallopian Transfer

Gland an organ that produces and secretes essential body fluids or substances, such as hormones

Gonadotropins the hormones produced by the pituitary gland that control reproductive function: follicle stimulating hormone (FSH) and luteinizing hormone (LH)

Gonadotropin releasing hormone (GnRH) the hormone produced and released by the hypothalamus that controls the pituitary gland's production and release of gonadotropins

Gonads organs that produce the sex cells and sex hormones; testicles in men and ovaries in women

Gonorrhea a sexually transmitted infection caused by the bacteria *Neisseria Gonococcus* that can lead to infertility

Granuloma a ball of inflamed tissue, commonly formed after vasectomy due to sperm leaking from the vas deferens

Habitual abortion repeat miscarriages

Hamster test a test of the ability of a man's sperm to penetrate a hamster egg stripped of its outer membrane, the zona pellucida. Also called Hamster Zona-Free Ovum (HZFO) Test or Sperm Penetration Assay (SPA)

Hemizona assay a laboratory test of the ability of sperm to penetrate into a human egg; first the egg is split in half, then one half is tested against the husband's sperm and the other half against sperm from a fertile man

Hirsutism excessive hair growth

Hormone a substance, produced by an endocrine gland, that travels through the bloodstream to a specific organ, where it exerts its effect

Host uterus procedure a woman carries to term a pregnancy produced by an infertile couple through in vitro fertilization

Hostile mucus cervical mucus that impedes the natural progress of sperm through the cervical canal

Human chorionic gonadotropin (hCG) the hormone produced early in pregnancy to keep the corpus luteum producing progesterone; may be injected to stimulate ovulation and progesterone production

Human menopausal gonadotropins (hMG) see Pergonal

Hydrotubation injection of fluid, often into the fallopian tubes to determine if they are open

Hyperprolactinemia excessive prolactin in the blood

Hyperandrogenism excessive production of androgens in women, frequently a cause of hirsutism and also associated with polycystic ovarian disease (PCOD)

Hyperstimulation excessive stimulation of the ovaries that can cause them to become enlarged

Hypothalamus the endocrine gland at the center of the brain that produces gonadotropin releasing hormone and controls pituitary function

Hypothyroidism underactivity of the thyroid gland

Hysterectomy surgical removal of the uterus

Hysteroscopy examination of the inner cavity of the uterus through a fiberoptic telescope inserted through the vagina and cervical canal

Hysterosalpingogram (HSG) an X-ray examination of the uterus and fallopian tubes

Immune system the body's defense against any injury or invasion by a foreign substance or organism

Immunoglobulins a class of proteins endowed with antibody activity; antibodies

Immunosuppressive drug a drug that in- terferes with the normal immune response

Immunotherapy a medical treatment for an immune system disorder that involves transfusing donor white blood cells into a woman who has had recurrent miscarriages

Implantation attachment of the fertilized egg to the uterine lining, usually occurring five to seven days after ovulation

Impotence inability of a man to achieve an erection or ejaculation

Incompetent cervix cervix with the inability to remain closed throughout an entire pregnancy; a frequent cause of premature birth

Infertility inability of a couple to achieve a pregnancy or to carry a pregnancy to term after one year of unprotected intercourse

Inflammation a response to some type of injury such as infection, characterized by increased blood flow, heat, redness, swelling, and pain

Intracervical insemination (ICI) artificial insemination of sperm into the cervical canal

Intratubal insemination (ITI) artificial insemination of sperm, which have been washed free of seminal fluid, into the fallopian tubes

Intrauterine insemination (IUI) artificial insemination of sperm, which have been washed free of seminal fluid, into the uterine cavity

In utero while in the uterus during early development

In vitro fertilization (IVF) (literally, "in glass") fertilization outside of the body in a laboratory; the term "test tube baby" is inaccurate since fertilization occurs in a small circular dish, not a test tube.

Karyotype a chromosome analysis

Klinefelter's syndrome a chromosome abnormality that prevents normal male sexual development and causes irreversible infertility due to the presence of an extra female (X) chromosome

Laparoscopy examination of the pelvic organs through a small telescope called a laparoscope

Laparotomy a surgical opening of the abdomen

Leiomyoma (fibroid) a benign tumor of the uterus

Leydig cells the cells in the testicles that make testosterone

LH surge the sudden release of luteinizing hormone (LH) that causes the follicle to release a mature egg

Luteal phase post-ovulatory phase of a woman's cycle; the corpus luteum produces progesterone, which in turn causes the uterine lining to secrete substances to support the implantation and growth of the early embryo

Luteal phase deficiency (LPD) inadequate function of the corpus luteum that may prevent a fertilized egg from implanting in the uterus or may lead to early pregnancy loss

Luteinized Unruptured Follicle (LUF) *syndrome* the failure of a follicle to release the egg even though a corpus luteum has formed

Luteinizing hormone (LH) the pituitary hormone that causes the testicles in men and ovaries in women to manufacture sex hormones

Menarche the time when a woman has her first menstrual period

Menopause the time when a woman stops having menstrual periods

Metrodin (Pure FSH) an injectable drug consisting of pure follicle stimulating hormone used to stimulate ovulation

Microsurgery reconstructive surgery performed under magnification using delicate instruments and precise techniques

Miscarriage spontaneous abortion

Morphology the study of form, such as assessing the shape of sperm during semen analysis

Motility motion, such as the forward swimming motion of healthy sperm

Mucus secretion from a gland that can be watery, gel-like, stretchy, sticky or dry; fertile mucus is watery and stretchy

Mycoplasma an infectious agent that falls structurally between a virus and a bacterium

Myomectomy surgical removal of a uterine fibroid tumor

Obstetrician-gynecologist (Ob-gyn) a physician who specializes in the treatment of female disorders and pregnancy

Oligomenorrhea infrequent and irregular menstrual cycles

Oligospermia a low sperm count

Ovarian cyst a fluid-containing enlargement of the ovary

Ovarian wedge resection surgical removal of a portion of a polycystic ovary to produce ovulation

Ovary the female gonad; produces eggs and female hormones

Ovulation release of an egg from the ovary

Pap smear removal of cells from the surface of the cervix to study microscopically

Parlodel see Bromocryptine

Patent open; for example, fallopian tubes should be patent after a sterilization reversal operation

Pelvic cavity the area surrounded by the pelvic bone that contains the uterus, fallopian tubes, and ovaries in women, and the prostate gland and seminal vesicles in men

Pelvic inflammatory disease (PID) inflammation of any of the female pelvic organs, usually due to infection from a sexually transmitted disease

Penetrak test a test of how fast sperm can travel up through cow mucus

Penis the male organ of sexual intercourse

Pergonal (hMG) the luteinizing and follicle stimulating hormones recovered from the urine of postmenopausal women that is used to induce multiple ovulation in various fertility treatments

Pituitary gland the endocrine gland at the base of the brain that produces the gonadotropin luteinizing hormone and follicle stimulating hormone, which in turn stimulate the gonads to produce sex cells and hormones

Polycystic ovarian disease (PCOD) a condition found among women who do not ovulate, characterized by multiple ovarian cysts and increased androgen production

Polyp a growth or tumor on an internal surface, usually benign

Post-coital test (PCT) microscopic examination of a woman's cervical mucus at the fertile time of the cycle to determine the number and motility of sperm following intercourse

Pre-embryo a fertilized egg in the early

stage of development prior to cell division

Progesterone the female hormone, produced by the corpus luteum after ovulation, that prepares the uterine lining for implantation of a fertilized egg and helps maintain the pregnancy

Prolactin the pituitary hormone that in high amounts stimulates milk production

Prostate gland the male gland encircling the urethra that produces the fluid that transports sperm into the ejaculate

Prostaglandins a group of hormone-like chemicals that have various effects on reproductive organs; so named because they were first discovered in the prostate gland

Reproductive endocrinologist an ob-gyn who specializes in the treatment of hormonal disorders that affect reproductive function

Reproductive surgeon an ob-gyn or urologist who specializes in the surgical correction of anatomical disorders that impair reproductive function

Retrograde ejaculation ejaculation backwards into the bladder instead of forward through the urethra

Salpingectomy surgical removal of the uterus

Salpingitis inflammation of the fallopian tube

Salpingitis isthmica nodosa an abnormal condition of the fallopian tube where it attaches to the uterus, characterized by nodules

Salpingostomy an incision in a fallopian tube, such as to remove an ectopic pregnancy

Salpingotomy an operation to open a blocked fallopian tube

Scrotum the sac containing the testicles, epididymis, and vas deferens

Semen the fluid containing sperm and secretions from the testicles, prostate, and seminal vesicles that is expelled during ejaculation

Semen analysis laboratory examination of semen to check the quality and quantity of sperm

Seminal vesicles the paired glands at the base of the bladder that produce seminal fluid and fructose

Seminiferous tubules in the testicles, the network of tubes where sperm are formed

Septum a wall that divides a cavity in half, such as a uterine septum

Sertoli cells the cells in the testicles that provide nourishment to the early sperm cells

Sexually transmitted disease (STD) a disease caused by an infectious agent transmitted during sex

Sperm male gamete or reproductive cell

Sperm bank a place where sperm are kept frozen in liquid nitrogen for later use in artificial insemination

Sperm count the number of sperm in the ejaculate (when given as the number of sperm per milliliter, it is more accurately known as the sperm concentration or sperm density)

Sperm penetration assay (SPA) see Hamster test

Spermicide an agent that kills sperm

Sterilization a surgical procedure (such as tubal ligation or vasectomy) designed to produce infertility

Sterilization reversal a surgical procedure used to undo a previous sterilization operation and restore fertility

Superovulation stimulation of multiple ovulation with fertility drugs; also known as controlled ovarian hyperstimulation (COH)

Surrogate mother a woman who becomes artificially inseminated with a man's sperm and carries the pregnancy for an infertile couple, who adopt the baby after its birth (the man being the biologic father of the child)

Testicle the male gonad; produces sperm and male sex hormones

Testicular biopsy the removal of a fragment of a testicle for examination under the microscope

Testosterone the primary male sex hormone

Thyroid gland the endocrine gland in the front of the neck that produces thyroid hormones, which regulate the body's metabolism

Tocolytic a drug that relaxes smooth muscles and therefore interferes with uterine contractions; frequently used to stop premature labor

Total effective sperm count an estimate of the number of sperm in an ejaculate capable of fertilization; total sperm count X percent motility X percent forward progressive motility X percent normal morphology

Toxin a poison produced by a living organism, such as by some bacteria

Tubal ligation surgical sterilization of a woman by obstructing or "tying" the fallopian tubes

Tuboplasty plastic or reconstructive surgery on the fallopian tubes to correct abnormalities that cause infertility

Tumor an abnormal growth of tissue that can be benign or malignant (cancerous)

Ultrasound (US) use of high-frequency sound waves for creating an image of internal body parts

Ureaplasma a microorganism similar to mycoplasma

Urethra the tube through which urine from the bladder is expelled

Urologist a physician who specializes in the surgical treatment of disorders of the urinary tract and male reproductive tract

Uterus the womb; female reproductive organ that nourishes the fetus until birth

Vagina the female organ of sexual intercourse; the birth canal

Vaginitis inflammation of the vagina

Varicocele a varicose vein in the scrotum

Vas deferens the tubes that conduct sperm and testicular fluid to the ejaculatory ducts

Vasectomy surgical sterilization of a man by interrupting both vas deferens

Vasectomy reversal surgical repair of a previous vasectomy for a man who wants to regain his fertility

Vasogram an X-ray study of the vas deferens

Venereal disease see Sexually transmitted disease (STD)

Virus a microscopic infectious organism that reproduces inside living cells

Zona pellucida the protective coating surrounding the egg

Zygote an egg that has been fertilized but not yet divided
Zygote Intra Fallopian transfer (ZIFT) in vitro fertilization with a transfer of the zygote into the fallopian tube; a combination of in vitro fertilization and gamete intra fallopian transfer

Index

About the Authors

GARY S. BERGER, M.D., is unique in being certified in the medical specialties of Obstetrics and Gynecology, Preventive Medicine *and* Epidemiology. He was one of the first American infertility specialists to bring female microsurgery techniques from England and has developed a technique of outpatient tubal sterilization reversal. He also reported the first birth following intratubal insemination. Dr. Berger has directed a private infertility practice, the Chapel Hill Fertility Center, for the past ten years, and is Adjunct Associate Professor of Maternal and Child Health at the University of North Carolina. He is also a charter member of the Society of Reproductive Surgeons of the American Fertility Society.

After receiving his medical degree from the University of Rochester, Dr. Berger was an intern at Duke University and a resident at Johns Hopkins and the University of North Carolina. He also trained in epidemiology in the U.S. Public Health Service at the Centers for Disease Control and obtained a Master of Science degree in Public Health from the University of North Carolina.

Dr. Berger is the author or editor of eight medical books and has written more than one hundred fifty articles for physicians on various subjects in the area of reproductive health. This is his first book written for the lay public.

MARC GOLDSTEIN, M.D., is the director of the Male Reproduction and Microsurgery Unit at the New York Hospital-Cornell Medical Center. He is also an Associate Professor of Surgery (Urology) at Cornell University Medical College, where he is a member of the in vitro fertilization team, and a Staff Scientist with the Population Council's Center for Biomedical Research, located on the campus of Rockefeller University.

Known for pioneering work in vasectomy reversals and microsurgical repair of varicoceles, Dr. Goldstein spends much of his time lecturing at infertility meetings around the world. He is the first American surgeon to operate on a Chinese citizen in China since its reopening to the Western World, and has spent time in China sharing his knowledge of microsurgery in exchange for information about a new Chinese method of nonsurgical vasectomy.

Dr. Goldstein has written chapters in more than a dozen medical textbooks and published more than fifty journal articles. He is the author of *The Vasectomy Book*, now in its second edition. He is also on the editorial board of the medical journal *Microsurgery*.

A summa cum laude graduate of the College of Medicine, State University of New York–Downstate Medical Center in Brooklyn, New York, Dr. Goldstein worked as a resident in general surgery at Columbia Presbyterian Hospital in New York and was trained in urology at the Downstate Medical Center. He continued his postgraduate training in reproductive physiology at the Population Council, Center for Biomedical Research, and at the Rockefeller University Hospital. He is a board certified urologic surgeon and member of half a dozen national medical societies dealing with male fertility and reproduction.

MARK FUERST has been a free-lance journalist for nearly a decade. His articles have appeared in popular consumer magazines such as *Family Circle* and *Woman's Day,* and he has written articles on infertility for *Good Housekeeping, Woman's World,* and United Features Syndicate. As a staff writer for *Medical World News,* he covered several infertility conferences and wrote numerous articles on infertility. He is also the co-author of *Computer Phobia: How to Slay the Dragon of Computer Fear.*

Mr. Fuerst earned a biology degree from Dickinson College and a master's degree in journalism from the University of Missouri at Columbia. He is a member of the National Association of Science Writers and the American Society of Journalists and Authors.

BOOK MARK

*The text of this book was composed
in the typeface Palatino
by Berryville Graphics,
Berryville, Virginia*

*This book was printed
by RR Donnelley & Sons
Crawfordsville, Indiana*

**BOOK DESIGN
BY LAURIE JEWELL**

Gary Berger, Marc Goldstein, and Marc Fuerst.

"The Couples Guide to Fertility"